D0500121

*The Keys to French Opera
in the Nineteenth Century*

The publisher gratefully acknowledges the generous contribution to this book provided by the following individuals and organizations:

John M. and Jola Anderson
Emily Callaghan
Frank A. Campini Foundation
Patricia S. Dinner
Eldorado Foundation
Ann and Gordon Getty
David B. Gold Foundation
William and Flora Hewlett Foundation

The publisher also gratefully acknowledges the contribution toward the publication of this book provided by the General Endowment Fund of the Associates of the University of California Press.

# The Keys to French Opera in the Nineteenth Century

HERVÉ LACOMBE

*Translated from the French by Edward Schneider*

*University of California Press*

BERKELEY    LOS ANGELES    LONDON

University of California Press
Berkeley and Los Angeles, California

University of California Press, Ltd.
London, England

© 2001 by the Regents of the University of California


Library of Congress Cataloging-in-Publication Data
Lacombe, Hervé.
[Les voies de l'opéra français au XIXe siècle. English]
The keys to French opera in the nineteenth century / Hervé Lacombe ; translated from the French by Edward Schneider.
     p.     cm.
Translation of: Les voies de l'opéra français au XIXe siècle.
Includes bibliographical references and index.
ISBN 0-520-21719-5 (alk. paper).
1. Opera—France—19th century.   I. Title.
ML1727.4.L35   2001
782.1'0944'09034—dc21                                        00-029869
                                                                      CIP

Manufactured in the United States of America
10   09   08   07   06   05   04   03   02   01

10   9   8   7   6   5   4   3   2   1

The paper used in this publication meets the minimum requirements of
ANSI/NISO Z39.48-1992 (R 1997) (Permanence of Paper). ⊚

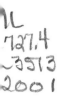

*To Anne*

# Contents

# Illustrations

# Preface to the English Edition

Only a short time has passed since this book was published in French, in 1997, and one might have thought that it would remain unaltered in translation, apart, of course, from the change of language. But since 1997, comments by friends and by critics, questions from students, and my own work and further reading have led me to expand on some points and to discover a number of additional elements and arguments, a few of which I shall mention here.

For example, in reading a considerable body of unpublished letters by Gounod, recently catalogued at the Bibliothèque nationale, and the Auber–Scribe correspondence edited by Herbert Schneider (Liège: Mardaga, 1998), I came not only upon new ideas but also upon new arguments supporting my thesis.

An invitation from the Musée d'Orsay in late 1997 to participate in a lecture series on the role of history in the nineteenth-century creative process in the arts made me think anew about the place of history in the creation of French operatic works and about the great implications of the historical dimension for the aesthetics, reception, and development of *grand opéra*. This gave rise to new passages on history as dramatic framework and on history as an aesthetic power.

I also want to explain something that has surprised some readers of the French edition: the absence of musical examples in a book about music. This was intentional. I set myself the challenge of writing about nineteenth-century French opera by entering into the spirit of the age. To a degree, I tried to adopt ways of thinking and writing about music that were those of the period under consideration, as so strikingly revealed in the work of the many music critics writing in both the specialized and the popular periodicals of the time. Berlioz and Saint-Saëns—among the greatest and ablest, in both literary and musical terms—showed me the way. Lyric theater—by its nature combining literature, theater, the history of taste, and so forth—lends itself especially well to this kind of writing. Moreover, I was aiming not to investigate a single factor but to show the diversity of the elements that constitute an opera, and the relationships among them, and to disassemble the components of that great machine. My essay is as much about society, the organization of theatrical institutions, and sensibilities as it is about music. This point of view made it possible not to interrupt the discursive style when moving from one element to the next, but rather to maintain a continuity of writing and thinking. Edward Schneider's lucid translation captures this stylistic continuity, in spite of my changes to the book—and my numerous "final" additions to it.

As part of the overall conception of the book, illustrations have been inserted into the text rather than being gathered in a separate section where they might have benefited from better reproduction. The point was not simply to embellish the book with pictures (which would nonetheless have been a perfectly praiseworthy goal), but to incorporate the illustrations into the writing and thinking on the opera under consideration. I also wanted to provide a sampling of the great variety of graphic documents that can enhance our understanding of an opera: caricatures, costume sketches, scenery, posters, illustrated title pages for plays or scores, paintings, photographs, and illustrated newspaper and magazine articles.

Let me conclude by mentioning the problem of finding an English title for the book. The French title, *Les Voies de l'opéra français au XIX^e siècle,* puns on *voies* (ways or paths) and its homonym *voix* (voices). *Voies* refers to the many directions taken by composers and to the various paths we must explore to arrive at an understanding of this genre. *Voix* refers to opera's central element—singing—as well as to my desire to construct this book on the basis of contemporary testimony and to use a great number of quotations to enable the reader to hear the nineteenth-century voices of those who fashioned this art and who wrote about it in their own style and with their own sensibility.

The English title, *The Keys to French Opera in the Nineteenth Century,* was suggested by Pierre Degott, a colleague in the English department of the University of Metz and an enthusiastic music-lover. Like *voies* in the French title, the word "keys" can function as a pun. Besides its meaning as a musical term, it signifies the action of identifying the keys (ideas, concepts, and principles) that will enable the reader to enter the world of French opera—that is, to understand it in accordance with its own laws, some elements of which it may have in common with other operatic schools. The title thus reflects the structure and objectives of this book. French lyric theater of the nineteenth century lay within a social and aesthetic space that, with rare exceptions, has long been closed off from our understanding and our sensibility. These keys are intended to make it more accessible.

# Introduction

Nineteenth-century French opera suffers on the whole from a poor reputation; out of a considerable repertory, only a few works such as *Faust* and *Carmen* appear to have stood the test of time. In approaching this subject, we must discard critical assessments inherited from Germany during the era of triumphant Wagnerism and adopt different criteria. French opera rarely aspired to sublimity, intensity, and depth of expression or density of composition. The preference was for the entertaining, pleasant, subtle, and light—and also for something that would surprise and impress. Bizet, and Gounod before him, would seem to fall between the two extremes. While it reflects particular attention to the orchestra, to the unfolding of the drama, to inventiveness, and to the quality of the writing, *Carmen* unquestionably remains part of the long *opéra-comique* tradition, particularly in terms of its structure and its lighter passages. The origins of this fusion are to be sought in the position of opera in mid-century France and in the variety of approaches it was taking.

Far from being the result of a free creative flowering, nineteenth-century French opera, perhaps more than any other art form, was governed by a complex set of codes and practices, and by a system of production that intruded on every level of composition, preparation, and performance. It was organized in keeping with a genuine system, with powerful structures, whose diverse components interacted and were governed by rules sometimes far removed from purely aesthetic considerations. Each stage in this system had its principal actors: the authors in the writing and composition of the work, the interpreters in its performance, and the public and the press in its reception. In addition, there were seemingly secondary players such as theater directors, publishers, and politicians.

In order to identify the foundations of this system and understand how it worked, we must look at a key phase in the history of French opera: the

Second Empire (December 2, 1852–September 4, 1870). Like all turbulent, questioning times, this period serves to point up sensitivities—by exacerbating issues, crisis makes them easier to identify. Viewing the Second Empire as the crossroads of many influences, we can observe the various paths taken by French opera during the century, some of them conservative, others more original, and a few of them completely atypical. Situated between Italy, the birthplace of bel canto, and Germany, the motherland of introspective romanticism, the French school sought to strike a balance that could only be achieved in the capital—the creative juices of the French nation flowed to Paris, and no composer could hope for wide success elsewhere.

In systematically retracing the creative process along the paths that any French composer had to follow in this unstable period if his music was to be heard, we need as our guide a work that will serve to illustrate each link in the chain of creation linking the artist to the spectator—a work that can shed new light on the repertory of contemporary French opera, illuminating the system that produced it and revealing its limits in seeking to emancipate it. Georges Bizet's *Les Pêcheurs de perles* perhaps best meets these requirements.

First performed on September 30, 1863, at the Théâtre-Lyrique, *Les Pêcheurs de perles* marked a decisive moment in the career of the twenty-five-year-old Bizet—and in the history of French opera, which was torn between devotion to tradition and a need for renewal. After eighteen performances, it was never again performed during the composer's lifetime and was forgotten for two decades. When it returned to the stage at the end of the nineteenth century and the beginning of the twentieth, its appearance changed several times. These revivals are a part of the opera's history and highlight something too often forgotten: the mutability of operas.

*Les Pêcheurs de perles* was the beneficiary of propitious circumstances in 1863 that enabled Bizet to make the transition from young supplicant to fulfilled creative artist very swiftly. He had to overcome many obstacles to gain entry to the great operatic institutions: to win the favor of a theater director, to be given a libretto, to try his luck with a publisher, to get his work published, and to have announcements placed in major periodicals. Variously occasioning surprise, irritation, and enthusiasm, Bizet's youth became a pretext for holding forth on the central problem of French opera: its renewal. That was the lot of young composers in the Parisian operatic system. Seemingly impossible to pigeonhole, this opera by a beginner was viewed as a rejection of the traditional categories of *opéra-comique* and *grand opéra,* and it provoked thinking about the concept of genre.

In *Les Pêcheurs de perles*, these basic issues are better combined than in other scores of the time. Gounod's *Faust* (1859), for example, sheds no light on the plight of a young composer, because Gounod was already well established, having had *Sapho* (1851) and *La Nonne sanglante* (1854) produced at the Opéra and *Le Médecin malgré lui* (1858) at the Théâtre-Lyrique.

The unfamiliar paths opened up by both the radical Wagner and the more conciliatory Gounod gave rise to controversy among Paris critics, whose reaffirmations of the traditional rules of French opera—which they saw as threatened—illustrate its aesthetics. "Good history . . . is history that asks a good question and tries to resolve it," Georges Duby remarks. "This is what gives an event its value: it makes it possible to pose and approach a problem better. The merit of an event is to be revelatory." And he adds: "The exceptional, sensational, unexpected, or surprising nature of an event spurs a rash of critical utterances, a sort of proliferation of chatter."[1] The 1863 production of *Les Pêcheurs de perles* was on the face of it a less notable event than that of *Tannhäuser* in 1861 at the Opéra. Nonetheless, critics expressed strong reactions and did not refrain from expounding their opinions.

In the numerous periodicals that published long articles on the theater (prominent in Parisian society of the day), operas were analyzed as works, steeped in various influences, that followed well-known outlines, employed tried-and-true forms, and were in general based on specific models. The libretto, score, and physical production of an opera—its dramatic structure, poetry, music, sets, and costumes—all clung to stereotypes. Operatic writing was subject to expressive conventions, blending the meaning of the verses with the evocative power of music and staying within categories specific to the period; this writing defined lyric drama.

This study is in three stages, rather like a series of overlapping and ever-deeper X rays. In the first part, I address the material conditions surrounding the creation of an opera, which determined the work's writing, performance, and reception. Then, in the second part, I turn to the laws of artistic structure that dictated the drama, the poetry, and the music of an opera. Finally, the third part seeks to identify the social, generic, and aesthetic foundations of the nineteenth-century French operatic system.

The period I explore has no precise boundaries. There were no sudden transformations—much less revolutions—in the history of nineteenth-century French opera; rather, there was gradual change. Various influences

overlaid and blended with fashions in taste; some forms and genres survived as their language evolved; repertory thought to be dead and buried
was resuscitated (the works of André-Ernest-Modeste Grétry, for example). Nonetheless, we can delimit a period of change between 1820 and
1830 during which *opéra-comique* acquired the form that would be viewed
as classic for the rest of the century; *grand opéra* emerged from its
chrysalis; and stage design underwent major changes at the Académie de
musique.[2]

The 1820s saw both the arrival in France of Rossini, who would play a
decisive role in French opera, and the first real appearance of Weber's operatic music on the Parisian stage. Despite major developments in musical
language and new expressive trends, however, the influence of tradition
was always substantial, and one of the strongest unifying factors in the
French operatic world until the eve of the Franco-Prussian War of 1870 was
Daniel Auber, whose long and successful career ran from *Le Séjour mili-
taire* (1813) to *Rêve d'amour* (1869).[3]

At the turn of the twentieth century, the music of Jules Massenet—
which without question dominated that period, thanks to its great success—
is in large part to be viewed more as reviving the operatic system described
in this book than as replacing it. "Reconciliation" is the byword of this
music: reconciling the old with the modern, Italian with German influences, and the primacy of the singer with the accurate rendering of the
drama.

To analyze nineteenth-century French opera from within, rather than
impose any particular view, I have called on contemporary witnesses.
Among the journalists of the day, I pay particular heed to musicians, especially Hector Berlioz (1803–1869), who left a body of criticism of no less
literary and historical interest than his musical output, and whose final article contains an account of *Les Pêcheurs de perles*. We shall also hear the
somewhat later—but very valuable—opinions of Ernest Reyer (1823–
1909), himself a talented composer, who succeeded Berlioz and Joseph
d'Ortigue at the *Journal des Débats*; Camille Saint-Saëns (1835–1921), the
true conscience of French opera, of which he wrote so well in classic style;
Reynaldo Hahn (1874–1947), who inherited and carried on the genre, and
who was also a remarkable writer and discerning analyst; and Alfred
Bruneau (1857–1934).

The persistence of a consistent French attitude to opera in the nineteenth century is also demonstrated by other contemporary commentators, among them writers such as Stendhal (1783–1842), Balzac (1799–
1850), Théophile Gautier (1811–1872), Alfred de Musset (1810–1857),

Charles Baudelaire (1821–1867), and Emile Zola (1840–1902). Composers other than the musician-critics named above also provide examples, such as François Adrien Boieldieu (1775–1834), Daniel François Esprit Auber (1782–1871), Louis Ferdinand Hérold (1791–1833), Giacomo Meyerbeer (1791–1864), Jacques Fromental Elie Halévy (1799–1862), Adolphe Adam (1803–1856), Félicien David (1810–1893), Jacques Offenbach (1819–1880), Victor Massé (1822–1884), Edouard Lalo (1822–1892), and, of course, Georges Bizet (1838–1875), as well as Emmanuel Chabrier (1841–1894), Jules Massenet (1842–1912), André Messager (1853–1929), Gustave Charpentier (1860–1956), and Claude Debussy (1862–1918). Among their works, a few have the status of genuine paragons of French opera, including especially Boieldieu's *La Dame blanche*—first produced in 1825, and considered the model *opéra-comique* for more than half a century thereafter—whose thousandth performance at the Opéra-Comique took place in 1862 in the presence of Napoleon III and Empress Eugénie.

In the course of 1863, there were performances, on January 20, of a revival of Auber's *La Muette de Portici* (1828) and, on November 4, of *Les Troyens* by Berlioz. Symbolically, the first performance of *Les Pêcheurs de perles* took place between the two, in September. Auber's score remained for many an "accomplished masterpiece of lucid, straightforward and easy melody, as radiant as the sun."[4] Berlioz's opera on the other hand was seen by the vast majority of the public as an "impossible" work that shattered the aesthetic framework of French opera. Bizet was thus confronted with these two emblematic models, one representing conservative tradition and the other innovative creative passion. But his deepest thoughts turned in a third direction: he was an admirer of Gounod. We shall proceed under the aegis of these three tutelary figures. Auber was the aesthetic and social model of operatic success under the Second Empire; Berlioz exemplified the frustration of originality and creative individualism; and Gounod took a middle road between these extremes, creating a new lyrical style and bringing about a perceptible renewal within the framework of that ambiguous genre, opera.

# PART 1

## GENESIS, PERFORMANCE, AND RECEPTION

# Chapter 1   The Genesis of an Opera

In nineteenth-century France, the genesis of an opera was not confined to the composer's and librettist's ateliers. Before the fine-tuning of rehearsals, even before the actual composition, an opera was structured and delimited through a process whose key element was the composer's admission to the constraining environment of an operatic institution.

## THE CONTEXT

Although it remained a powerful source of fascination for composers, *grand opéra*, the crowning glory of the Théâtre de l'Opéra during the directorship of the celebrated Dr. Louis Véron (1831–35) and thereafter, lost some of its luster in the second half of the nineteenth century. Meanwhile, *opéra-comique*, the other dominant French genre, badly needed an infusion of new life. Here one was "still dealing with the old eighteenth-century comedy," Charles Malherbe could write somewhat exaggeratedly, adding that "it was the defeat in the Franco-German war that profoundly changed the French outlook."[1]

During the Second Republic (February 25, 1848–December 2, 1851) and the Second Empire (December 2, 1852–September 4, 1870), Meyerbeer and Auber respectively still embodied the two genres that dominated French opera: *grand opéra* and *opéra-comique*. The two composers who would be best remembered by posterity, Gounod and Bizet, appeared on the scene at a low point, when opera seemed to be living on its past successes and no longer to have the energy needed for renewal. It was truly a time of crisis. The "lamentable drying-up of the live sources of inspiration"[2] that Gounod detected when he heard Halévy's *La Magicienne* in 1858 was a symptom of this situation. "The Second Empire was an essentially anti-musical period," Reynaldo Hahn would observe, with more than usual severity. "Its music resembled its furniture: it was ill-assorted, mediocre, and heavy, comprising elements of every genre and every period; its style consisted of a total lack of style."[3]

Here we must exclude the success enjoyed in the 1850s by the music of Giuseppe Verdi (1813–1901) at the Théâtre-Italien, especially *Rigoletto* and *La Traviata*.[4] Verdi contributed only *Jérusalem* (1847, based on *I Lombardi*), *Les Vêpres siciliennes* (1855), and *Don Carlos* (1867),[5] three works that did not immediately look as if they had a promising future, to the contemporary French repertoire. In December 1863, the director of the Théâtre-Lyrique, Léon Carvalho (pseudonym of Léon Carvaille, 1825–1897), successfully mounted *Rigoletto* in French. This initiative launched a new policy for that theater, geared toward translating works, something that until then had been done only for older foreign operas. But whereas the music of Gioacchino Rossini (1792–1868) had had a profound influence on French operatic writing in the first half of the nineteenth century, Verdi's does not seem to have had anything like the same impact.

The Paris musical hierarchy might have been invented to obstruct the development of new forms of operatic expression. The directors of the traditional theaters gave young composers hardly any opportunity to be heard and were even more wary of those who advocated reforming the operatic genres. "Serious modern music…owes its reputation for decadence to the scant importance attached to it, to the very silence that is imposed upon it," Gustave Chadeuil objected in 1863.[6] "So few new works, and so many revivals in twelve months!" exclaimed Paul Smith (pseudonym of Edouard Monnais), adding that Paris audiences "complain to all and sundry that their theaters no longer produce anything for them, because, thanks to the railways, foreigners and provincials constantly fill their auditoriums and their coffers."[7] Smith listed two new works at the Opéra (*La Mule de Pedro*, an opera in two acts by Philippe-François Pinel Dumanoir and Victor Massé, and *Diavolina*, a ballet in one act by Saint-Léon and Pugni), and regretted that at the Opéra-Comique "the ration of new pieces has never been so meager." Berlioz too attacked the Opéra sharply: "As for the Théâtre de l'Opéra, it still occasionally puts on *La Favorite* and the other masterpieces of the immortal repertory; it is wrong to criticize it for never doing anything new—it has given up."[8] It was all the more bitter to be kept waiting outside the doors of the Opéra when foreign composers such as Gluck, Rossini, and Meyerbeer had so often passed through them. Hence this 1870 definition of the Académie impériale de musique: "Grand French theater consecrated by the French taxpayers to the glory of foreign composers."[9]

We tend to underestimate the extent to which, in this climate, the works of Gounod brought about a renewal of French opera. In the words of Reynaldo Hahn:

> For a long time, despite a few bright glimmers, French dramatic music lay lifeless; one overwhelming reason was the singing itself, and another major factor was the melodramatic element; grim, ghastly *coups de théâtre* followed mawkish cavatinas; spirited coloratura gave way with the greatest of ease to parental maledictions, demonic apparitions to laryngological graces. All of this lacked genuine, straightforward, sincere flavor, real feeling—in short, life. It also lacked something else: poetry, that is color, mystery, what we call today ambiance or atmosphere. Moreover, it lacked musical beauty itself, the beauty that comes from the musical language, the quality of the melodies, harmony, organization, expressive choices, variety of musical vocabulary—in a word, style. But all these elements emerged together in 1851, in the first work of a young musician: in Charles Gounod's *Sapho*.[10]

Yet this work had no direct impact on the public, which rejected it. Some musicians took note, however, and accurately gauged the importance of Gounod's aesthetic conception. "To me, *Sapho* is an *immortal masterpiece*," Bizet wrote to his publisher.[11] Berlioz was carried away by the last act and declared: "It is beautiful. Very beautiful. Miraculously beautiful!"[12]

In 1859, *Faust* was to confirm Gounod's originality and importance. "Go back fifty years," wrote Camille Bellaigue in 1910, "open all the scores of the time, and nowhere will you find the character, what I might call the tone, or the half-tone, of that sensitivity and that poetry."[13] Bizet, who was a fervent admirer of Gounod, was beginning his career at a time when his senior was making a name for himself and when many journalists remained biased against operatic expression that appeared to destabilize tradition. To some writers, the critical phase through which the French school was passing could be seen in the lack of balance in the influences that marked the nation's repertory: "At present," wrote Nestor Roqueplan after hearing *Les Troyens*, "French music is leaning more toward Germany than toward Italy.... Will audiences follow our composers in this transformation, which is so out of keeping with our traditional outlook? This we do not know, but what we wish above all is that the question should be resolved, that the chaos in which we are floundering should be dispelled."[14]

After winning first prize in the Institut de France's 1857 Prix de Rome competition, Bizet spent a few years at the Villa Médicis in Rome, and when he returned to Paris tried to gain entry to the sanctuaries of the major opera houses. Let us now consider the various possibilities open to this ambitious young composer.

## THE PARISIAN OPERATIC INSTITUTIONS
## AND THE THÉÂTRE-LYRIQUE

Despite many attempts to mount operas in various other theaters, operatic activity in Paris was centered around the Opéra, the Opéra-Comique, and the Théâtre-Italien, three institutions with little interest in change. Moreover, one of them, the Théâtre-Italien, was entirely devoted to Italian repertory (apart from a few summer visits by German or English companies on tour).[15]

At mid-century, in a generally rather dreary musical climate, the Théâtre-Lyrique provided a touch of life. Its establishment in 1853 was "the culmination of a long struggle among musicians, the government and men of letters to secure the opening of a third operatic stage, with plenty of room for young composers, Conservatoire graduates, and winners of the Prix de Rome, and give a larger and broader public access to the French repertory, both old and modern."[16] To this brief list, we must add the auditoriums that welcomed the nascent genre operetta. In 1855, Jacques Offenbach (1819–1880) was authorized to open a theater, the Bouffes-Parisiens, the success of which is well known. Also around 1850, Florimond Ronger, known as Hervé (1825–1892), made an attempt of his own, first at the Folies-Concertantes then at the Folies-Nouvelles.

In 1863, Léon Carvalho stood out in an otherwise lackluster operatic scene. Gustave du Taillys compared Carvalho's Théâtre-Lyrique favorably with "the Opéra and the Opéra-Comique, which are somnolent."[17] Gaston de Saint-Valry agreed: "We note that this theater—which is now playing *Les Noces de Figaro* and *Joseph,* and at the same time preparing Berlioz's *Les Troyens* and Gounod's *Miréï* [*Mireille*]—was opened to newcomers as soon as state subsidy permitted this. It is at present the most interesting and the most active of our musical theaters."[18]

The Théâtre-Lyrique's repertory was a careful blend of translations of foreign operas (particularly by Mozart and Weber), adaptations of older works (including those of Grétry), contemporary operas of conventional cut (such as those of Adolphe Adam), and more original works such as Gounod's *Faust.* It laid down certain standards of quality and originality for its productions, although sometimes compromising on originality in order to please a broader public. In seeking to attract an audience with tried and true operatic genres, however, it had every reason to fear the hostility of older institutions such as the Opéra-Comique, which jealously guarded their repertories and their exclusive association with them. In the late 1850s, therefore, Carvalho turned to translations and encouraged the composition of so-called *demi-caractère* operas. Because of his personal tastes, and in order to make an impression on audiences—influenced here by the example of *grand opéra*—he accustomed the public between 1856 and 1860 "to richness of stage setting and to developed dramatic action, which were indeed necessitated by the large-scale works toward which he was inclined by preference."[19] After a two-year hiatus (1860–62), during which Charles Réty directed the company, Carvalho resumed his post, and on Thursday, October 30, 1862, he opened a new auditorium on the Place du Châtelet.[20] There he aimed to venture further along the new paths that would distance his theater from the well-trodden byways of *opéra-comique.* Recounting the events of 1863, Albert Soubies noted: "It was at the end of the year that M. Carvalho, demonstrating even more than in his first directorship his preference for opera, would in rapid succession present two very important new works, which unfortunately did not gain the success that they deserved: *Les Pêcheurs de perles* and *Les Troyens.*"[21]

FRENCH MUSICAL CULTURE: AN OBSTACLE TO CREATIVITY

Art that sought to break with routine had little hope of recognition in France: "On the basis of the principle that only works sanctified by time can be masterpieces," wrote Ernest Reyer, "it is always with a certain mistrust and with great reservations that [the public] greets anything attributed to a living being, anything that is modern."[22] As one might imagine, the musical culture of a middle-class listener was closed in upon itself. The composer Henri Maréchal (1842–1924) recalled that in his youth "the *concerts du dimanche* did not exist" and that "for the Parisian middle classes, the Opéra-Comique remained the alpha and omega of the art of music."[23] "The real piano literature," he went on, "was absolutely unknown to the ordinary music-lover, and only arrangements [of well-known operas] had any standing."[24] For their part, the followers of Italian opera, isolated in their bastion, the Théâtre-Italien, constituted (especially in the first half of the century) a clique that was not notably open to other operatic styles. They formed a social or aesthetic aristocracy: "rich and poor alike are elites," wrote Frédéric Soulié, "the former in their elegance, the latter as music-lovers. The boxes amount to seigniorial property; the orchestra seats tend to be a musical club. The Opéra is a fashion and a taste; the [Théâtre des] Italiens is a *need* and a *passion.*"[25]

Even musicians themselves had but a limited view of the overall repertory. Using the salon composer Paul Henrion (1819–1901) as an example, Maréchal tells us that Henrion "had taken as 'his gods'—as he freely admitted—Boieldieu, Hérold, Auber, Rossini, and Meyerbeer. In his day, these were virtually the only deities known in Paris to the broader public." And Maréchal added: "This point must always be borne in mind when speaking of a French musician of this era."[26] Berlioz had bitter experience of all this, and his writing often reflects his indignation. To be perfectly fair, it should be noted that chamber music[27] and symphonic concerts (especially on the impetus of the famous *concerts du conservatoire*) were expanding and gradually winning an audience of their own. In the second half of the nineteenth century, the musical culture of composers and music-lovers alike broadened and, thanks to influences from Germany, became more demanding. Yet the notion that the whole purpose of an opera was to gratify public taste at any price defined an attitude toward composition that can be viewed as the most prominent characteristic of the French school. Massenet—who was often criticized for his "concessions"—was the most striking example of this attitude at the turn of the twentieth century. This seems to be the defining question for French opera, and we shall return to it. For the moment, let us note that artistic considerations were more often than not relegated to a secondary position.

SUBSIDIZING A THEATER—COMMISSIONING
AN OPERA—CENSORSHIP

Throughout the nineteenth century, French opera was organized around institutions governed by a complex system of subsidies, privileges, and *cahiers des charges,* or contracts between the state and the director of a theater specifying the composition of the company, subsidies, the kinds of works that could be performed, scenery, and so forth. These were especially important in defining the framework in which operas were created, as the example of *Les Pêcheurs de perles* demonstrates. It would hardly have been possible for Bizet to compose such a work before the recent opening of the Théâtre-Lyrique, and for Carvalho to launch such an ambitious project, he needed a subsidy. Just when *Les Pêcheurs de perles* was being conceived, however, he was granted 100,000 francs, and we may assume that it was when he learned of this windfall that Carvalho gratefully commissioned an opera in three acts from Bizet and his librettists.

The *Exposé de la situation de l'Empire* distributed to the members of the Corps Législatif in 1863 states that at "the end of its last session, the

Corps Législatif expressed the wish that a subsidy be granted to the Théâtre-Lyrique to encourage praiseworthy efforts and reward outstanding successes. This desire has lately been fulfilled. It having been possible to assess the management of the Théâtre-Italien under new circumstances, and the proprietor himself having offered to undertake that management without state assistance, the annual sum of 100,000 francs that thus became available has been allocated to the Théâtre-Lyrique."[28] The report of the budget committee presented to the Corps Législatif in mid April 1863 noted: "Because part of the money no longer needs to be put to its present use, the committee considers that it would be both just and liberal to use it to encourage the Théâtre-Lyrique, which is to be commended for its persistent efforts, for the artistic nature of its management, and for the talents it has produced."[29]

The subsidy was granted by a decree dated June 5, 1863. It was noted that "during the two terms of his management, M. Carvalho, while striving to conform to the terms of his *cahier des charges,* has been unable to devote an adequate share to performances of modern works, particularly those by young composers and by winners of Institut [de France] prizes." This decree adjusted various points in the *cahier des charges* issued on November 10, 1862. The new version of article 2 stipulated that "each year the director of the Théâtre-Lyrique should arrange the performance of at least one piece in *three* acts, whose music shall have been composed by student stipend-holders or former stipend-holders of the [French Academy] in Rome who have as yet had no work performed in Paris."[30] The November 1862 *cahier des charges* had been less rigorous: "The [winners of the] first prize for musical composition, in the two years following the expiration of their stipends, shall have the right to priority in the production at the Théâtre-Lyrique of a work of their composition, in *two* acts."[31]

The selection and commissioning of a work also depended heavily on its theme, on how interesting its plot was, and hence on its standing in what we might call the theatrical marketplace. The law of supply and demand applied, along with the element of surprise. To win an audience, attention had to be paid to the themes being portrayed in other theaters. Sometimes a popular theme was declared a surefire hit, and other theater directors had no hesitation in making use of the same subject. But at the same time they had to ensure that their themes were not in direct competition. Gounod and the director of the theater for which the production of *Faust* had been planned decided to delay that work because the Théâtre de la Porte-Saint-Martin was to perform a piece on the same subject. Gounod informed one of his librettists of this decision: "Dear friend, I saw Carvalho last night. He and I had a final discussion on our business [the production of *Faust*]. We have definitely been upstaged by the Porte-Saint-Martin. Still: *absolute silence about our plans; they will resurface one day or other.*"[32]

The creation of a work was thus dependent on institutions and their internal structures. The state shaped the repertory through the granting of subsidies and privileges. Another means of control was censorship, which during the nineteenth century was employed intermittently and with varying degrees of stringency: it would even change its stance now and then on such delicate questions as the portrayal of religious subjects on stage, a position that was by turns anticlerical and punctiliously respectful. The July Revolution of 1830 against King Charles X inaugurated five years of freedom. Theatrical censorship was restored in 1835, halted in 1848, and reinstated once again in 1850; apart from a brief suspension in 1870, it thereafter remained in force until 1906.[33]

Although the libretto of *Les Pêcheurs de perles*, which Carvalho submitted to the censorship office on August 11, 1863,[34] was well received, that of *Sapho* was subjected to harsh criticism. The censorship office imposed changes intended to weaken the meaning of Emile Augier's verses, which made too explicit allusion to the morals of some of the characters. The musicologist Steven Huebner quotes an excerpt from the original duet between Pythéas and Glycère:

> Oui, je comprends mignonne
> Ton désir,
> Le mystère assaisonne
> Le plasir.
>
> Yes, my darling, I understand
> Your desire;
> Mystery adds spice
> To pleasure.

In the censored libretto, this was amended to:

> Oui, j'aime ton caprice
> De candeur,
> Le mystère est complice
> De bonheur.
>
> Yes, I like your whim
> For innocence;
> Mystery is the ally
> Of bliss.[35]

Moreover, the authorities could not accept the revolutionary stance of Alcée, who sought to overthrow the tyrant Pittacus. For the last two performances, in December 1851, major cuts were made to cleanse the plot of anything hinting at a conspiracy.

These hidden participants in the creation of an opera—the members of the censorship committee—did not always play such a major role. On the other hand, theater directors, librettists, and publishers held considerable power over creative activities, as we can see from the examples of Carvalho, Cormon, Carré, and Choudens.

## THEATER DIRECTOR, LIBRETTIST, PUBLISHER

Léon Carvalho, a former singer, seems to have sought to substitute active participation in rehearsals for appearing on the stage himself, and to have made every effort to put his stamp on the works he produced. Not only did he interfere with composers' work, he even imposed changes during rehearsals. He was a romantic character, and his originality and long career made him without doubt one of the most important figures in the Parisian operatic life of the day. As we have seen, he served as director of the Théâtre-Lyrique from February 1856 to March 1860 and from October 1862 to May 1868, then worked at the Opéra and at the Théâtre du Vaudeville before succeeding Camille Du Locle and Emile Perrin as head of the Opéra-Comique in August 1876.[36] He was imprisoned in the wake of a fire at the second Salle Favart in 1887, but was exonerated in 1891 and resumed his functions until his death. During this final term, there were revivals of many works dating from his time as director of the Théâtre-Lyrique.

When Carvalho assigned Bizet the libretto of *Les Pêcheurs de perles,* which had obviously been written in haste and without enthusiasm and had in the course of a few months undergone repeated changes, the end result was far from an unalloyed success. Still, both librettists were well known in contemporary theatrical circles, and were skilled craftsmen. In the course of a long life (1811–1903), Eugène Cormon (pseudonym of Pierre-Etienne Piestre) wrote a large number of dramatic works, many of them for the operatic stage. Michel Carré (1819–1872), the better known of the two, gained his renown in tandem with Jules Barbier (1825–1901), with whom he devised the librettos for the majority of the most influential works of the second half of the nineteenth century, including *Faust* (1859) and *Roméo et Juliette* (1867) for Gounod; *Mignon* (1866) and *Hamlet* (1868) for Ambroise Thomas; and *Les Contes d'Hoffmann* (1881) for Offenbach.

In *Le Ménestrel* of August 23, 1863, Gustave Bertrand outlined the coming season, and noted that "all these works—*Mireille, Les Troyens,* and *Lélia* [sic] [*Les Pêcheurs de perles*]—are the property of M. Choudens... who in the most honorable manner has staked his claim as the publisher of the young French school." Although at this stage there were plans to purchase Bizet's opera, publication ran into difficulties. Despite a misunderstanding between the composer and his publisher, the newspapers in October 1863 published the first announcements for the score and its individual numbers—an important link in the chain of an opera's existence. Publishers and musicians alike had long viewed an opera as a mine of arias and hit numbers. In 1840, in an article on the new Opéra-Comique production of *La Perruche* by Louis Clapisson (1808–1866), a success at the time but completely forgotten today, a critic wrote: "The overture contains the obligatory galop, without which no publisher will view a score as viable. (The galop is the net in which the composer ensnares the publisher.)"[37] Auber's lasting success is connected to the wealth of pleasant numbers in his music, of a kind that spread rapidly among the French public. In his review of *L'Enfant prodigue* (1850), the publisher J.-L. Heugel referred to "a mass of delightful little items, both for singing and for dancing, which will soon gain recognition at our salons and balls."[38]

A publisher could simultaneously play both a direct and a more covert role. Gambling on a score's success, he would organize a paid claque of applauders and seek to influence journalists. Thus, "Heugel, who had purchased the score [of *Mignon*] after the fourth [performance] from the authors for 15,000 francs, was determined to make the work succeed. His actions followed his words. They cut, they trimmed, they changed.... Forty or fifty people were planted in the auditorium, and there was advertising as well."[39]

THE MANY IDENTITIES OF AN EVOLVING OPERA

Far from being an individual, isolated, intrinsically perfect creation, a nineteenth-century opera was subjected to the ordeal of rehearsals and productions each time it was revived. As shown by the various sources that have come down to us (see Appendix 1), *Les Pêcheurs de perles* exemplifies the mutable nature of an operatic score. As in the case of nearly all such nineteenth-century works, the documents that form the basis of our knowledge of the opera—librettos and scores—set out the various states of a work that thus appears to have many identities.

*Les Pêcheurs* was never revived during Bizet's lifetime. After attempts to achieve success through sundry versions (see Appendix 2), however, the opera ultimately gained popularity and a place among the most-performed works in the repertory. As with many other works—such as Gounod's *Mireille* (1864), whose initial failure led to the introduction of constant changes at successive revivals until World War II—the opera is no longer the same as the score played at the first performance; it is extremely difficult to determine the authorship of the changes, cuts, and additions that have been a part of its subsequent history. To discover the original form of a nineteenth-century opera, it is very often necessary to go back to its beginnings. Clearly, this difficulty is nothing new, and performers often face the difficult problem of different versions and traditions, which at times involved major changes. Thus, the life of an opera cannot be reduced to a mere chronology divided into the three stages of creation, performance, and reception. A work's genesis—the process of shaping it—could continue well beyond the first performance.

Cormon and Carré's libretto was conceived as an *opéra-comique*, in which spoken sections, written in prose, alternated with verse intended to be sung. It was subjected to major revisions even before it was circulated. The scenes of dialogue were shortened to the point of containing only a few exchanges. The few remaining lines were put into verse and became the texts for new recitatives. Revised in this way, the work became an *opéra* in the sense of a work containing no spoken dialogue. A chorus was added, and three roles (two witches and a nonspeaking character) were eliminated. Again, such revisions were normal at the time, and many works were transformed from one genre to another. Examples are *Robert le Diable*, conceived as an *opéra-comique* but destined to be Meyerbeer's first *grand opéra; Faust*, which began as an *opéra-comique* and was then recast as an opera with music throughout; and *Mignon*.

Bizet responded quickly to Carvalho's commission. As with every other opera composer of the time, his task was eased by conventions based on stereotyped numbers of predetermined form, easily copied from one work to another. (In part 2 of this book, which is devoted to the dramatic craft, we shall see how an opera could be constructed on the basis of models.) Moreover, Bizet followed the age-old practice of fleshing out the three acts of his score by adapting numbers he had already written (see Appendix 2), a system he would use all his life—including in *Carmen*, where, for example, the famous tenor line "La fleur que tu m'avais jetée" was taken from an incomplete work entitled *Grisélidis*. To return to the example of *Sapho*, we know that Gounod adapted two of his songs to create numbers for the title role: "Le Soir" (in the act 1 "Ode de Sapho"), and "La Chanson du pêcheur" (in the act 3 "Stances de Sapho"). For his part, Massenet drew upon a fragment and a section not used in the duet for Salomé and Jean in *Hérodiade* for the Hôtel de Transylvanie theme in *Manon* and for a portion of the duet between Chimène and Rodrigue in *Le Cid*.

A score would often be altered in the course of rehearsals. This could include minor variations in the vocal line, changes in the text, simplification of the accompaniment, transpositions, and cuts. The latter might involve only a few measures or might extend to lengthier passages. The longer cuts reflect the search for a more realistic and lively unfolding of the plot. In this connection, the act 2 finale of *Les Pêcheurs de perles* was subjected to many changes. It was necessary to decide which of the various characters would discover the pair of guilty lovers, and how this would come about (see Appendix 3). Similarly, the final scene was turned upside down several times. All the loose ends of an excessively complicated drama had to be tied up, and the fate of the characters had to be determined. And cuts were made even in the course of the performances (see Appendix 4). It is very difficult to know who decided on which changes, and whether or not the composer was in full agreement with them.

That was a brief outline of the creation of an opera. The changes of genre and of action and the cuts of all kinds were made gradually. When the composer delivered his manuscript to the theater, the opera remained incomplete; it remained an evolving work. There was nothing unusual about this; it was, indeed, a long-standing practice. In the early nineteenth century, for example, we might cite *Aladin, ou la Lampe merveilleuse*, a work (produced posthumously at the Opéra in 1822) by Nicolas Isouard, known as Nicolò (1775–1818), a popular composer for the Opéra-Comique under the Consulate (1799–1804) and the First Empire (1804–1814). The publishers explained in the preface to the libretto that the musician and Opéra administrator François-Antoine Habeneck (1781–1849) was determined "to devote himself to the exhausting labor of rehearsals and to make the cuts and additions that are always necessary."[40] Shortly after the completion of Halévy's *La Juive* (1835), a journalist expressed his satisfaction that "a number of apt cuts have been successfully essayed."[41] In 1859, one critic wrote that after "the inevitable additions and deletions, *Faust* has just been produced."[42] Nearer to our time, we know that Debussy had to lengthen the interludes in *Pelléas et Mélisande* at the last minute to accommodate scene changes. The reality check of performances and theatrical practice was decisive. The performers would bring the characters to life; the theater would impose its rules; the goal of making an impact on the audience would necessitate changes; singers would request transpositions so that their arias would be better suited to their voices.

Corrections could also be made by a composer dissatisfied with his work. Meyerbeer was a perfectionist, famous for his intensified activity during rehearsal periods. The musicians' long faces during the dress rehearsal of *Le Pardon de Ploërmel* at the Opéra-Comique could be blamed on the composer. "Poor musicians!" wrote one columnist. "Last night they were in their places for an ordinary performance. At midnight, Meyerbeer delivered a revised finale, which had to be learned immediately."[43]

Before rehearsals began, the task of creating the work did not have only two stages—writing the libretto and composing music to it. It is obvious from drafts and manuscripts, and from the correspondence of librettists and composers, who provide fascinating observations on the creation of their works, that in fact these two stages overlapped rather than taking place in succession. It would be more correct to say that there were three stages, because the librettist's work was itself often divided into two parts, hence the many teams, such as Barbier-Carré and Meilhac-Halévy, where one member would be responsible for the dramatic framework and the other for the verses. Gounod's letters to Jules Barbier provide a remarkable account of fruitful teamwork between composer and librettist. A letter regarding the composition of *Mireille* shows how the composer would sometimes think of a situation and of a musical color, to which the librettist would then give literary form:

> Dear friend, for the opening of our *Marche religieuse* in the last scene you must write me two stanzas, the theme for which I found at Saintes-Maries, in the rite for the saints; here is the Latin text, which contains a charming legend. [Here Gounod gives the Latin text and a translation into French.] For each of these stanzas, I would like you to write six lines, to which I shall add as a refrain the following two lines, which I have already set to music, in order to set the tone for the number: "Aimons tendrement (*bis*) / Un si bon maître qui nous aime tant!" I think you will be pleased with the coloration I have given this.[44]

The correspondence between Scribe and Auber also demonstrates that the dramatic structure of an opera was the result of a constant back-and-forth between libretto and music, to the point where the librettist might think of some music and the composer of some text. On September 4, 1843, Scribe told Auber of numerous changes in the *opéra-comique La Sirène* (1844). Concerning a duet in act 3, he wrote:

> I have made a few changes, first because I remembered that you did not like this duet, and also [because] the new structure of the scene and of the plot demands that there should be great briskness; first of all, I have cut the very slow sort of aria sung by Mlle Lavoye [Zerlina]. You will tell

me that for you this was the best part. No: because this big aria tired her out for her final aria, and had always been less effective than the latter. So I begin the duet with a declaimed melody, as in the couplets "Je ne vous vois jamais rêveuse, jamais de palpitations" in *Ma tante Aurore* [an *opéra-comique* by Boieldieu], except that there there they are sung by an old woman and here by a very young girl, and that there there they were comic couplets and here the feeling will be one of innocence....I shall continue with the same declaimed text until "C'est horrible à dire et pourtant...," and shall then begin the theme of the duet and the melody "Oui malgré moi-même ...," a theme that she begins alone and that her lover will accompany.[45]

When the composer wrote vocal music with a situation in mind, but lacking a text from his librettist, he would draft what was known as a *monstre:* bogus verses that served as a frame for the vocal line, which the librettist would then transform into real verses. The point was to use this throwaway text to define the musical form or rhythmic structure of the number.

### THE CREATIVE ENTITY

The composer and librettist might deem some of these changes useful, but other imposed alterations were sometimes harder to accept. Reyer describes very clearly the aggravation an opera composer had to endure, and speaks out against, among other things, one abuse that theater directors "considered to be one of the most valued prerogatives of their profession. These are the cuts to which every new work is subjected to as a matter of course and which are all too often imposed even on old works."[46] Any and all justifications could be invoked in support of a given modification, and "if one had not been through it oneself, [no one could] invent the multitude of poor reasons the theater director could summon up to prove to the composer that a number was too long or that it should disappear completely. Theatrical requirements dictate this; the audience's weariness at that point in the evening absolutely demands it; the prima donna will be exhausted—or she must be kept backstage long enough for the audience to forget her; the number is beautiful, very beautiful, but it is not in the right place; etc., etc." Under these repeated onslaughts, "the composer would finally yield, and would let the red pencil wander to and fro over the pages of his score." Anyway, it was better to respond quickly to the performers' wishes, because "singers are obsessed with requesting changes, which as such fine musicians they will take it upon themselves to make if [the composer] does not agree to them."[47] Eugène Ritt, director of the Opéra-

Comique from 1862 to 1870, recalled that "Marie Cabel, who was playing Philine [in *Mignon*], asked Thomas to write her a grand aria in the garden scene. He regretfully did so."[48]

Major singers would make their own "contributions" to a work; here the Italians seem to have been the most active, as a journalist observed in 1841: "It is common in Italy to hear operas—and I refer to those which have had the extremely good fortune to survive a year or two after their inaugural season—in which barely three or four of the composer's numbers have been retained; everyone adds his own. The most important is always the one that each singer refers to as his *quaresimale*, or Lenten piece: this ordinarily shows off everything he is capable of doing."[49]

With his sense of humor and his scathing irony, Berlioz noted on the manuscript of *Les Troyens à Carthage*[50] the various cuts he had to make in 1863 both in response to the many pieces of wise advice that were lavished upon him and to adapt to circumstances. Hence Berlioz's marginal notes, an exceptional source, which speak volumes about the composer's exasperation. With regard, first of all, to the "Chasse royale et Orage": "Note for the *intermède:* If the theater is not huge enough to accommodate a spirited and grandiose production of this *intermède;* if it is impossible to induce the female chorus members to move about the stage with disheveled hair and the male chorus members dressed as fauns and satyrs to cut grotesque capers while shouting, 'Italy!'; if the firemen are afraid of fire, the stagehands of water, and the director of everything; and above all if the scene change before act 3[51] cannot be effected quickly, this *symphonie* should be omitted." The aria and the duet for Anna and Narbal[52] were omitted "without regard for the logic of the action, the necessary explanations contained in the scene, or the new form of the duet. It was considered that it produced what in theatrical slang is called *un froid*—a chill." Iopas's *strophes*[53] fared no better, and were abandoned "because there was no lyric tenor who could sing this number well." "I forgot to mention," added Berlioz,

> that one could also…omit the soldiers' duet,[54] whose somewhat vulgar informality is in such marked contrast to the sailor's melancholy song, which precedes it, and to Aeneas's impassioned aria, which follows it. It has been observed in France that mixing the tragic and comic genres is dangerous, even intolerable, in the theater, as though the opera of *Don Giovanni* were not an admirable example of the fine effect produced by such a mixture; as though the hordes of plays performed daily in Paris did not contain excellent uses of this system; as though, finally, there were no Shakespeare. It is true that for most of the French, Shakespeare means even less than sunlight means to a mole—for at least a mole can feel the sun's warmth. So I mark this cut also, as I contemplate the

pleasure experienced by directors, actors, and conductors, by firemen, stagehands, and lighting men when they insult an author and disfigure his work; I would be very sorry if I did not do all I could to facilitate the gratification of such noble instincts.[55]

Later, at the turn of the century, the same struggle for influence would continue. In 1897, the directors of the Opéra, Pedro Gailhard and Eugène Bertrand, prevented Alfred Bruneau and his celebrated librettist, Emile Zola, from making changes, while imposing alterations of their own. Bruneau reported that the "ballet [in *Messidor*] was the focus of interminable discussion between them and us. They had an unshakable belief in the use of the 'tutu.'... We considered, on the contrary, that it was essential that our ballerinas should wear costumes." And the model of the golden cathedral angered the two authors: "We did not like the second model any better," the composer went on. "At the dress rehearsal, the tutus and the dreaded scenery were unanimously thought so absurd that we wanted the ballet to be completely eliminated. Bertrand and Gailhard resisted. Their detestable notion was to shift this poorly executed choreographic scene from the middle of the libretto to the beginning; this made for an incomprehensible and bizarre prologue."[56]

The published score is often the last place to look for an idea of the work as it was heard by an audience on a given date. Every rehearsal, then every performance, could give rise to changes. Press accounts supplement the information we can glean from primary sources. For example, a column by Auguste Durand in *L'Esprit public* on November 13, 1863, notes that the poetic stanzas declaimed at the beginning of *Les Troyens* "were broken up on the night of the first performance by a few notes on the harp, the effect of which did not appear particularly felicitous; the first sacrifice was that these pizzicati were eliminated on the second day."

The more successful an opera, the more it was performed and the more it became public property, and it would be revised by performer after performer, all of them leaving their personal stamp on it. When the tenor Adolphe Nourrit took on the role of Licinius in Gaspare Spontini's *La Vestale* in 1834, he found that he needed to make a number of alterations. Berlioz wrote in *Le Rénovateur* of August 16, 1834, that "the role, which had been written for a second tenor, obliged him to make some transpositions in the low strings, from which the expressiveness of the recitatives and the beauty of the melodies still suffer a little." As operas "ply the ocean of success under full sail," Saint-Saëns observed, "singers, instrumentalists, conductors, *chefs de chant*, and stage directors all make fast to their sides, so that their progress is first hampered, then completely impeded."[57]

The author's ideas are seen, "most of the time, only in veiled and unrecognizable form." In 1917, Saint-Saëns beseeched his friend Gabriel Fauré (1845–1924), then director of the Conservatoire: "While you are in the process of introducing reforms in the Department of Singing, I would be delighted if you would ax those abominable 'traditions'! that habit of doing things the composer never thought of and for which he has to pay the price, of throwing rhythm to the winds at every pause in the accompaniment, of always holding high notes, etc."[58]

If one sought to reconstruct a nineteenth-century French opera thinking it to be the work of a single composer, whose score definitively established the progression of its dramatic and musical elements, one would encounter major problems. Moreover, it is not always easy to demonstrate that the creator had a precise idea of what he wanted to achieve. Edmond Galabert tells us that, when he met Bizet, the latter spoke of *Les Pêcheurs de perles* as a work of no value, but later said that he was nonetheless "pleased to have been able to write a few of its passages at so young an age."[59]

The history of the famous *romance* from *Mignon*, "Connais-tu le pays," provides a good example of the creative community that could shape an opera. According to the creator of the title role, Célestine Galli-Marié, Ambroise Thomas composed "two versions of the music." Since the singer liked both equally well, "it was the orchestra musicians, whom we consulted, who made the decision."[60] Singers sometimes played a part even while a work was still being written. Adolphe Nourrit, a cultivated and intelligent singer, wrote the text of the famous aria "Rachel, quand du seigneur" from *La Juive,* and was an active participant in the creation of *Les Huguenots.* Moreover, most librettists and composers conceived roles in the light of the vocal capabilities, physical appearance, and temperaments of the available singers, who would in turn be determined by the roster of the theater that was to produce the work. An 1845 letter from Scribe to Auber, regarding the *opéra-comique La Sirène* (1844), is most illuminating in this regard: "I have arranged the principal role for [Gustave-Hippolyte] Roger....When I wrote the part for [Jean-Baptiste] Chollet, I had no other option, but it distressed me. Because Chollet, who can still be good in burlesque or fantastical roles, is dreadful when truth, verve, and, above all, interest are required."[61] At times, the relationship with singers could be conflictual. A good example of this comes from Gounod's *Mireille;* as noted in *Le Ménestrel* of February 7, 1864, the singer Mme Miolan-Carvalho and the composer had to agree to "mutual concessions."

Like Italian opera, traditional French opera was the work of a strange, divided creative entity: the nexus of the tensions among several individuals.

These tensions would be heightened if the principal participant, the composer, was in a weak position—because of his youth, for example. They would diminish if, on the other hand, the composer's fame and creative energy were dominant, as was the case with Meyerbeer. Adaptation and revision show that an opera is not an aesthetically self-contained, perfect artifact, but a living thing whose acclimatization must take into account the circumstances and evolution of its milieu. Meyerbeer fashioned his scores so that they could be adapted to the capabilities of various theaters and performers. For example, *Le Prophète* contains many instructions for cuts, arrangements, and simplifications. The role of Fidès, written for the uncommon voice of Pauline Viardot, had to be open to simplification: "Every time the vocal line, written to show off Mme Viardot's exceptional compass, rises or falls above or below the normal mezzo-soprano range, a way to avoid this extension will be found, written in small notes," Meyerbeer explained.[62]

### TRANSLATION, ADAPTATION, AND RE-CREATION

Less than a year after arriving in Paris in August 1824, Rossini completed his final Italian work, *Il Viaggio a Reims,* written to mark the coronation of Charles X. Then, while his older works were enjoying an enormous success at the Théâtre-Italien, he prepared to write a French opera. For practice, he began by adapting *Maometto II* (which became *Le Siège de Corinthe*) in 1826, and *Mosè in Egitto* (*Moïse*) in 1827. These two works were not merely translated, but were rebuilt and adapted both to the conventions of the Académie de musique and to French declamation. They are two re-creations that hold an important place in the history of the incipient French genre of *grand opéra*. In writing *Le Comte Ory* (1828), Rossini drew on many elements from *Il Viaggio*. Then, finally, he wrote a completely new score, *Guillaume Tell* (1829).

Such adaptations are more disturbing when done after a composer's death. The light orchestration of Grétry's operas, for example, was deemed too thin and was filled out (notably by Adolphe Adam) to bring it into line with the kind of sound that a mid-nineteenth-century audience would expect. Even worse, there were pastiches of foreign operas, such as *Les Mystères d'Isis,* based on Mozart's *Die Zauberflöte,* which was produced in Paris in 1801, and *Robin des bois*—Weber's *Der Freischütz* vastly revised by Castil-Blaze—put on at the Théâtre de l'Odéon in 1824.

Mozart's opera was turned into a hodgepodge of arias taken, according to the press in 1801, from *Don Giovanni, La Clemenza di Tito,* and *Le Nozze di Figaro*—and, indeed, from *Die Zauberflöte* itself—as well as from

scraps of music by Haydn, Pleyel, Sacchini, and Lemoyne, all linked together by recitatives specially composed for the occasion. The whole affair
was cobbled together by the Czech-born Parisian Ludwig Wenzel Lachnith
(1746–1820).[63] The adaptation of *Der Freischütz* was just as much the work
of Castil-Blaze, assisted by the librettist Thomas Sauvage, as it was
Weber's. In the relationship between opera and audience, it was the former
that had to adapt to the latter—whose requirements were shaped by national tastes and rules. "Experience has already shown that German plays
and operas could not be naturalized in France without being adjusted and
made to conform to our theatrical customs, which are so different from the
romantic excesses of such as Schiller and [Friedrich] Kind," a journalist observed in 1824.[64] Here again, the opera offered to the spectator was little
more than a proposal that was subject to change. "The clearly expressed
opinion of a large and well-informed audience persuaded the librettists to
make the changes that taste and effect seemed to demand," the same journalist added. Even when a German company came to Paris in 1829 to give
a series of performances in the original language, they took care to use
every means to ensure success. After the first performance, on May 14, cuts
were made, and the tenor Haitzinger, "who found . . . little to display his talent in the awkward vocal lines of *Der Freischütz*, inserted into the third act
a most charming aria, mimicking the Italian style, which gave him scope
for cadenzas and roulades."[65]

When *Don Giovanni* was produced (as *Don Juan*) at the Opéra on
March 10, 1834, the director of the theater had no hesitation in adding an
entire ballet made up of fragments from a variety of Mozart's works. But
what most scandalized Berlioz, who wrote an account for *Le Rénovateur* of
March 16, 1834, was not the addition itself, but the musical choices that
had been made:

> Since you wanted a dance *no matter what,* it would have been better,
> more honest and fairer to have someone compose some genuine ballet
> pieces, and to admit that these had nothing to do with the composer of
> *Don Juan,* rather than using shreds violently torn here from an operatic
> duet, there from a piano concerto, all drawn out, truncated, dislocated—
> from which you have made nothing other than a horrible mixture,
> whose worst defect is that it is no good for dancing.

But from the very outset there was a group who opposed these barbaric
translations. "The musical world," wrote a critic in 1834, "is talking of
nothing but *Der Freischütz* (*Robin des bois*), which, full of lovely numbers,
makes such an astonishing effect in a piece from which, thanks to the

Figure 1.    Title page of *Le Chasseur noir,* the first French edition of Weber's *Der Freischütz,* published in 1824. It is remarkably faithful to the original compared with Castil-Blaze's reworking of the score, produced in the same year and published under the title *Robin des bois.*

admirable arrangement of M. Castil-Blaze, all the outstanding numbers have been either eliminated or whittled away."[66] For that reason, the journalist recommended to his readers the score published by Schlesinger under the more promising title of *Le Chasseur noir*[67] (see fig. 1), rather than that of Castil-Blaze.[68]

But the phenomenon of translation/adaptation is not unique to music: it is found also in literature. It is something that has been fundamental to the history of cultural interchange—which takes place above all by adopting foreign works of art as one's own. This in turn involves a whole range of manipulations. Specific national characteristics, extremely powerful and vigorously championed as part of the French identity, had long demarcated a tightly secured cultural space that was virtually closed to outside elements, which to some extent limited the public's receptiveness. François-Victor Hugo (1828–1873), in the "Observations" that opened his translation of the complete works of Shakespeare, explains the approach taken in the 1770s by the author of the first French translation, Félicien Letourneur:

> It must not be forgotten that Letourneur's version, which served as a model for all other translations published thus far, dates from the eighteenth century; that is, the first interpreter of Shakespeare had to make, and did make, many concessions. It was already rather audacious to present to the narrow literary critics of the day a kind of drama that ignored the distinction between tragedy and comedy, and that violated the law of the unities—even without adding to these liberties its stylistic liberties. It should therefore come as no surprise if Letourneur's translation is full of paraphrase, if it shrouds the thoughts of the poet in so much circumlocution, and if it remains so far from the original despite the conscientious efforts of M. Guizot [the author of an 1821 revision of Letourneur's translation] to bring it closer.[69]

Along the same lines is the case of F.-A. Loève-Veimars, a German émigré living in Paris, who between 1829 and 1833 published twenty volumes of translations of the tales of E. T. A. Hoffmann. These prove to be adaptations that willfully stray from the German originals.

As audiences became culturally able to absorb various national styles, rewriting that drastically changed a work from top to bottom was abandoned in favor of more limited adjustments. In 1841, Berlioz himself, who had harshly censured Castil-Blaze's tampering—*tripatouillage* as it was called at the time—agreed to revise Weber's score so that it could be played at the Opéra. This included substituting recitatives for the spoken dialogue (forbidden on the stage of the Opéra), and orchestrating the famous "Invitation à la valse," as well as some fragments from *Oberon* and *Preciosa*—

this to abide by the Opéra's conventions regarding ballet. But this more respectful attitude was by no means universally acclaimed, and indeed *La France musicale* was able to write: "M. Castil-Blaze was a man of keen mind and good taste who entirely understood that what was a masterpiece for the Germans might very well not be so for the French, and that one might, through certain modifications, enhance even further the merits of a work."[70] A few weeks before the premiere of this new version of *Der Freischütz*, on June 7, 1841, Wagner published two articles in the *Revue et Gazette musicale*, expressing his concern at seeing so essentially German a work adapted to conform to French conventions. This exceptional score, he said, would have warranted the Opéra making an exception to its rules about recitatives and ballet.[71] At the time of the 1876 revival of the Berlioz version at the Palais Garnier, Saint-Saëns said more or less the same: "This is a small-town *grand opéra*, something essentially Germanic that is difficult to acclimatize everywhere else."[72]

In its turn, the French repertory was translated for performance in foreign theaters. In Italy and in the many Italian opera houses in other countries, it was unthinkable to perform an opera with spoken dialogue, such as a French *opéra-comique*. That is why in the 1880s and 1890s, *Carmen* triumphed worldwide in the version that included the recitatives added by Ernest Guiraud. Massenet, who lived to see his music gain international success, was himself open to this sort of arrangement, and composed recitatives for the Italian performances of *Manon*. In 1857, it was altogether normal for a columnist to announce in *Le Ménestrel* of March 22 that the Italian opera in London would "next season give Auber's *Fra Diavolo*, with recitatives expressly written by the celebrated composer, a new *romance* for Mario, and a new finale."

Finally, the notion that a work should always remain the same is a very recent one. "Nowadays perhaps," warily wrote Albert Soubies in 1899, "it would no longer be permissible to insert into the first act [of Gluck's *Orphée*] the *vocalises* that appear in the score 'conforming to the performance' " at the Théâtre-Lyrique in 1859. "That was," he continued, "a concession to the taste of the time."[73] Similarly, it was not considered necessary to perform an opera in complete form. On the contrary, there were performances of operatic excerpts. Liszt was against this and condemned "this new kind of vandalism that assails the most admirable masterpieces, *Guillaume Tell, Moïse, Don Giovanni;* which dismembers them, mutilates them, by chopping away two-thirds of them; and that hands them to the audience only in broken-up fragments on the pretext of putting together an appealing show."[74]

An older work was viewed as similar to a foreign work, and many people felt that, removed from its context, it no longer made any sense. "Whatever can be said about Gluck, Piccini, Sacchini, and the other masters of yore," wrote Théophile Gautier,

> is on the bookshelves and the pianos of music-lovers. They are inexhaustible sources of exercises for virtuosos, but a living audience requires living works. Nothing can replace the contemporary atmosphere. However great an admirer of the past one might be, one is left somewhat cold by the performance of an ancient masterpiece; one feels that these are dead words, dead melodies. Their soul has fled; they no longer have the sense of life that an audience in communion with the author imparts to a piece. Those tossed-off words, those sentences left hanging, which everyone would have filled out in accordance with the common notions of the time, are no longer understandable except through a retrospective intuition of which few minds are capable.[75]

That is why the writer-critic came to the defense of the work of the reviser: "Certainly, the score of *Le Déserteur* [by Monsigny] has greatly aged; but it is full of gay, singable melodies that remain popular.... M. Adolphe Adam has updated... certain parts of the accompaniment that had become completely outmoded, which will undoubtedly earn him the charge of vandalism leveled at him in connection with [Grétry's] *Richard* by some toothless fanatics who cannot bear anyone touching their idols, even to remove the dust with which they are covered."[76]

The attitude of Victor Wilder in a column in *Le Ménestrel* dated December 7, 1873, was still the same, for, like the vast majority of his contemporaries, he believed in evolution in the arts: "In the flow of the libretto, a few inconsequential changes have updated Sedaine's prose. As to the music, we know that Adolphe Adam had already altered the orchestration for the 1841 revival. Indeed, it is in that respect alone that the operas of Grétry have acquired a few wrinkles, and it is impossible to see why it should be forbidden to remove them."

Theater directors and performers were not yet taking the "authentic version" approach. Yet early on we see the beginnings of a movement to rediscover old music, and there were scattered signs of a change in thinking. When François-Joseph Fétis organized the *concerts historiques* in 1832, he said that he was "working on ways to give the performance of... pieces the local color and tradition of each period."[77]

The whole problem in the task of revising was to know how far you could go, according to what criteria, and at what point the work would become disfigured. To put it differently, when exactly did a loss of identity occur? The image of the omnipotent creator left to us by Wagner must not obscure this way of thinking, which governed most of the operatic world. The master of Bayreuth himself began by accepting this system, or at least tried to abide by its practices, if only by revising for the French stage an opera originally written in German, *Tannhäuser*. In a way, it was good to understand that a work had to be adapted to a given theater, to a given audience, and to the conventions of a given national repertory—even though for the sake of dramatic realism, Wagner refused to move the danced divertissement from the first to the second act.[78] His attitude gradually changed, and the system was reversed. It was no longer a matter of trying to adapt a finished work to each audience; rather, it became obvious that it was the job of the audience to abandon all its prejudices so as to hear the author's message in its original form, and to make contact with the quasisacred work of a godlike creator. And to be sure, it would be hard to imagine a performance of *Parsifal* today translated into French (or English) with cuts, changes, or indeed expansions in some of its scenes, and with the addition of a ballet. This evolution has taken place in all countries and has been accompanied by a transformation in the social function of opera.[79] Such thoughts could not have been further from the minds of Gounod and Bizet, even though, like so many of their contemporaries, they must have bridled at the limited power enjoyed by the composer.

Performances succeeded genesis—or overlapped with it. The work emerged from its gestation period in the fluid form of an opera. The opera and its creators now had even less freedom of action than at the time of its birth. In appearing before the public, they were entering the territory of a society that lived by a rigorous code.

# Chapter 2   Performance

More than any other theatrical form, opera is subject to the vagaries of managing a company whose principal tool is a particularly fragile one: the human voice. The complexity of productions; the selection of performers; dealing with authors, singers, instrumentalists, scene painters, and so forth; and the heavy workload of rehearsals: these are but a few of the many problems confronting a theater director. "Preparing an opera is nothing like preparing an ordinary play," Alfred Bruneau wrote in 1931:

> It takes far longer and is more complicated and more fragmented. First, the singers individually learn the music and words of their roles with a pianist whose job it is to guide them and motivate them. They are not brought together—they do not do the so-called ensembles—until they can perform their parts from memory. During these difficult and slow explorations, the chorus is at work in a hall of its own. Then comes the stage direction: the positioning of each character and the gestures best suited to his mood and actions are decided on the stage itself. Meanwhile, the orchestra—either divided into string, woodwind, and brass sections, or all together—defines and balances the instrumental sound. But that is not all. Before the decisive test of the dress rehearsals, all these various groups are brought together for a so-called *répétition à l'italienne*, where everyone is seated and concentrates only on the rhythmic gestures of the time-beaters. Let me add that if there is a ballet, the men and women dancers carry out their preparatory tasks on their own.[1]

In 1852, the Théâtre-Lyrique tried a new approach to performances, alternating two casts for Adolphe Adam's *Si j'étais roi*. This novel practice won practically no converts, and the press observed that the audience came out only on days featuring the better of the two.

Producing an opera called for a strategy that took into account not only the artists, theater director, and scheduling but the struggles over influence (and sometimes over politics too) that dogged the workings of any theater. The difficulties were not only internal, and did not involve only the performers and the orchestra. Gounod spelled out these problems in September 1861 after completing the score of *La Reine de Saba*:

> On Monday I went to the Opéra with the intention of immediately beginning preparations with my artists. Unfortunately, I found quite a different situation from what I expected. First, *Alceste*, which will not take place until early October, has deprived me of my chorus. Secondly, the Prince [Poniatowski] has asked for a revival of [his opera] *Pierre de Médicis* and is using my principal performers. Thirdly, Royer [the Opéra administrator] also spoke to me about a revival of [Halévy's] *La Reine de Chypre* ordered by the minister. Confronted with all these obstacles, I can do nothing but wait: the minister is in Biarritz, and I cannot turn to him to clear up the situation.[2]

Diplomacy vis-à-vis the major artists, politics, management, and financial questions all influenced the choice of dates for rehearsals and performances. Since it was difficult—indeed, impossible—to predict a success, it was important to control all the elements that could pave the way to one. Scribe expressed concern to Auber about the future of *Haydée:*

> First of all, the first two acts have become known. There is nothing more we can do about them. Secondly, if we wait to put act 3 together, this brings us right into December, and you know that is the worst time of all: it is automatic death to success. Moreover, if we move it back to January, you know that Roger [the tenor] is leaving at the end of April, and that our piece—which his departure will kill forever—will have had barely three months of life. Finally—and this is the key point—our work seemed to be destined for great success, but the longer we continue, the more impossible our young Greek slave seems to me. So what will happen with the third act? I fear that this may jeopardize everything.[3]

Let us return to 1863 and *Les Pêcheurs de perles*. After having been closed for three months (from June to August 1863), the Théâtre-Lyrique reopened on September 3 with Mozart's *Le Nozze di Figaro*, in the 1858 French-language version by Barbier and Carré. The work had not been performed in this theater since 1860. The opening night had been scheduled for September 1, but it was delayed for two days by the indisposition of Mme Ugalde and of Mlle Brunetti. *Les Pêcheurs de perles* was to have opened the new season, as announced in *Le Ménestrel* on May 31, 1863, but the premiere was delayed several times. The role of Léïla, initially assigned to Mlle Ebrard, a student at the Conservatoire, was in the end given to Léontine de Maësen. But the illness of the new soprano again delayed the performance, and revivals of Grétry's *L'Epreuve villageoise* and of Méhul's *Joseph* were announced pending the production of Bizet's new three-act opera. In his column, Berlioz wrote of a cold that kept the singer away from the theater for more than ten days.[4] The management had to accept this situation, and "*Les Noces de Figaro* helped us to be patient," a writer in the *Guide musical* noted.[5]

The quality of a performance depended in part on how well known the composer was. Marie Escudier commented that Léon Carvalho had put on "the work of a virtually unknown composer at great expense, and with as much care as would be devoted to a work of Meyerbeer or Auber."[6] Léontine de Maësen (Léïla, soprano), Jean-Vital Ismaël (Zurga, baritone), and François Morini (Nadir, tenor), it was noted, "are three highly worthy artists who can bear comparison with the best of Paris's other operatic theaters."[7]

The brilliance of the September 30 premiere quickly tarnished, and the dwindling success of Bizet's opera dimmed Carvalho's hopes. The table showing the works performed at the Théâtre-Lyrique between September 27 and November 28, 1863 (see Appendix 5), goes to the heart of the problems of managing a theater, and puts *Les Pêcheurs* in the theatrical context in which it was conceived. At that time it would have been unthinkable to devote a whole block of time to a single work. Opera houses were meant to be places of entertainment and had to offer several works in rotation. The older theaters, such as the Opéra and the Opéra-Comique, operated on the basis of their own proprietary repertories, which always enabled them to return to a tried-and-true score, either complete or, sometimes, in the form of individual acts. The Théâtre-Lyrique, which like the Opéra-Comique was burdened with daily performances, had been founded only a few years earlier and thus had a limited repertory.

Here is a good example relating to all these matters. In December 1902, only a few months after the April 30 premiere of *Pelléas et Mélisande* at the Opéra-Comique, *La Revue musicale* published the daily box-office receipts of the Opéra and of the Opéra-Comique (see table 2.1). A comparison of the two scheduling systems and the two sets of figures is revealing. The *Revue* entitled this table "The Musical Barometer" and prefaced it with a brief note on how to interpret the data:

> In reading the table . . . one must not forget: that some performances were for a broad audience [*populaires*], or at reduced prices; that others were subscription evenings where a portion of the take was guaranteed; that others owe much of their high figures to a major guest artist. . . . Finally,

Table 2.1.

| Theater | Opera Performed | Date [1902] | Receipts (francs) |
|---|---|---|---|
| Opéra | Lohengrin | November 19 | 17,195.76 |
| Opéra | Les Huguenots | November 21 | 15,332.41 |
| Opéra | La Valkyrie | November 22 | 16,751.00 |
| Opéra | Les Barbares, Bacchus (premiere) | November 26 | 12,237.26 |
| Opéra | Les Barbares, Bacchus | November 28 | 13,683.41 |
| Opéra | Rigoletto, Bacchus | December 1 | 14,173.41 |
| Opéra | Les Huguenots | December 3 | 14,160.26 |
| Opéra | Roméo | December 5 | 13,946.91 |
| Opéra | Rigoletto, Bacchus | December 6 | 12,082.50 |
| Opéra | Don Juan | December 8 | 12,880.91 |
| Opéra | Faust | December 10 | 16,357.26 |
| Opéra | Les Barbares, Bacchus | December 12 | 13,255.91 |
| Opéra | Salammbô (reduced prices) | December 13 | 10,819.00 |
| Opéra | Bacchus, Les Barbares | December 15 | 10,856.95 |
| Opéra | Paillasse, Bacchus | December 17 | 14,234.26 |
| | | | |
| Opéra-Comique | Louise | November 18 | 5,679.50 |
| Opéra-Comique | Mme Dugazon, La Vie de Bohème | November 19 | 3,143.50 |
| Opéra-Comique | Le Médecin malgré lui, Cavalleria | November 20 | 8,938.50 |
| Opéra-Comique | Pelléas et Mélisande | November 21 | 4,939.50 |
| Opéra-Comique | Le Médecin malgré lui, Cavalleria | November 22 | 9,481.50 |
| Opéra-Comique | Mignon | November 23 (mat.) | 7,436.50 |
| Opéra-Comique | Lakmé | November 23 (eve.) | 4,533.00 |
| Opéra-Comique | Cavalleria | November 24 | 5,595.50 |
| Opéra-Comique | Mme Dugazon, La Vie de Bohème | November 25 | 3,455.50 |
| Opéra-Comique | Louise | November 26 | 5,651.50 |
| Opéra-Comique | Le Médecin malgré lui, Cavalleria | November 27 (subscription) | 9,348.50 |
| Opéra-Comique | Mireille | November 28 | 4,270.50 |
| Opéra-Comique | Pelléas et Mélisande | November 29 | 7,646.00 |
| Opéra-Comique | Lakmé, Les Noces de Jeannette | November 30 (mat.) | 8,569.00 |
| Opéra-Comique | Carmen | November 30 (eve.) | 6,147.50 |
| Opéra-Comique | Cavalleria (Mme E[mma] Calvé) | December 1 | 9,064.50 |
| Opéra-Comique | Manon | December 2 | 6,393.50 |
| Opéra-Comique | Le Roi d'Ys | December 3 | 3,637.50 |
| Opéra-Comique | Mme Dugazon, La Vie de Bohème | December 4 | 5,716.00 |
| Opéra-Comique | Louise | December 5 | 4,691.00 |

Table 2.1. *(Continued)*

| Theater | Opera Performed | Date [1902] | Receipts (francs) |
|---------|-----------------|-------------|-------------------|
| Opéra-Comique | *Pelléas et Mélisande* | December 6 | 6,384.00 |
| Opéra-Comique | *La Fille du Régiment, Le Médecin malgré lui* | December 7 (mat.) | 6,819.00 |
| Opéra-Comique | *Manon* | December 7 (eve.) | 4,964.50 |
| Opéra-Comique | *Mignon* | December 8 ("popular") | 3,851.50 |
| Opéra-Comique | *Le Maître de Chapelle, La Vie de Bohème* | December 10 | 3,157.00 |
| Opéra-Comique | *Louise* | December 11 | 6,958.00 |
| Opéra-Comique | *Carmen* | December 12 | 5,548.50 |
| Opéra-Comique | *Mireille* (subscription) | December 13 | 7,557.50 |
| Opéra-Comique | *Pelléas et Mélisande* | December 14 (mat.) | 5,709.00 |
| Opéra-Comique | *Maître Wolfram, Le Domino Noir* | December 14 (eve.) | 3,512.00 |
| Opéra-Comique | *Maître Wolfram, Lakmé* | December 15 | 6,743.00 |
| Opéra-Comique | *La Carmélite* (premiere) | December 16 | 2,213.00 |
| Opéra-Comique | *Manon* | December 17 | 6,203.50 |

one must understand this: every time the weather is inclement (rain, frost, snow, too hot or too cold, fog, etc.), the receipts—which are just as sensitive as the stockmarket is to the political situation—are invariably affected.... Let us recall that the maximum for the Opéra [in 1902] is 22,500 francs, and 9,500 francs for the Opéra-Comique."

*Les Pêcheurs de perles* alternated at the Théâtre-Lyrique with Mozart's *Figaro*. To reverse the definite downward trend in the receipts for the first five performances (from around 3,000 to around 2,000 francs per performance), the director tried to draw a larger audience by preceding Bizet's three-act opera with a more easily accessible score he had just revived: Grétry's *L'Epreuve villageoise*. The curtain time was moved forward by forty-five minutes, from 8:00 to 7:15 P.M.

Since *Les Pêcheurs* was not a great success, the theater was obliged to capitalize on *Figaro*, which continued to do well, thanks to a brilliant performance by Mme Carvalho. To instill a sense of urgency among theatergoers, announcements of the "final" performances appeared in the newspapers, such as this one from *L'Entr'acte* of October 15, 1863: "The Théâtre-Lyrique Impériale announces the final performances of *Les Noces de Figaro*. That work will be performed only six more times. The first performance of *Les Troyens* by Berlioz will take place at the beginning of

November.... Immediately following this, the Théâtre-Lyrique will revive *La Perle du Brésil* by Félicien David." The management wanted to publicize the activities of the theater, which could not simply rest on the laurels of a prior success. The advent of *Les Troyens* made it possible to space out the performances of Bizet's opera. In a final effort, Grétry's *L'Epreuve villageoise* was scheduled as the first item on a program that included *Figaro*—which repeatedly survived its "irrevocable final performance." Bizet's opera was taken off without warning after November 24, when the box office took in the paltry sum of 674 francs; meanwhile, another work with an exotic theme, *La Perle du Brésil*, was revived on November 26.

## THE THEATER AND MANNERS

Every operatic performance was governed by rules and took place in stages that the audience both understood and expected. As soon as a planned production was announced, a buzz began, which was picked up by the press and sustained the curiosity of a public always hungry for theatrical gossip. Seating arrangements followed a true social topography. For instance, in the 1830s, Frédéric Soulié said of the Académie de musique:

> Apart from the members of Paris society who go to the Opéra, there is an operatic public. The most permanent, the most inevitable, is the public of *la fashion*, that harbinger of vogues, who have come to be called *petits maîtres, incroyables, merveilleux, élégants*, and *dandys*.... In general, they inhabit the balcony and the boxes; they know the opera—by which I mean the singers, the dancers, and the management—by heart. The real music-lovers, the artists, and the journalists generally sit in the orchestra.[8]

Traditions were lovingly preserved by the regulars, who felt completely at home in the theater. Any change in etiquette would precipitate conflict or commotion. Halanzier-Dufrénoy, director of the Opéra from 1871 to 1879, was harshly criticized when he decided to admit women to the orchestra seats.

Ordinarily, one of the artists would announce the opera's composer and librettist at the end of the performance. In the case of *Les Pêcheurs de perles*, the announcement indicated that Bizet had won the Prix de Rome in 1857, to which people objected. "Ismaël [the baritone] appended to M. Bizet's name, 'Prix de Rome for 1857.' What did this mean? And what does it matter to the audience? When they perform *Les Troyens* will they also say, 'M. Berlioz, Prix de Rome for 1830, Chevalier de la Légion d'Honneur, member of the Institut, Librarian of the Conservatoire, etc., etc.?' If need be, M. Berlioz will sort this out."[9]

This first gaffe was noted by more than one journalist, but there was another, more serious one: Bizet came on stage to take a bow. While the young
Emmanuel Chabrier understood "the training of a young composer, eager
and proud to thank both the audience that had commended the fruit of his
labors and the fine orchestra that had performed it,"[10] the majority of writers viewed Bizet's appearance as crude, especially since (in a third error),
"over his black suit," he wore a gray *paletot*, albeit "of a pleasing shade," as
Nestor Roqueplan noted.[11] This poor garment was written about in papers
as diverse as *L'Illustration, Le Journal amusant, L'Opinion nationale,* and
*L'Art musicale.*[12] Albert Wolff jokingly imagined a hysterical scene had *Les
Pêcheurs* been a success: "reckless friends would have torn [it] to shreds...
and would have distributed the pieces as everlasting mementos of that
lovely evening."[13] Gustave Bertrand offered the scatterbrained young man
a lesson in manners: "There was general surprise to see him appear on stage
to greet the audience at the end of the work. This may be the custom in
Italy, but we are in France, and M. Bizet is French. We here do not permit
such exhibitions except for an absolutely exceptional success, and even then
the author ought to be dragged out against his will, or should make it appear
so."[14] Bizet's divergence from the rules of etiquette was far more serious
than one might think: "By appearing at the end, M. Bizet alienated many
people: modesty is seemly in a young man, and a conscript who has gained
a victory will sometimes delay his commissioning as an officer."[15]

Verdi took a bow when he conducted *Aida* in Paris in 1880, and his appearance and the attendant commotion by no means pleased the traditionalists. Adolphe Heulhard stormed in *Le Télégraphe* on March 24, 1880:
"Parisians, buffeted last night by a wind that blew in from Italy, turned the
return of *Aida* into a ceremony that did not in any way succeed in being
impressive. The inarticulate cries of enthusiasm, the *successi stupendi,* the
thundering applause, the tumultuous calls for the maestro at the end of the
*capolavoro* are not acclimatized to French soil."

The unfortunate experience of *Tannhäuser* in 1861 was first and foremost the result of a breach of customary behavior. For a portion of the audience, the *Tannhäuser* scandal may have been an opportunity to show
their opposition to the regime of Napoleon III. But the factors involved in
this affair were so numerous, contradictory, and diverse that we must be
circumspect and, in the absence of any primary sources revealing what was
in the minds of the demonstrators, must refrain from trying to put words
into the mouths of those who are long dead and gone. The waters are
clouded by the fact that the issue was a blend of nationalism (France versus
the Germanic countries), aesthetics, morality, style, and musical language.

It is a well-known story, so let us just recall that the members of the Jockey Club[16] joined in a cabal against Wagner, who had not agreed to insert a ballet into act 2, which was the time when these gentlemen would habitually come, after dinner, to admire their protégées among the ballerinas. Despite the presence of the emperor, the tumult and whistling made the composer withdraw his work after only three performances (on March 13, 18, and 24). "One cannot recall such an evening in the precincts of our great Opéra, normally so calm and serene," a writer reported after the second performance.[17] Finally, the press published a letter from Wagner addressed to the director of the Opéra: "The opposition that has been expressed to *Tannhäuser* proves to me how right you were when, at the outset of this business, you commented to me on the lack of a ballet and other stage conventions to which the Opéra's subscribers are accustomed. I regret that the nature of my work prevented me from conforming to those requirements."[18] Wagner omits to say that he had needed 163 rehearsals and that he had moreover come up against the habits of the orchestra pit. Wagner had been dissatisfied with the work of the conductor, Pierre-Louis-Philippe Dietsch, and had officially requested permission to conduct the work himself. The minister of state, Count Alexandre Walewski (Napoleon I's illegitimate son), replied on March 8: "Never in France—whether relating to works by our own composers or to those of foreign masters such as Rossini and Meyerbeer—has the orchestra director been stripped of the right to remain at the head of his corps of performers."[19]

What is more, by failing to submit totally to the laws and proprieties of Franco-Italian opera, and by destabilizing the reign of singing and of the performers, Wagner was committing yet another error and was breaking with the dominant aesthetic code.

SINGING REIGNS SUPREME

Audiences were inordinately fond of vocal exploits and fashionable prima donnas such as the two daughters of Manuel Garcia, Maria Malibran (1808–1836) and Pauline Viardot (1821–1910). The first of the two died prematurely and was immortalized by one of her admirers, Alfred de Musset, in a poem entitled *A la Malibran*, whose eighth stanza extols her singing:

> O Ninette! où sont-ils, belle muse adorée,
> Ces accents pleins d'amour, de charme et de terreur,
> Qui voltigeaient le soir sur ta lèvre inspirée,
> Comme un parfum léger sur l'aubépine en fleur?

Où vibre maintenant cette voix éplorée,
Cette harpe vivante attachée à ton coeur?

O Ninette—beautiful, adored muse—where are
Those tones full of love, charm, and dread
Which floated of an evening o'er thy inspired lips
Like a delicate perfume o'er the flowering hawthorn?
Where does that tearful voice stir now—
That living harp joined to thy heart?

Even today, particular types of voices are designated in French by the names of some of these singers. The *baryton martin* is named for the brilliant, smooth, wide-ranging voice of the Opéra-Comique's Jean-Blaise Martin (1768–1837), for example, while the roles known as *jeunes dugazon* and *mères dugazon* refer to his colleague Louise-Rosalie Dugazon (1755–1821), who in the course of her long career there played first ingenues, then mothers. Similarly, a *soprano falcon* is essentially a dramatic soprano of the type of Cornélie Falcon (1814–1897)—nominally a mezzo-soprano but with a range that extended from low B to high D—who created the roles of Rachel in Halévy's *La Juive* and Valentine in Meyerbeer's *Les Huguenots* at the Opéra.

The voice of the coloratura soprano Marie Cabel (1827–1885) helped define Auber's Manon, Meyerbeer's Dinorah, and Philine in Thomas's *Mignon,* and, later in the century, Sybil Sanderson (1865–1903) inspired and created Massenet's *Esclarmonde* and *Thaïs.* The composition of an opera naturally involved such performers, whose talents had an influence on the composer and who sometimes played an active role in the creative process. Indeed, the power of their singing and acting alone could keep a work in the repertory. The success in 1856 of Louis Clapisson's *La Fanchonnette* and Victor Massé's *La Reine Topaze* cannot be dissociated from the personality of their lead singer, Marie Miolan (1827–1895), known as Caroline Carvalho after her marriage to Léon Carvalho in 1853, who had one of the most beautiful voices of the day and was "a performer...of ideal refinement and rare elegance."[20] This singer, who portrayed the heroines in Gounod's principal works, lent her support to operas whose signal merit was that they provided her with an opportunity to shine. The euphoria kindled by the vocal sparks of her coloratura kept audiences on the edge of their seats and nearly always aroused enthusiastic applause. Although the box-office takings of the Carré-Barbier version of *Figaro* in the 1850s and 1860s might be construed as reflecting public recognition of Mozart's art, the fact is that Mme Carvalho's Chérubin (Cherubino) was at the root of the production's success. Similarly, when *Orphée* was revived at the Théâtre-Lyrique in 1859, listeners were struck not by Gluck's genius but by the presence on stage of Pauline Viardot, and their cravings were satisfied by the vocalises she added to the score.

Vocal feats were especially gripping when they involved a rivalry with instrumental virtuosity. Caroline Carvalho triumphed in *La Reine Topaze*, for example, with her dizzying act 2 variations on "Carnaval de Venise," a "monumental and delightful tour de force" that *Le Ménestrel* likened to the "miraculous fantasias of the late Paganini."[21] The contrast between voice and instrument reached its apex in the nightingale (or other songbird) arias that were so common, which combined the agility of a flutelike voice and the flexibility of a flute in the orchestra. Audiences loved to hear a soprano soar into the stratosphere of ultra-high notes—it seemed impossible that a human voice could reach such frequencies. Never at a loss for a witty turn of phrase, journalists drew on current events to describe this seemingly supernatural phenomenon—Auguste Vitu, for example, called Sybil Sanderson's high G in Massenet's *Esclarmonde,* first produced during the 1889 Exposition Universelle, for which Gustave Eiffel built his tower, "the tone of a genuine piccolo,...the 'Eiffel Tone' of the Opéra-Comique."[22]

During the first half of the century, coloratura had reigned at the Théâtre-Italien. It was the basis of a type of vocal training rejected by Liszt, who used the felicitous expression *entrechats de gosier,*[23] "throat entrechats," to describe singers' virtuosic antics. This was a weighty judgment: as the apostle of new music and the champion of Berlioz and Wagner, Liszt advocated a society in which theaters would be wide open to young authors rather than "warming over successes from Naples and Milan."[24] And Liszt, who reformed many genres (although not opera) and transformed the language of music, certainly could not appreciate the dying embers of a vocal aesthetic whose sources lay in eighteenth-century *opera seria,* which was based on instilling wonderment and on the creation of an imaginary world ruled by singing for singing's sake.

When Théophile Gautier saw Marietta Alboni[25] in Rossini's *La Cenerentola,* he admired "that unrivaled evenness; that astonishing perfection; those lavishly strung necklaces of auditory pearls; all her beautiful singing that is so bold, so clear and so pure, so classic and so youthful, so full of elegance and strength, in which no sign of fatigue or effort can be discerned."[26] When the singer made her debut in that opera in December 1847, Gautier clearly described the close connection between virtuosity and wonderment that was at the heart of the bel canto aesthetic:

What an astounding tour de force was the performance of the final *rondo*—one of the most difficult of all passages to sing. Alboni uttered it with unimaginable perfection. Anything more flexible, more mellow, more brilliant cannot be imagined. All those risky leaps were executed effortlessly. There was no jolting in the most abrupt passages. The sound—whether it was climbing in its golden slippers the crystal staircase of the scale and glistening in the light atop that tower of sound built of several stories of octaves, or whether it was descending with a more somber footfall down to the lowest steps of the musical staircase, ever phosphorescent in the shadows of those lower purlieus—was always pure, strong and sweet; the echo of not a single footfall went astray.[27]

With his characteristic use of imagery, Gautier succeeded in finding words to express the full magic of such singing:

When we hear a Rossini aria, a patch of blue sky appears overhead; the sun shines; a sea of blue dotted with white sails extends to the horizon; lemons and oranges, as in Mignon's song, suddenly ripen beneath emerald leaves; dark eyes sparkle and white smiles gleam from dusky faces.... The happy, carefree spirit of southern climes, which inspires nimbleness of gesture and volubility of language, breathes in these easy, light melodies, dazzling rockets of sound that suddenly take off, first bursting into radiance and then vanishing.[28]

The drama was outstripped, or rather condensed, by vocal expression. "Singing in a dramatic manner," wrote Gautier, "does not mean, as is too often believed, pacing the stage, flailing the arms, rolling the eyes; it means stressing the forceful passages and expressing passion and feeling by vocal inflection, by the accents that the soul lends to the word, and not by exaggerated gestures." The writer, who was so passionate about opera, then put the case of the tenor Giovanni Battista Rubini (1794–1854), "who had always been considered as a wretched actor when he was not actually grotesque." Rubini, he insisted, nonetheless "rose...to the highest level of dramatic expression in the last scene of *Lucia*. No tragedian has ever produced more profound, moving, and harrowing emotion. All the lacerated fibers of the soul would quiver in that delirious finale in which pain is raised to the most otherworldly lyricism. Yet this whole denouement took place in the throat of Rubini."[29]

In the 1820s, Stendhal's columns on music give us a precise idea of the practices of Italian singers, their creativity, and their inventive ornamentation: all elements of the art of singing that the French were to imitate, adapt, modify—and distort. Two examples may be cited from Stendhal's columns in the *Journal de Paris*. In bel canto, all voice categories had the option of ornamenting their parts: "In his beautiful bass voice, Zuchelli performed, with perfect ease and astonishing mellowness, embellishments and *fioriture* that in Italy were the glory of the [castrato] soprano Velluti. Twenty years ago we would have refused to believe in such a miracle" (article dated November 25, 1824, on a performance at the Théâtre-Italien of Rossini's *L'Inganno fortunato*). Ornamentation should be adapted to the expression of emotions:

> Mlle Mombelli sings the beginning of her duet with Malcolm exceptionally well, but with the most ridiculous misinterpretations. She says to her lover, "Il padre impone / Ch'io non pensi a te [My father has ordered / Me no longer to love thee]." But it is with the most radiant joy and the gayest, most brilliant ornaments that Mlle Mombelli announces this good news to her lover. . . . Mlle Mombelli, if she stands warned by the silence of the audience, has talent enough to embellish this duet with sorrowful ornaments. Note that we need never criticize our sublime Madame Pasta for such misdeeds. [30]

This bel canto technique seems to have been applied indiscriminately to all scores. Laure Damoreau-Cinti (1801–1863), who made her Théâtre-Italien debut in 1816, sang Zerline (Zerlina) in *Don Juan* at the Opéra with ornamentation that Berlioz criticized in *Le Rénovateur* on March 16, 1834: "Mme Damoreau-Zerline sings like the flute of [the celebrated flautist] Tulou; unfortunately, she always wants to be playing a concerto, and the ornaments slip out, so to speak, unwittingly. True, they are always perfectly charming, but in such original music with such firmly fixed outlines, these vocal frolics are nonetheless the cause of unspeakable torment among the admirers of Mozart."

Along the same lines, it can be said that Rossini's transformation from Italian to French composer was a turning point in the adaptation of virtuoso singing to the concept of "realism" in musical drama. Runs and other bel canto practices were gradually reduced until they appeared only in a few specific types of scenes (see page 116) or vanished completely. Here, too, the change was gradual: it came about not by discarding an old practice in toto, but by diluting it until it finally disappeared. Italian vocal luxuriance was thus confined to the printed score rather than being its unchanging essence. It was retained in *grand opéra* because of its expressive and entrancing qualities; it was distorted in cadenzas, where the composer tried to exploit every effect he could extract from it. The works of Meyerbeer contain these inflated cadenzas, which singers needed several breaths to complete. Free ornamentation was practiced with less and less imagination; it was confined to the high voices and lost its original significance.

In 1841, Berlioz denounced the harmful direction that singers were taking by substituting effect for art and emotion. His scapegoat was the *ténor au zénith*: "He has observed that certain ornaments, certain vocal fireworks, certain trite endings, certain squalid rhythms, have the power all by themselves instantly to evoke spontaneous applause. This seems to him more than sufficient reason to want them to be used, even to demand them, in his roles, with no regard for expression, originality, or dignity of style, and to evince hostility to works of an independent, lofty nature." Finally, "there is no more melody, no more expression, no more common sense, no more drama, no more music; there is only voice, and that is the important thing."[31]

We must therefore understand vocal virtuosity from two main perspectives. The first is as the continuation of a legitimate art, bel canto, of which Rossini can be considered to have been the last genuine representative;[32] this died out in the first quarter of the nineteenth century. The second perspective is that of more or less gratuitous virtuosity in pursuit of effect, aimed solely at impressing listeners who were more enthralled by any kind of vocal display than mindful of the music. A more syllabic type of vocal writing emerged, and fuller, more powerful singing was demanded of performers. "The tradition of Rossinian music," Gautier grumbled in January 1847, "has long been lost at the Opéra. That vivacious, bold, brilliant music requires great lightness of technique, flexibility, and skill in trills and runs, possessed at present by no artist on the rue Lepeletier,[33] apart from Mademoiselle Nau, who learned from Madame Cinti-Damoreau the pure method of Italian singing. The practice of so-called dramatic shrieking and acts of violence engaged in by today's singers has made their larynxes resistant to such subtleties."[34] Vocal distinction was now based on new criteria.

## THE EVOLUTION OF THE TENOR

A good example in this connection is the evolution of the high male voice. Tenors, explained Berlioz in 1837, "with their several registers composed of a mixture of tones—of head and chest voices—display infinite variety. One might have only three or four head tones; another might have many more: Rubini had six; most reach only A in chest voice; Nourrit has a B-natural, Duprez reaches C, and Haitzinger could hit a C-sharp."[35] Bel canto singing favored the merging of the two registers and great flexibility. The trend during the nineteenth century gradually came to dictate a powerful vocal style that required the use of the chest register in its high ranges, especially in *grand opéra*. The public was fascinated by this preternatural achievement. "For them, all the interest in the revival of *Guillaume Tell*," Berlioz continued, "lay in that diamond of a C; that out-of-reach C. The libretto, the score, the chorus, the orchestra, the singers are nothing—nothing but the framework that is unfortunately necessary for that pyramid of a C." Whereas Adolphe Nourrit (1802–1839) had created the role of Arnold in *Guillaume Tell* in 1829 employing a vocal technique that used falsetto in the high range, Gilbert Louis Duprez (1806–1896) made his Opéra debut in 1837 in the same role, but sang it entirely in chest voice. In a way, the domination of broad singing was a return to the school of Gluck as it was understood by Berlioz, who wrote in *Le Rénovateur* on August 31, 1834, that "nothing is basically more difficult than broad, sustained singing. Out of twenty sopranos who sing the most complicated vocal lines with ease, you will not find one who can first understand and then properly perform an aria by Gluck that contains nothing but half-notes and quarter-notes."

The tenor craze inspired journalists to put pen to paper. One columnist described the situation in the August 29, 1841, issue of *Le Ménestrel*, in an article entitled "L'Europe et ses cent cinquante ténors" (Europe and its 150 tenors):

> It has been calculated, based upon a reasonable average figure, that the 150 lead tenors who service all the opera houses, from the San Carlo [in Naples] to the Queen's Theatre in London, and from the Theater Royal in Lisbon to the Imperial Theater in Saint Petersburg, obtain each year from the music lovers of Europe the not inconsiderable sum of 7,500,000 francs. Under the Empire, the job of soldier was the world's leading profession; today, it is the job of tenor. A conscript arriving at his regiment held the baton of a maréchal de France in his cartridge pouch;[36] a voice student who leaves a conservatory with a high C from the chest bears in his throat a guaranteed income of 50,000 francs. So it is that tenors have supplanted the sons of the French nobility in winning the hands of the heiresses with the amplest dowries.

A few years later, a high C-sharp was to draw crowds all by itself. Again, it was the Théâtre-Italien that "introduced Tamberlick and his high C-sharp";[37] people counted the number of times it appeared in an opera; it eclipsed everything around it and took on an apocalyptic complexion. A columnist reported that Michot "launched [at the Théâtre-Lyrique] a number of these bombs *à la* Tamberlick, known as C-sharps."[38] In 1863, the Italian tenor Enrico Tamberlick (1820–1889) "repeated that dazzling wonder, his famous C-sharp—the Palais-Royal cannon moved to the Rue Ventadour so to speak. Never perhaps has this vocal bomb exploded so

Figure 2.   Title page of *L'Ut dièze* (The C-sharp) by Eugène Grangé and Jules
Moinaux (Paris: Michel Lévy Frères, [1868]). Here, M. de Flanpanné gives his
daughter's hand in marriage to his nephew, who has performed the feat of
singing a high C-sharp from the chest (the specialty of the great tenor Enrico
Tamberlick) in Rossini's *Otello*.

marvelously as in the duet in [Rossini's] *Otello*, which served as its gun-
carriage. Everyone in Paris will want to hear that unfailing C-sharp
again."[39] It was such a wonder that it came to be a sociological phenomenon. The best testimony to this is the curious one-act *bouffonnerie* by
Eugène Grangé and Jules Moinaux, which was performed at the Théâtre des
Variétés on July 3, 1858, and was entitled simply *L'Ut dièze* (The C-sharp)
(see fig. 2): ever since that note was mentioned in the newspapers, Monsieur de Flanpanné, a "rather nice elderly music-loving gentleman," has
longed for nothing more than that dizzying auditory experience. To quell
his "C-sharpomania"—his *utdiésomanie*—he decides to have the celebrated tenor abducted. But instead of Tamberlick, his servant mistakenly

kidnaps one Jean Bernique, a peasant. After a series of misunderstandings, M. Flanpanné's nephew Octave, a student of singing at the Conservatoire, produces the astounding note with the assistance of one of his friends, a bass. In the end, Flanpanné tells him, "You have given [me] a C-sharp, and I give you my daughter."

The changed technique of the tenor in *grand opéra* by no means meant that from the 1840s every single opera was sung in this new way. In fact, it is a terrible misrepresentation when we hear today's tenors (with voices of greater or lesser power) consistently singing in chest voice, even though much of the French and Italian operatic repertory contains passages calling for head voice in order to reach high notes lightly, or for *voix mixte*—and in general for great vocal flexibility. It must be admitted that late-twentieth-century tenor technique has become almost uniformly rudimentary and monotonous. This is particularly awful in *opéra-comique* (*Carmen*, for example, where, without necessarily demanding the use of falsetto, the role of Don José is full of subtle nuance and calls for a varied palette of vocal colors), which is bloated by performers devoid of vocal subtlety or charm. Even in *grand opéra*, we cannot fail to deplore the bellowing often inflicted on us in works such as Halévy's *La Juive* or Auber's *La Muette de Portici*. There is also a confusion between agility and register: a fairly light tenor, briskly singing the coloratura in a Rossini aria, views it as a challenge to use the same chest voice from the lowest to the highest pitches, and most of all to shine out with a powerful high register, which imposes a certain aggressiveness or force on vocal tracery whose delicacy was intended to charm the ear. This delicacy can be achieved only if the singer abjures a powerful high register and adopts a flexible voice that can shift imperceptibly from chest to head tones. In this connection, note that the expressions "head voice" and "falsetto" are sometimes synonymous but sometimes refer to different timbres, depending on the singing method and on the author. In his famous method, published in 1840, Manuel Garcia (the brother of Maria Malibran and Pauline Viardot) differentiated among no fewer than five vocal registers: chest, falsetto, head, *contrabasse*, and *voix expiratoire*.

### AUDIENCE ATTITUDES

Despite the public's infatuation with vocal derring-do, we must remember that—at least for a substantial group of people—going to the opera was above all a social occasion. The Académie de musique was a school of elegance. People went to sample pleasures that sometimes had little relation

Figure 3. A box at the Opéra, engraving by Robinson after Eugène Lami, from *L'Ete à Paris* by Jules Janin (1844). Three of the occupants are engrossed by the grandiose production, while the couple at the back of the box ignore the performance in favor of a presumably amorous dialogue of their own.

to the music, which provided a backdrop for a variety of activities: to be seen; to engage in conversation; to meet friends; to pursue an *amour*; to "protect" a ballerina (see fig. 3).[40]

Berlioz—perhaps in pique—had horrid things to say: "For the vast majority of Opéra habitués, it is neither for the drama nor for the music that they come to that theater, but only for the incidentals. And as for the remainder, who think that what they like in an opera is the opera itself, it is not the beautiful that suits them; nor is it the bad: it is the mediocre—which is what they resemble."[41] Indignant that the Opéra had rejected the composer of *Les Troyens*, the critic Pier Angelo Fiorentino struck much the same note: "They have no right not to perform it, especially when they are dragging along from revival to revival and have not played a note of new music for two years. I know that the auditorium is always full, but they go there to keep warm, to chatter, and to ogle the ballerinas, and I know that the surest way to make big profits is not to perform anything at all."[42] Basically, Reynaldo Hahn summed up in 1925, "that pleasant and lightweight public, greedy for pleasure and hostile to complexity, was taken first and foremost with the pleasures of listening to singing, of comparing rival artists and of ranting about everything that surrounded the music, rather than of listening to and appraising the music itself."[43]

Patrick Barbier paints the following picture of the routine at the Opéra in the first half of the nineteenth century:

> Five minutes before the rise of the curtain, half [of the members of the audience] would still be in the lobby or in the corridors. When the foot-lights were lit, doors to boxes would be opened noisily and people would lean forward to greet a well-known individual or wave to friends, ignor-ing all requests for silence. . . . Maintaining silence during performances was another problem. In this respect, the audiences of the Paris Opéra fell somewhere between those of theaters in Italy, who only kept their places and remained quiet for the great arias, and those of the Théâtre-Italien in Paris, who wanted to hear every note and who considered si-lence to be obligatory. Members of Opéra audiences did their best to listen to the work's most important scenes, yet welcomed the first oppor-tunity to be inattentive.[44]

Literature reflected this behavior. When the great authors—and those who are today less well known—moved their protagonists through the streets of Paris, they often placed them in the vicinity of an opera house or had them attend a performance, for lyric theater was closely linked to other social activities. The examples in Balzac's *La Comédie humaine* and in Stendhal are well known, as is that of Zola's *Nana* (1880), a novel built around the world of operetta, symbolic of the decadence of a Second Em-pire given over to bawdiness and the unrestrained fulfillment of desires. (*Nana* hinges on the stage, as seen from three different points of view: the first chapter describes the Théâtre des Variétés from the standpoint of the audience, chapter 5 a performance seen from the wings, and chapter 10 a performance seen from the stage itself, during rehearsal.)

Even in the prestigious preserve of bel canto, people liked to be seen. Théophile Gautier recalled this in his description of the 1841 renovation of the Théâtre-Italien:

> Before speaking of the birds, let us say a few words about their cage, which was made to be as gilded as it could be; for the Bouffes [the Théâtre-Italien] is as much a salon as a theater, and its audience— drawn almost entirely from the world's fortunate—absolutely de-mands the full pursuit of comfort and elegance. . . . The first circle, which is shaped like an upended basket, is made of pierced copper, whose openings enable one to glimpse the hems of the dresses of the women seated behind it. So beware of ugly feet—or of badly made shoes, which amount to more or less the same thing.[45]

Performances were punctuated by expressions of the audience's pleasure or discontent; the former could extend to calling for the repetition of a number right in the middle of the opera (the practice of performing such encores persisted into the first decades of the twentieth century). The audience demonstrated its mood according to a code that varied from theater to theater: applause, voiced interjections (even shouts), or murmuring. On October 19, 1825, a columnist in *Le Corsaire* wrote of a fiasco surrounding a duet in the final performance of Rossini's *La Gazza ladra* at the Théâtre-Italien (the Salle Louvois) and took the opportunity of observing that "the *dilettanti* rejected it with those *chut* noises that at the Salle Louvois are the equivalent of the sharpest whistling at other theaters." Such responses were not always those of the audience proper; sometimes they were the work of a claque.

## THE CLAQUE

The emperor Nero may have been the first to come up with the idea of a claque: when he sang in the Roman amphitheater, he seeded the audience with battalions of young men whose job it was to applaud. In allusion to these ancient Roman *claqueurs*, people paid to applaud were often called "Romans" in nineteenth-century Paris.

The first attempts to establish a permanent claque go back to the time of Napoleon I. After the Restoration, the claque became institutionalized; only the Théâtre-Italien contrived to keep it out. "Apart from the latter attraction," we read in Larousse's *Grand Dictionnaire universel,*

> all theaters have organized claques; the Opéra's is the most highly disciplined. The chiefs of the claques claim the title of entrepreneurs of dramatic success; from the management they receive no subsidies, but rather a certain number of seats, to which they have access each night for their own profit, which would be insufficient to account for the 10,000, 20,000, 30,000, or even 40,000 francs that some of them earn each year thanks to the vanity and weakness of artists who, in order to have a large share of the allocation of bravos, give cash gifts commensurate with the quantity of applause they desire.[46]

During final rehearsals, the chief of the claque would carefully prepare the interventions of his troops, who were known as the Knights of the Chandelier because they occupied the center of the orchestra level. After several evenings, "all the words or situations to be applauded are set, frozen forever, and even if the piece were to be performed a hundred times, two hundred times, they would applaud, laugh, or weep at the same passages."[47] Although the claque was repugnant to some, others viewed it as necessary to encourage the performers; it survived until the end of the century, especially in opera houses.

Some observers of the Paris musical scene feared that claques had invaded the entire world of music. On January 22, 1868, Johannès Weber devoted a portion of his "Critique musicale" column in *Le Temps* to this problem:

> The principal argument of those who defend the claque is that without this institution, theatrical performances would be very cold, and that the *claqueurs* serve as coaches [for the audience]. The truth is quite the opposite. In provincial theaters there is no claque. "But," comes the response, "there are cliques"—as though the claque precluded these in Paris. At concerts of rubbish, everyone is applauded and no one is hissed or whistled at; an artist who is not called back on stage after a number has committed a fiasco. At recitals by string-quartet societies, the audience is also fairly indulgent—although without disguising its feelings. At the concerts of the Conservatoire and the Cirque Napoléon [directed by Jules Pasdeloup], there is not a trace of a *claqueur*, either official or unofficial; are these cold occasions?...The freedom and spontaneity with which [the audience] expresses its feelings constitute one of its unquestionable merits.

Anyone who wanted to succeed in the theatrical world had to learn to negotiate with the claque. Balzac, in fact, devotes several scenes in *La Comédie humaine* to this: the naive but ambitious provincial Lucien de Rubempré is amazed at the consideration and status that his friend Etienne Lousteau accords the chief of the *claqueurs:* " 'Is Monsieur Braulard in?' he asked the doorkeeper. 'Monsieur!?' said Lucien. 'The chief of the *claqueurs* is a "Monsieur"?' 'My dear fellow, Braulard has an income of 20,000 francs; he has the endorsement of the boulevard playwrights, all of whom have an account with him, just as they would with a banker.' "As Lucien (who had come for his protégée) listens to this man, whom he had been ready to despise, he is astonished to hear him assess the talents of authors and performers alike. " 'Coralie has won out,' Braulard told him with the air of a competent judge. 'If she behaves herself, I'll secretly support her against the cabal at her Gymnase debut. Listen: I'll have some men in the galleries for her, who'll be smiling and murmuring to encourage applause. That's the kind of game that'll set a woman up.' "[48]

At the Opéra, the claque expanded during the 1830s and was centered around Auguste Levasseur (died 1844),[49] who ably commanded a veritable regiment of *claqueurs*. He negotiated with management, singers, and dancers, and viewed his work with seriousness and a marked sense of hierarchy, looking down on his counterparts at inferior theaters such as the Opéra-Comique.

Musicians' letters too bear witness to these practices. In 1872, shortly before the premiere of his little *opéra-comique Djamileh,* Bizet wrote to his librettist, Louis Gallet, "The head of the claque came to annoy me because of his emoluments. De Leuven [director of the Opéra-Comique], whom I consulted, advised me to give fifty francs for the *première* and fifty at the twentieth performance."[50]

## THE GLAMOUR OF SPECTACLE

The visual elements of a performance (except for *opéras-comiques* of the kind that had tangled plots, and for the Théâtre-Italien) were decisive, especially in *grand opéra* with its staggering magnificence. *La Juive* (see fig. 4) marked the acme of this phenomenon and gave rise to concern "that the incredible splendor of the stage production would itself be the sole focus of all the audience's attention, its noisy glamour cloaking and suffocating the more delicate, nobler language of the music."[51] Forty-two years later, a columnist could still write of the premiere of Massenet's *Le Roi de Lahore* (1877): "Never in our opinion have so many splendors been combined in a single work on the stage of our Grand Opéra; the third act alone—the Paradise of Indra—would be enough for all of Paris to run to see it."[52] On the other hand, a poor production could have unfortunate consequences. "A bad set," Zola wrote to Bruneau, "often means the death of an act; it is cut at the last moment."[53]

Along with the scenery, danced divertissements added to the glamour and contributed their own visual effect. In the *Revue des Deux Mondes* of March 14, 1833, Alfred de Musset wrote an account of Auber's *Gustave III,* in which he jokingly marveled at the considerable part played by dance:

> Once, one would have thought that people went to a royal academy of music to hear music. For my part, I am no musician.... But I really do not think I had any need of it this time. The loveliest thing in *Gustave* by way of music and libretto is a galop.... Anyone who has not seen this galop [in act 5] has not seen anything. The sparkle of candles, the noise of a party, the aroma of flowers, music, folly, beauty: never have these provided an hour of pleasure that can compare with this. Never have the thousand colors of exciting masks and the bizarre mixture of costumes, dominos, and grotesques rippled with greater grace and wit under the dazzling glow of the chandeliers. Never has a student reading *A Thousand and One Nights*

Figure 4.   Halévy's *La Juive,* act 1, crossroads at Constance. Lithograph by Eugène Ciceri, P. Benoist, and Gaildrau, based on the scenery by Léon Feuchère, Charles Séchan, Jules Dieterle, and Edouard Despléchin (1835). The conventional setting of a city square has been expanded and combined with medieval and religious images.

seen in his night-time dreams a more voluptuous or intoxicating phantasmagoria.

The importance accorded to splendid stage sets is one of the most characteristic elements of nineteenth-century French opera. Stage design underwent a revolution during the first decades of the nineteenth century, but there were signs of change in the theater much earlier. Marie-Antoinette Allévy observes that as early as "the first quarter of the eighteenth century, the art of the theater had already begun to change its techniques on the way to the decisive transformation that was to take place in the Romantic era."[54] Purely symmetrical sets and unvarying perspectives disappeared. More and more, there was an attempt to approximate the apparent disorder of nature; the spectator was to envision a space larger than the stage itself and to imagine elements hidden from view. Local color and historical accuracy brought more impact and power to scenery; all manner of techniques were used in an attempt to heighten scenic illusion. At the beginning of the nineteenth century, the most striking efforts were seen on the stages of the popular theaters. Gradually, an increasing number of different scenes and pictur-

esque and fantastical effects joined with stage movement to powerfully create atmosphere and mood. During the Restoration, the boulevard theaters,
which were the realm of *mélodrame*,[55] evinced an inventiveness and diversity that dazzled the spectator. Some theaters specialized in purely visual
spectacles and presented silently moving "paintings" as well as panoramas.
Louis-Jacques Daguerre (1789–1851) changed the placement of sets and
skillfully reproduced natural phenomena. And Pierre Luc Charles Ciceri
(1782–1868) made scenery into true paintings, establishing "the nature of
theatrical design as it was to be unceasingly practiced on all stages, with an
irritating lack of change, for more than a century."[56]

Among the most important technical improvements, gas lighting made
it possible to vary the illumination; it made a major contribution to stage
illusion. In Nicolò's *Aladin, ou la Lampe merveilleuse,* first performed on
February 6, 1822, Ciceri and Daguerre introduced this new technique to
the Opéra; it lent new brilliance to the supernatural scenes and found its
raison d'être in the Palace of Light in act 5. The groundwork was laid for
the new concept of set design that emerged in the Romantic era. "Nature
was called upon to provide its locales," Allévy writes, "peoples their customs, history its monuments; all the sciences—topography, ethnology, and
archeology—were employed in re-creating that 'color of the times' of
which the Romantic school was to make such a display. More than ever before, the scene painter, the stagehand, and the costumer were to occupy a
first-rank position in the theater."[57]

No matter what the subject, there was a quest for verisimilitude in sets
and costumes. Eugène Ritt of the Opéra-Comique wrote in connection
with *Mignon* (1866): "I took such great care that I had the chorus costumes
made near Forbach by local seamstresses so that they should be absolutely
accurate."[58] And indeed, while there is much to say about the scenery, we
must not neglect the beauty of the costumes (see fig. 5). Paul Lormier designed the costumes for *La Juive* on the basis of documentation in *La Vraie
et parfaite science des armoiries* by the seventeenth-century historiogra-
pher Pierre Palliot. Along with the props and with armor made of metal,
these took the stage in the famous procession, "with its heralds, its banner-
bearers, the emperor Sigismund on his caparisoned horse, wearing a
cuirass draped with an ermine-lined purple mantle edged with red woolen
damask with floral designs in gold, and bearing his broadsword and his
orb."[59] Like all the other components of operatic theater, scenery tended to
evolve in the direction of excess. A good example of this was the set for the
crossroads at Constance in the first act of *La Juive*—an expanded and more
sumptuous version of a normal city square, blended with medieval and

Figure 5.   Costume sketch by Alfred Albert for Balkis in act 3 of Gounod's *La Reine de Saba*. The magnificence of the costumes added to the splendor of the production.

religious imagery (see fig. 4). Exoticism provided an opportunity to display both a concern for accuracy and the results of enriching the visual elements—indeed, of amassing them.

The preference for scenic accuracy was so marked that fussy journalists would scorn inaccuracies that had once been tolerated. Hence the 1847 review in *L'Illustration* of the Opéra production of Verdi's *Jérusalem:*

The historical accuracy of the costumes was matched only by the faithful way in which the locales were depicted. Every detail appeared to have been the subject of special archeological studies. But we must exclude the use of Sax's instruments, which, while they produce an excellent effect from the musical standpoint...are none the less an odd anachronism—indeed incomprehensible coming from M. Duponchel....[It] would have been more logical to leave the saxhorns and saxophones back stage...and to show on stage exact copies of genuine medieval musical instruments, whose forms are hardly known except to enthusiastic devotees of old bas-reliefs.[60]

If operatic set design in nineteenth-century France attained what contemporaries in other countries thought a matchless standard, this was thanks to a distinguished line of designers, including Ciceri, who has already been mentioned; Edouard Désiré Joseph Despléchin (1802–1871); and Philippe Marie Chaperon (1823–1906). They turned opera performances into living paintings that combined forms and colors of dazzling splendor. To deal with the massive job of building a production, from the 1830s on, the Opéra turned to a crew and workshops of its own. The jobs were divided among several artists. For example, when *Faust* was first given at the Académie de musique, Jean-Baptiste Lavastre and Edouard Despléchin built the sets for scenes 1, 3, 9, and 10, Charles Cambon those for scenes 2, 4, 5, and 6, and Auguste Rubé and Philippe Chaperon those for scenes 7 and 8. The costumes were the work of Paul Lormier.[61]

The role of the stage director as we understand it today took shape only gradually. At the Opéra, Edmond Duponchel, an architect by training, worked with the director, Louis Véron, to make the performances even more splendid. Called by his contemporaries the "Alexander of stage production," he "brought water into the theater to supply jets and waterfalls," "installed the first 'English' traps, which facilitated the appearance and disappearance of fantastic characters," invented "the '*rideau de manoeuvre*' [or front cloth], making it possible when necessary to effect complicated scene changes without...recourse to the difficult and awkward manipulations of changes in full view," and "constantly [improved] the state of gas lighting."[62] It was he who polished the production of Meyerbeer's *Robert le Diable* in 1831. The way in which his official title changed is significant: first, he was inspector of stage equipment (*inspecteur du matériel de la scène*) from January 1829 to June 1831, then he became stage manager (*directeur de la scène*) from June 1831 to September 1835, and finally production director (*directeur de la mise en scène*) from June 1840 to October 1841. Commonly, theater directors, too, were active participants in the development of a production. We have already seen how Léon Carvalho used his authority to control every aspect of a work, both musical and visual.

In his excellent *Dictionnaire du théâtre,* published in 1885, Arthur Pougin drew a distinction between the "human" production, which concerned stage action, and the "material" production, which related to all the physical equipment required for that action. More generally, he offered the following definition:

> Production is the art of determining stage action in all its facets and in all its aspects, not only as regards the individual or combined movements of each character who collaborates in the performance of the work that is being given, not only as regards the movements of crowds—groups, marches, parades, fights, etc.—but also as regards properly combining these individual and collective movements with the set decoration, the furnishings, the costumes and the props, both as a whole and in their details.[63]

## THE PRODUCTION COMES TO LIFE

*Les Pêcheurs de perles* provides a great deal of information about the production of an opera, and enables us to grasp the scenic ideas of the time (see Appendix 6). For a precise idea of contemporary productions in France, we can turn to published production notebooks, such as the valuable collections of Louis Palianti, who was assistant stage manager of the Opéra-Comique from 1836 to 1872.[64] These describe a large number of works in great detail, with diagrams showing the position of sets and groups (chorus and soloists) and lists of objects and of the movements and expressions of the performers (see figs. 6 and 7). The spaces, shapes, and colors of nineteenth-century opera appear also in the numerous and often beautiful documents that have survived intact, and of which the Library-Museum of the Paris Opéra contains many examples:[65] three-dimensional models of stage sets, drawings, sketches, photographs, posters, scores, and production notebooks. Some documents are actual canvases, such as the set for the church scene in Gounod's *Faust* painted in tempera by Charles Antoine Cambon (1802–1875). Illustrated papers such as *L'Illustration* devoted considerable space to drawings or caricatures of operatic performances.[66] Paintings also indicate the contemporary view of opera, such as *Le Trio de "Robert le Diable"* (i.e., Nicolas Levasseur, Adolphe Nourrit, and Cornélie Falcon), oil on canvas (1835), by François Gabriel Guillaume Lepaulle, in which the characters are portrayed in expressive poses (see fig. 8).

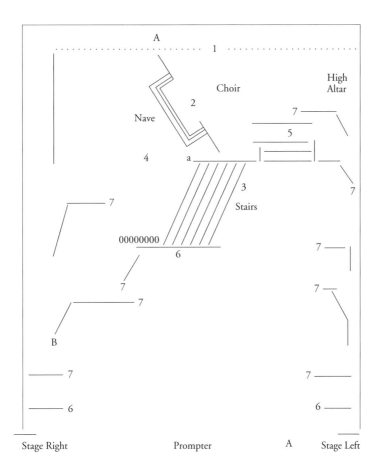

Figure 6.   Floor plan of Louis Palianti's set for Meyerbeer's *Le Prophète,*
act 4, the cathedral. 1. Backdrop depicting the nave of the church. The
perspective fades into the distance stage left. 2. Gilded railing. 3. Marble
steps lead to the choir, of which the audience sees only a portion, and to
the high altar, which is completely hidden from view. 4. Nave. 5. Three
steps supposedly leading to the ambulatory that surrounds the choir
and high altar. 6. Drapery. 7. Flats depicting the church. Through the
top part of an opening in one of the stage-right flats (B) it is possible to
see a portion of the backdrop and flats positioned upstage. The column
(A) is duplicated on the backdrop. The ramp (6) is duplicated in painted
form on the column (flat a). The stage orchestra is located atop the
steps, in the place marked 00000000.

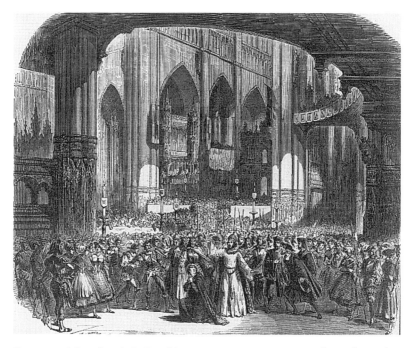

Figure 7.   Meyerbeer's *Le Prophète,* act 4, scene 2, coronation of Jean de Leyde in Münster cathedral (*L'Illustration,* April 28, 1849).

The press was full of accounts of operas, which provide us with numerous clues and, above all, with a lively view of performances, peppered with comments that convey the audience's impressions, almost at firsthand. With respect to *Les Pêcheurs de perles,* columnists highlighted the richness of the sets and costumes—even if these could not equal the splendor to be seen at the Opéra, with its considerable technical and financial resources. Indeed, one journalist noted that "the sets have been seen before, but they are still fairly fresh."[67] This was very probable: it was still usual to reuse sets from other productions that belonged to defined types (e.g., rustic landscape, town square, oriental palace). Even though in theory the Opéra had abandoned such recycling in the 1830s, traces of the practice were still to be seen in the second half of the century. Reyer's *Sigurd,* which premiered at Brussels in 1884, was first performed at Paris with sets previously used for *Françoise de Rimini, Guillaume Tell, Le Comte Ory,* and *Der Freischütz.*[68] Certain kinds of sets defined the visual space of an era, such as the gallery opening on a landscape that was so widely used between 1810 and 1832 (see fig. 9).[69]

Before their expressive and realistic functions came into play, sets defined the locale of the action through emblematic elements and helped

Figure 8.  *Le Trio de "Robert le Diable,"* oil on canvas by F. G. G. Lepaulle (1835): Nicolas Prosper Levasseur (Bertram), Adolphe Nourrit (Robert), and Cornélie Falcon (Alice). The painting isolates the three principal characters and depicts their theatrical poses; actors would convey the emotion controlling their characters with eloquent gestures and exaggerated facial expressions.

present the story. Thus, palm trees, a seascape, and pagodas would instantly transport the spectator to exotic lands (see fig. 10). Organizing the space in different ways made it possible to create special scenes, such as the heroine left alone atop a rock (see fig. 14), dances of death in the disquieting surroundings of an impenetrable forest, and so forth.

Where were the performers placed within this scenic space? The few attempts that were made at innovation in the way the performers moved did not much appeal to the critics. In the finale to act 1 of *Les Pêcheurs de perles,* the soprano is supposed to sing while raised several meters above the ground, and the tenor is supposed to sing his act 1 *romance* lying down. Pier Angelo Fiorentino was outraged and forcefully reminded his readers of the artificial nature of opera:

> O realism, look what you have perpetrated! If an opera were written on *Charlotte Corday,* Marat, for the sake of greater verisimilitude, would sing in his bathtub. We have seen actors speak with their backs to the audience because they think this is more natural than standing downstage

Figure 9.   The gardens of the palace of the duc d'Arcos in act 1 of Auber's *La Muette de Portici*. Lithograph by Engelmann after P.-L.-C. Ciceri. An open gallery overlooking a landscape was one of the types of set most often used by designers from the 1810s to the 1830s.

in a row, like onions. They forget that everything in the theater is convention. First and foremost, the audience must not miss a word of what the actors are saying; beyond that, they should manage as best they can. Thus, the first law, the first requirement of the operatic art is that the singer should be in a position that favors voice production. . . . By trying too hard to approach reality, they lapse into absurdity.[70]

In 1875 Bizet made an enormous effort to see to it that the chorus in *Carmen* moved about in small groups and performed actions rather than remaining static. Columnists found the first Carmen, Marie Célestine Laurence Galli-Marié, too realistic. Not all the elements of the production were ordinarily intended to convey an entirely realistic picture of the drama, apart perhaps from the sets and costumes, which aimed at a meticulous re-creation of reality. The gestures and poses we see in illustrations and photographs of the period (see fig. 8)—which today we might consider grandiloquent—along with the lighting, all went to heighten the presentation of the drama. Nineteenth-century staging favored an aesthetic of

Figure 10.   Set for the act 2 finale of Bizet's *Les Pêcheurs de perles*. Illustration from *Il Teatro illustrato* (Milan), April 1886, for the La Scala premiere. Exotic vegetation forms a harmonious visual composition with picturesque structures, with the sea visible in the distance.

bombast over a realistic understanding of movement and gesture. Operatic time and space resulted from the definition of moments that combined to form stage pictures; the succession of these pictures culminated in a final scene that ended by immobilizing the actors against the backdrop. The singer interpreted his role through a catalogue of expressive gestures, as is still borne out by press accounts in the early twentieth century. Describing the skills of Mlle Bréval in Saint-Saëns's *Henry VIII*, Debussy wrote that she had "a marvelous musical sensitivity and an instinct for the needed gesture, which in the last act enabled her to find her inflections and her postures."[71]

Opera lives only in performance. Without revivals, it perishes. And when an opera is revived, its appearance changes, even if only through being interpreted by different performers. Revivals succeed creation, and new links are added to the work's chain of life. Opera depends on a strategy for disseminating it and on the evolution of tastes. *Les Pêcheurs de perles* is a particularly significant example, for it raises all the problems mentioned above, such as differing versions, translations, and so forth, and enables us to cast light on the question of dissemination in parallel with that of the evolution of opinions and of tastes.

## THE FATE OF A WORK: CHANGING TASTES
## AND STRATEGIES FOR DISSEMINATION

In the latter half of the 1880s, *Les Pêcheurs de perles* was performed in Italian (premiering in Milan on March 20, 1886), and then traveled the world: Lisbon in 1886, London, Barcelona, and Mexico City in 1887, Buenos Aires in 1888, Saint Petersburg in 1889, and more. It was also translated into languages including German, Hungarian, Czech, Russian, Danish, Croatian, and Polish.[72] It was even performed in French now and then (Geneva and Brussels in 1887; New York in 1916). This fresh interest in the work, which now enjoyed an "enthusiastic reception,"[73] was part of a more general rediscovery of Bizet following the international success of *Carmen*. In 1889, Arthur Pougin explained that "the triumphal career that *Carmen*...has enjoyed abroad for the past ten years gave Italian singers the idea of tackling Bizet's earlier works. *La Bella fanciulla di Perth* does not seem to have been terribly successful, but *I Pescatori di perle*...appears on the contrary to have been very favorably received on Italian stages."[74] The initiative lay with the Italian publicist, impresario, and music publisher Edoardo Sonzogno, "a sincere friend of France," in Pougin's words, "who for ten years has constantly striven for the growth of French art in Italy."[75]

Sonzogno used the press to convey his enthusiasm, and he was the director of *Il Secolo*, "one of the first organs in Italy to defend French interests."[76] Moreover, this enterprising man was the publisher of the Milanese illustrated paper *Il teatro illustrato*, in which it is an easy matter to follow the spread of French repertory throughout Italy. For some scores, one can truly speak of a triumphal tour, of which characteristic descriptions by many Italian journalists survive.[77]

Adolphe Jullien described the publishing policies of Editions Choudens that this renaissance concealed: "After *Carmen*...had gained irresistible momentum in America as well as in Europe, the publishing house that owned the works of Bizet took advantage of these restored fortunes by causing to be performed in Italy, in Belgium, and elsewhere an opera [i.e., *Les Pêcheurs de perles*] that is very easy to mount, with three principals, few secondary performers, and indifferent scenery."[78] In 1886, the composer of *Le Roi d'Ys*, Edouard Victor Antoine Lalo, expanded on this thought in explaining to Edouard Blau the actual haggling in which the French publisher engaged:

> Choudens is the most powerful and most energetic publishing house in Paris with respect to the theater; it owns the biggest contemporary successes with the principal operas of Gounod and with *Carmen*, and it uses these successes to impose upon foreign theater directors works that would otherwise never see the light of day; that is how the obligation to produce *Noé*, an inferior work by Halévy [completed by Bizet], was imposed on Berlin. Choudens said to Berlin, "You want permission to perform *Carmen*? Very well, but on the condition that you perform *Noé*. You want *Mireille*? Perform *Les Pêcheurs de perles*."[79]

Publishers also tried to feed the fresh interest in Bizet in ways other than the production of operas, and his music was heard also at concerts and in salons. It took several years, however, for *Les Pêcheurs de perles* to earn the support it needed for a place in the Parisian repertory. Simultaneously, the work gained momentum in provincial theaters, before reappearing in the capital on April 20, 1889, at the Théâtre de la Gaîté—sung in Italian by Sonzogno's troupe.

The press, which initially had great reservations, gradually changed its view, and many formerly skeptical critics changed their minds—sometimes suddenly.[80] Following the revival that took place on March 17, 1932, *Les Pêcheurs de perles* became one of the treasures of the Opéra-Comique, alongside the great hits of Jules Massenet, Ambroise Thomas, and Gustave Charpentier.[81] A work that was nearly avant-garde for 1863 audiences ended up being viewed as an "easy" opera and, paradoxically, as representative of the nineteenth-century French repertory.

Moreover, with these various revivals, differing versions of the opera came into being, sometimes changing an entire act, cutting a number, or, conversely, including new passages (see Appendixes 1 and 2). It was only in 1964 that serious study began of the relationship among these various versions and of the question of their authenticity. Times have changed. Undoubtedly following the example of early-music performers, traditional operatic circles have begun to question the validity of the scores they have been using. The facts are astonishing. Even if one could (or should) restore an opera to the state of a given production, one has to be able to do so on the basis of reliable documents. Very few works are published in high-quality editions, and the state of the French repertory is particularly disastrous. The works of Offenbach, Gounod, and Bizet, to name but a few, have been distorted and are performed from incomplete material riddled with errors.

Simultaneous study of an opera's creation, "death and transfiguration," and dissemination clearly reveals the overlap—specific to music and even more so to opera—of "artistic" matters (all tasks relating to the opera as a work of art) and sociological matters (the fate of the work in performance, which is dependent upon a given society). Because a nineteenth-century French opera had to be performed if it was to live, because it was the work of a divided creative entity, and because it had to make money, its very existence depended on complex variations in the operatic repertory and in tastes.

# Chapter 3    Reception

We must remember that theatrical and operatic events had a considerable hold on nineteenth-century minds, somewhat like that of television today. Every major newspaper worthy of the name had to have its own column devoted to the theater and the opera. Can we imagine regular accounts of operatic activities in, say, *The Sporting News* or its French equivalent, *L'Equipe?* But these were indeed to be found in their nineteenth-century counterpart, *Le Sport,* in its column "La Vie à Paris."[1]

Here again, the first decades of the nineteenth century saw the establishment of practices that would remain in place throughout the century—even though, to be sure, there were changes in the content and length of the articles, and in the attitudes and tastes of the critics.[2] This chapter will not recount the entire history of the Paris musical press and of the numerous columns that appeared in newspapers and magazines of all kinds. Musicologists have yet to study this considerable body of documents in any great detail.[3] Rather, I shall identify a few principles that guided musical criticism and that decisively shaped the way in which French operas were received. Certain themes were widely discussed in the press; their context changed and their meaning evolved, gradually but radically. Among these, Wagnerism and the concept of a Wagnerian style particularly deserve fresh consideration. Rather than looking at these points on the basis of the dual assumption that Wagnerian art was aesthetically superior and that its dominance was inevitable—in other words, rather than projecting onto the entire nineteenth century in France an assessment that came to prevail only at the very end of that century—it is important for anyone with a genuine interest in understanding the world of French opera to retrace the development of Parisian criticism of Wagner and his music, and of French works that were labeled "Wagnerian."

## THE STRUCTURE OF A REVIEW

Articles about an operatic performance typically followed a precise outline that covered the following points: (1) an introduction based on something that was of interest to the critic (the type of opera, the atmosphere surrounding its first performance, the composer's career, circumstances specific to the premiere, and so forth); (2) a synopsis of the libretto; (3) general comments on the music; (4) a description of outstanding numbers, or of those that most appealed to the audience; and (5) a critique of the performance and the staging.

It is amusing to see critics juggling these conventions. In his account of performances of Adolphe Adam's *Si j'étais roi* (in *Le Ménestrel* of September 12, 1852), J. Lovy was in such a hurry to write about the composer that he neglected the traditional order of a music column and began by describing the music itself. After a while, he took himself in hand and chided himself for this departure from convention: "But observe: without noticing it, I have reversed the order of my account. As a well-schooled columnist, I shall begin with the libretto."

Generally speaking, columnists described a performance by focusing on the merits or defects of the performers and by writing of their origins and their careers. Only exceptional or troublesome elements of the performance or the staging were noted. Finally, a few comments (which may provide clues for modern performers) sought to convey the singers' vocal attributes.

These articles invariably combined criticism of the work itself, criticism of the performance, and an account of the audience reaction. Apart from personal issues and corruption, journalists followed a tradition, were proponents of a given style or school, and approached the opera they were analyzing in terms of how normal a link it was in the history of lyric theater. Moreover, they were aware of belonging to a well-defined milieu, to which they often made allusion, and this sometimes led to a certain mutual echoing and to changing the subject from the opera in question, and aesthetics in general, to current Parisian topics and the Paris press.

## RECEPTION AND PRE-RECEPTION

The actual reception of an opera commenced when the public first confronted the work. Before this, there was a "pre-reception": before it was ever seen, a work was introduced into the sphere of conversation—where fashion was made, where enthusiasms and prejudices were generated, where an idea gradually formed of what would be seen on stage. The skill of theater directors lay in their ability to pique public curiosity. The buzz (of which we have already spoken) that preceded the first performance prefigured the public's judgment of the work and stimulated expectations and anticipation among the future spectators; Hans Robert Jauss has written about this, employing the useful term "horizon of expectations." On the basis of operatic tradition and the nature of the particular theater, and in the light of their own cultural background and of current fashion, spectators would imagine a probable version of the opera. This was the "advance work" that they expected to see, and on the basis of which they formed an "advance opinion." It was therefore important to make people talk about a new work without the talk becoming boring—and without evoking an excessively precise image of the work, which could result in disappointment in the face of the realities of the production. It was also important not to make them wait too long. François-Joseph Fétis observed of the constantly postponed premiere of *Le Prophète* that "for anyone but the author of *Robert le Diable* and *Les Huguenots,* these long delays in producing a work that has become nearly mythic would have worn out the public's attention. Curiosity would have given way to indifference."[4]

A few words in the press following the dress rehearsal sometimes succeeded in amplifying the buzz, attracting attention for one final time and readying the spectator for an original score. "The dress rehearsal of *Les Troyens* aroused enormous curiosity; . . . no one left his seat before the end of a work that is so far removed from present-day habits and the tastes of our times," noted *L'Art musical* (November 5, 1863). The "Chasse royale" was dropped after the first performance, but Charles Desolmes felt that good publicity could have prepared the spectators for that rather strange scene: "We are strongly convinced that if the poster had announced this unsung scene in explicit terms, the impression would have been as it should have been—that is, entirely favorable."[5]

*Les Pêcheurs de perles* thus inspired rumors: "All the members of M. Carvalho's company who are not involved in learning this musical composition, who do not appear in it and who have no roles are nonetheless attending all the rehearsals, so struck are they by the beauties of this *Lélia* [*sic*]."[6] But the journalists sometimes bridled: "For the nearly four months since this work was announced, it has been spoken of as an event," *L'Europe artiste* observed in October 1863. "A great deal of good is said of it in advance; its beauties are extolled; these are discussed neither more nor less than if this had been the work of a proven master. So much buzz is not without danger for M. Bizet. How often have we seen reputations made in advance come to grief and collapse when the public has had an opportunity to judge them!"[7]

Parisians were skittish about the unknown and happiest in a familiar cultural environment, with "nearby horizons" and "expected surprises." Fétis observed in the *Revue et gazette musicale* of September 20, 1863, that the public had

> its habits, its traditional enthusiasms, and the guarantees offered to it by famous names, which do not force it to use its intelligence to form the judgments that are required by a new work. It knows that it is going to experience pleasure at a passage that has tickled it for thirty years, and it is delighted in advance: it likes only the surprises it already knows. It is a respectable public that is proud of what it thinks of as its classicism, which is synonymous with narrow-mindedness.

As has often been noted, a work's reception was a dynamic two-way process between its creators and the audience. The latter (whether in France or in Italy) approached a new opera from the standpoint of the conventional operatic forms, which it expected to find, no matter what the work's subject, and which it was prepared to demand. We see this clearly in an anecdote told by the composer Louis Ferdinand Hérold about his experience of having an opera produced in Italy:

> The piece ended with these words: "Zitti, Zitti si faccia silenzio"; I therefore wrote a very gentle, brief little number in which the prince quietly sends everybody away. Nearly everyone raised a hue and cry: "What? An opera that ends without drum and trumpets?" . . . Even though I know perhaps better than anyone the flaws of my music, I cannot believe that I was wrong with that final number; but to please the Neapolitans I wrote them a new one, and the next day, at the very moment when they were preparing at least to have a laugh at my expense, a new finale of exactly their type shut their mouths and opened their hands.[8]

## CRITICAL ATTITUDES

Most columnists were more literary than musical figures, and they enjoyed writing criticism of the many librettos that were open to attack. The worst among them, such as the dreaded Julien Louis Geoffroy (1743–1814),[9] simply vented their spleen (in the early 1800s, Belinda Cannone observes, Geoffroy "hailed or panned operatic works that nothing qualified him to judge").[10] And their attitude toward new talent was rarely dispassionate; they were all too happy to get their claws into their youthful prey and to flaunt their knowledge by trying to detect in a new opera features that belonged to other works. In Jules Ruelle's words:

For years all the Paris journalists hounded the theater directors with a single righteous voice: "Give the young people a try! Give the young people a hearing! How stubborn you are! Barbarians!" So [the work of] a young man is played, and the choice rightly falls, with or without pre-meditation, upon M. Georges Bizet, a composer of great talent, who has written a fine work. And the press sets to work furiously, almost passion-ately, criticizing him; and where even a little exaggerated praise might have been reasonable, they go overboard in panning it.[11]

Pondering the meaning of Cormon and Carré's libretto for *Les Pêcheurs de perles* in 1863, Benoît Jouvin observed: "At that time in the distant past when critics would happily pass judgment on a work with a witticism, they would not have failed to say as they left the theater that there were neither fishers in the libretto nor pearls in the music. Even if the composer had cre-ated a masterpiece, he would have been as good as dead: the critics would never have given up an epigram."[12] Now more serious-minded, Jouvin ar-gued, journalists had outgrown this kind of glibness. Evidently, however, not all of them had: Henri Vignaud could not resist saying that he found in *Les Pêcheurs de perles* everything "but pearls and style."[13]

Some journalists claimed the function of educating the composer, who, "enlightened by experience and guided by a wise critic who is without prejudice but who feels duty-bound to hold the beacon as high as possible over the road he should travel, will later give us a work in which he will more evenly balance knowledge and inspiration."[14] Even composers of ac-knowledged skill were vouchsafed a few lessons. Berlioz himself had the route that would unfailingly lead him to success traced for him by a dis-cerning columnist:

And now, some advice for the master. He is well known; he has talent, knowledge and experience; he handles the orchestra like few others among our composers...; he knows very well the power and resources of the human voice; he knows, finally, what pleases the public, what charms it, what draws it in and what enraptures it...; in the future he should select lively subjects dominated by emotion, and he should give melody a large role to play.[15]

French musical criticism had long been fettered by a national tradition that thought of music very offhandedly and accorded it only a secondary place among the arts. In addition to this terrible handicap, the formidable Paul Scudo noted two reefs on which a column might founder: on the one hand, excessive technical detail and a vocabulary overloaded with words un-intelligible to the great majority of readers; on the other, reliance on elegant, but uninformed, phrases to depict the emotions evoked in the writer by the music. To satisfy to both professionals and amateurs, Scudo concluded, these two critical approaches should be merged.[16] Berlioz's music criticism often in fact achieved this ideal, to the probable irritation of Scudo, who was hostile to the music and the thinking of the composer of *Les Troyens*.

A critic would either stress the background of a work or confine himself to analyzing its form; he functioned as a musical historian or a musical technician, usually attempting to describe the dreams, ideas, and emotions that the music and the production aroused in the listener's mind, sensibilities, and imagination. Some championed the theories or principles that had shaped their judgments, while others aimed at an unattainable impartiality. Too much time was spent on the ideas behind the work and on the reactions to it. E. Mathieu de Monter emphasized the diversity, and hence the richness, of such journalistic art:

> What diverse tribes! What temperaments! Some have the knowledge, the writing skill, the scholarship, the imagination. No sooner does a new work appear than they expound so wonderfully on the subject—or near the subject—they expand on their thoughts, they take a place on stage, they tell you of their feelings or share their knowledge with you. . . . Others, on the other hand, hound us with their irony and strike us to the very heart; they cast a cold eye on our enthusiasm and thus extinguish it. . . . Some of them are sincere—knights-errant of the truth, so to speak—but at the same time are masters of invective who insult and abuse with conviction whenever someone does not share their views, their opinions, or the system to which they adhere at the moment. . . . The salient feature of contemporary music criticism is that it is eclectic.[17]

A new opera would evoke all sorts of musical memories, giving journalists the chance to show off their acquaintance with the repertory. This way of looking at a work was sometimes employed in a kind-hearted critique of a beginning composer, but it could also be the starting point for a harsh judgment along the lines of "being preoccupied with imitating, the composer has forgotten to create."[18] This was also the time to examine the score. Here the opera became a sort of memoir that fused the tastes of a period and summed up a number of trends: a score in which diverse stylistic leanings and aesthetic movements met. Although columnists would sometimes give a few examples in their reviews, they preferred to write in more general terms about the techniques of the composer who had served as a model for the author of the new work under consideration.

Obviously, the vocal writing and the talents of the singers both as musicians and as actors counted for a great deal in how an opera was received.

Reviews would judge both libretto and music by existing standards, compare schools of singing technique, expound on the various vocal types and
their development, cite learned professors, and recall great performers. The
act of listening to music was inseparable from comparative memory. First
and foremost, a work was the expression of a culture, and the job of the
critic was to show his readers the landmarks that would enable them to find
their way through the labyrinth of styles, schools, and influences.

### THE MUSICAL COLUMN AS LITERARY GENRE

Aside from the images they conjured up to illustrate an aural impression
or evoke a musical emotion, it was in the synopsis of the libretto that journalists were best able to exercise their style and their wit. A musical column had its own high points, and, like the work that was its raison d'être,
it too had to respond to the expectations of an audience: its readers. These
reviews developed into a genre with norms of its own.

Columnists knew how useful a well-crafted synopsis could be, and
many mastered the art of writing one. Berlioz habitually employed it to
exercise his acute sense of caricature, exaggerating and distorting images,
emotions, and ideas, often by piling them up. He particularly disliked the
conventional *opéra-comique* of the period: "But let us turn to the new
piece; ... although it would be less disagreeable to me to have a tooth pulled
than to analyze a one-act *opéra-comique* for you, I think it best to be brave,
just as with a decayed molar, and show up for the 'operation' on time."[19]

A caricatured synopsis could be merciless: rather than driving out the
evil spirits, Léïla's song in *Les Pêcheurs de perles* "addressed sweet nothings
to the local sharks," Arthur Pougin jibed.[20] For Pier Angelo Fiorentino, the
condemnation of the two lovers to death was a scene of sadism: "Zurga is
inflexible: 'Light the pyre,' he says, 'and be sure to use green wood so that
the scoundrels will be burnt over a slow fire.'"[21] Journalists often sacrificed
critical rigor for the sake of being witty, a style incompatible with subtleties
of thought. In assessing whether Berlioz "was right to try to be both word-
smith and musician," Nestor Roqueplan neatly summed up: "The verses of
*Les Troyens* are as anyone could have written them; the piece is as no one
would have wanted to write it."[22]

There was some opposition to this ascendancy of style, which basically
meant a complete lack of ideas or an intrusive, self-centered critic. Advocating a sparer style, one critic wrote in 1870: "I wish that ... the language [of
writers], when they must give an account of a concert, were just as simple
as it is when they assess the proceedings of a Ministry or of the Chamber

[of Deputies]....I wish, in a word, that expressions of their satisfaction or their censure, as well as of their impressions, were kept within the bounds of reality."[23]

This style was still in vogue at the end of the century. In 1893, Johannès Weber, who admired the work of Massenet but not that of his librettists, parodied the plot of *Werther* in lapidary style: "In the first act, a fiery-tempered young man who enjoys getting drunk on his own words falls for a girl who is about to be married. In the second act, he makes a first attempt, after which he is able to believe that all hope is not lost. In the third act, he considers that the time is ripe to mount an assault; he is repulsed. In the fourth act, he kills himself."[24] At other times, columnists liked to build up a good rhetorical head of steam, as in Benoît Jouvin's blast at the musical uproar of the storm in *Les Troyens:*

> But I beg pardon of the author of *Les Troyens.* He is not—he could not be—guilty of a deception that amounts to a cruel and horrific torture. To the butchered composer I expose a conspiracy, or perhaps a mere distraction by the members of the orchestra, who, being insufficiently rehearsed and wishing to get themselves out of trouble, haphazardly blew the trombones, the horns, and the trumpets, whistled the piccolo, honked the oboe, quacked the clarinet, and used a bow unsullied by rosin to scrape the large and small members of the violin family. No, a thousand times no: M. Hector Berlioz is not the perpetrator of this audacious hullabaloo, which was committed with premeditation—this robbery of renown, this auricular burglary—by night in an inhabited auditorium! Yet again, in headlong flight with his troops, M. Deloffre [the conductor] has lost his head and cried: "Save yourselves if you can! And play if you like!"[25]

THE MATTER OF "WAGNERIAN" MUSIC

After the squabbles about Italian music, it was the turn of German music to be the target of the critics. We see again and again how Weber defined a decisive stage in the penetration of the German aesthetic into the Parisian operatic repertory. Criticism of Wagner's music shows a heightening of passions that were first aesthetic and then nationalistic. To understand this phenomenon and its considerable influence on the way in which French music was received, we must identify its critical origins. So let us return to 1863 and *Les Pêcheurs de perles.*

The "din and the cries" of which many columnists complained when they heard Bizet's opera were related to the most recent trends in dramatic music. It could have been the bad influence "of the new Italian school" of which "the composer inevitably heard the cries during his stay in Rome."[26]

But it was, of course, the German school that was the prime target. The very negative assessment was based more on a vague notion of the Wagnerian aesthetic than on any precise understanding of its principles. In 1870, the *Dictionnaire musico-humoristique* defined "noise" as "the modern sonority," and in defining "cacophony" made reference to Wagner's Music of the Future.[27] Marie Escudier described the "sense of weariness" the audience felt at the end of *Les Pêcheurs*, which was "the result of the musical system with which the young pupil of M. Halévy appears to have affiliated himself more out of pedantry than out of conviction. This is the system of Richard Wagner, in other words the negation of melody as we admired it in the masterpieces of Mozart, Rossini, Meyerbeer, Hérold, and Auber."[28]

Like many of his contemporaries, Sigismund Neukomm referred to the "music of the future" and to Wagner's writings: "M. Bizet is a musician with a brilliant future—so long as he does not get too caught up in the 'future'; unfortunately, it seems that he has a preference for this new school. At least, this is what I thought I detected at the first performance of *Les Pêcheurs de perles*, from which I emerged as from that forest of which M. Wagner has spoken."[29] This is a reference to a famous passage in the "Lettre sur la musique" that Wagner had published in Paris in 1861 as a preface to his *Quatre poèmes d'opéras:*[30]

> In conclusion, I turn again to metaphor to describe great melody as I conceive it, which encompasses the entire dramatic work; to that end, I shall focus on the impression that it must of necessity produce. Its infinite variety of detail must be apparent not only to the expert, but also to the layman, to the most unschooled mind once it has engaged in the necessary reflection. Hence, it must arouse in the soul a mood similar to that which a beautiful forest at sunset arouses in a walker who has just fled the noise of the town.[31]

The Parisian public had had little opportunity to get to know Wagner's music. Occasional concerts—one in 1841 and two more in 1850 and 1858—had programmed a few minutes of it. On January 25 and February 1 and 8, 1860, however, the composer himself organized and conducted concerts at the Théâtre-Italien. These included the overture to *Der Fliegende Holländer*, excerpts from *Tannhäuser* and *Lohengrin*, and the prelude to *Tristan und Isolde*. More was heard in 1861, the year of the production of the French version of *Tannhäuser* at the Opéra on March 13.[32] These beginnings marked the first stirrings of Wagnerism in writers such as Théodore de Banville and the Parnassians, followed by the symbolists. As early as 1849, Charles Baudelaire mentioned Wagner in his correspondence, and on February 17, 1860, having heard the excerpts from *Lohengrin* and *Tannhäuser* at the Théâtre-Italien, he wrote to the composer to thank him for "the greatest musical pleasure I have ever experienced."[33] Villiers de l'Isle-Adam (1838–1889), another fervent admirer, featured Wagner and praised his music in several columns in his *Revue des lettres et des arts* in 1867. Wagnerian music-drama and the concept of the *Gesamtkunstwerk* enriched the French idealist (later symbolist) theater.

As opposed to French critics such as Scudo and Fétis, the realist writer Champfleury (pseudonym of Jules Husson, 1821–1889) saw Wagner as an innovative artist who had to be defended against the conventional thinking that prevented the development of art.[34] The majority of French music critics, who were often ill-tempered about it, nonetheless had only a confused idea of Wagnerian style, based on their own listening and on Wagner's writings and those of others, such as Liszt, about his work.[35]

"A number of listeners without bias or prejudice quickly recognized the powerful skills of this artist and the regrettable leanings of his system; a larger number seemed to recognize in Wagner only a violent will and in his music only tedious and irritating noise," Berlioz wrote of the first 1860 concerts.[36] While ranking the overture to *Lohengrin* a masterpiece, Berlioz remained unreceptive to the musical language of *Tristan*, whose prelude proceeded "with no theme other than a sort of chromatic groaning...full of dissonances." After discussing the works he had heard, Berlioz set about considering the Wagnerian school, labeled "the school of the music of the future, because it is considered to run counter to the musical tastes of the present time, but to be certain, on the other hand, to accord perfectly with those of a future era."

Wagner responded on February 22, 1860, in the same paper, with "To M. Berlioz," saying: "You should know, then,...that the coiner of [the phrase] 'music of the future' was not I, but M. Bischoff, professor at Cologne.[37] The incident that gave rise to that hollow expression was my publication a decade ago of a book entitled *The Art Work of the Future*," which "contained none of the absurdities attributed to me" and dealt "in no way with the question of the grammar of music." In fact, however, a columnist in the *Berliner musikalische Zeitung* had originally coined that hated expression in 1847—ironically, in an article criticizing the music of Berlioz himself: "M. Berlioz is understood to be setting up an orchestra of his own; then he will be able to indulge himself to his heart's content and perform his musical hocus-pocus, adorned with the title of 'new music' or 'music of the future.'"[38]

From the 1850s to the 1870s, columnists made hardly any mention of specific works by Wagner, which is significant in the light of the great number of references to other composers, from Grétry to Verdi. Journalists knew very little of Wagner's music. Only a few composers and critics studied his scores in depth, and even the best prepared found some of Wagner's bolder strokes incomprehensible. We have seen the case of Berlioz, which was complicated by his personal relations with Wagner and by his bitterness at the production of *Tannhäuser* at the Paris Opéra when he had been unable to get his own work, *Les Troyens,* performed there. In 1864, Ernest Reyer, too, remained ignorant of *Tristan;* it was only in 1884 that he published an article praising it.

Jules Ruelle was better informed about this matter than most of his colleagues, and in 1863, he chided them harshly for their insincerity: "To lend power to their thrusts, they freight them with a great absurdity: they bring Wagner into it, claiming that M. Bizet's music resembles his."[39] This same phenomenon can be seen in press accounts of the first performance of *Carmen* in 1875.

The majority of critics based their judgments on an academic notion of opera and were unaffected by endeavors aimed at renewing the lyric theater. The concept of the leitmotif was utterly unknown. For French audiences of the mid nineteenth century, thematic repetition was essentially associated with the pleasure of re-hearing a beautiful phrase. This is why the theme of the Nadir-Zurga duet (which is heard eight times in the course of *Les Pêcheurs de perles*) is generally viewed as unconnected with any dramatic context.

Operatic columnists displayed many characteristics of a Franco-Italian aesthetic understanding. It took the power of the chorale handled as brilliantly as it was by Meyerbeer in *Les Huguenots* or really striking evidence of a theme connected with events (such as a celebration scene or a trumpet call) for them to recognize the dramatic or theatrical value of a mnemonic motif. In their reviews of Massenet's *Werther* (1893), more than thirty years after the Paris premiere of *Tannhäuser,* the best-informed critics had to devote considerable space to correcting misconceptions. "It cannot be said," Reyer hastened to note, "that the score of *Werther,* in which, incidentally, leitmotifs appear only very rarely—and take care not to confuse these with the characteristic phrases that M. Massenet uses—it cannot be...said that this score is a Wagnerian score. Here and there at most."[40] Although Massenet "was inspired by Wagner's techniques, his style is completely different from that of the German master," Victorin Joncières added. "The latter made leitmotifs the very framework of his instrumental designs....

M. Massenet's approach is less complex: he confines himself quite simply to recalling a theme, without even modifying it according to the various episodes that bring it back."[41] Note that, in order to make clearer the differences between the two aesthetics, Joncières to some extent caricatures Massenet's approach, which is not merely a repetition of themes.

THE RISING TIDE OF WAGNERISM AS SEEN BY THE PRESS

What, then, were the musical ingredients that the press called "Wagnerian" in the 1850s through the 1870s, and beyond? In Henri Vignaud's words, they were "highly learned techniques" and "beauties concealed by harmonic profundities."[42] Wagner's influence was seen "in atrociously harsh dissonances,"[43] in "the misuse of violent modulations and of laboriously achieved stunts,"[44] in "harmonic eccentricities," and in "melodic recitative." Obscurity, fog, unbearable volume, the struggle of voice against orchestra, the loss of melody, melodic recitative, harmonic harshness, symphonic music, and affected writing were typical formulas to denote the supposed Wagnerism of a score. As it happened, the term "fog" was also used of Gounod's music, and the composers of *Faust* and of *Tristan* were also evoked together when it came to identifying the leaders of the school of "symphonic opera." Several trends were thus lumped together.

In short, it seems that the most common image of the German composer was that of a grotesque and symbolic figure to be dangled before the public in order to denounce a work. It is no distortion of the views of the journalists of the time to say that the pejorative term "Wagnerian" evoked noise and complexity (see fig. 11). It was also applied to any music that forsook the traditional relationship between melody and accompaniment (some of Rossini's operas were once called "German" in their native land). No one was safe from this murderous epithet. Even Offenbach, at the very opposite end of the operatic spectrum, was called Wagnerian by critics (Berlioz among them) when he forgot proper decorum and used a few dubious harmonic effects—and, worse still, barking noises—in his madcap *Barkouf* (first performed in 1860 at the Opéra-Comique), in which a dog is appointed governor. "M. Offenbach's new work swarms with harmonic eccentricities that the discordant apostles of the Music of the Future would not disavow," Oscar Comettant wrote. "With that blend of charlatanism and faith that characterizes German thinking, [the new German school] is pursuing its voyage to discover the ideal in music, which it believes it can discern beyond a turbulent ocean of sour notes and nettlesome modulations."[45]

**RICHARD WAGNER, par GILL.**

Figure 11.    Caricature of Wagner in *L'Eclipse*, April 18, 1869. Here, Wagner's music is likened to noise that endangers the listener's hearing.

This was, in fact, aesthetic misappropriation: Wagner's art was stereotyped in terms such as "Music of the Future," "infinite melody," and so forth, which were ridiculous when taken out of context; this revealed the critics' taste for fashionable phrases and their need to use anti-German rhetoric (referring, after 1861, to the *Tannhäuser* scandal) to condemn anything that did not adhere to the canons of French taste and that could be identified with the stereotypes of the German school: heaviness and complexity. The conservative voices in the press (long the most influential) combined to chorus traditional values and to reaffirm the omnipotence of a national taste and a national aesthetic—but without at this stage taking on the aggressive, nationalistic tone that would dominate after the Franco-Prussian War of 1870 and even more so during World War I, when it culminated in Saint-Saëns's dreadful *Germanophilie,* in the preface to which the aging composer and critic indignantly wrote that

> Germany, taking up the role of Christianity, but in reverse, has been seized by…evil instincts.…[She], who claims to be religious, who invokes divine protection, and who boasts of a superior culture, trumpets the supremacy of brutal force over moral force, scoffs at goodness and pity, and establishes cruelty as a principle and as a system. This is the violent decline of Civilization, a return to ancestral Barbarism.
>
> In the face of this situation, how can one say one is a Germanophile? Germanophilia is either a deception or a crime.
>
> You choose.[46]

To understand this, it is necessary to have a grasp not only of the historical context but also of the spectacular reversal that took place in the last quarter of the nineteenth century, profoundly changing the way in which educated audiences perceived and reacted to music. Wagner was now seen as a model with so great an influence on the worlds of art and criticism that it seemed vitally important to oppose him. Although Wagner's "Aristophanic comedy" *Eine Kapitulation* (A capitulation: Comedy in the antique manner),[47] which on the face of it ridiculed the French, was added to the concept of the Music of the Future to bolster the arguments of the nationalists and the anti-Wagnerians, this negative influence could not slow the powerful movement to disseminate Wagnerian music and ideas. Between 1876 and 1886,[48] the number of concert performances of Wagner's works in France increased, as did the number of French Wagnerians. Among the more important critics, Saint-Saëns managed during the 1870s to distinguish between the man and the composer. He was at pains to state his fondness for the music of Wagner without succumbing to the Wagner-mania that he mentioned in passing: "For the Wagnerians, music did not exist before the works of Wagner—or rather, it existed only in embryonic form. Wagner raised it to the level of an art." Furthermore, "no matter what the product of the master, even the ballet from *Rienzi,*…it hurls [the Wagnerian] into a state of exaltation that is hard to describe."[49]

A letter dated Bayreuth, July 31, 1882, from Ernest Guiraud (who composed the recitatives for both *Carmen* and Offenbach's *Les Contes d'Hoffmann*) to Mme Chabrier gives us a glimpse of the lunacy that touched the Wagnerians of the day:

> Amid the fanatics, would-be musicians, and minor musicians of all lands who are here, amid these folk whose distinctive trait is to wear soft hats and huge eyeglasses with round lenses, and to have dirty fingernails, I feel the need to take refuge with you to chat as reasonably as I can after escaping from these lunatics. I heard *Parsifal* yesterday. Before telling you my impressions, I shall want to gather them together; to do this I shall take advantage of the time when I have no more Wagnerians on my heels. If you only knew how awful these people are! Here they rip you to shreds if you are so foolhardy as to venture the least criticism. Even enthusiasm is forbidden—or at least one is not permitted to show any sign of it during a performance. Only ecstasy is tolerated. I must confess to you, who are no Wagnerian, that I was a trifle ecstatic, because the work has beauties of the first order that signify a great musician.[50]

Edouard Dujardin's *Revue wagnérienne* published its first issue on February 8, 1885. In the French musical press, there were increasing numbers of analytical articles, aesthetic studies, and accounts of concerts. Ever greater numbers of pilgrims headed for Bayreuth. Albert Lavignac's *Le Voyage à Bayreuth* (1897) was the climax of this celebration. It contained "a genuine practical guide to Bayreuth for the Frenchman" in which the author sought to describe "in what frame of mind one should" undertake the journey, and the "appealing preliminary studies to which one should commit oneself if one wishes to enjoy it fully."[51] A "rough list of the French who have attended performances at the Bayreuth Festival Theater from its opening [1876] to 1896," which was updated in each successive edition, added to the interest of this work.

Although it was possible to hear Wagner's music in concert, producing his operas continued to pose problems. *Rienzi* was performed on April 6, 1869, at the Théâtre-Lyrique and was given thirty-eight performances before the collapse of France in 1870. It was then not until May 3, 1887, after much intrigue in the press, that a French version of *Lohengrin* was heard at the Eden Theater, when the run was curtailed in the face of growing hostility. For Théophile Gautier *fils*, this was not an aesthetic or patriotic issue, but an economic problem: "On the matter of *Lohengrin*, it is very important to end up by speaking the truth.... This whole business is the eternal struggle between protectionism and free trade.... [The] day when the marvelous harmonies and genuinely human melodies of Wagner's works are heard, enhanced by the magic of a stage production, the infantile imitations of the members of the young French school of music will fade away like indistinct murmurings. Saint-Saëns and Massenet will no longer be anything more than dim shadows."[52]

But it was not until the 1890s that the music dramas of the composer-poet were performed in France. To give a few examples, the first performance of *Lohengrin* at the Opéra took place on September 16, 1891; *Le Vaisseau fantôme* (*Der fliegende Holländer*) was premiered in France at Lille on January 28, 1893; on May 12, 1893, *La Walkyrie* was performed at the Opéra (it had been given in 1887 at the Théâtre de la Monnaie in Brussels); and *Les Maîtres chanteurs* (*Die Meistersinger*) was heard at Lyon on December 30, 1896. Audiences were thus able to take in all the various styles of Wagner's work: the traditional operas, such as *Rienzi*; the romantic operas drawing on legends, in which Wagner developed the initial elements of a compositional technique based on the manipulation of motifs and the lengthening of scenes, such as *Lohengrin*; and the true music dramas, based on a continuous leitmotif structure and new aesthetic concepts, such as *Tristan und Isolde* and *Der Ring des Nibelungen*. (When speaking of Wagnerian music, it is always necessary to specify to which Wagnerian style or period one is referring.)

In 1893, Zola observed in an article on French lyric drama: "The Wagnerian system—so logical, so complete, so total—has gained supremacy, to the extent that it has long been thought that nothing excellent or new can be created outside that system. The ground has been taken; it will now yield only works that are the offspring of the master."[53]

As a result, the reception in France of music in general, and of opera in particular, was transformed—or more precisely, the modes of perception that partly defined the process by which works were received at any given time were reversed. This period saw the beginning of the retreat of French music as it had been conceived and viewed (and as this book attempts to understand it) before it came to be dominated by Germanic thinking and aesthetics. Here, the words of the poet and essayist Camille Mauclaire are illuminating: "People today can never fully understand what Wagner was for us in 1892, the vast region of light that his magic opened up to us, the groundswell he provoked in our souls, *the horrible disgust he aroused in us for anything that was not him*" (emphasis added).[54]

# PART 2

## DRAMA, POETRY, AND MUSIC

Opera is where theater and music meet. Even more, it is where we see cross-fertilization between the two arts: music is a continuous presence in the performance of the drama, and the play is given life by taking on a musical form. Catherine Kintzler has described the concept of a "poetic text" that reflects this close relationship between music and theater, and in which "the guiding presence of a literary text" is of great importance.[1] Her comments are applicable well beyond the time of the French *tragédie lyrique* and remain relevant in the period we are discussing. In her words, operatic music "is defined in an essentially theatrical way"; it "carries out a fully-fledged poetic function because, from the point of view of both author and spectator, it is itself a genuinely fictional means of creating a text and of contributing to the dramatic design."[2] I shall adopt this first essential idea. The arrangement of an opera's musical components (recitatives, ariosos, arias, choruses, ensembles, finales, ballets, and so forth) follows a dramatic order. But the proposition must also be reversed: an opera's libretto is defined, almost always very obviously, in *musical* terms. In other words, the literary material is shaped by, or for, the music. The dramatic design and the manner in which the libretto is written depend on elements of musical structure and form, such as the recapitulation of musical passages and the structure of ensembles. Even more, the "final text"—the text heard by the audience—is not contained in the libretto, but rather in the score. It is the score that determines such factors as the libretto's pacing, the repetition of words, and when several texts are to be sung simultaneously.

The literary work—the libretto—must obey rules of its own, which are based on its need to be suitable for setting to music. The poetic text may be read on three levels. The first involves the arrangement of the story, the drama as a whole, and the way it is set out. This is the product of dramaturgy in the ordinary sense of the word, "the art or technique of dramatic composition and theatrical representation" (*Webster's*), and I refer to it here as the "dramatic framework." The second level, which relates to the realization of this framework in literary form, and is the product of a highly formalized art, I call "poetic writing." The third level is the poetic expressiveness itself, the result of the combined powers of the libretto and the music, which I refer to as "operatic poetry."

Before laying out the drama, it was necessary to choose a setting for the action and a subject that had dramatic and expressive potential. Authors were frequently inspired by existing works or specific events: borrowings (or references) were a fundamental principle of operatic dramaturgy. Librettists used all kinds of techniques, formulas, and rules; manipulating these was the basis of the dramatist's craft.

# Chapter 4 The Construction of a Drama

In every libretto, the setting of the action may be distinguished from the subject. The former comprises an external environment and a social environment with its own organization and cast of characters. Natural elements of this external environment (such as landscape, plants, animals, and natural elements and cycles) are combined with those built by human hands (such as dwellings, other kinds of buildings, and architectural ornaments) to create a distinctive and structured space. Settings vary from highly urbanized places (or interiors) to depictions of pristine nature; a balance is often struck by portraying nature as organized by human beings.

The space in which the action of *Les Pêcheurs de perles* takes place is structured around a Hindu temple, staircases, columns, and statues (see fig. 10). The natives, who come to these places only during the time of pearl fishing, are heirs to a past civilization whose architectural splendor lends grandeur to their religious rites. The environment is the expression of a society, in addition to performing a decorative and symbolic function.

Many librettos reflect the staying power of a concept that the Romantics held dear: the close link between nature and drama. Harmony between a landscape and a state of mind, an emotion, or even an event made it possible to fuse description and expression. The setting for the action thus mirrored the forces working upon the hearts and minds of the characters. Wagner described to perfection the operatic dramatist's interest in a good relationship between the setting and the music. In his discussion of Halévy's *La Reine de Chypre*, he observed that "the external form is made up of two distinct parts determined by the locale in which a given scene takes place. Diversity in the locales of the scenes has never been so important as it is in this drama, where

87

Figure 12. Gounod's *Mireille*, act 1, mulberry-picking scene. Lithograph by A. Lamy.

it makes a special mark both on the action and on the forms in which it appears. If you listen carefully to Halévy's strains, you will understand how this diversity of locale can be expressed in sound."[1]

*Les Pêcheurs de perles* opens with a radiant sun in a clear sky, and a sea that one imagines to be of a cerulean blue. Love is in the air under the starlit heavens. A storm bursts at the moment of disaster: the discovery of the two lovers. The pearl fishers perform their dance of death by the glimmer of braziers, alone in the disquieting depths of a forest. In a fine, noble monologue at the beginning of act 3, Zurga endeavors to regain the calm that is a prerequisite for wisdom so that he can disentangle the threads of duty and of passion. At the very outset, he links the natural disaster at the end of act 2 with the emotional torment that has shaken him so profoundly: "The storm has calmed. Already, the wind is dying down, / Just as anger is subsiding."

In keeping with a simple code, places had a meaning that added power to the drama and that the audience was able to decipher. They followed a typology based on real, if sometimes rudimentary, images—for example, those of country towns such as Epinal (in the Vosges), which were used in

Figure 13. A medieval setting for the duel between Faust and Valentin in the town square, in Gounod's *Faust* (*L'Illustration,* March 6, 1869). A contemporary critic described, "A square surrounded by feudal, gothic architecture, in which cathedral spires are combined with the arched posterns of towers.... The silhouette of the town, with the striking outlines of Prague or Nuremberg, bristles with battlements and turrets" (Amédée Achard, "Revue dramatique," *Le Moniteur universel,* March 8, 1869).

depictions of the countryside and of village life, including those in Adolphe Adam's *Le Chalet* and the mulberry orchard scene in Gounod's *Mireille* (see fig. 12). A well-chosen setting instantly transported the spectator to the time and place of the action. The troubadour style and its many off-shoots throughout the century provided a whole palette of highly expressive and dramatic effects, locales, motifs, atmospheres, and themes: in act 4 of Gounod's *Faust,* for example, a duel is set against the backdrop of a me-dieval city (see fig. 13).

Dramatists, who built up their plays in a series of contrasting scenes, based their work on a pictorial conception of the stage. It was this kind of the-atrical writing that accounted in large part for the success of Boieldieu's *La Dame blanche* in 1825; that work then became a model in this sphere, as a journalist observed in 1870: "What we must point out in *La Dame blanche* is the very individual color that the composer has given his work.... Here we must also praise the librettist [Scribe], who supported him with all his might and with rare skill, by making each of his acts into a picture, some-times colorful (the mountains of Scotland, the rustic fête, and the storm) and sometimes strange and poetic (Georges's exploration of Avenel Castle…), but always lively, and each completely different from the others."[2] At the other end of our period, Massenet's *Werther* heightened this trend: "The episodes follow one another like a series of genre paintings; each act bears a title [The Bailiff's House; The Lime Trees; Charlotte and Werther; Christmas Night; The Death of Werther] as though it were a painting or a chapter in a picture book," Gottfried Marschall notes.[3] In *Esclarmonde*, Massenet and his librettists went so far as to reject narrative time in favor of a pictorial conception of this fable set in the Middle Ages. Its six central scenes blend the glamour of fantasy with knightly settings: the terrace of a palace at Byzantium; the enchanted island; a room in the magic palace; a square near the city of Blois; a room in the palace of King Cléomer; the forest of the Ardennes. A prologue and an epilogue (both constructed with the same musical elements) frame the entire work in the resplendent setting of the basilica at Byzantium with its holy iconostasis. With this recapitulation, the authors bring the audience back to the very beginning of the drama, which thus seems to have taken place outside time—or, to be more precise, according to the laws of an eternal time of legend.

### OPEN SPACE AND CLOSED SPACE

In many operas, one function of the setting is either to open the action onto the outside world or, on the contrary, to close it in upon itself. Either abruptly or by degrees, the scene would change from an open space to a closed space, just as the drama, generally speaking, moves from collective to individual expression. The open space of a sunlit beach at the beginning of *Les Pêcheurs de perles* gives way to the more enclosed space of the temple and the terrace (Leïla's isolation, the nighttime love scene, and the subsequent discovery of the lovers), which in turn yields to the completely closed space of the tent (Zurga's monologue and his confrontation with Leïla). Life in the open air is followed by an "interior life" centered around individual characters and their domestic environment (see figs. 14 and 15). It would be nonsensical to ignore this principle in the design of a production. The final setting, which brings all the protagonists together in a great mass scene full of savagery, returns to a space in nature—but in the disturbing darkness of the forest and the night, illuminated by a pyre. From exposition to denouement, the drama unfolds in accordance with a rhetoric of decor.

This theatrical motion—opening or closing the scenic space and moving from day to night and from the collective to the individual—was firmly es-

Figure 14.   Open space. Bizet's *Les Pêcheurs de perles* act 1 finale (*Il Teatro illu-strato*, April 1886).

tablished by Boieldieu and Scribe. The first act of *La Dame blanche* takes place by day, in a country setting, amid a crowd of people. The libretto indicates that "the stage represents the interior of a Scottish farm; the rear, which is open, provides a view of a picturesque scene, trees, rocks, and a path descending from the mountain to the farm." In striking contrast, act 2 begins with an "intimist" scene (the servant Marguerite seated at her spinning

Figure 15.    Enclosed space. Bizet's *Les Pêcheurs de perles*, act 3, duet for Léïla and Zurga (*Il Teatro illustrato*, April 1886).

wheel), in the depths of night, in a closed space: "The stage represents a great Gothic hall." This is precisely the same sequence that demarcates the first two acts of *La Juive*, the first of which takes place in the town square and the second inside Eléazar's house. The grandiose scene of the Catholics celebrating the opening of the Council session takes place in the open air, while Passover is celebrated in secrecy. The basic conflict of the drama is thus tellingly conveyed through the scenery. The first two scenes of *Faust* offer another example. In the first, the scholar expresses his metaphysical weariness and considers suicide; the austere, somber setting of his study reflects the way in which Faust himself is closed in upon himself: it is his interior world. By contrast, the exterior world, first evoked by the off-stage chorus, is depicted in the lively and colorful kermesse of the following scene.

Figure 16.    Two spaces superimposed. Gounod's *Roméo et Juliette,* act 5, ruined monastery above an underground crypt. Sketch of stage set by P. Chaperon (1872).

Sometimes, rather than juxtaposing two kinds of space, designers superimposed them, translating the tensions of the plot into visual terms. Thus, for example, the score of Jean-François Le Sueur's *La Caverne* (1793) describes the well-known scene, involving two Spanish noblemen who have been taken prisoner by brigands, on which the drama is built, as follows: "The stage represents a cavern hewn into the rock. . . . The stage is divided horizontally; above the cavern is a forest. . . ."[4] The same idea is repeated in the *grand opéra Guido et Ginevra* by Scribe and Halévy, whose third act depicts the Duomo of Florence and underground vaults. In act 5 of *Roméo et Juliette* (1867) by Gounod, Barbier, and Carré, the oppressive atmosphere of the subterranean crypt is intensified by the contrast with an upper level showing a ruined monastery surrounded by trees and illuminated by moonlight (see fig. 16).[5]

A final example, from *Carmen*—which without question is exceptionally successful in this sphere—demonstrates how the authors used these same principles to adapt the theatrical space to the drama. The public space of act 1 (the great square in Seville) is contrasted with the closed space of act 2 (Lillas Pastia's tavern). The collective scene defined by social relationships

Figure 17.   Space of rejection. Bizet's *Carmen*, act 4, entrance to the Seville bullring. Sketch for stage set by Emile Bertin (unidentified revival).

(between the cigarette women and the soldiers; between the tobacco factory and the guardhouse) yields to individuals whose fates will be juxtaposed and intertwined. The public space—initially light and well ordered, then disrupted by the agent of the drama, Carmen—is replaced by a murky space that is closed in upon its individual inhabitants. Act 3 brings breathing room and the mystery of a natural space by night (rocks and a wild, picturesque landscape), which can sometimes be poetic and sometimes disturbing; here, passions take a fateful turn. Finally, act 4, which is set outside the bullring, shifts the meaning of that place, as the drama tilts toward tragedy. The arena begins as the site of the corrida; but it then, so to speak, absorbs the crowd. The stage area, now empty, becomes a space for rejection (or exclusion) in which the final, fatal confrontation takes place, outside of society, between Carmen and Don José (see fig. 17).

On a smaller scale, stage movement, too, reflects a semantics of theatrical space. When Léïla swears her oath in act 1 of *Les Pêcheurs de perles*, the written stage directions indicate in concrete terms the young woman's accession to the status of priestess: she "mounts the path leading to the temple ruins, followed by Nourabad." The balcony scene in act 2 of Gounod's *Roméo et Juliette* is particularly significant in this regard: the balcony opens Juliette's inaccessible bedchamber to the world. The characters' actions acquire meaning in relation to this space, which is suspended between interior and exterior, between society and intimacy, between earth and sky, between the threat of detection and the promise of secret love. At the center of this dramatic structure, Juliette and Roméo appear, hide, and disappear, first separately, then together. The movement of people and places reflects the movement of souls. Maeterlinck recalled this technique, but used the tower in act 3 of *Pelléas et Mélisande* as a sign that the reconciliation of the two protagonists was impossible, in spite of the strength of their love.

### RELIGIOUS RITUAL AS THEATER

An opera plot was constructed on the basis of the practices of a group, or of the members of a social category, often combined with the interplay of tensions between individuals and the community. The social codes of a given environment could be the essence of the dramatic fabric. The pearl fishers' microsociety has its own ways and customs, which the librettists describe both with an eye to realism and because this social framework supplies the action with essential motivations: tribal structure and religious ritual are at the root of the drama. The locales and events of an exotic world demanded that specific spaces be created. For example, act 2 of Saint-Georges's *La Pagode* (1859, music by Fauconnier) began with a scene of worship and offerings in the East Indies, with a pagoda, altar, and incense burners. As native practices, the customs of distant lands also lent a kind of plausibility to the ballet (see fig. 18).

Contrasting different groups is another potent principle of dramatic writing, and it was used extensively in *grand opéra*: Christians against Jews in *La Juive;* Protestants against Catholics in *Les Huguenots;* an oppressed people against its oppressor in *Guillaume Tell*. Two of those three examples involve religion. The inclusion of religious scenes and religious practices in operatic typology was a major focus of nineteenth-century lyric theater.[6] Just as Chateaubriand, in his *Génie du christianisme*, stressed the poetic and emotional richness of Christianity, French operatic writers would explore its dramatic potential, applying this initiative to a broad spectrum of religions. The plot of *Les Pêcheurs de perles* is built precisely around the beliefs of its Ceylonese fisherfolk. In the course of the drama, we see a high priest, solemn oaths, ceremonies, a propitiatory hymn, and an expiatory sacrifice. Exotic subjects added variety to the array of religious scenic effects.

Figure 18.    Gounod's *La Reine de Saba,* first performed at the Opéra on February 28, 1862. Anonymous woodcut after the act 2 scenery for the premiere, by Charles Cambon and Joseph Thierry. Exotic subjects made it easy for the plot to accommodate the ballet demanded by the lavish staging of *grand opéra.*

Librettists and composers alike understood the extraordinary emotional and theatrical potential of religious practices, whether external (such as ceremonies and processions) or more intimate (such as prayers). Following the path taken by Gluck, notably in *Alceste,* they made use (especially in *grand opéra*) of the liturgy's inherent theatricality and pomp, and of many theatrical high points related to religion. Spectators could relate to these from their own experience, and they aroused the deepest and most powerful emotions. There was a proliferation of oaths, marriages, coronations, anathemas, and prayers.

The scenic interest of these was their dependence on clearly identifiable settings such as churches, which made it possible to add a touch of the Gothic to the production and to engender a religious atmosphere. A church seen from the outside would lend itself admirably to a scene with off-stage musical effects. In act 5 of *Les Huguenots,* for example, we hear the prayer of the women gathered inside the church. Its interior could be a grand setting for ceremonials of all kinds, or it could be the site of a tryst. At the apex of this genre is the church scene in Gounod's *Faust,* which added an intimate atmosphere to its theatrical elements.[7] It is clear, too, that Wagner profited by these experiences—in *Parsifal,* for example.

Writing of the premiere of *La Juive,* a critic whose name has unfortunately not come down to us felt that this theme should be viewed as the basis of a new operatic aesthetic:

> The new subject of *La Juive* is an entirely Catholic, apostolic, and Roman subject. The advances here are more visible than ever before. Mythology has long been dead at the Opéra: the Middle Ages have replaced mythology; the Devil has taken the place of Jupiter; the powers of Hell have dispersed the hordes of minor deities...; no more rose coppices, but instead fine Gothic cathedrals...; this was one fantasy replacing another fantasy, invisible powers taking the place of invisible powers. Christianity had finally arrived at the Opéra, roughly driving out flamboyant, impassioned paganism. But until *La Juive,* Christianity remained hidden. Its beliefs and superstitions had been set to music, but its ceremonies—much less its ministers—had not been put on stage.[8]

The article concludes: "The revolution has taken place.... Now, the Catholic Church is on stage; now, and for a long time to come, we shall not turn away from the subject of Christianity."

It was not the elimination of the supernatural but rather a change in its nature, as Chateaubriand expressed it, that this extraordinary success placed at the center of the "new world" of ideas and feelings that fueled the arts, taste, and even morality of the whole first part of the nineteenth century. Opera would be the theatrical extension of this new world. In the preface to the first edition of his *Les Martyrs* (1809), Chateaubriand wrote, "In an earlier work [*Le Génie du christianisme,* 1801], I suggested that the Christian religion seemed to me more conducive than paganism to the development of characters and the handling of emotions in a historical epic; I said further that the 'supernatural' of that religion might be able to hold its own against the 'supernatural' borrowed from mythology."[9] Moreover, Christian themes found favor because of the popularity of history, as Chateaubriand wrote in the preface to the third edition of the same work: "To treat a subject drawn from modern history, it is necessary to make use of Christian supernatural elements, for the Christian religion is today the religion of the civilized peoples of Europe." It was thus possible to use religion to combine the new demand for historical realism with the long-standing taste for the supernatural. Yet, apart from *Robert le Diable* and a few other scores, such as Halévy's *Le Juif errant* (1852), this new kind of supernaturalism was soon stripped of its magical dimension, retaining only its external form and becoming what we might call a realistic super-naturalism. In his modern epic *Les Martyrs*, Chateaubriand created a tangible world, magnificent word paintings that spur the imagination, and scenes that, along with other works, made a lasting impact on the thinking of the century. His writings bear out the dominance of the aesthetic of weeping and of opening the heart and soul, as introduced by Rousseau; this influenced the style of the *romance* and of many operatic arias, including the famous "Pleurez mes yeux" (Weep, my eyes"), sung by Chimène at the beginning of act 3 of Massenet's *Le Cid* (1885), and Charlotte's "tears" aria, "Va! laisse couler mes larmes," in *Werther* (Vienna, 1892; Paris, 1893). In book 15 of *Les Martyrs*, Chateaubriand's Christian hero Eudore is able to confide to the beautiful Cymodocée, "Daughter of Homer, my God is the god of gentle souls, the friend of those who weep, the consolation of the afflicted." In contrast to this kind of emotion and sensitivity, the author also reveals the powerful dramatic potential of Christianity, specifically the theme of anathema, which would become a standard scene in *grand opéra*. The passage in book 6 in which Eudore recounts that in his scandalous youth he had rejected the Christians might have come from an opera, with its striking groups of people on a stage set with medieval scenery, with a tremendous bass solo and an outburst from the chorus:

> Deacons, priests, bishops—silent, motionless—were gathered over the nearby tombs, like newly resurrected souls at the Last Judgment....I tried to advance; an exorcist blocked my way. Simultaneously, the bishops extended their arms and raised their hands against me, turning their heads away. Then the pontiff spoke in a terrible voice: "Anathema upon him whose ways defile the purity of the word 'Christian'! Anathema upon him who no longer draws near the altar of the true God! Anathema upon him who views with indifference the abomination of idolatry!" All the bishops cried out, "Anathema!"

Scribe and Meyerbeer succeeded in rejuvenating this theme and in giving dramatic form to its philosophical meaning. Théophile Gautier explained:

> *Robert le Diable* is Catholicism with its superstitions, its mysterious half-light, its temptations, its long cloisters tinged with blue, its demons and its angels, all its fantastical poetry. *Les Huguenots* is the analytical mind, rational fanaticism; the struggle of ideas against beliefs, duty against passion, denial against affirmation; it is history replacing legend, philosophy replacing religion. *Le Prophète* is hypothesis, utopia, the still-unclear form of things that do not exist, all outlined in an extravagant sketch.[10]

The church had such a position on the stage because it had developed a dramaturgy of its own, and in Paris had become, perhaps more than in earlier centuries, a place to be seen. Jules Janin, who exemplified the qualities and flaws of a Parisian man of letters, described this phenomenon to perfection in 1842, in a witty book that enjoyed a brisk success, *Un hiver à Paris:*

> After the Opéra, which is far and away the center of Parisian life, what the *beau monde* of Paris prefers to any other pleasure…is a religious ceremony—but a beautiful ceremony, something that smacks of pomp and dramatic sparkle: a burial, for example, or a wedding, or, better yet, a sermon. In Paris there is a certain church that is mentioned for the brilliance of its lighting, for the aromas of its incense, for the beautiful voices of its cantors, for the great number of its choirboys. They speak of the priest's lace, the sumptuousness of his vestments, and the embroidery on his surplice just as they would speak of the shawl and the gown of a great lady of fashion.[11]

Everything was arranged to provide a "feast for the eyes"; the church became a theater, the chapel a boudoir; and the singers came from the Opéra to be heard. Then, when the Divine Office was over, "everyone departed, casting a curious eye over their neighbors. Then the conversation became noisier and more lively: they asked whether Monsieur So-and-so had sung well, or whether he hadn't sung better at the Opéra the other day; whether the priest was feeling well. The priest passed, and they greeted him with a little smile that meant, 'The Mass was lovely!' "[12] In this way, "the Church played its part in all the pleasures and all the sorrows of these curious people. Like the Opéra, it had its fashions, its practices, its attire and its loyal subscribers. And in recent times, it has been involved more than ever in the excitements, needs, and expectations of everyday life."[13]

Yet, for the sake of propriety, the censors saw to it that the true Catholic liturgy was not belittled by being depicted on stage. It would be interesting to piece together the background of religious scenes from the standpoint of how closely the music and the libretto resemble actual practice. We can, however, note that it was not the *Kyrie eleison*—an obvious borrowing from the liturgical text—sung by the retinue of the bishop of Blois in act 3 of *Esclarmonde* (1889) that as late as 1923 prompted an official initiative on behalf of the greatest luminaries of the Catholic world aimed at revising the score for its first performance at the Opéra. The director of the Opéra, Jacques Rouché, wrote to the minister of fine arts that the work, "it appears, will violate dogma by showing on stage a Byzantine bishop betraying the secrecy of the confessional."[14] Despite its happy ending, this

incident is nonetheless astonishing. What is more, Massenet's opera, with a libretto by Alfred Blau and Louis de Gramont, included a rather uncommon sort of religious scene: an exorcism (see fig. 19).

Massenet's output should be viewed as the final development of religion in the French opera of a wide-ranging nineteenth century. Among other works, *Hérodiade* (1884), *Thaïs* (1894), and *Le Jongleur de Notre-Dame* (Monte Carlo, 1902; Paris, 1904) exploited the dramatic and stylistic potential of religion, while also expressing Christian supernatural themes, the marriage between sensuality and spirituality, and sometimes the torments of the flesh—a force that ran counter to the yearning for existential fulfillment (or for a spiritual life), a yearning that Thaïs nevertheless fulfills at her death. The sinner of Massenet's oratorio *Marie-Magdeleine* (1873) bears the features of a Manon or a Thaïs. Adolphe Jullien wrote in *Le Journal des Débats* on May 20, 1906, that "the composer's youthful inspiration...seemed, as it had from the very outset, to be completely permeated with a voluptuous tenderness and with a sensual mysticism that was not very religious but rather affectionate and captivating, at least for those who require only that music charm and soothe them." The eternal feminine is seen in the light of a fin de siècle aesthetic that does not draw a boundary between bodily and spiritual pangs, or between Christian and amorous feelings. "Everything about the love between Salomé and John the Baptist bears the sure mark of a master. M. Massenet's somewhat sickly and love-besotted muse excels in describing this mystical passion, this passion of the sacristy, these burning dreams of seminarians," we read in one review of *Hérodiade*.[15]

Act 3, scene 2, of *Manon* takes place in the visitors' room of the seminary at the eighteenth-century church of Saint-Sulpice in Paris, whose setting is used to uncommonly good effect, taking on different meanings as the events of the drama progress. The action begins with a quintessentially theatrical scene: the sounds of the organ and the chorus of the faithful, which contrast with the previous scene on the Cours la Reine. The arrival of the Comte Des Grieux breaks this mood of collective religiosity. Community gives way to family confrontation. The site, initially a space for

Figure 19.   *Opposite:* Massenet's *Esclarmonde,* scene 6, a room in King Cléomer's palace: the exorcism (*L'Illustration,* May 18, 1889). The bishop, followed by monks and executioners, takes Roland and Esclarmonde, whom he associates with the devil, by surprise. "As Roland steps forward to defend Esclarmonde, and as the priests and executioners prepare to seize him, fiery spirits appear and surround him" (libretto [Paris: Hartmann, 1889], p. 45).

communal practices, becomes the symbol of isolation from the world and from society, a refuge of existential malaise: "I have found only bitterness and disgust in life," replies the young man to his father, who has come to remove him from the seminary ("Marry some nice girl," he advises). The drama closes in and the hero is alone. This is when the theme of the struggle between faith and the call of memory comes into play ("Ah, fuyez, douce image"—"Ah, begone, sweet image"). An external event (the distant music of the organ) reminds Des Grieux of his duty: the Divine Office. Now the mood of the scene changes with the arrival of Manon, who remains alone during the religious ceremony whose echoes she hears from off-stage, and in which Des Grieux is a participant. The seminary becomes a hostile place ("Ces murs silencieux"—"These silent walls.... The chill air I breathe..."). Manon has carried out the opposite action to her lover's: she has returned to the world by detaching it from religious commitment. Before the confrontation, Manon ventures a "loving prayer,"[16] which is followed by a duet full of a very special emotion—for in this place Manon's struggle to rekindle Des Grieux's love becomes a struggle between human love and faith ("Ne parle pas d'amour ici..."—"Do not speak of love here; it is blasphemy"). The dramatic apogee of this duet comes with the second signal that the church sends to Des Grieux: the bells summoning the faithful to prayer. The scene ends with the striking contrast between the austere walls of the church and the surrender to the carnal by the Chevalier, dressed in his cassock, in the arms of his mistress.

Apart from the remarkable dramatic and scenic interest of such scenes, their inclusion provided an opportunity to enrich the musical vocabulary. Composers drew on styles associated with Church music and with ancient practice, which did not normally appear in their scores (see pages 165–67). Note that the prayer long remained a nearly obligatory type of number in all genres, even the most frivolous, such as operetta. The chorus "Le front dans la poussière, amis, prosternons-nous" ("Faces in the dust, friends, let us bow down") from *Les Mousquetaires au couvent* (1880) by Louis Varnay is a notable example of this.

### HISTORY AS A FRAMEWORK FOR DRAMA

Driven by such factors as the French Revolution (an upheaval that to some extent created its own historical era), and under the influence of a return to origins, the exploration of vanished worlds, and the new attention being paid to ancient ruins and old documents, there was a desire to bring the past to life in the social sciences and in the arts. Once again, Chateaubriand became the exemplar of this movement. A whole school of young historians regarded his *Les Martyrs* as a model of historical revival; it was admired by both François-Pierre-Guillaume Guizot (1787–1874) and Augustin Thierry (1795–1856). Just as in the case of religious themes, and propelled also by the vogue for the romantic novel inspired by the works of Sir Walter Scott (1771–1832), history overran opera librettos, proving to be a considerable reservoir of subjects and ideas for constructing a drama. *Grand opéra* in particular brought together the two trends of romantic historiography: that which depicted the grandeur of past splendors, and that which described the sufferings of the oppressed, popular movements, and mighty struggles—picturesque history on the one hand, and dramatic history on the other. Jules Michelet (1798–1874), a historian in the epic style, succeeded in merging the taste for diversity and the aspiration to unity, something *grand opéra* had great difficulty in achieving.

In spite of that difficulty, a well-chosen historical subject could be a windfall for all the artists who collaborated in producing an opera. Commenting on the first performance of *La Juive* (see fig. 4) in *Le Constitutionnel* on February 25, 1835, a columnist wrote:

> M. Scribe was fortunate to have guided his Muse of operas and librettos onto the path of the fifteenth century and the Council of Constance. For the composer, there were pious chants, military marches, and choruses hailing the triumphal entrance of the cardinals and the emperors into the fair city of Constance; for the set designer, Gothic churches with ancient stone saints and soaring spires, gabled houses and tortuous streets, mysterious chapels with stained-glass windows, and palaces with great flowing tapestries; for the painter, costumes with an incredible variety of original and magnificent garments...; as for the stage director, he lacked neither marches nor countermarches, nor splendid rites, nor crowds coming, going, running, climbing onto roofs.

Another journalist, in *Le Courrier français* of February 27, 1835, was most impressed: "What diverse and priceless things for a skillful poet, for a composer of great talent and promise, and for the designers and painters under the guidance of an artist eminently gifted with a genius for picturesque archeology." On March 11, 1835, *Le Constitutionnel* concluded: "An opera like *La Juive* is a veritable dramatic bazaar." History was viewed as a kind of Aladdin's cave, from which limitless wares could be extracted and lavishly strewn in a mass upon the stage. It was this that led some critics to write of a nouveau-riche aesthetic.

The convention was that the various elements of an opera each played a role of its own. To oversimplify, the libretto was responsible for conveying the drama; the visual elements for local color, pomp, and luxury (which had become an aesthetic category in itself); and the music for expressing emotions. But in fact these elements did not merely complement one another; increasingly, the goal was a merger of expressive and descriptive resources. In that sense, all the arts could participate in setting out the drama and could collaborate in expressing the nature of a situation. In his account of *La Juive*, the critic of *Le Constitutionnel* added: "In the first act, the religious chorus, supported by the playing of the organ, depicts a pious, Catholic respectability; the people's inveighing against the Jew Eléazar is clearly and exactly conveyed; Cardinal Brogni's aria is of a calm profundity and religious solemnity that aptly delineate a priest who is simultaneously harsh and tolerant." Here, the composer is conveying not so much local color as the nature of a situation that is defined by history. A vaguely religious musical style, suggested by the fifteenth-century plot, is heard when a Gothic church or old village is seen; this becomes part of a general evocation of olden times. We shall see in chapter 6 how composers used pastiche and a variety of other techniques to express local or period color in their music.

As we have seen, while some stage settings depicted a period with fantasy, others were the result of meticulous research and reflected a real concern for re-creating the original. In 1828, *Le Courrier des théâtres* noted that it was possible "at last to travel to Naples in a few hours" by going to see Auber's *La Muette de Portici* (*Masaniello*). For some, this concern with literal reproduction and with accurate detail bordered on obsession: as Nicole Wild shows, for the production of Saint-Saëns's *Henry VIII* at the Opéra in 1883, the painter Eugène Lacoste carried out historical research that took him to Liverpool, to Hampton Court palace, to Windsor Castle, to the Tower of London, and to the British Museum—and, in France, to the museum of musical instruments at the Conservatoire. "My labors were... but a serious exercise in historical research," he said. His endeavors gained from the physical stature of Jean Lassale, who sang the title role, and who looked like a reincarnation of Henry VIII as painted by Hans Holbein (1498–1543).[17]

STEREOTYPED CONSTRUCTION—THE MODEL OF EUGÈNE SCRIBE

Once the setting, the subject, and the general features of the action were outlined, it remained to give dramatic form to the story. Librettists and composers were helped in this by the stereotyped layout of an operatic work. Scene followed scene in line with a principle of continuity that aimed at an unbroken exposition of the action. As with the works of classical authors, the text would contain elements that were sufficient to enable the spectator to imagine how the action continued when a character was off-stage. The causal relationship among events and their placement in time generally followed the classical progression: exposition (sometimes with an additional deferred exposition), development, peripeteia (or change of fortune), and conclusion (or denouement).[18] Yet it was sometimes hard to grasp all the ins and outs of the plot, because librettists favored situations at the expense of clarity. This criticism was often made by journalists, including the columnist who wrote that Cormon and Carré had "made" (*confectionné*, as a garment or a stew) the libretto of *Les Pêcheurs de perles:* "We say 'made' on purpose, because we know no other expression to describe the type of canvas of which a handful of authors are the favored suppliers."[19]

Dramatic situations were repeated over and over again: "You know the scene: a happy meeting and indescribable transports of joy, followed by heart-rending remorse."[20] Some observers noted that the characters were always based on the same models. The soprano-tenor-baritone triangle always obeyed conventional rules by which certain types of roles were associated with specific voice categories: "Léïla…accepts Nadir, whom she loves because he is a tenor; she does not love Zurga, because he is a baritone. That rule applies in India [i.e., Sri Lanka] just as it does in Europe, so it seems. Poor baritones! They are loved less and paid less than tenors."[21] Zurga "is a loyal baritone; as a tenor, Nadir has a less steadfast heart."[22]

Operatic overproduction in the nineteenth century turned the theater into a commodity that did not meet very strict aesthetic standards. The era of "industrial literature" that Saint-Beuve deplored in 1839[23] did not come to an end until the following century. *Vaudevilles,* melodramas, and serialized novels with virtually interchangeable scenes were mass-produced. Patrick Berthier counts 2,802 new plays between 1836 and 1845 (1,924 of them *vaudevilles*), and also tells us that between 1831 and 1872, Jules Janin published some 2,500 drama columns in *Le Journal des Débats*.[24]

The leader of the authors who viewed their art as a craft was Eugène Scribe (1791–1861), who is quoted as saying that "a well-made play" was based "on an art of dramatic composition that [owes] much to the recipes of the trade and to the conviction that it [must] 'work' for the spectator." [25] According to Ferdinand Brunetière, it was he "who managed to reduce the art of the playwright to a set of models."[26] In an article written in 1877, on the occasion of the publication of Scribe's complete works, a journalist described him as the master "of theatrical concoctions of gripping effect."[27]

The changes in operatic dramaturgy brought about by Scribe were significant. One of the key concepts was the incremental unfolding of the plot—or, more precisely, of the drama's sequence of events. Scribe sought to diversify the action and to slow it down. As *Le Ménestrel* observed on December 7, 1851:

> In the past, in plays with surprises in the plot, the audience was taken into confidence from the outset; only the actors did not learn the secret of the play until the end...but since M. Scribe and his wonderful *Le Domino noir,* there has been a complete revolution in the poetic theory of the genre, and neither the audience nor the actors see things clearly until the final scene—which is incontestably far cleverer and more interesting.

This dramaturgic technique differed from that of the Italians, who tended to set out the facts of the conflict immediately.[28] In *grand opéra*, Scribe's expertise coexisted with the inevitable divertissements, which by their nature slowed the action. The succession of new developments and the suspense provided by the incremental unfolding of the plot would give a fresh start to the action after it had thus been interrupted. Long after Scribe's death, authors continued to apply his principles, by employing a "framework" over which they could "spread any kind of plaster."[29]

### SOURCES OF INSPIRATION

Ultimately, operatic subjects were very rarely original. Librettos were normally conceived as adaptations of other works, such as novels or plays. Librettists also drew upon fashionable themes, combined multiple sources, and took inspiration from recent events. The vogue for historical novels, begun by Sir Walter Scott, made a major contribution to the emergence of *grand opéra,* just as the taste for the fantastic and for poetry about the night and tombs permeated the theatrical and operatic repertories, as in the nuns' ballet in *Robert le Diable* (1831). *Le Pré aux clercs* (1833), *Les Huguenots* (1836), and *Carmen* (1875) were inspired by Prosper Mérimée. *Faust* and *Mignon* were based on originals by Goethe, but also on boulevard plays.

The authors of *Les Pêcheurs de perles* opted for an exotic subject, a type that by that time was quite mature. Their intention was to renew it by drawing, it appears, upon a book that had just appeared at the time the libretto was conceived, and that has now been identified: Octave Sachot's *L'Île de Ceylan et ses curiosités naturelles.*[30] It is all there: detailed descriptions of the pearl fishery and its attendant superstitions, of the locales (with rocks overlooking the sea, and a ruined temple) and of the huts built by the natives. Even the sorceresses who were first included but then scrapped by Cormon and Carré appear in Sachot's description.

To serve for a plot, this information was combined with elements from *La Vestale* (1807), a *tragédie lyrique* in three acts by Gaspare Spontini to a libretto by Victor Joseph Etienne de Jouy. A series of changes was made to this libretto, notably the expansion of a secondary theme, the friendship between Cinna and Licinius. Despite everything that the 1863 libretto owes to that of 1807, the two works are quite different in spirit. By the middle of the nineteenth century, librettos were losing their status as literature. We have moved far away from the aesthetic of *La Vestale*. In a preface to the original edition of that libretto,[31] Jouy defends the literary genre of *tragédie lyrique*, which he refuses to view as a minor one; he invokes Racine in explaining the liberties he took. The differences between the two librettos were connected also to changes in the political context. *La Vestale* glorifies Licinius (i.e., Napoleon), while *Les Pêcheurs* forsakes historical drama with a contemporary resonance for a timeless drama of passion and exoticism.

Consider the example of Shakespeare's *Hamlet,* as adapted for the operatic stage by Jules Barbier and Michel Carré and set to music by Ambroise Thomas. Inevitably, much was added to meet musical requirements. But other requirements, cultural in nature, also had to be addressed: operatic conventions and audience tastes, to name but two. Let us look at a few significant scenes. The coronation scene with which the opera begins depicts the new monarchs' wedding festivities and the coronation of Queen Gertrude, which are only mentioned in the play. This grand presentation brings on stage the entire cast of characters, apart from Hamlet. Following operatic dramaturgy's law of contrasts, this festive scene is duly set against the solitude and isolation of the main character; moreover, it provided an opportunity for large-scale musical development and for the splendor that was suited to the stage of the Opéra, where the work was first given in 1868. As Théophile Gautier wrote in his March 16, 1868, column in *Le Moniteur universel,* "This portrayal on stage of an earlier event, which Hamlet often recalls with such bitter sadness, has the advantage of being clearer and of providing the musical opportunity for songs, choruses, and marches of dazzling color, serving as a good contrast with the dark heart of the action."

The naming of the murderer—which is strictly confidential in the play, where only Hamlet and Horatio share their knowledge, and where Claudius is not openly accused until the final scene—becomes a public accusation in act 2 of the opera; this unleashes passionate condemnation by all present and produces a striking dramatic effect. In the play, Ophelia's suicide is disclosed in a brief statement by the queen; in the opera, it is the occasion for a scene: in the world of opera, the mad scene (with coloratura) followed by a suicide had proven its worth, and the librettists did not deny themselves that device.

When, in act 5 of the opera, a despairing Hamlet is preparing to join Ophélie in the next world, the ghost returns to remind his son of his duty. The reappearance of the ghost toward the end of the work is unquestionably effective, and in terms of music, provides an opportunity for an ensemble involving the chorus and all the characters, apart from Polonius.

Other additions are weaker. The act 1 chorus "Nargue de la tristesse!" seemed, as Ernest Reyer wrote in the March 14, 1868, *Journal des Débats*, "to have been put there only to fill a gap." The same is true of Hamlet's drinking song in act 2, which angered Gaston de Saint-Valry, who wrote in *Le Pays* on March 17, 1868, "A comic-opera drinking song, sung by Hamlet—ah, the old cliché, forever triumphant!" Ophélie's act 4 "Ballade de La Willis," "Pâle et blonde," is absolutely devoid of dramatic import, but is nicely set to music and furnishes a poetic moment. The villagers' songs and the spring festival are nothing more than the obligatory divertissements: "There can be no lyric drama without *entrechats*, without *ronds de jambes*," jeered Reyer, "and it is absolutely necessary that at a given moment the action will be interrupted so that we can see Mlle Fiocre or Mlle Fioreti, or some other ballerina vastly famous for her talent or her beauty."

In spite of the cuts—which were inevitable, because the way time passes in music limits the length of the text—and in spite of the liberties taken with the main outlines of Shakespeare's play, the libretto remains reasonably cohesive. Some scenes are even very similar to their counterparts in the play—which is sometimes irrelevant, as in Hamlet's monologue, whose philosophic dimension can hardly be credible in musical terms. Moreover, like *Faust* and many other great literary myths, *Hamlet* is open to interpretation. In recognizing the aesthetic value of a work—in this case, Shakespeare's—we are liable to forget that it is only one version of the myth, and that other versions, too, have legitimacy. It is worth noting in this connection that although Barbier and Carré were criticized for leaving their Hamlet alive, whereas he dies in Shakespeare's "version," they were in effect going back to the original historical legend as set out by the medieval Danish historian Saxo Grammaticus.

## BORROWINGS AND STRUCTURAL REFERENCES

In addition to the actual sources of a subject, we can identify three levels of borrowings or structural references to preexisting elements that contributed to the construction of a libretto: the use of schemas, the use of models, and the reuse of material. The schema is the most abstract of these, and provides only general features or outlines. Authors used the frameworks imposed by habit and custom. Classical dramatic structure, referred to above, and the layout of the scenes (introductory chorus in the first act, love scene in the second, and so forth) defined a general plan that no playwright could claim to have invented.

Critics quickly took to revealing this kind of automatic writing and the absurdities it engendered. After listening to Adam's *Le Chalet* in 1836, one wrote: "Following habitual practice, when the curtain rises we see a troupe of villagers, men and women, who announce that 'The horizon is tinged with the color of the first light of day' and who repeat in chorus, for a long time, 'Let us leave, let us leave for the town,' without, however, giving up an inch of ground."[32] Indeed, the introduction was one of the most unchanging parts of the libretto, although various types of construction were used,[33] such as choruses, solo arias, and huge scenes for both soloists and chorus. Yet again, *La Dame blanche* provides a perfect example of the most common formula, which is found also in *Les Pêcheurs de perles:*

## TYPICAL INTRODUCTORY SCENE

| *La Dame blanche* | *Les Pêcheurs de perles* |
|---|---|
| A. Chorus with dance (rejoicing). | A. Chorus with dance (rejoicing). |
| B. Some characters break away from the group and have a dialogue with the crowd. | B. Zurga has a dialogue with the crowd. |
| C. Entrance of the hero (Georges Brown) on the mountain ("But who is this outsider?"). | C. Entrance of the hero (Nadir) among the rocks ("But who comes there?"). |
| D. Introduction of the characters. | D. Introduction of the characters. |
| E. Aria for Georges Brown, ending with a chorus. | E. Aria (curtailed) for Nadir, ending with a chorus. |
| A. General jubilation: reprise of the chorus. | A. General jubilation: reprise of the chorus. |

If such a very general schema did not spark the authors' imagination, they had to model their creation on a specific opera. And, finally, writers could have recourse to their own verses, abortive projects, and discarded arias; or they might even extract a few well-phrased monologues from an old libretto. Here we can speak of reuse. These three kinds of borrowing defined a standard type of writing, a true manufacturing process.

Hence, librettists drew on a corpus of situations that enabled them to put together their texts quickly, while still meeting the expectations of the audience. The recurrence of conventional schemas made for easy reading. Writers showed their originality by refurbishing established formulas or quite simply by reassembling old elements: making the right choices was a substitute for inventiveness. The critics harshly berated the coterie of dramatists for doing nothing but "turning [the frayed cuffs] of old suits and restitching the worn trimming on the repertory of the past,"[34] which was regularly rejuvenated with fashionable themes and new literary trends.

An example will demonstrate how the handling of a stereotyped scene evolved through exaggeration of the original idea. A *romance* or serenade beneath a balcony—to guitar accompaniment if possible—was nearly obligatory for Spanish subjects.[35] Such scenes were invented to be either dramatic or tenderly poetic moments: in the act 2 finale of Grétry's *Les Fausses Apparences, ou l'Amant jaloux* (1778), Florval, to the accompaniment of pizzicato strings and two mandolins, sings the serenade "Tandis que tout sommeille" beneath Léonore's windows, thus inciting Alonze to jealousy.

This type of scene was then diverted from its original purpose to become a comic situation, a form in which it would proliferate. In *Les Pontons de Cadix* (1836, libretto by Paul Duport and François Ancelot, music by Eugène-Prosper Prévost), the French military officer Savenay plays the guitar, then strikes up a *romance*, while Héléna and her niece Olivia sing a fandango—as a kind of "counter-*romance*"—in order to drown out her suitor. In act 3 of *Le Duc d'Ollone* (1842, libretto by Scribe and Saintine, music by Auber), three men arrive simultaneously to declaim, each in his own fashion, beneath the balcony of the woman they love. The classic situation is rendered ridiculous by such exaggeration, as well as by the text of the libretto, which emphasizes the characters' amorous extravagance, and indeed their foolishness. Act 1 of *Don Pèdre* (1857, libretto by Cormon and Grangé, music by Ferdinand Poise) contains a reversal of this type of scene: it is the beautiful Nérédha who, from her balcony, sings to her own mandolin accompaniment, while her two suitors (the king in disguise and Fabio) find themselves face to face. The cliché reaches its apex in Massenet's delightful *Chérubin* (1903). The librettists, Francis de Croisset and Henri Cain, focus the scene on one man (played, in fact, by a woman): in act 2, beneath the windows of an inn under the cover of darkness,

Chérubin must woo three women at once—the ballerina l'Ensoleillad, the baroness, and the countess, each of whom sends him a token of her love. Chérubin describes himself as "bombarded with love."

## SCHEMAS, CLASSICAL AND MELODRAMATIC

In the classical schema, the hero reaches his goal only by overcoming a series of obstacles that are the basis of conflict and that make up the peripeteia: reversals in the action or sudden changes in the situation. Traditionally, the female character would stand on the sidelines, but we know how *Carmen* shattered that idea.

Normally, the denouement comprised "the removal of the final obstacles or the final peripeteia and the events that could result from them; these events are sometimes described by the term 'catastrophe.'"[36] Authors used—and abused—the formula of a reversal of the situation, knowing that, as Boileau wrote in his *Art poétique*, audiences always understood "that in a...plot shrouded in a secret, as soon as the truth is known, it changes everything and gives everything an unexpected dimension." One basic law of dramatic writing is that "the fate of all the major characters should be revealed, and that none of the problems set out in the play should go unresolved."[37] In *Les Pêcheurs de perles*, the librettists abandoned that principle by discarding the social and religious aspects of the drama at the end of the opera.

The melodramatic schema was basic to the advent of *grand opéra*, and it was often used to supplement the classical unfolding of the drama—in the face of ever harsher journalistic protests. Throughout the century, *mélodrame* was "both relished by the broader public and despised by critics and literary historians, who rarely forswore their attitude of condescending irony and automatic derision."[38]

A caricature of the genre, exemplified by the playwright R. C. Guilbert-Pixérécourt (1773–1844), is to be found in a little book entitled *Traité du mélodrame*, published in 1817, whose recipe found its way into many librettos: "A ballet and a scene for the entire company should be placed in the first act; a prison, a *romance*, and some chains in the second; fighting, *chansons*, a fire, etc., in the third."[39] Many operas were derived from these "dramas of chance encounters and speedy unraveling of a crisis (whose threads had been knotted twenty years earlier)."[40] Wide use was also made of recognition, that fundamental principle of *mélodrame*. Recognition marks the end of persecution and comes about through the "voice of kinship" or "my mother's crucifix." In *Les Pêcheurs*, Cormon and Carré skillfully combined these two terms, along with the broad emotions they represent: morality, filial bonds, and a maternal figure. An *opéra-comique* by Aimé Maillart, composed to a libretto by Lockroy and Adolphe Philippe Dennery (or d'Ennery), and first performed at the Opéra-Comique in 1852, went so far as to take its title from this approach: in *La Croix de Marie*, act 1, scene 2, the young Marie's father entrusts her with the melodramatic object par excellence:

> This evening, at the monastery,
> Bring with you this token of good fortune.
> It is your mother's cross;
> Set it over your heart.

Dennery (1811–1899), who "came to be viewed as the inventor of 'my mother's crucifix,' " was dubbed "the people's Shakespeare."[41] His 1874 *Les Deux Orphelines* took melodrama to extremes, and he was sharply criticized by a certain part of the elite for bad taste and long-windedness, but he enjoyed great popular success. The eleventh-hour resort to a necklace in *Les Deux Orphelines*, a critic observed, was nothing other than " 'that famous succor that is never lost,' and that is the salvation of *opéra-comique* victims."[42]

In the last quarter of the nineteenth century, these models did not really fall into disuse; rather, they were melded with other forms and combined with various literary and aesthetic trends such as naturalism, Wagnerism, and symbolism.

STRUCTURAL MODELING AND REUSE

As we have already seen, Cormon and Carré structured the drama of *Les Pêcheurs de perles* on the model of Jouy's *La Vestale*, in terms not only of the characters and subject but of the very outline of the libretto, which, like the earlier work, is divided into three acts. The relationship between acts 1 and 2 of the new work and of its model is shown in tabular form below. In both works, moreover, act 3 includes a change of scene. The denouements differ, but both are centered on the theme of fire. In *La Vestale*, thunder and lightning incite alarm ("O terreur! O disgrâce!"), and an ensuing volcanic eruption is accompanied by a miracle. In *Les Pêcheurs de perles*, the final conflagration terrifies the pearl fishers and gives Zurga a chance to free the two prisoners. To close the opera, Bizet's librettists had considered a reprise of the duet between Nadir and Léïla (no. 14, "O lumière sainte"), which is what Jouy did for Spontini by inserting the act 2 duet into the final scene.

## COMPARISON OF THE OPENING SCENES OF *LA VESTALE* AND OF *LES PÊCHEURS DE PERLES*

| *La Vestale* | *Les Pêcheurs de perles* |
|---|---|
| Models | Copied Portions (Sequence in Score) |
| 1. Preparations for a celebration; games; dancing | Chorus with dancing (1) |
| 2. Friendship duet | Friendship duet (3) |
| 3. Prayer of the Vestals | Prayer of the pearl fishers (5) |
| 4. Julia and the High Vestal | Léïla and Nourabad (4) |
| 5. Coronation of Licinius | Selection of Zurga as leader (2) |

## COMPARISON OF SECOND ACTS OF *LA VESTALE* AND OF *LES PÊCHEURS DE PERLES*

| *La Vestale* | *Les Pêcheurs de perles* |
|---|---|
| Models | Copied Portions |
| 1. Evening Hymn | 1. Chorus: "L'ombre descend des cieux" |
| 2. Julia and the High Vestal | 2. Léïla and Nourabad |
| 3. Julia alone | 3. Léïla alone |
| 4. Arrival of Licinius and *grand duo* | 4. Arrival of Nadir and *grand duo* |
| 5. The sacred flame burns out, which draws attention | 5. The lovers are discovered (storm) |
| 6. Licinius flees | 6. Nadir flees |
| 7. The people demand vengeance | 7. The natives demand vengeance |

It is far harder to detect the reuse of material: authors never advertised self-borrowings or the refurbishment of old projects. But I have been able to discover a hitherto unpublished example in the text of the *chanson* "De mon amie fleur endormie," no. 8, act 2, of *Les Pêcheurs de perles*. The source of the two stanzas of this may be traced to no. 11 in act 2 of an early version of Félicien David's *opéra-comique Lalla-Roukh*, composed to a libretto by Michel Carré and Hippolyte Lucas, which had its first performance at the Opéra-Comique on May 12, 1862. In David's score, after a spoken scene for Baskir and Mirza (act 2, scene 8), the guzla[43] of Noureddin (who is in love with

Lalla-Roukh) is heard from off-stage; he enters and begins a barcarole. Similarly, in *Les Pêcheurs de perles,* "the sound of a guzla is heard off-stage" at the beginning of no. 8, signaling the arrival of Nadir, who is heard "from far away," then ever closer. In both the piano-vocal and the orchestral scores of *Lalla-Roukh,* the text of the barcarole is, in fact, a second version (see below). But in the printed libretto (Paris: Lévy, 1862), we find in its place two stanzas that match Nadir's *chanson* word for word. In 1863, when Carré, along with Cormon, had in short order to write a libretto for the young Bizet, he would have remembered the original verses of no. 11 from *Lalla-Roukh,* which were a perfect fit for the situation in no. 8 of *Les Pêcheurs de perles.*

THE TEXTS OF NOUREDDIN'S BARCAROLE

| *First version of the barcarole, as later used in* Les Pêcheurs de perles *(act 2, no. 8)* | *Second version of the barcarole, as used in* Lalla-Roukh *(act 2, no. 11) to replace the first* |
|---|---|
| I | I |
| De mon amie, | O ma maîtresse, ô mes amours! |
| Fleur endormie, | Fuyons ensemble et pour toujours. |
| J'ai vu, dans l'onde | Avec ivresse et sans effroi |
| Claire et profonde, | Je braverai la mort pour toi, |
| Etinceler le front joyeux | Comme autrefois, comme autrefois. |
| Et les doux yeux. | Ma bien-aimée! l'âme charmée, |
|  | Je veux entendre encore ta douce |
| II | voix! |
| Ma bien-aimée |  |
| Est enfermée | II |
| Dans un palais d'or et d'azur. | Rose vermeille, étoile d'or! |
| Je l'entends rire | Je veux te voir, te voir encor. |
| Et je vois luire | Mon amour veille et te défend |
| Sur le cristal du gouffre obscur | Ange adoré, rieux enfant! |
| Son regard pur. | Comme autrefois, comme autrefois. |
|  | Ma bien-aimée! l'âme charmée, |
|  | Je veux entendre encore ta douce |
|  | voix! |

There are symmetrical structures at two levels. The rhythm and meter of the verses must follow regular patterns corresponding to a rhythmic or melodic motif and to the regular phrase structure of the music; and, especially in numbers for more than one singer, the rhymes and what might be called the "semantic symmetries" must make it possible to superimpose melodic lines—and therefore words—and must lead all the vocal parts to the same rhyme or the same refrain. The well-known but rarely analyzed relationship between music and libretto in terms of symmetry deserves a thorough study of its own.[44]

### NUMBER OPERA AND ITS VARIATIONS

Librettos followed a form that was divided into scenes; in the musical score, these were replaced by recitatives and other items whose names—aria, chorus, finale, and so forth—referred to their musical content. In the list of the pieces that made up an opera, these items were numbered in the order in which they were to be heard (for example, no. 1, chorus and scene; no. 2, recitative and duet; no. 3, chorus; no. 4, *romance*; and so forth). This succession, interspersed with recitatives (or with spoken dialogue in *opéra-comique*) constituted a "number opera." Each number is autonomous and has its own thematic and harmonic logic. Even more so than French opera, Italian opera clung to the practices of the number opera, which made it possible to reuse elements in other works and facilitated what amounted to operatic mass production.[45] In 1841, Blondeau caricatured these practices in the form of a recipe, in an article entitled "How Operas Are Made in Italy." In spirit, it was no less applicable to French opera:

> The organization of an opera is always more or less the same, whether it be comic or serious, and follows the following order: first, some sort of overture.... [This] overture, which moreover no one will ever listen to, has no kind of relationship with the work, and is always in D major, with trumpets.... If the overture ends with anything but the famous crescendo, that touchstone for any piece of music, it will be mercilessly whistled.... After the overture we hear: a chorus, an aria by the second male singer, an aria by the second female singer, a comic aria, a duet, and a finale in E minor. That covers the first act. The second act is always an arena for discussions and negotiations about which of the two—the *prima donna assoluta* or *[prima donna] di cartello* or the *primo tenore assoluto* will sing the first number of the second act.... Finally, once every concession has been debated and agreed upon, we hear an aria by the *prima donna*, in the key and tempo, and including the main passages, that it has pleased her to prescribe to the composer—who must submit, however vexed he may be, or must resign himself to its not being sung; then comes an aria by the first tenor, who will sing only on those same terms; after this there is generally a duet for the first male and female singers, either preceded or followed by the obligatory polonaise; then a quintet or a sextet; a bit of filler; and a finale.[46]

Although the classification of the numbers was less rigorous than it had been for the previous century's *opera seria*, the operatic dramatist remained faithful through most of the nineteenth century to a kind of catalogue of arias and situations. Here are a few examples. Although it was the target of increasing criticism, the coloratura aria, whose essential goal was to let the singer shine and to kindle wonderment in the audience, remained a major ingredient of a hit opera. Léïla's act 1 aria falls into this category, as does the polonaise "Je suis Titania la blonde" sung by Philine in act 2 of *Mignon,* which was composed to show off the soprano Marie Cabel. Nearly twenty years later, audiences could delight to Manon's bravura aria "Je marche sur tous les chemins" in act 3, scene 1. This piece was an "obvious concession to the virtuosity of the soprano,"[47] as one critic did not hesitate to observe. Still, it must be said that librettists and composers sought to justify coloratura by using it in particular situations. In the case of *Manon,* it reflected the heroine's vivacity, gaiety, and laughter; in other instances, it was employed to express madness or the supernatural. The coloratura passages sung by the automaton Olympia in *Les Contes d'Hoffmann* reflect that creature's artificial nature as a kind of music box with a vocal mechanism.[48]

Léïla's *cavatine* in act 2 of *Les Pêcheurs de perles,* in which the horn plays a particularly important role, belongs to a category of aria with obbligato instrument that was favored both in *opéra-comique* and in *grand opéra.* Ferdinand Hérold provided a near-archetype in Isabelle's lovely aria "Jour de mon enfance" in act 2 of *Le Pré aux clercs* (first performed at the Opéra-Comique in 1832); its introduction contains a violin solo worthy of a concerto. Gounod, even in the context of a *demi-caractère* opera—more "serious" and less conventional—did not break with tradition, and wrote Faust's *cavatine* "Salut demeure chaste et pure" with a violin solo. The Méditation from *Thaïs* (1894) is the culmination of this trend, as it consists of an "aria for violin," accompanying a silent heroine who is deep in thought.

Number operas had the virtue of great clarity—a key element for audiences. Gounod's reaction when he first heard *Tannhäuser* in 1860 bears this out. He wrote to Jules Barbier, "My wife and I went . . . to hear *Tannhäuser* at Carlsruhe. . . . Carré does not believe this work can be successful in Paris; I do not agree; I think it is possible. It is a way of expressing things that in any event is much farther from the conventional than most of today's works. I fear only that musical numbers do not play a large enough part; Wagner clearly cannot stand them."[49]

The evolution toward continuous music following the events of the drama without the shackles of preestablished forms was therefore perceived as an obstacle to understanding, especially as it was accompanied by the transformation of lyric phrasing into an unbroken sung declamation that listeners found wearying. Louis Roger, who did not like Berlioz at all, did not fail to highlight this regrettable trend in *Les Troyens*. Apart from a few clearly identifiable numbers, he said, "the score is a tedious recitative that spreads boredom even into the lobby. The ushers fell asleep in their chairs. All of the established facts about the composition of an opera have been rejected by M. Berlioz. Overture; trios; quartets; ritornellos; *couplets;* cadenzas; flourishes: he will permit none of these. His interminable, exhausting recitative leaves you not a minute of respite. Where the libretto indicates an aria, you will find a funereal melody."[50] Henri Vignaud wrote, "yet it is not arias that are lacking in *Les Troyens;* the libretto indicates plenty of them. But I challenge even the most practiced ear to detect the exact point that separates one of M. Berlioz's arias from the recitatives that precede and follow it."[51] What audiences found disconcerting was the elimination of a clear demarcation between narrative and expressive styles and the general use of free vocal expression blended with orchestral melody. There was, indeed, nothing new about using arioso passages and flexible, irregular declamation. The various types of recitative; *parlante*—minimalized declamation over rich orchestral activity; monotone declamation; a variety of musical phrases molded by the form of the verse without a preestablished musical structure; and the many kinds of aria: all these constituted a rich store of possibilities, from which an academically trained composer would cautiously take just a few elements to fashion a number.

Gounod, as Steven Huebner has shown, occupied a median position, which lets us see clearly the subtle interplay among musical form, vocal style, and the course of the drama. He did not reject the old system; rather, he incorporated more numerous long passages that did not comply with its codes, although retaining clearly defined sections and often making use of models, which he would condense or abbreviate. Hence, at the beginning of *Faust*, Huebner observes, the tenor's

> solo musings are largely conducted in non-periodic declamation.... Nevertheless, the scaffolding of a conventional *grand air* with slow section and *cabalette* is still faintly visible, since on two occasions Faust does start a passage that appears to be the beginning of a complete periodic section. The first ("J'ai langui triste et solitaire") has the earmarks of a lyrical slow section, but after only eight bars a modulation to the mediant and a change of texture is effected. The second beginning ("Salut! ô

mon dernier matin") has the cut of a martial *cabalette* and it is also interrupted, this time by young people outside.[52]

True continuous melody rejects the typical harmonic articulation of
phrases in regular, symmetrical structures. To Auguste Durand, some passages in *Les Troyens* were "utterly incomprehensible" because of a "total
lack of cadences," which he defined as "a fall in the phrase," "point,"
"breath," and "rest." The perfect cadence "is the most necessary and the
most often used; it is this that determines the key and that truly gives rest
to the listener's mind." But, lamented that critic, "Berlioz knows, or uses,
only broken cadences. His phrases begin but do not end. Imagine any book
in which an entire chapter several pages long consisted of one single
phrase. You would never consider starting a second chapter. Similarly, in
*Les Troyens* the entire act is one single phrase. So when the curtain falls,
every chest is seen to expand as though breathing had long been suspended."[53]

Press and public alike were slow to accept the complete abolition of
numbers. Johannès Weber, while well informed about Wagnerian theory,
had no misgivings about writing in 1893 that "so-called conventional
forms are not objectionable unless they conflict with the progress of the action on stage; if they do not, why avoid them? Let me say more: Why not
seek them out?"[54] Massenet, who felt it was very important to build a musical drama appropriate to the language of the late nineteenth century and
to theories of dramaturgy and realism, was also aware that if he was to
please his audience, he could not completely reject the old forms. He moved
from one genre to another, never decisively taking a single approach. The
critic and composer Victorin Joncières, a Wagnerian, criticized him for this,
writing that his about-faces were the sign of "a lack of conviction" and of a
"a too-exclusive preoccupation with success."[55] Even in *Werther,* the symphonic framework and the continuous musical discourse throughout an act
could not mask references to typical arias and situations. "Werther," wrote
Ernest Reyer, "enters, then sings an invocation to nature, an invocation
that has every feature of a *cavatine*—without the *cabalette,* it is true, but a
*cavatine* nonetheless—and one that, I assure you, has nothing Wagnerian
about it."[56] Similarly, Marcel Rémy noted that "the bravura aria, although
concealed, still gleams in *Werther,*" and concluded that "the importance
given the role of Sophie is nothing but a pretext for *romances.*"[57] A decade
earlier, a critic had observed that the number-opera model still played a
major role in *Manon:* "M. Massenet has tried...to avoid the so-called
number with its defined, symmetrical forms; but nevertheless, the number

constantly returns to his writing, disguised to a greater or lesser degree, with its opening theme, its middle section, and its reprise of the first theme."[58]

Massenet replaced the traditional spoken dialogue of *opéra-comique* with *mélodrame* (spoken text with a musical accompaniment), which carried on and expanded an old French tradition. But the result—constant melody, either on stage or in the orchestra—could be perceived as a result of the influence of the Wagnerian school. "This is not every-day *opéra-comique*," commented one journalist in 1884. "This is not opera, with its recitatives. This is the practice of continuous melody, of which Wagner has made himself the apostle, applied to the French stage."[59] The same columnist realized the "foolishness of a system that halts the action of a play to let a musical number unfold" but did not very much appreciate "the charm of dialogue that is constantly supported by orchestral chattering of greater or lesser significance."

All this leads to questions about the subtle relationship between musical form and dramatic form, and about the apportionment of expression, or of meaning, between text and music.

# Chapter 5   Space and Time
*Manipulating Reality*

As they moved within the defined space of the stage and followed the chosen dramatic form, plots and characters came to life and began to exist in another dimension: time. The lyric stage had special requirements in addition to the conventions of theater in general, and a work would be created with two kinds of aims: dramatic and musical. This complicated the already subtle relationship between theater and reality and obliged librettists to employ special techniques in constructing their texts. They had to augment normal theatrical conventions—such as diction of varying degrees of refinement, the use of verse, the employment of asides—with a more complex manipulation of time, a broadening of space, and the use of specific operatic techniques, such as off-stage singing.

Once spectators accepted the operatic convention whereby singing replaced speaking, they soon understood that librettos made use of two devices exclusive to music: reprises and overlay (singing by more than one character at once). A section of text may be repeated for reasons of form, for example, in the ABA form of a da capo aria; and voices may be overlaid, as in ensembles and choruses. To give the impression of reality, writers had to construct their librettos in a way that would develop situations in as logical a manner as possible.

Opera, which had long been dominated by fantastical subjects, retained its propensity for manipulating locales and diversifying space and scenery. Changes of scene had four functions in a performance. First, they fulfilled the requirements of realism and provided a suitable setting for the action. Second, they could have a psychological and poetical function by reflecting the emotions felt by the characters. Third, by providing contrast, they served as a powerful dramatic force in themselves. And finally, the progression of scene changes helped to convey a sense of the dimension of time.

CONTINUOUS TIME AND TIME ELUDED—INTRUSION OF THE PAST

Opera could truthfully depict all the ongoing events of the drama. When it was impossible to do this before the eyes of the spectator, off-stage techniques could give the illusion that the audience was witnessing an event without its actually being enacted. The transition from one act to the next, often with an intermission, poses problems of temporal logic. Should the audience take account of the "black hole" of the intermission? Authors had a number of solutions to hand. The simplest was to frame the two acts as contiguous; the time between them was to be disregarded. At the beginning of act 3 of *Les Pêcheurs de perles*, we suddenly find ourselves inside Zurga's tent. Only when we hear, at the beginning of the act, the last throes of the storm that had broken out at the end of act 2 do we link the two incidents. Time appears to have been condensed. One asset of the technique of eluding time is dramatic foreshortening: it propels the story forward.

Librettists could heighten this impression of foreshortening by juxtaposing two acts whose action is separated by a long lapse of time, as in acts 1 and 2 of *Carmen*. The first ends with Don José's misconduct in allowing the heroine to escape, and the second begins in Lillas Pastia's tavern, where Carmen is reunited with José, who has been released after serving a two-month prison sentence.

Within the time continuum that inescapably linked successive scenes, the authors would sometimes have the characters recall past events; such instances are momentary windows in time that allow the past to burst into the drama. These were often clearly demarcated incidents: a character thinking aloud, or relating events to an attentive companion, in the past tense; such accounts would often continue in the narrative present tense. Yet the boundary between past and present action was not always clear.

The well-known tenor-baritone duet for Nadir and Zurga (no. 2 in *Les Pêcheurs de perles*) is a good example of this. After a few exchanges, the friends recall the moment in the past when they witnessed the appearance of a veiled woman. Initially, their description follows the conventional sequence for narrative, first using the past tense, then the narrative present. But when they describe the amorous turmoil and the consequent jealousy that have disrupted their lives, Nadir and Zurga give the impression of actually reliving the event. Sharing the narrative of past events between two characters makes possible a dialogue, and hence an illusion that the action is taking place in the present. The present-tense style takes over, and spectators forget that they are listening to a narrative.

With greater originality, Offenbach's *Les Contes d'Hoffmann* is completely built on the basis of what cinematographers call flashback. To choose one among the many incarnations of this opera, it is clear that the five-act version actually takes place in the tavern (acts 1 and 5); this is the present, which Hoffmann suspends by casting the audience back into his recollections. Hoffmann tells the tales of his past loves, which are then brought to life on stage: Olympia in act 2, Antonia in act 3, and Giulietta in act 4. Stella, as the hero says, combines "Three women in the same woman! / Three souls in a single soul! / Artist, girl and courtesan!" Toward the end of act 1, the librettists summed up the duration of the drama:

| | |
|---|---|
| HOFFMANN: | Do you want to hear the tale of these mad loves? |
| THE STUDENTS: | Yes! Yes! |
| NIKLAUSSE: | What do you have to say about your three mistresses? |
| HOFFMANN: | Have a smoke! |
| | Before this dead pipe is lit again, |
| | You will certainly have got my meaning.... |

Finally, it is important to note that the librettists reflected the Hoffmanesque theme of division in a sort of *mise en abîme,* by having the narrative of the hero's three loves take place during a performance by Stella. Lindorf, who understands Hoffmann's intentions, says to himself, "Before the opera [sung by Stella] is over, / I shall have the time to listen too!"

Apart from such endeavors, librettists created their texts with a view to their being set to music. The writing had to meet additional demands, unknown in the spoken theater, concerning the way in which time moved forward.

### MUSIC AND TIME—ENFOLDED TIME

Music by its nature involves essential relationships with time. According to Claude Lévi-Strauss, "the characteristic that myth and music share" is that they are both "languages which, in their different ways, transcend articulate expression, while at the same time—like articulate speech, but unlike painting—requiring a temporal dimension in which to unfold."[1] But, he continues,

> this relation to time is of a rather special nature: it is as if music and
> mythology needed time only in order to deny it. Both, indeed, are in-
> struments for the obliteration of time. Below the level of sounds and
> rhythms, music acts upon a primitive terrain, which is the physiological
> time of the listener; this time is irreversible and therefore irredeemably

diachronic, yet music transmutes the segment devoted to listening to it into a synchronic totality, enclosed within itself. Because of the internal organization of the musical work, the act of listening to it immobilizes passing time; it catches and enfolds it as one catches and enfolds a cloth flapping in the wind.[2]

One can view the notion of the suppression of time in the context of our subject, and can even observe that spoken—or, even more so, written—discourse functions precisely on the basis of the paradoxical relationship between diachrony and synchrony: between the way that things change in the course of time and the multiple events that occur simultaneously. This occurs on several levels. At the level of the individual word, the perceived succession of sounds that constitute the word (the diachrony) is fused into a whole (the synchrony): the word itself, and its meaning. At the level of the sentence, the series of words of which it is composed becomes a complex entity. The same observation holds for larger formal units—paragraphs, sections, and so forth—depending on the nature of the narrative or the text. This is true also for music. The diachronic succession of musical elements, which becomes a synchronic whole, takes place at various levels, which vary in number and whose structuring depends on the era. For example, a motif made up of a succession of notes, a phrase made up of a series of motifs, and a section created by linking several phrases are all elements in the perception of which a role is played by the incongruity between diachrony and synchrony. By repeating this process, it appears to be possible, by means of a sort of temporal *mise en abîme,* to see music as an assembly of layers—or rather dimensions—of time, all of them involved in the overall movement of the work, which eclipses them.

Perhaps music deeply touches human beings because it functions as we do, as our double, through the inexorable march of continuous time—time, however, that is constantly rewritten or enfolded as though it had been halted. This enables it to have a unity, or an identity, and to constitute a completely structured whole, which also depends on reminiscences and memories.

Moreover, in traditional operatic theater, two temporal planes interact. "Dramatic time"—both continuous time and narrative time—is regularly punctuated by "lyric time." This distinction may be oversimplified to the relationship between recitative and song. The listener, in the former, is asked to follow the progress of the action, and, in the latter, is drawn away from the realm of dramatic time and taken out of the real world by the magical power of music.

Carl Dahlhaus defined this capability of music as "the ability to give a fleeting moment an unreal duration, and hold it fixed for contemplation."[3] Alfred de Musset hailed the ability of the librettist Baron Dupaty (1775–1851):

> One of M. Emmanuel Dupaty's most remarkable talents is to be able very skillfully to, as they say in the theater, set a scene, that is, to grasp the opportunity, the occasion, the exact moment when, with interest and curiosity gradually heightened to a certain point, the action can stop and passion and pure emotion can emerge and unfold.... *[O]péra-comique*... of all genres is the very one in which we see most clearly these pauses, these points of demarcation between action and poetry. So long as the actor speaks, the action moves forward—or at least *can* move forward; but when he sings, it manifestly stops.... Melody takes charge of emotion; it segregates it; whether it concentrates it or pours it out at length, it draws out its supreme traits.[4]

The emotion thus experienced in a kind of ecstasy is the result of a focus (the melody) on a feeling. Time is opened out or suspended by the music. In this repertory, it makes no more sense, while an aria is being sung, to expect characters to engage in vigorous action or artificially to introduce additional events than to impose movement on something whose very point is to draw out an instant in time. This would be to fail to understand that at that moment, the space of the stage has shrunk down to the character alone—indeed, to the character's voice (whence the concept of tightening the beam of the spotlight around the singer), or that it has completely merged with the emotions of that character.

There is another way of organizing time that must be superimposed on the overall understanding of a piece of music as a block of time. The requirements of a closed musical form conflict with those of the open form of the continuous unfolding of events, an observation that played a leading role in Wagnerian reforms. The linear nature of the time the spectator actually spent in the theater during a performance did not meet the requirements of nineteenth-century composers; they needed repetitions and reprises. These concepts gave rise to refrains and reexpositions of material; in the libretto, they were often reflected in textual repetitions, which do not exist in ordinary plays (see pages 130–31). During the nineteenth century, the use of continuous music and the disappearance of the distinction between recitative and aria would gradually change the face of operatic time, by seeking to enrich dramatic time with a layer of lyric time. Hence, some *drames lyriques* are much better suited than number operas to continuous action in the stage production.

Dialogue divides discourse into a series of distinct moments; time moves forward, pulsing with alternating rejoinders. In true ensembles, utterances seem to enfold themselves; they overlay one another. Music here exercises all its power by eliminating the diachrony of dialogue and replacing it with the extraordinary synchrony of polyphony, or the combining of several voices at once. This was a major element in the magic of opera, which some would try to abandon for the sake of dramatic realism.

On the scale of the opera as a whole, time could be rearranged in a series of recurrences, something that was relatively recent in the history of the lyric theater, although rudimentary examples can be found in Monteverdi's *L'Orfeo*, at the very dawn of opera. These could appear in a given number to recall a musical idea that had been stated earlier in another number and that was linked to a meaning or simply to a situation. Arias, ensembles, and choruses had previously been freestanding musical entities, independent blocks of time, each sealed off from the others, that paced the drama, so to speak, in fits and starts. Now the barriers between numbers became permeable, which caused time leakages. The recurrence of motifs within a score strengthened the thread of musical discourse and enhanced the meaning of the words and actions of the protagonists; further, it projected the listener back into the work's past. Little by little, composers in the nineteenth century would seek to replace the disjointed dribble of musical numbers with a continuous dramatic stream by opening the barriers between numbers—as in the forward-looking final act of Rossini's *Otello* (Naples, 1816)—ultimately to grow into the broad river Wagner, whose flow is interrupted only when each act comes to an end.

## OFF-STAGE MUSIC—COORDINATING COMPLEX SCENES— STAGE SPACE AND MUSICAL SPACE

When the space on stage proves too limited, the use of off-stage areas can effectively suggest a greater expanse. One of the advantages of opera over spoken drama is its ability to make use of off-stage effects throughout a number: it is hard to imagine a character or group of characters in a play speaking off-stage for several minutes at a time. Thanks to the impressive effect of mysteriously muted music issuing from the wings, opera can exploit an intermediate space between the actual space of the stage and the imaginary space of the narrative. Cormon and Carré took particular advantage of this[5]—excessively so in the view of some critics.

Toward the end of the eighteenth century, Grétry and his librettists were the pathfinders, and *Zémire et Azor* (1771) was a prototype.[6] A deep impression was made by the magical scene in act 3, which was accompanied by clarinets, horns, and bassoons positioned behind the characters (Sander, Fatmé, and Lisbé) whom Azor causes to appear. In the scenes leading up to the final scene of act 4, Grétry enhanced the spatial effects inherent in the text: Zémire is searching for Azor, who is dying in a cave; the only response to her call, sung from the wings, is the echo of the horn. The composer used music to amplify the dramatic idea: the echo then moves from the horn in the orchestra pit to a horn on the stage, then to a third, more distant, horn. Another motif, this time in the flute, is given the same treatment.

There are two ways of using this approach: to depict two very different actions[7] taking place in different places but at the same time, and to suggest the approach or departure of a character, in what one might call a "sonic zoom."[8] We may note two examples in *Carmen:* Don José singing "Dragon d'Alcala" as he arrives at Lillas Pastia's tavern, and Escamillo retreating into the distance at the end of act 3. In act 2 (no. 17), Bizet overlays the distant call of the bugles onto the gypsy dance: two independent actions competing for the tenor's attention. The two places symbolize the struggle between love here and now (depicted on stage) and duty at a distance (off-stage); between the throbbing voice of sensuality and the rigid music of the army. The hero is torn between the two spaces.

In the historical opera *Henry VIII* (1883), Saint-Saëns and his librettists Léonce Détroyat and Armand Silvestre used off-stage music to construct one of the repertory's longest and most striking scenes. At the end of act 1, the king and his court are welcoming Anne Boleyn. While the king sassily woos her, we hear from off-stage the sounds of a funeral march as Buckingham (who had unsuccessfully sued for mercy for Queen Catharine) is led to the torture chamber. Ladies-in-waiting and nobles rush to the window, while Anne and the king converse down stage. The sounds of the funeral march grow nearer, and a chorus of monks is heard (*"De profundis/* Que Dieu dans sa miséricorde / Au pécheur repentant accorde / Une place en son paradis!"—*"De profundis!/* May God in His mercy / Grant the repentant sinner / A place in His paradise!"). Anne's visions of glory ("Mon coeur s'emplit de rêves insensés"—"My heart fills with mad dreams") yield to a nightmare ("Une hache! du sang! / O sombre vision de l'enfer envolée! / J'ai peur!"—"An axe! Blood! / O dark vision of Hell arising! / I am afraid!"). The king's avid love too is colored with a sinister tinge, which disappears as the march fades into the distance ("C'était un sombre rêve / Qui s'envole et s'achève"—"It was a gloomy dream / Which is fleeing and coming to an end").

Off-stage elements could thus be part of complex ensembles. Let us look briefly at the act 1 finale of *Les Pêcheurs de perles*, which is especially rich in lessons on the techniques of dramatic structure. When the number begins, Léïla has just sworn her oath, and the fishers have gone to the shore to prepare for their pearl-diving. The use of off-stage elements and the layout of the scenery make it possible to coordinate three actions in three different nearby locales—simultaneously, thanks to the capacity of a musical form that can combine multiple voices. The ensemble moves toward a common action. In the first part (*scène et choeur*), the various components are set out, singly and independent of one another: the fishers, at a distance, celebrate the fine weather ("Le ciel est bleu"—"The sky is blue"); Léïla is led up to the rock by Nourabad, who commands her to begin her propitiatory chant; Nadir, who remains downstage, is lost in dreams ("Adieu doux rêve"—"Farewell, sweet dream"). The three spheres of action defined in this way are depicted in time based on theatrical convention, which makes the chosen moment stand out in a series of moments that also correspond to a series of places. The three spatial-temporal subparts of no. 5a are set out in the table below:

## SPACES AND ACTIONS IN NO. 5A OF *LES PÊCHEURS DE PERLES*

| Location on Stage | Setting | Characters | Action |
| --- | --- | --- | --- |
| 1. Off-stage | Shore | Pearl fishers | Preparation for pearl diving |
| 2. Backstage | Rock | Léïla and Nourabad | Nourabad commands Léïla to sing |
| 3. Downstage | Beach | Nadir | Reverie |

Initially, it is necessary to present the three elements sequentially if the spectator is to absorb the information needed to understand the next phase, when they are overlayed. In no. 5b (*air et choeur*), the action is focused on Léïla's prayer. The librettists then devised a progression that gradually merges the scene's three components until they are finally united. In physical terms, this merging is expressed by Nadir's appearance at the foot of the rock. The timing of these three spheres makes "diffracted" time develop into "simultaneous" time. Whereas the libretto is limited to the direction *Ensemble* (Together) for an exchange, the score specifies when each character is to speak vis-à-vis the others. Here we see the boundary between the opera as planned in its libretto and the work in its final form.

The presentation of complex scenes was one of the most spectacular elements of an operatic performance, especially when the musical forms and techniques provided a true translation of the stage space and of the action. This idea was neither new nor restricted to the Théâtre de l'Opéra—which, however, remained the chief place for such structures. *Jeannot et Colin* (1814), a three-act *opéra-comique* by Nicolò, provides a notable example of musical form adapted to the drama. The act 2 party scene (no. 9) appears to have been inspired by the three on-stage orchestras in act 1, scene 20, of Mozart's *Don Giovanni.* Three quadrilles—(a) "les Bergères" in 6/8 time; (b) "les Basques" in 2/4; and (c) "les Troubadours" in 2/4—each distinct both musically and in terms of instrumentation, are first presented in succession and are then overlayed, in the following sequence: a-b-(ab)-c-(abc).

At the Opéra, this type of structure profited from theater's considerable stage resources and, particularly, from the imposing size of the chorus. By fusing stage movement and musical "movement," authors could thus achieve a true "theatrical sculpture" (*plastique théâtrale*), to use the term Wagner employed in describing Auber's *La Muette de Portici.* For example, in *Guillaume Tell* (1829), Rossini composed the finale of act 2 by musically following the movements of the actors. Guillaume, Arnold, and Walter are at the center of this structure; men of the three Swiss cantons join them each in turn to plot the expulsion of the Austrian oppressor. The gradual movement of these three groups toward the center of the action is magnified by the musical characterization of the three choruses that portray the groups. The overall effect is striking. In fashioning his *grand opéra*, Rossini drew on elements he had tested during his Neapolitan period. The final scene of act 1 of *La Donna del lago* (1819) had conformed to the drama by presenting in succession a chorus of bards ("Già un raggio forier") accompanied by harp, pizzicato violas and cellos, and a single double bass, then a chorus of warriors ("Su! Amici! Guerrieri!") accompanied by trumpets and a small stage band; the two choruses were then overlayed.

In a similar way, Meyerbeer, so to speak, absorbed the performance space into the score of *Les Huguenots.* In act 3 (no. 14), stage movement becomes a polychoral musical structure: Huguenots, Catholic women, and clerics from the basilica form three distinct groups that contend and combine. After the soldiers' *couplets* ("Ra-ta-plan") and the litany of the Catholic women ("Vierge Marie") are presented separately, the two are overlayed, punctuated by interjections from the third group. Counterpoint, that abstract principle of composition, here becomes a concrete, sculptural theatrical technique.

In act 1, scene 2, of *Gwendoline* (Brussels, 1886; Paris, 1893), Chabrier, with exceptional compositional virtuosity, combines soloists and multiple choruses when the Danes attack the Saxons. The enemies' cries grow nearer, and the Saxons burst onto the stage, pursuing their adversaries and sowing terror, then intoning their war chant ("Eheyo! / Entamons les cuirasses"). All of this develops logically into a vast polyphonic passage of sumptuous sonorities.

## INSERTIONS INTO THE MAIN ACTION—"CLOSE-UPS"

Librettists could anticipate the musical effects that composers would be able to draw out of the situations in their texts. They would on occasion introduce a secondary element into the main action—just as they might construct the chronology of the drama to include forays into the past. Such elements, relating to a past event or to one peripheral to the plot, gave the composer scope to work with musical forms and to write contrasting sections. The continuous time of the main action would be suspended to accommodate the insertion of time.

At the end of act 1 of *Les Pêcheurs de perles*, Cormon and Carré included a passage along those lines. Having finished his *romance*, Nadir is dozing. Nourabad and Léïla appear on the rock overlooking the sea; the priest asks Léïla to sing (no. 5a). The tenor interrupts this scene, although no one is supposed to hear him, with the single line "Adieu doux rêve, adieu!"—"Farewell, sweet dream!" which, as in a dream, refers back to his *romance*.

Moreover, the librettists anticipated a cinematic technique for isolating one portion of a larger scene: the close-up. In act 3, scene 2, we find Nadir in the forest amid a wild scene of drinking, dancing, and singing. Initially, the audience sees these "furious dances"; then, as though the stage has shrunk to Nadir's space, everything comes to a halt, and only the tenor is heard. This is later reversed, and the scene ends with a return to the chorus. The *grande scène dansée* in act 2 of *Faust*—unified by the waltz "Ainsi que la brise légère," which was to become popular in its own right—works in the same way. The chorus, dancing the waltz, becomes a blurred background shot (to retain our cinematic terminology) from out of which the primary shot comes into focus: that of the principal characters, Faust, Marguerite, Méphistophélès, and Siebel. Again, the composer reverses the process and returns to the choral scene.

REQUIREMENTS OF CLOSED MUSICAL FORMS—
TEXTUAL REPETITION—FINAL TEXT

If you read an opera libretto as a normal play, you will be surprised by all the special traits noted above, and perhaps even more by the many and varied repetitions that would seem to be anti-dramatic: to name but a few, an entire chorus reprised at the end of a scene; several lines repeated during a monologue; one character in a duet repeating unchanged the words of the other when the two sing together. In the context of operatic reality, as already noted, the skill of a librettist lay in making reprises, repetitions, and overlays seem as logical as possible.

There are two categories of repetition: formal (external or generalized) and structural (internal or localized). The first, on a large scale, includes repeating one or several lines of text in order to delineate the shape of a standard musical form. In the second, on a smaller scale, the composer makes the characters repeat words because of the temporal requirements of the musical texture encompassing the voices; these repetitions thus appear in the score but not in the libretto. Here the words are often reduced to a mere support for vocalism. Oddly, however, listeners seem to be capable of reconstructing the original text and following its meaning—so long as the singer's diction is clear.

The dramatic form of the opening scenes of act 1 of *Les Pêcheurs de perles* was structured in the libretto as a buildup of independent events (an open form). In its musical form, this section was conceived as a great crowd scene with soloists, concluding with a reprise of the opening chorus (a closed form).

Librettists and composers used several techniques to free themselves from drama based on closed forms. The pairing of the arrival of a group and the departure of the same group provides an opportunity to use the same music to accompany the symmetrical stage movement that demarcates one or several musical numbers. This technique was common, even at the end of the century, for example, in the Epithalame in act 2 of Chabrier's *Gwendoline*. Better known is the children's chorus in act 1 of *Carmen* (no. 3), which is entirely built on this framework: the dialogue between Moralès and Don José takes place between the two marches (the arrival of the relief guard and the departure of the old guard).

It is important to recall that setting a text to music changes that text. Léïla's *cavatine* early in act 2 of *Les Pêcheurs* is a good example of a composer reorganizing the literary structure, thus creating what I shall call the "final text." Bizet repeats words in order both to sustain the vocal line and to reinforce transitional sections and the coda of the aria (see table 5.1). In the ensembles, Cormon and Carré set out the verses in a symmetrical manner, but the composer adapted the text, sometimes substituting a few verses of his own (see Appendix 7).

By combining the continuous unfolding of events with a constantly evolving musical flow, opera ultimately did away with closed forms. Librettos abandoned textual repetition, and melodic phrases turned away from regular, symmetrical structures. Note, however, that composers still liked—plot or psychological situation permitting—to include in their scores occasional passages containing repetitions, with a guaranteed impact on the audience. Even Wagner opted for regular structures suggested by events, for example, in the successive transformations of Alberich in scene 3 of *Das Rheingold* and in the powerful scene in which Siegfried forges his sword, Notung (*Siegfried,* act 1, scene 3). There, the hero's elation is conveyed in the refrain "Notung, neidliches Schwert!" and his fervor in the repeated cry of "Hoho! Hohei!" Indeed, in its overall construction, the *Ring* cycle is a huge closed form, beginning with the Rhinemaidens at the opening of *Das Rheingold* and ending with the same creatures in act 3 of *Götterdämmerung:* a world born of the river and returning to the river, to which the gold stolen by Alberich is finally restored.

## TRUTH THROUGH PROSODY—THE CONSTRUCTION OF A MELODY

In an opera constructed in accordance with conventional rules, the exigencies of musical setting obliged librettists to devise rhyme and metric schemes that could be translated into musical structures and rhythms (see Appendix 7). On the other hand, some composers would write melodies on the basis of a situation or emotion, without having the words in front of them. In such cases, librettists had to conform to the framework and to the rhythm of the melody as they wrote the aria's text. This is the practice of using a *monstre* (see page 22). The process was so firmly rooted in the thinking of the time that it was unimaginable for the majority of mid-nineteenth-century French musicians to free themselves from it. The back-and-forth between textual and musical composition was such a matter of routine that librettists and composers alike made unquestioning use of symmetrical forms and structures, often without attempting to adapt them to the true flavor or emotions—indeed, without any longer knowing whether the libretto was imposing its framework on the music or the other way around. Gounod, who led the way to a radical transformation of French musical prosody,[9] did a good job of

Table 5.1.  Relationship Between Literary and Musical Form in Léïla's
*Cavatine* (Act 2, No. 7)

| Musical form | Literary Form in the Score ("Final Text") | Literary Form of the Libretto |
|---|---|---|
| A | Comme autrefois dans la nuit sombre,<br>Caché sous le feuillage épais,<br>Il veille près de moi, dans l'ombre,<br>Je puis dormir, rêver en paix!...<br>Je puis dormir, rêver en paix!...<br>Il veille près de moi, | Comme autrefois dans la nuit sombre,<br>Caché sous le feuillage épais,<br>Il veille près de moi, dans l'ombre,<br>Je puis dormir, rêver en paix!... |
| Concluding section | Comme autrefois, comme autrefois. | |
| B | C'est lui! mes yeux l'ont reconnu!<br>C'est lui!...mon âme est rassurée!<br>O bonheur!...Joie inespérée!<br>Pour me revoir il est venu! | C'est lui! mes yeux l'ont reconnu!<br>C'est lui!...mon âme est rassurée!<br>O bonheur!...Joie inespérée!<br>Pour me revoir il est venu! |
| Transition | O bonheur, il est venu, il est là,<br>Près de moi, ah! | |
| A | Comme autrefois dans la nuit sombre,<br>Caché sous le feuillage épais,<br>Il veille près de moi, dans l'ombre,<br>Je puis dormir, rêver en paix!...<br>Je puis dormir, rêver en paix!...<br>Il veille près de moi, | Comme autrefois dans la nuit sombre,<br>Caché sous le feuillage épais,<br><br>Il veille près de moi, dans l'ombre,<br>Je puis dormir, rêver en paix!... |
| Concluding section | Comme autrefois, comme autrefois. | |
| Coda | Je puis dormir,<br>Je puis rêver en paix.<br>Il veille près de moi.<br>Oui, comme autrefois,<br>Je puis rêver. Ah! en paix. | |

describing how tyrannical the regular structure of librettos that had been versified in the traditional way could be: "The symmetry of verse gives the musician a far easier framework—sometimes dangerously easy, in the sense that once he is drawn in by the rhythm that the first line in a sequence awakens in his mind or in his ear, the musician in a way becomes the slave of the dialogue rather than remaining its master and, no longer in control, surrenders himself to the purely rhythmic consequences of his first impression."[10]

Operatic music in France was rooted in the often ambiguous, even conflictual, relationship among prosody, the pure melody of the vocal line, and the rearrangement of the verses for expressive purposes—as when the composer would add, repeat, or delete words, or hastily pass over some, while dwelling at length on others. This is at least in part a result of adapting Italian lyric forms to French opera. Indeed, by the beginning of the nineteenth century, melody had come to dominate every other musical element through the rejection of what had once been the foundation of French operatic aesthetics: declamation. Writers no longer thought in terms of syllabic quantity or of correct prosody. Duration, intonation, and stress patterns at the level of the syllable, then of the word and of the line, vary from language to language; in French, these pose formidable problems for setting text to music.[11]

As noted, all these matters fall within the more general framework of the overall creation of an opera. At other levels of reading, the junction between a recitative and an aria corresponds to those between dramatic time and lyric time, between dominance by language and dominance by melodic idea, and between open form and closed form.

By its nature, traditional *opéra-comique* contains a variety of shifts between language and music and between spoken text and orchestral melody, through a range of intermediate forms of varying degrees of subtlety and richness: ordinary recitative, dramatic recitative, arioso, aria, and coloratura aria. In France, the dominant approach—once there was a renewed awareness of correct prosody—was to increase the number and the refinement of these forms rather than, like Wagner, to combine them into continuous lyric declamation. Among the many techniques with which French composers experimented to link music and language more closely, *mélodrame*—spoken or nonrhythmic declamation to an orchestral accompaniment—was frequently used. These experiments often yielded extremely effective results, as seen in the works of Thomas, Meyerbeer, Gounod, Bizet, Delibes, and Massenet. An example may be found in Gounod's lovely but little-known *Le Médecin malgré lui* (1858).

In the sextet (act 2, no. 8), Sganarelle must diagnose the muteness of Géronte's daughter. Having ascertained that Géronte does not understand Latin, he launches into a lengthy explanation in dog Latin, which he elucidates using the most fantastical brand of French medical jargon. Gounod composed an extraordinary sequence over orchestral chords and tremolos. Sganarelle nonrhythmically declaims "Cabricias arcithuram" on the single note of D, accented at the start of each phrase with a rising octave leap; he switches to speaking when he returns to French ("Et pour en revenir à notre raisonnement"—"And to return to our argument"). The shift from one to the other is so swift that the listener can detect no break. Apart from its comic purpose, the move from one kind of vocal production to another here plays a structural role. It emphasizes the use of two languages: the language of science, impenetrable to ordinary mortals, and the language of Sganarelle's explanation, which in fact is just as incomprehensible.

As composers strove for more realistic declamation, vocalization was increasingly viewed as undesirable, and syllabic setting came to dominate. In the second half of the nineteenth century, French opera turned back to the concerns that had led to the creation of *tragédie mise en musique,* as early French operatic works were often called. In chapter 4 (see the section entitled "Number Opera and Its Variations"), it was noted that to make it possible to include coloratura arias, of which a large segment of the public remained fond, librettists and composers used unusual situations to justify the vocal exuberance. The bel canto concept of beauty for beauty's sake had been completely abandoned, and when coloratura elements were found elsewhere than in those well-defined passages, they had to reflect a need to broaden either the prosody (to give greater weight to a particular syllable, for example) or the expressive qualities. The function of vocal ornament had changed.

Léïla's *cavatine* "Comme autrefois dans la nuit sombre" (*Les Pêcheurs de perles,* act 2, no. 7) is preceded by a recitative in which Bizet takes this approach. The first lines describe the setting: "Me voilà seule dans la nuit. / Seule en ce lieu désert où règne la silence"—"Here I am alone in the night. / Alone in this desolate place where silence reigns." The anxiety that grips the heroine is expressed by the orchestra, *allegro agitato,* through motifs that are vigorous and tonally unstable. Léïla then expresses her feelings: "Je frissonne, j'ai peur"—"I am trembling; I am afraid." She is comforted when she thinks of her beloved: "Mais il est là mon coeur devine sa présence"—"But he is there; my heart senses his presence." The flourish on the word *coeur* reflects the externalization of the emotion, the lyric scent of a heart in love, which perfumes the setting of the following words, *devine sa présence.*

## VERISIMILITUDE IN CHORUSES, ARIAS, AND ENSEMBLES

The special characteristic of choruses and ensembles is that they enable several individuals to speak at once, something that is not found in the spoken theater for longer than a fleeting moment and a few words. Opera requires such elements, and these contribute to its splendor. In his list of the precepts for libretto writing, Antoine (Anton) Reicha (1770–1836) suggested that "scenes with several actors together should most often end with an ensemble piece, and the final scenes that bring a major act to an end should be fully set to music to yield a remarkable and exciting finale, in which most of the singers should be heard."[12] As distinct from other parts of a libretto, which could be declaimed as though in the theater, ensembles and finales required of the librettist a special kind of writing that was comprehensible only when set to music.

Yet the chorus could be one of the most realistic elements of the drama. It would appear in situations which in real life would allow—or require—it to sing as a group. Put briefly, the dramaturgy of the chorus drew in turn on a logic of realism (when a particular situation required the use of the chorus) and on a musical logic (when the various voices of a group came together for reasons of operatic aesthetics). The orderly group of a ceremonial is replaced by the collective character—invented in Greek theater and revived in opera.[13] But this collective character is possible only when the crowd is part of a preestablished structure that suppresses the individual in favor of the collective, and that consists only of members of a particular entity, such as monks, peasants, or soldiers.

But extreme situations could justify, or even require, diversity in the chorus. That was the case in scene 2 of *Gwendoline,* which we considered earlier in this chapter. Here, it was natural to depict the Danish attack on the Saxons by tangling the voices of the crowds. The terror of the Saxon girls justifies the "disorder" of their utterances, while the savagery and brutality of the Danes are expressed through their war cries. The Roman Carnival scene in act 1, scene 2, of Berlioz's *Benvenuto Cellini* (1838) is another good example of disorder organized through music, with lines sung by the crowd and by the protagonists bursting from all sides.

As authors tried to strike a balance with verisimilitude, ensembles were probably the hardest element to draw into the drama, and this was why they were virtually absent from *drame lyrique.* Because they expressed the thoughts of an individual, arias had natural roots in a variety of situations: when they were required by the plot, or when they were the voiced expression of a lone character's thoughts or reveries. By focusing on a single feeling, an aria could justify textual reprises and repetitions: the singer would always return to the initial idea. To some extent, operatic characters display a manic preoccupation with their obsessive thoughts.

When voices no longer alternate but are overlaid, we are in the sphere of the ensemble, a sphere limited to the lyric theater. Structurally, ensembles follow a logical course, which is generally organized around three elements: an explanatory dialogue; a dialogue including symmetrical musical phrases; and an ensemble section. The order of these elements could vary depending on the action, which could introduce sudden twists in the plot and could supplement the original form with choral sections of various kinds, new characters, or special stage effects.[14] The love duet is traditionally cast in this mold: the meeting of the lovers is generally delayed by all manner of circumstances, and explanations are offered first of all. The two characters then express their feelings in turn, and finally give themselves over to amorous outpourings.

Librettists used three main techniques to bring dramatic credibility to their ensembles. Two of these relate to the elemental antagonism between love and hatred (see Appendix 7). The protagonists, depending on whether they view themselves as enemies or friends, as allies or, indeed, as lovers, fall into a pattern of opposition or of accord. In the first case, they move toward rupture, with their simultaneously expressed anger; in the second, toward fusion of their thoughts. The sequence gradually leading to the overlay of the voices takes the form of an increasingly stormy encounter, with a simultaneous explosion of anger. An exception is the crisis situation, used to warrant the apparent disorder when a number of characters depart from the socially normal path of dialogue and of hearing one another out, and have their say irrespective of the others.

The third technique is simply to set out the individual feelings of a number of characters reacting simultaneously to a single situation; this is an expansion of the theatrical aside.

The long duet for Zurga and Léïla in act 3 of *Les Pêcheurs de perles* combines contrasting and contradictory emotions in a particularly spirited form. The beginning of the duet brings Léïla into Zurga's tent to speak with him. Their encounter frightens the heroine and deeply troubles the man, who is in love with her. The libretto heads each of these two speeches with the indication *à part* (aside); this implies that the librettists wanted the characters to express their thoughts in succession. But Bizet opted to have Léïla and Zurga speak nearly simultaneously. The duet begins with an imitative phrase first sung by the soprano ("Je frémis, je chancelle") then repeated by the baritone ("Je frémis devant elle"). These dramatic and psychological events are reflected in the music. Individually, both characters are experiencing confusion.

Let us turn to the quartet in Gounod's *Roméo et Juliette* (act 4, no. 15). Roméo has just left Juliette; Gertrude tells Juliette that her father is on the way. When he arrives, Capulet says that Tybald, before he died, had chosen a husband for her, Count Paris. While Capulet sings of duty ("Nous devons respecter la volonté des morts"—"We must respect the wishes of the dead"), Juliette, Gertrude, and Frère Laurent simultaneously voice their own feelings: Juliette swears loyalty ("Ne crains rien Roméo"—"Fear nothing, Roméo"); Gertrude spurns the injunction of the count ("Dans leur tombe, laissons en paix dormir les morts"—"Let us leave the dead to sleep in peace in their tombs"); and Frère Laurent is worried ("Elle tremble et mon coeur partage ses remords"—"She trembles, and my heart shares her remorse").

## MNEMONIC MOTIFS AND LEITMOTIFS

The Wagnerian leitmotif has had such an impact that we forget its origins and the widely varied forms that preceded it—especially in the French repertory. To understand this, it is important first of all to separate the basic principle (that of recurrence: the return of an element in the course of a work) from the many ways in which it was adapted, both in drama and in music. Myriad examples of the use of recurrent motifs may be seen, from simple mnemonic motifs employed to recall a situation, to motifs that are brought back for the sake of musical structure, to atmospheric motifs that lend color to a scene or an act, to the true leitmotif, which is both a symbol and a nearly continuous thread that weaves the musical fabric. Critics referred to these various kinds of motifs as "characteristic" or "typical" phrases. Their defining features could vary greatly: the musical traits of the motif (such as melody, rhythm, harmony, timbre, and structure) and the meaning linked to the motif (character, idea, feeling, object, and so forth). Finally, an analysis should consider the recurrences of such motifs and their density in a given work, along with the ways in which they are combined and developed—whether they are invariable or whether they undergo development or modification, or even whether they are subjected to variation (as in "theme and variations"), which is unusual.

This technique of composition resulted both from the pursuit of unity within a large-scale structure and from a desire to experiment with a new expressive and dramatic tool. Since the end of the eighteenth century, composers had sought to establish relationships among the various movements or parts of a work. In the classical period, composers greatly exploited the potential of organizational techniques and the unifying power of tonality (think of Mozart in *Don Giovanni*), but they also turned their attention to using thematic elements to tighten symphonic construction. Among the pioneers were Haydn, who was popular in France, and Beethoven, who was admired by Berlioz, then by Bizet, and who gradually came to be admired by discerning listeners. Think of the rhythmic motif that opens Beethoven's Fifth Symphony and that returns in later movements, and of the recurring themes in the Ninth Symphony. And in the finale of Etienne Nicolas Méhul's Fourth Symphony (1810), the composer brings back a motif from the adagio. This ultimately leads to the cyclical principle of which César Franck was so fond.

In opera, the ambition to broaden scene units paralleled a desire to establish links among self-contained musical forms. In no. 7 of *Moïse*—the French version of *Mosè in Egitto* (Naples, 1818) prepared for the Paris Opéra in 1827—Rossini employed an instrumental motif as a unifying element in a very large-scale number that included both soloists and chorus. As the century progressed, traditional numbers were gradually abandoned in favor of larger scenes; ultimately, composers would envisage their musical forms in terms of whole acts, then of the entire opera.

Carl Dahlhaus demonstrates how Wagner moved forward in stages before achieving true music drama founded on continuous development of leitmotifs. In between this—the through-composed opera—and the number opera, he places the "scene opera," which in his analysis of *Der fliegende Holländer* he discusses in the following way: "The process of drawing separate arias, duets, ensembles and choruses together in complexes, instead of having them succeed one another as separate items—a process adopted in act-finales in eighteenth- and early nineteenth-century operas—was extended in *Der fliegende Holländer* to the whole work, though without there being any question of calling it a through-composed music drama."[15]

Once again, Gounod takes the middle road: act 1 of *Mireille* uses an extended form of the typical introductory scene (see page 109). Characters converse with the crowd; and the heroine arrives, then after a dialogue sees Vincent. Here a duet replaces the traditional aria. The whole is flanked by the joyful chorus that opens and closes the act and that serves as its center point. Acts 1 and 2 of *Roméo et Juliette* were also composed as single scenes. The first, the Capulets' ball, is framed by the music of the mazurka, and the second, which takes place in Juliette's garden, by a lovely diaphanous theme.

The final act of *Sapho* was conceived as a unified whole progressing toward the poignant aria "O ma lyre éternelle" and the heroine's suicide. Several numbers of that act are punctuated by appearances of the first motif played by the orchestra. This depicts the motion of the waves; its full meaning is revealed when it accompanies Phaon's words, "Je n'entends que le bruit des flots qui vont me transporter sur la rive étrangère"—"I hear nothing but the sound of the waves that will transport me to foreign shores." This descriptive line evokes the hostility of the water, which symbolizes the hero's departure, the lovers' separation, and the abyss into which Sapho is to plunge herself.

The desire of the Romantics to bring words and music closer together and to express thoughts and feelings in sound led composers to invest musical ideas with more than formal significance. They came to think of the ordering of motifs in dramaturgical terms; their recurrences could have extramusical significance. This evolved in program music. Berlioz translated the constant image of the beloved woman (the idée fixe) into a melody that spans the entire *Symphonie fantastique* and that undergoes the changes demanded by the fifth-movement nightmare. Liszt explored these possibilities in his one-movement symphonic poems, as well as in his *Faust Symphony* (1854, 1857), which was dedicated to Berlioz; here the musical connections among the motifs reflect the links that connect the characters of Faust and Méphisto. The concept of thematic metamorphosis made it possible to follow psychological development through musical development.

Broad-scale thematic development came late to French opera, although the simple return of motifs caught on early. In his *Poétique de la musique* (Paris, 1785), Etienne de Lacépède suggests that at weak points in their operas, composers should repeat "the most moving of the pieces that have already been heard." This inverts the procedure of the composer who writes a potpourri overture by combining a selection of the opera's best passages. The overture could be reduced to nothing in order to pitch the spectator directly into the action, but it could also serve as a foretaste that, by extracting essential themes linked to the drama, would set a particular tone and sometimes provide an interpretation or synopsis of the work, as does the grandiose overture to Lalo's *Le Roi d'Ys*, which is true program music. Here we find not so much mnemonic as premonitory motifs.

A simpler procedure was to compose a brief prelude that developed a theme, which would then be used in the opening scenes. Such a building-block motif would lend cohesion to the exposition of the drama, and could sometimes create a particular atmosphere. This is what the prelude to *Les Pêcheurs de perles* does; it is a mysterious 32-measure orchestral introduction that later returns to accompany the entrance and the exit of the unknown priestess.

Outside the realm of opera, the theatrical genre of *mélodrame* made use of a dramaturgic form that associated certain stereotypic scenes with music, which the playwright would specify for various places in the production. This was effective in terms of characterization, and no less so in terms of the action, where it added emphasis to the high points. The writers of *mélodrames* normally supplemented their stage directions "with a highly encoded form of dumb show and a particular musical phrase, to announce and accompany the entrance of the various characters."[16]

The lyric theater was heir to this tradition, especially since many librettists, including the prolific Eugène Scribe, worked in a variety of genres.[17] Very often, it was the librettist who suggested to the composer musical recurrences that could serve as markers in the score, as that master of *mélodrame* Adolphe Philippe Dennery and his co-author, Lockroy, so obviously did in Aimé Maillart's *La Croix de Marie*, where they asked the composer to repeat in the orchestra, both in act 2 and then in act 3, "the motif that in the first act accompanied the kiss that Marie's mother gives her daughter." But in the musical flow of an entire opera, the spectator did not perceive such reprises in the same way as in the spoken theater, where music appeared only as an exception, and where it was linked from the outset to the ideas it was intended to bolster. Mid-century French opera audiences would usually have been aware of the return of a phrase without connecting it to the drama, except when the plot included clearly identified flashbacks. When at the end of Gounod's *Faust*, Marguerite, in her prison cell, sees her lover once again, her vocal line echoes the melody of the garden scene. She then recalls their first meeting ("Voici la rue / Où votre main osa presque effleurer mes doigts"—"Here is the street / Where your hand was bold enough nearly to brush my fingers"). The orchestra then plays the waltz that had accompanied that scene in act 2.

Here again there are notable similarities between operatic and cinematic dramaturgy. In Michael Curtiz's film *Casablanca* (1942), the haunting song "As Time Goes By" adds its own emotional resonance to the narrative: it is quoted to signal the lovers' encounters; it regularly reappears during their meetings throughout the drama; and it is played in a more extended form when the film evokes the past love of Rick (Humphrey Bogart) and Ilsa (Ingrid Bergman), effectively recalling the origin of the despairing hero's sorrowful thoughts.

In 1784, Grétry viewed the *romance* "Une fièvre brûlante" in *Richard Coeur de Lion* as "the pivot around which the entire work turns," and kept up audience interest by changing it for its various appearances.[18] Méhul and Cherubini, at the turn of the nineteenth century, made sometimes subtle use of recurrent motifs. In his *Ariodant* (1799), Méhul depicted feelings of hatred and vengeance with a complex motif whose component parts vary over the course of the drama.[19] Specific musical styles corresponding to typical scenes, such as church scenes or scenes of rejoicing, helped adapt recurring motifs to their purposes and at the same time made it easy for audiences to grasp their meaning.

With very subtle operatic dramaturgy, act 3 of Boieldieu's *La Dame blanche,* after Anna's opening aria, is conceived as a painting framed by the charming chorus "Chantez, joyeux ménestrel." In a way that might be seen as pre-Proustian, this chorus unearths recollections that had been buried in Georges Brown's memory. Brown tries to remember the melody he has just heard the chorus sing, in a scene that also delves into his visual memory. The whole scene works on the melodramatic principle of recollection followed by revelation: as a child, Julien d'Avenel, alias Georges Brown, had been deceived by one of his father's servants, who concealed his identity and his wealth.

Meyerbeer then opened up new horizons. In *Les Huguenots* (1836), he combined this technique with that of musical quotation by creating a motif on the basis of a Lutheran chorale, which tints the entire drama with its particular color. This chorale is a full-fledged melody, organized into several phrases; it also influences the opera's striking dramatic rhythm by evolving, in ever-tauter form, as the final disaster approaches.[20] The same opera introduced the concept of a motif based on timbre: the majority of Marcel's utterances, which represent the Protestant world, are accompanied by cellos. Perhaps Meyerbeer knew Mendelssohn's revision of that monument of Protestantism, Bach's *Saint Matthew Passion,* which had been played in 1829 at Berlin; both the music and the text of that work are punctuated by chorales. Note that for the second performance, at Leipzig in 1841, Mendelssohn—could he have been influenced by Meyerbeer?—replaced the piano accompaniment of the *recitativo secco* with a pair of double-stopping cellos and a double bass: a striking effect that, as we have seen, is also found in *Les Huguenots.* Berlioz, too, in *Harold en Italie* (1834), had experimented with using an "instrumental protagonist": Harold is portrayed by the viola. And in a more rudimentary way, Boieldieu would contribute to the association between timbre and character by linking the harp with the mysterious White Lady in *La Dame blanche,* just as Adolphe Adam would connect the flute to the character of Tracolin (a flute player by trade) in *Le Toréador* (1849).

Gounod, Thomas, Reyer, and Bizet each used recurrent motifs in accordance with his own style, and the practice ultimately became a reflex, especially in the last quarter of the century. At mid-century, motifs were not so well developed and were rarely combined. In this sense, the score of *Les Pêcheurs de perles* is among the most original of its day. The use of recurrent motifs correlates perfectly with the opera's theme of memory. The network of motifs mirrors the construction of the action through the connotations of each recurrence of those motifs. In his *Samson et Dalila* (Weimar, 1877; Rouen, 1890), Saint-Saëns retained a classic musical architecture, modeled at times on that of eighteenth-century works, while at the same time making use of motifs, of which some twenty are found in the opera.

In the late 1840s, Liszt brought to the attention of French music-lovers the dramatic and expressive potential of the techniques with which Wagner had been experimenting:

> In *Tannhäuser*, he has made a striking operatic innovation, in which melody not only expresses but actually represents certain emotions by recurring when these reappear, and by being duplicated in the orchestra independently of the singing on stage, often with modulations that depict the passions to which they correspond. Such recurrence not only gives rise to moving recollections; it reveals the emotion it expresses. Barely glowing when these impressions still stir only vaguely in our heart, [the melody] vigorously unfolds when they forcefully grip it once again.[21]

For motifs to grow more numerous and to continuously follow the development of the characters and of the drama, we have to wait for Chausson's *Roi Arthus* (Brussels, 1903) and especially Vincent d'Indy's *Fervaal* (Brussels, 1897). Those composers had carefully studied and assimilated Wagner's late scores, not merely imitating them but adapting them to their own musical language; motifs grew more numerous and continuously paralleled the development of the characters and of the drama. The "heroic masculine" theme in *Fervaal* is a good example. In the prologue alone, it appears in augmentation during the brief orchestral introduction; it is distorted when Fervaal is wounded; and it is played under vocal declamation when Guilhen questions the hero's origins and when Fervaal is laid out on a stretcher. Finally, it is expanded and combined with its own augmented form. Another motif derived from it evolves simultaneously: the war theme.

A number of scores were composed to librettos directly inspired by the *Ring;* this could lead one to believe in their total Wagnerism, but in terms of their music, they remain far from having thoroughly assimilated Wagner's language. Reyer's *Sigurd* (Brussels, 1884; Lyon and Paris, 1885), in spite of its subject drawn from Nordic sagas and the tale of the Nibelungen, and in spite of its numerous thematic recurrences, is far removed from the artistic achievement of the *Ring*. Indeed, the composer affirmed that he had not known the post-*Lohengrin* operas when he was working on *Sigurd,* which was completed in 1872.

Alfred Bruneau began by repeating motifs without really modifying them, as in *Le Rêve* (1891); later he would increase their number, combine them to the point of surfeit (as in *Naïs Micoulin,* 1906), and transform them.[22] For his part, Massenet,[23] notably in *Werther* (Vienna, 1892; Paris, 1893), attempted a synthesis of the Franco-Italian tradition of vocal melody and the Wagnerian heritage of lyric drama based on motifs and on continuous musical and dramatic movement. His works swing between the two extremes, favoring sometimes one and sometimes the other (*Esclarmonde* is his most clearly Wagnerian score). In general, Massenet sought to sustain a color (a *tinta* in Verdian terms) by using motifs linked to situations or to atmosphere relating to a particular act, while employing other thematic elements to express the feelings or personality of the characters throughout an opera.

What we should remember is the diversity of the ways in which recurrence was used in French opera, rather than any notion of a steady evolution toward ever-greater complexity in the handling of motifs.

# Chapter 6    Poetic Expression and Musical Expression

In an opera, text becomes music, prosody becomes rhythm, poetic images become tone paintings. Sounds augment or replace words as expressions of the poetry, of situations, feelings, and impulses of the heart.

## POETIC WRITING

Just as operatic plots followed preexisting schemas or models, the actual writing of the libretto borrowed from poetic stereotypes. Verses flowed effortlessly from the pen; it would not be an exaggeration to speak of automatic writing drawn from the huge database of situations and formulas available to a librettist in any given period. Some of the clichés were hoary indeed: lines written by Marmontel for Ali's aria in the first act of Grétry's *Zémire et Azor* (1771)—"L'orage va cesser / Déjà les vents s'apaisent"— "The storm is ending / Already, the winds grow calmer"—are echoed nearly verbatim by Zurga at the beginning of act 3 of *Les Pêcheurs de perles:* "L'orage s'est calmé, / Déjà les vents se taisent, / Comme eux les colères s'apaisent"—"The storm has calmed; / Already, the winds are growing silent; / Like them, tempers are growing calmer." The poetry of birds—or anything able to fly—invariably rhymed *léger* (light) with *voltiger* (flutter). Love duets repeated, ad nauseam, images that it would be difficult to describe as truly poetic. Even in *Les Troyens*, rich in mythological references, which Berlioz revived with a classicism that was viewed in 1863 as anachronistic, it is an easy matter to detect a few of these formulas—for example, in the amorous utterances of Didon and Enée.[1] Let us in fact compare them with the words of Nadir and Léïla in an early version of their act 2 duet.[2]

| Les Troyens | Les Pêcheurs de perles |
|---|---|
| Ensemble | Ensemble |
| Nuit d'ivresse et d'extase infinie, | Nuit d'ivresse, nuit d'amour! |
| Blonde Phoebé, grands astres | Ciel parsemé d'étoiles, |
| de sa cour, | Etends sur nous tes voiles |
| Versez sur nous votre lueur | Et retarde le jour! |
| bénie; | O nuit d'amour! |
| Fleurs des cieux, souriez à | |
| l'immortel amour. | |
| Together | Together |
| Night of euphoria and | Night of euphoria, night of love! |
| unbounded ecstasy, | Star-studded sky, |
| Fair Phoebe and great stars of | Spread thy veil over us |
| her court, | And delay the day! |
| Cast upon us your blessed glow; | Oh, night of love! |
| Flowers of the heavens, smile | |
| upon immortal love. | |

We might also compare the text of Lakmé's prayer with choral response with its twin in the first act of *Les Pêcheurs de perles*, Léïla's prayer with chorus:[3]

| Les Pêcheurs de perles | Lakmé |
|---|---|
| Prière de Léïla | Prière de Lakmé |
| O dieu Brahma, | Blanche Dourga, |
| O Maître souverain du monde. | Pâle Siva! |
| Blanche Siva, | Puissant Ganeça! |
| Reine à la chevelure blonde. | O vous, que créa Brahma! |
| Esprits de l'air, esprits de l'onde, | Apaisez-vous, |
| Des rochers et des prés et des bois, | Protégez-nous! |
| Ecoutez ma voix. | |
| O god Brahma, | White-skinned Durga, |
| O sovereign master of the world. | Pale Siva! |
| White-skinned Siva, | Powerful Ganesha! |
| Blonde-tressed queen. | O thou, created by Brahma! |

Spirits of the air, spirits of the          Be assuaged,
    waves,                                   Protect us!
Of the rocks and the meadows
    and the woods,
Hear my voice.

"What does it matter," exclaimed Castil-Blaze at the beginning of the nineteenth century, "that the poet uses the same words to signify the same feelings? All expressive variety is the province of the composer's talent."[4] Still, many critics complained about the overuse of formulaic verses and of certain situations: "Asia and America have great appeal, but through overuse they have been stripped of poetry," wrote Johannès Weber in 1863. "After *Jaguarita, La Perle du Brésil, La Statue, Lalla-Roukh, La Reine de Saba,* and other operas...the public simply does not care whether the action takes place in Delhi, Timbuktu, or Chile—or in Quimper-Corentin [in northwestern France]. Allah and Brahma are beginning to be no less discredited than Jupiter and Apollo; they will soon have nothing left but, like the Olympian gods, to strut about at the Bouffes-Parisiens."[5]

Although at mid-century most critics were still trying to encourage a certain level of quality in librettos, an opera's literary merit was increasingly no longer the decisive criterion it once had been. In 1849, F.-J. Fétis took note of a change Meyerbeer had made to the libretto of *Le Prophète:* at the beginning of act 1, he had substituted an eight-syllable line ("O liberté! c'est la victoire!") for the ten-syllable original. "Could one say that these words make no sense? I would, but they are musical, and that is what an opera is all about," Fétis commented.[6] And another journalist wrote in 1875: "As for the libretto, it doesn't much matter what language it speaks; feelings and passions can make do with a kind of summary expression; it is *situations* alone that are preeminent."[7]

The conclusions of Catherine Kintzler's analysis of the Abbé de Mably's observations about *tragédie en musique* apply especially well to nineteenth-century opera: "The elliptical, condensed, coarse, and repetitive character of the writing was...dictated by the nature of lyric theater. It is precisely because a poetic space must be left for the music that the strictly literary poetic content must be restricted and must, so to speak, occupy only half the territory."[8] The written text of a libretto was shorter than that of a spoken play, and the writing reflected an inclination to exaggerate. Clichés and ready-made phrases were "used in the same way that a fresco painter works, with a hint of coarseness that would 'scare' a portraitist. This practice is justified by a law of perspective; one must leave room—sufficient space to allow the music to work in a poetic fashion."[9] Librettists had to forsake much of their artistic ambition and, at least to some extent, think of the special purpose of their work. The need for interesting situations overwhelmed the pursuit of literary quality, and the requirements of musical setting won out over painstaking preparation of the text. As we have seen, it had to be possible to translate the text into a musical form.

Even more, it seemed as though the libretto was to be nothing more than raw material, an indispensable element that would relinquish all its own worth. Charles Malherbe had no hesitation in saying, in a chapter on Auber and Meyerbeer, that "lyric poetry in the theater must be mediocre—more, it must even be bad."[10] He explains: "From the day when the musician took precedence over the poet, the latter saw the pointlessness of asserting his own personality, and contented himself with providing the composer with elastic, neutral material that would enable the melodist to exhibit his abilities with complete freedom." The verses could be inept; if the musician had enough talent, he would incorporate their "elastic" material into his own aural domain. "In that connection," continued Malherbe, "Scribe, with his felicitous prosaicness, freed the composer from all constraints and, thanks to the wide variety of meters appropriate to music, provided broad scope for his inspiration. Hence those choruses, whose words are ridiculous in themselves, but which still today produce an unfailing musical effect."[11] When *La Muette de Portici* was revived in 1863, the critic Ralph (Léon Escudier) pointed out that since a libretto was not a masterpiece of poetry, it was the librettist's job to tailor his verses to fit the music. He gave this example: "The Neapolitan fisherman's song written by Auber is delightful; it communicates the poet's idea and expresses the situation. If the accentuation is faulty, why did Scribe not change the line?"[12] Note, however, that in the second half of the nineteenth century, a reverse trend can be seen, leading to a restoration of the libretto's status.

It is sometimes impossible in studying an opera's expressive qualities to separate literary from musical writing, for an opera is the result of the fusion of these two elements: an aria may be viewed as "poetic" even though it does not rise above the commonplace as literature. A study of poetic writing draws us subtly from literature to music and enables us to identify the expressive tools of a kind of "operatic poetry."

## THE CONCEPT OF "OPERATIC POETRY"— THE EXPRESSIVENESS OF MUSIC

Let us try to form a notion, if not a precise definition, of what constitutes poetic expression in an opera, and to set the development of the French repertory in the mid nineteenth century in that context.

The word "poetry" is routinely used to describe something that is poetic, that is touching or inspiring, or that makes us dream—as in "the poetry of Nature" or "a painting full of poetry." That is Paul Valéry's first definition of the word in his "Première leçon de cours de poétique": it "designates, first of all, a class of emotions, a special emotive state, which can be induced by very diverse objects or circumstances."[13]

The external form of a text must not be confused with its content, as Théophile Gautier reminds us: "Nothing is more unpleasant than this dexterous mediocrity, these correctly rhymed lines that look like verses without containing an atom of poetry."[14] Whether it is the product of the imagination and sensibility, or a breath from the soul, or a clear perception of the beautiful, or a striking and idealized imitation of nature, we are interested here in poetry insofar as it is linked to images and feelings, and in terms of its ability to capture and communicate an emotion or a moving incident, which adds a sympathetic charm to the verses.

Valéry's second definition is that poetry "makes one reflect on an art, an odd enterprise whose purpose is to reconstruct the emotion to which the first meaning of the word refers. To restore poetic emotion at will, in isolation from the natural conditions in which it is spontaneously produced, and by means of the artifice of language: that is the goal of the poet, and that is the idea connected with the word 'poetry' in its second sense."[15] Poetic emotion results when all the elements that have been employed "make one another resonate as though they corresponded harmonically. The poetic universe defined in this way is markedly analogous to what we are able to surmise about the universe of dreams."[16]

Poetry's "indissolubility of sound and meaning"[17] finds new expression in opera. It is as though the alchemy inherent in poetic verse, which merges the sound and the meaning of its words, was operating between the text (which is almost solely the bearer of the meaning) and the music (which is by nature the bearer of the sound). The role of scenery comes into play as well: the stage creates a primary framework that defines both the literary space and the musical space.

Whether or not an opera is "poetic" depends on the composer's ability to bring to life a series of emotions or images, to make them as brilliant and as moving as can be. The music flows into the poetic framework comprising scenery, verses, and dramatic situations, and reveals its own beauties, which the listener will then associate with the meanings and sensations indicated by that framework (see fig. 20). The composer magnifies the resonances between the poetic framework and the music by his use of evocative devices (musical devices aimed at directing the listener's imagination or at

Figure 20. Gounod's *Faust,* Marguerite in the garden (*L'Illustration,* March 6, 1869). The scenery and all other elements of the staging work together to create a poetic setting. Here the artist has combined two poetic incidents: the garden scene and the spinning scene, which actually takes place in Marguerite's bed chamber.

evoking an image, feeling, or idea) and stylistic connotations (religious, military, or pastoral music, for example). In this sense, "operatic poetry" must be understood in relation to the ways of a collective culture and a collective imagination. Usage determines meaning, and the relationship between signifier (the musical elements) and signified is based on conventions that, depending on the period, are part of a cultural "total immersion" from which the cultivated spectator benefits, although not necessarily consciously.

Operatic music completely fulfills a poetic function, because it is a means of producing emotions, because it creates an atmosphere (through its link with the meaning of the text, of the situations, and of the settings), because it intensifies and drives the drama, and because, like a book that creates a world according to its own rules, it reformulates the time and space of the narrative in order to transform it into an aesthetic object. While we may view Berlioz as the theoretician of this operatic poetry, it is Gounod's lyric works that were its clearest and most influential embodiment in the mid nineteenth century; it was this model that Bizet admired, to the point where he was afraid he would be unable to shake it off.

Such an understanding of poetry is inseparable from an aesthetic by which music wields expressive power. As a composer, Berlioz championed the concept of music that was inherently expressive, and whose meaning, moreover, could be defined through specific techniques:

> Music...speaks first and foremost to a sense that it delights, and the stim-
> ulation of which, spreading throughout the body, results in sensuous
> pleasure that is sometimes gentle and calm, sometimes fiery and violent—
> which one would never think possible without having experienced it. By
> linking itself to ideas, which it has a thousand ways of inspiring, music
> heightens the intensity of its effect through the omnipotence of what is
> commonly called poetry. It is itself already ardent; by expressing passions
> it harnesses their flame. Sparkling with rays of sound, it refracts them
> through the prism of the imagination. It embraces the real and the ideal
> simultaneously.[18]

Drawing on the writings of the Italian critic Giuseppe Carpani (1752–1825), Berlioz distinguished between physical imitation (the "direct [imitation] of natural sounds and noises") and emotional imitation (which "seeks through its sounds to evoke in us an idea of the various affections of the heart and, by addressing only the sense of hearing, to arouse feelings that human beings ordinarily experience only through the other senses").[19] This second kind of imitation is "the aim of expression, of painting, and of musical images." As a musician, Berlioz then adds, "As to expressive power, I doubt that the draftsman's arts or even poetry possess this to the same degree as music."

The expressiveness of music and its evocative and signifying powers were greatly developed by the Romantic movement, along with a work's emotional content, especially in program music. Liszt wrote, "my piano, thus far, has been my self, my word, my life; it is the intimate repository of all that quaked in my brain in the most ardent days of my youth."[20] The composer of the Faust Symphony believed deeply in the expressive power of music and of its sonorities. In his analysis of *Tannhäuser,* Liszt observed that the "motifs are so characteristic that they bear within them all the affective meaning that is demanded of musical thoughts, consigned to the instruments alone."[21] It was clear to him that this reflected progress in the arts, combined with an evolution in the increasingly large audiences toward seeking something more than mere auditory hedonism: "Nowadays the public includes many cultivated minds who by no means limit themselves to experiencing a vague pleasure, a gentle and rhythmic thrill, but prefer to use analogous thoughts and images to interpret the meaning of all music."[22]

CORRESPONDENCES AND METAPHORS—
THE COLOR AND EXPRESSIVENESS OF INSTRUMENTS

It quickly becomes clear from reading the nineteenth-century Paris musical press that operatic music was viewed essentially in terms of its relationship to the libretto. It "created an image" or a "feeling"; it evoked emotions. One gradually becomes aware that all the factors of authorship had
to unite to achieve a common goal: the musical "yield" of the drama in
every respect from the most utilitarian to the most exalted. It was in that
regard that Fétis admired the charming scene early in Meyerbeer's *Dinorah, ou le Pardon de Ploërmel* (act 1, no. 2), whose style, orchestration, pacing, and form depict the actions of Dinorah and her goat, and the successive
emotions experienced by the girl, who has gone mad: "The elegant and fine
interplay of the instruments as the character runs; the rhythmic, bounding
gait of the goat; the melancholy ritornello when Dinorah returns exhausted; her gentle, sad recitative; the brief, gay distraction caused by a
fresh idea in her delirious imagination; and finally, the return at the end of
the recitative to the initial emotion: with boundless artistry, all this precedes and leads into the delightful *berceuse* [lullaby]."[23]

Critics seek to attach meaning to what they hear. Berlioz was without
question one of the most zealous in this regard, both as a composer and as
a journalist, and it is to his writings that we shall turn for guidance. One of
the main aims of his columns was to find images that, through metaphor,
could describe the impressions that a work produced. Moreover, metaphor
made it possible to demonstrate the profound relationship among the arts,
a concept the Romantics held dear. Liszt began his memoir of Chopin by
affirming that "The many forms of art [are] but various incantations intended to evoke feelings and emotions, to make them perceptible, somehow
tangible, and to communicate their trembling."[24] And in an 1861 article on
Wagner, Baudelaire wrote, "What would be really surprising would be for
sounds to be *unable* to suggest colors, for colors to be *unable* to give the
idea of a melody, and for sound and color to be unsuited to conveying ideas,
because things have always been expressed by mutual analogy since God
created the world as a complex and indivisible whole."[25] The concept of
correspondences, which the author of *Les Fleurs du mal* (1857) so wonderfully turned into a poetic system, was more than a mere attractive notion:

Comme de longs échos qui de loin se confondent
Dans une ténébreuse et profonde unité,
Vaste comme la nuit et comme la clarté,
Les parfums, les couleurs et les sons se répondent.

Il est des parfums frais comme des chairs d'enfants,
Doux comme les hautbois, verts comme les prairies[.]

Like fading echoes confused in the distance
Into a gloomy and deep unison
As vast as the night or as the daylight,
Scents and colors and sounds become equals.

There are perfumes as fresh as a child's flesh,
As sweet as the oboe, as green as the meadows[.]
        (*Spleen et Idéal*, IV—"Correspondances," ll. 5–10)

For Baudelaire this was a reality; it is no less present in the works of Berlioz, where it influences even his instrumental music. To supplement the quotations on opera that are scattered through this book, let us recall one famous example from outside the lyric repertory: the symphonies of Beethoven. According to Berlioz, the slow movement of the Second Symphony contains "a pure, ingenuous song" and a "beautiful painting of innocent pleasure, barely darkened by a few occasional notes of melancholy."[26] In the finale of the Third Symphony, he "sees" "a B-flat struck by the violins and immediately taken up by the flutes and oboes, in the manner of an echo" and compares "the nuance that differentiates [the instruments] to that which distinguishes blue from violet." The particular combination of a modulation and a crescendo in a passage in the first movement of the Fourth Symphony seemed to Berlioz analogous to "a river whose calm waters suddenly disappear and emerge from their subterranean bed only to fall with a roar in a foaming cascade." The orchestra's voice could moan or threaten; a theme could sparkle with verve; an oboe phrase could be of beautiful freshness; melodies could express feelings of melancholy tenderness, impassioned exhaustion, dreamy religiosity, and so forth.

There are correspondences among the works of great authors, whether they be painters, composers, or poets. Berlioz thus sensed in the funeral march in Beethoven's Third Symphony "a translation of Virgil's beautiful lines on the procession of the young Pallas" and in the scherzo "true funeral games...like those the warriors of *The Iliad* celebrated around the tombs of their leaders." And the "remarkable landscape" of the Pastoral Symphony "seemed to have been laid out by Poussin and drawn by Michelangelo." There are a great many more such examples. Like the poet, the composer is aware of "horizontal correspondences, or syntheses, by means of which sensations evoke one another, in a reversible way."[27]

In composition, Berlioz drew a distinction between musical painting—the "painting of visible objects," for which he did not at all care—and "images or comparisons that give rise to sensations for which music unquestionably possesses analogues."[28] Analogy is a resemblance whose origins lie in the imagination: "In order that the original for those images may be recognized," continued Berlioz, "the listener must be informed of the composer's intent by some indirect means, and the point of comparison must be obvious." Thus, "Weber created moonlight in the accompaniment to Agathe's aria in the second act of *Der Freischütz*, because the hazy, calm, and melancholy color of his harmonies and the chiaroscuro sonorities of his instruments are a faithful image of those pale glimmers and, moreover, perfectly express the reverie into which the lovers so willingly let themselves fall at the sight of the nighttime orb whose assistance Agathe is now imploring."[29]

Nowhere but in opera is the relationship between visual and aural elements so powerfully expressed. Yet certain subjects are more conducive than others to creating real sonic/pictorial paintings—fantastical themes, as in *opéra-féerie*, particularly so. Massenet's *Esclarmonde* (1889) was among the last of this kind. Its writing reflects the survival of a lyric style of poetry, based on images and sensations adapted to the realm of sound. In the prologue, referred to earlier (see chapter 4), the composer took advantage of a setting rich in imagery: Phorcas, standing before the closed iconostasis, addresses his subjects in austere tones. He then gives the order, "Open the golden doors of the revered altar, bathed in light." The image moves; the light gleams: "In a cloud of incense, Esclarmonde appears, veiled, crowned with a tiara, adorned with precious stones; she could be taken for a Byzantine idol."[30] The stark atmosphere (in the key of C) gives way to gleaming orchestration in D-flat major. The chorus "O divine Esclarmonde" is accompanied by penetrating figures in the oboes, English horn, clarinets, first and second horns, and solo trombone, while some of the strings (first and second violins and violas, all divided) join the harps in sketching out a D-flat arpeggio in various forms; this expresses a shimmering glow, translating into sound a thousand points of light that could easily have been painted by Gustave Moreau. The flutes and piccolo mirror this harmony with a pattern of repeated notes. And the crystalline sparkle of the triangle punctuates the ensemble with a final glitter, softened by a subtle, pianissimo halo of harmonies in the cellos, basses, bassoons, and third and fourth horns.

The role of the instruments is twofold: they color and they express. To identify the exact meaning attached to them, we must turn to the tradition of instrumental typology, of which Berlioz acted as theorist, as brilliant exponent, and as impassioned propagandist and champion. In his *Mémoires*, he writes of how by careful listening at the Théâtre de l'Opéra, he discovered the "subtle connection between musical expression and the technique of instrumentation."[31] The notion of deepening this relationship and even of codifying it in a theory had been brewing for some time, as indicated by the ambitious title chosen by Georges Kastner for his 1837 treatise on orchestration, *Cours d'instrumentation considéré sous les rapports poétiques et philosophiques de l'art*. Among other instruments, Kastner describes the harp, whose "character has something both of the celestial and of the gentle about it, which is ideally suited to prayers, invocations, or other scenes of that kind"; the clarinet, "instrument of love and of tender feelings"; and the horn, "perhaps the most romantic of the instruments."[32]

In addition to its expressive and coloristic functions, timbre took on a role in the spheres of development and structure. But Berlioz's extraordinary notion that timbre could generate a musical discourse,[33] which culminated in his *Symphonie fantastique*, would truly bear fruit only in the twentieth century. It was as an inventor of new sonorities and as a poet-theoretician that his colleagues viewed Berlioz: "Do you have Berlioz's treatise on instrumentation?" Bizet asked Paul Lacombe. "If not, get hold of one as fast as you can.—It is an admirable work: a vade mecum for any composer who writes for the orchestra.—It is absolutely complete.—It is full of examples.—It is indispensable."[34]

THE POETIC MODEL OF GOUNOD—
EXPRESSIVENESS IN THE ORCHESTRA

Reference was made in chapter 1 to the appalling state of French music around 1850 and to Gounod's importance as a reformer. We must now return to this point and discuss it from the perspective of operatic poetry. Saint-Saëns, who knew Gounod well, saw his *Sapho* as "a milestone in the history of French opera" and emphasized the great contribution made by Gounod's personality and "the concern for purity, the fine style, [and] the fitting expression" in his work, a view later echoed by Reynaldo Hahn.[35] Berlioz, whose career began before Gounod came on the scene, and who thus witnessed that composer's arrival, held a similar view. In his column on the premiere of *Sapho*, he defined the two principal directions open to the operatic composer (apart from traditional *opéra-comique*). The first was that of effect and overwrought dramatics; this was the dominant direction in the France of the day. The other, the direction for which Gounod opted, was the subtler path of apt emotion and the poetic exploration of a given situation. Berlioz catalogues the beauties of the work and the poetic themes that emerge, concluding: "It thrilled me; it enthralled me; it touched my heart; it moved me; it uplifted me; it cast me into a deep, delightful turmoil,...while so many other operas that pass for extremely 'dramatic' bore me and tire me with their thousand details; offend me with their very pretension to being interesting; and displease me because of the obsequious prosaicness of their industry."[36] The idea of an operatic poetry was not, of course, new; what was new was its development to the point where it became an essential goal for the composer.

Gounod preferred poetry to the dramatically prosaic. Let us look a little more closely at how this is reflected in *Sapho*. The most interesting passages are to be found in act 3, the whole of which Berlioz judged to be "very beautiful; extremely beautiful; poetically worthy of the drama."[37] He wrote: "Everything there is musical, grand, harmonious, well crafted, thoroughly clear, aptly and deeply expressive; the orchestral coloration is sometimes dark like a winter night, sometimes brilliant and mild like a lovely spring morning....It is a broad and poetic creation." When the work was revived, he added, "It is all so unusual: passion nobly expressed, common sense in art, poetic naturalness, simple truth, grandeur without bombast, strength without brutality! And, oh, a work dictated by the heart in our age of machine-ism, of mannequin-ism (and of neologism) and of industrialism disguised to a greater or lesser extent under a pretense of art!"[38]

It is clear from these comments that a tone of simplicity and truthfulness (contrasted with music that strove solely for effect), depth of expression, and density of musical discourse, along with the orchestration, are the essential elements of the operatic poetry in act 3 of *Sapho*. It was principally the last element, orchestration, that was to bear fruit and give rise to a glorious branch of the French school, whose ramifications would reach as far as Ravel. Let us consider what this consists of for Gounod.

Beginning with Phaon's curse in the third act ("O Sapho! sois trois fois maudite!"—"O Sappho, be thou thrice accursed!"), Berlioz sees "monumental, perfect, admirable orchestration":

> Each instrument says what it should say, the whole of what it should say, and nothing but what it should say. The artistry is so complete that it disappears. One thinks of nothing but the sublimeness of the overall expression without being aware of the means the author has used. It is a broken heart beating its last; it is outraged love that breathes its final moan; it is the roar of the sea awaiting its prey; it is all the mysterious

sounds of deserted beaches, all the cruel harmonies of smiling Nature, unaware of human sorrow.[39]

The orchestra "spoke," expressing the human heart as well as it could express nature. To achieve this, the composer used figurative devices and the evocative powers of timbre, as this 1859 review of *Faust* reminds us: "Seated at her spinning wheel, Marguerite…sings as she spins. The orchestra completes the picture. A violin figure imitates the sound of the wheel. The harps accompany this figure with a mysterious harmony over which the gentle, veiled sounds of the horns spread misty hues. This is effected with enormous finesse entirely worthy of the exceptional symphonic talent of which Monsieur Gounod has already given so much evidence."[40] In his correspondence, the composer himself explained his working methods. Referring to a barcarole in act 2, scene 2, of *Polyeucte,* he wrote to his librettist, "As best I could, I have given this piece a character that signifies a person of distinction, through *melodic form,* and I have entrusted the orchestra with expressing the entire *picturesque* aspect of the scene. It therefore has an aspect of refinement and Epicurean sensuality intended to express pagan society, as well as an aspect thoroughly descriptive of nature, of the place, of stillness, of the night, etc."[41]

The adherents of the Italian school viewed this trend toward creating sound pictures and making the orchestra speak as the ruination of a lyric theater based on vocal melody. Such criticism of Gounod would gradually vanish, but in the 1880s, it was taken up again by the detractors of a composer who may be viewed as Gounod's heir in this sphere: Massenet. Raoul de Saint-Arroman faulted *Manon* (1884) for its "congestion of pictorial effects": "I have no difficulty with the abundance or the relevance of the descriptive, imitative harmonies in the third act, but the phantasmagoric instrumentation stunned me like the blaze of a lightning bolt." The entire musical interest of the death of the heroine "is concentrated in the orchestra, which is moved and which weeps far more than the spectator. I would prefer the opposite."[42]

To return to Gounod, Saint-Saëns tells us that "his great concern was to find a beautiful color on the orchestral palette; far from taking ready-made effects from the masters, he looked on his own for the tones he needed for his brush strokes in a study of timbre and in fresh combinations."[43] Gounod was a colorist who worked through subtle strokes rather than through the sharply contrasting and even violent brush work of a Meyerbeer. As Saint-Saëns said, Gounod, who "had painted, knew that it was not obligatory to spread his entire palette on the canvas, and he restored restraint—the source of apt coloration and delicate nuance—to the theater orchestra."[44] Conveying impressions, sensuality, the creation of an atmosphere, and the expression of feelings all lie within the domain of orchestral writing.

The shepherd's song in *Sapho* shows how Gounod could create a poetic moment by translating into music the characteristics of a given situation. It may have been this scene that inspired Puccini (a Francophile) to write one of his loveliest poetic passages, the opening of the third act of *Tosca*, where a shepherd boy sings, completely carefree, unaware of the despair and death that are at the heart of the drama. "The poetic and picturesque novelty," wrote Camille Bellaigue of the scene in *Sapho*, "lies in this figure of a carefree child, indifferent to the tragic fate that would take place nearby. And the folklike air of his languid musette, the sighs of the chalumeau[45] that frame it, and the persistent basso ostinato that supports it and seems to cradle it are what constitute the, so to speak, specific originality of the music itself."[46]

According to critics, Gounod's great contribution in this sphere was in expressing love through music: "Before Gounod, music spoke of it all the time, but it did not understand it, did not feel it, did not express it. Every opera in the French repertory since Lully is about love; not a single one of them lets us feel it." The music of Gounod was "genuinely imbued with love," for the composer succeeded in "arousing the idea . . . , the sensation of desire, of sensuous pleasure."[47] In his review of *Faust*, Léon Escudier recognized this suggestive power: "The duet between Marguerite and Faust is very poetic; here the composer was equal to the situation; a really delightful feeling of loving tenderness pervades this passage; everything until Marguerite's farewell is interesting. The orchestra sighs its gentle caresses, and with charming grace weds its sweet harmonies to the voices of the two lovers, full of emotion."[48] Many columnists agreed with this view. Joseph d'Ortigue described Marguerite's discovery of love thus:

> Marguerite enters her chamber, appears at the window, upon which the moonlight falls, and there, deeply inhaling the perfume of the flowers, she speaks in dulcet melody of the first transports of this unknown feeling that is causing her very being to tremble. And all this seduction, all this elation, all the throbbing and fluttering of a virginal heart are expressed in veiled tones, in timid notes, in delicate nuances, in the mellow outlines of that enchanted orchestration. The author of such a scene is not merely a great musician; he is also a great poet.[49]

Between the extremes of comic and tragic, of slightness and grandiose pathos, Gounod was able to cast a spectrum of feelings, emotions, and poetic forms that made it possible to express the experiences, thoughts, and turmoil of the characters with greater truthfulness. Nadir in *Les Pêcheurs de perles*, a dreamy hero with delicate feelings, was the direct beneficiary of this. Reynaldo Hahn explained that Gounod brought naturalness to French music: "Until him, operatic characters could express themselves only with grandiloquence and affectation; *opéra-comique* characters were nothing but bluster or artificial joviality. With Gounod, they sing as one speaks, they say what they have to say—more prettily than in real life because their speech is notated in music and because a subtle lyricism elevates them. But all conventional artifice has disappeared from their language."[50]

Curiously, if we go strictly by appearances, the operatic poetry that Gounod developed was linked to the advance of the nineteenth-century realist aesthetic. Saint-Saëns noted:

> He set his sights high, but, as with everything to do with realism, his constant concern for expressiveness inevitably brought him back to earth from time to time. This realism itself opened a fertile and absolutely new musical path. For the first time, the depiction of the union of hearts and souls was joined by that of the communion of the flesh, the perfume of unknotted tresses, the exhilaration of breathing in the fragrance of spring. I have seen chaste and highly discerning minds take fright at these innovations and accuse Gounod of having given in the theater a debased, materialistic view of love. If only others were so fortunate as to merit such a rebuke![51]

Once again, Massenet followed that path and aroused the same kinds of reaction. In 1884, Raoul de Saint-Arroman wrote of the amorous atmosphere of *Manon* in terms that might have been employed by certain critics of *Faust:* "How the lovers adore each other, and how the composer's music underscores the beating of their hearts! Is the orchestral sketch that accompanies their romantic banter not shimmering? And how those light harmonies reflect the exquisite sweetness of the letter—'On l'appelle Manon'—and support Des Grieux's fervent reply."[52] And in 1889 Massenet broke new ground with the love scene between Esclarmonde and Roland. Camille Bellaigue wrote: "It was proper to conceal from view the passion relating to the frenzy of Esclarmonde and her lover [in act 2]. Through a remarkably expressive orchestral peroration, we understand what we do not see. I do not think there has ever been so accurate, so detailed a sonic description of the physical manifestations of human love. With its sounds, the orchestra challenges decency; M. Massenet's instrumentation was already luxuriant—now it is luxurious."[53]

### DISCOVERING NEW POETIC VISTAS

The color, mystery, and atmosphere that Reynaldo Hahn found in Gounod are present in most of the major scores of the second half of the nineteenth century. Hahn claimed, with some exaggeration, that no comparable music existed by composers before Gounod:

> The evocative element...had completely disappeared from dramatic music. For some time there had been no question of distinctive color or descriptive poetry in opera. Countries and locales no longer existed for the composer. In *La Muette de Portici*, Auber had made a few felicitous efforts at being evocative, but then decisively abandoned all such nonsense as unworthy of a sensible middle-class gentleman dwelling on the rue Le Peletier. Rossini passed for a great artist because he inserted a *ranz des vaches* in *Guillaume Tell* to remind us that we were in Switzerland....As for Meyerbeer, no matter what the time and place of the action were, he irrevocably adopted a sort of all-purpose Dufayel[54] style. With *Sapho*, Gounod put the poetry back into music.[55]

Hahn was wrong to underrate Meyerbeer and Rossini like this. To be sure, Meyerbeer used the orchestra principally to spectacular ends, in line with his preference in *grand opéra* for effect and theatricality over subtle poetry or the creation of delicate atmospherics. But he discovered new sounds and served as a model for many composers in the sphere of orchestration. Berlioz cited him on many occasions in his treatise, and Liszt, writing of the premiere of *Les Huguenots,* did not fail to emphasize the power of his imagination: "The instrumentation...is if possible even more skillful [than that of *Robert le Diable*], and the orchestral effects are so cleverly combined and diversified that we have never attended a performance of *Les Huguenots* without fresh feelings of surprise and admiration for the artistry of a master who had the ability to tint the rich fabric of his musical poem with a thousand nuances, so delicate that they are barely discernible."[56]

As for Rossini, mid-nineteenth-century musicians never forgot act 2 of his *Guillaume Tell* (1859),[57] which was even performed on its own. The horn calls' "wild harmony" of which the hunters sing gives way to the songs of the shepherds ("Au sein de l'onde qui rayonne") heard from afar in the mountains in *mezza voce* accompanied by the harp. The description of the day's end transforms the poetry of the open air and of nature into a nocturnal poetry. With the repeated text "Voici la nuit"—"Night approaches," Rossini links four root-position common chords (C, B, A, and G in the basses), in long note values, separated by rests; this produces a sense of strangeness that the listener associates with the text and with the scenery depicting a deep valley being engulfed by the night: "The stage represents the Rütli mountains, looking out over the lake of the Waldstätte or the Four Cantons. Upon the horizon can be seen the summit of the Schwitz mountains; below is the village of Brunnen. Dense pines standing on either side of the stage add to the solitude." The sounds of the harp fade, mingling with the peal of the village bells, and yield to the strings accompanying the words of a hunter. Then, distant horn calls extend the sonic space, in which snatches of the hunters' voices are heard. Also in the ensuing *romance* for Mathilde, "Sombre forêt, désert triste et sauvage," Berlioz found,

> in addition to the enormous worth of the melody and the harmony,... a melancholy accompaniment in the violas and first violins, as well as a pianissimo effect in the timpani at the beginning of each stanza that keenly sharpens the listener's attention. You think you are hearing one of those noises whose cause is unknown and which you notice at the quietest times deep in the forest; one of those vague murmurings, those sighs of nature, that intensify the impression of silence and isolation. This is poetry; this is music; this is beautiful, noble, pure art.[58]

In an 1835 article, Berlioz reaffirmed the importance of Meyerbeer and Rossini, saying that "before the appearance of *Robert le Diable* and of the second act of *Guillaume Tell*, it would have been madness to expect the score of *Don Giovanni* to achieve such a magnificent success at the Opéra. The audience's sensitivity had been numbed; it was revived thanks to the positive influence of those two models on the art of disbursing treasures of instrumentation."[59]

But even before those two works, a foreign opera had managed to arouse sensitivity to unprecedented expressive forms. The 1824 production of Weber's *Der Freischütz* on a French stage was a major event in the discovery of new poetic vistas for opera—even though that work had been mutilated; even though the Parisian public took its entertainment primarily from the deviltry and the opera's other eccentricities. "However much it had been interfered with," recalled Berlioz in his *Mémoires*, "the score emitted a wild perfume whose delicious freshness intoxicated me. I admit to having grown somewhat tired of the solemn mien of the tragic Muse, and the quick, sometimes charmingly sudden, movements of the wood nymph, her dreamy attitudes, her naive and virginal passion, her chaste smile, her melancholy flooded me with a torrent of hitherto unknown sensations."[60]

Weber's opera demonstrated how to create a landscape and poetic emotions of great intensity through musical language and the sonic spell of the orchestra. "The listener misses nothing," wrote Berlioz about Agathe's scene and aria in act 2, "of the orchestra's sighing during the prayer of the young virgin awaiting her betrothed....Never before has any German, Italian, or French master given voice successively within a single scene to prayer, melancholy, anxiety, meditation, the slumber of nature, the silent eloquence of night, the harmonious mystery of the starry skies, the torment of waiting, hope, half-certainty, joy, ecstasy, emotional transport, and delirious love!"[61] The act 2 finale—where the magic bullets are cast—marked a high point in achieving a fantastic style in music, drawing on the deepest sources of German romanticism. Berlioz thoroughly analyzed this and then integrated it into some of his finest passages,[62] as other French composers too would gradually come to do.

## WEBER, THE FANTASTIC STYLE, AND FRENCH ADHERENTS

Weber conceived the Wolf's Glen scene[63] by bringing together the whole range of scenic and musical elements to create a grippingly intense atmosphere and emotional level. Before they were coordinated by musical form, all the elements used to build this great edifice had an extramusical basis: that of the plan reflected in the stage production and in the libretto. Through the scenery, spectators found themselves in a highly evocative picture typical of German romanticism: pine forest, high mountains, waterfall, full moon, and withered tree, all brought to life by the storm and the mysterious presence of nocturnal birds, and then by a series of apparitions. The human voice—sung or spoken, murmured or shouted—melds with descriptive orchestral passages; choral utterance evokes invisible spirits; the protagonists express them in articulate language, and also in mime.

Apart from making use of chromatic movement and diminished seventh chords, Weber developed his fantastic style by exploiting the suggestive power of the orchestra and by employing all the resources of the language of music. The finale begins with a calm expanse of sound generated by the pianissimo rustle of the first and second violins and the violas, tremolando (restricted to a medium-low register and colored first by the clarinets, then by the bassoons). From this expanse comes the droning utterance of the chorus, which becomes an inhuman cry magnified by woodwinds and horns, with a fortissimo octave leap. The finale is driven by contrasts of all kinds: calm metric writing versus heavily stressed rhythms; harmony versus melody; monotone versus gushing melodic figures; chromatic melismas versus wide leaps; quiet versus booming sounds; repetition versus fleeting motifs; and contrasts in timbre, register, and dynamics.

The introductory section concludes with a sustained diminished seventh in the oboes, first and second clarinets in low register, violins and violas, punctuated by the timpani doubled by pizzicato low strings. The ensuing section (agitato) brings with it a fresh battery of mainly rhythmic effects. Over an ostinato triplet figure that recalls the infernal ride of Schubert's *Erlkönig,* a melody begins in the first violins, with disjointed rhythms and interrupted by the spoken voice of Samiel cloaked in the diminished seventh motif that concluded the preceding section. This second section closes with a chromatic line in the strings (violins and violas) and flutes, fortissimo.

After several transitional measures, the third section (allegro) contrasts three melodic measures in the strings, on a motif with off-beat and syncopated rhythms, with two measures of crescendo chordal writing for the woodwinds. These techniques are increasingly used and combined in this finale, sometimes yielding breaking waves of sixteenth notes or halting on sustained tremolos. When at last the time comes for casting the magic bullets, Caspar's voice is supported simply by delicate sonic strands: the resonant, cavernous sounds of two flutes playing in low register, then the strings punctuated by the timpani-pizzicato combination we have already heard. The texture grows more intense, blending an increasing number of motifs; it changes with the casting of each bullet, ending with a tutti (presto) on the prominent theme first heard in the overture.

The score is impregnated by emotional turmoil, the frenzy of contrasts, Max's anguish, the unreal nature of the locales, and the supernatural atmosphere, all of which heighten its expressive power. From this time on,[64] infernal or fantastic scenes would become part of the typology of the situations and musical styles used by French composers. *Robert le Diable* (1831), *Faust* (1859), *Mireille* (1864), *Hamlet* (1868), and other works were inspired by *Der Freischütz* either in a general way or in detail. Even Auber wrote in a fantastic style, in the act 2 *couplets* for the soothsayer in *Gustave III* (1833) and in his musical depiction of the "dreadful place" in act 3.

Steeped in German culture and possessing a keen sense of the spectacular, Meyerbeer understood all the effects he could draw from this style. In his first *grand opéra*, he found a dramatic framework that allowed for many scenes in which it would cause wonderment. "Imitation of reality is prominent in *Robert;* here is the weak and passionate man drawn toward good and toward evil by two opposing influences; Robert is Max-Faust; Bertram is Gaspard of *Le Chasseur noir* or Goethe's Mephistopheles set to music by Spohr," a columnist wrote in *Le Français.*[65]

*Le Courrier de l'Europe* admired the instrumental combinations in *Robert le Diable* and noted that "not only the expression of all emotions, but also all the noises of nature and the voices of spirits and genies, are expressed by this fantastic orchestra."[66] In the act 3 *Valse infernale* (no. 10), Bertram hears the Satanic crew's bursts of infernal joy. "These are raucous shouts, hoarse and shrieking cries; these are footsteps and leaps that are as heavy as a stone statue's dance; this is a mixture of death rattles and madmen's cackling; all is confused, mixed into a long hullabaloo that seems to pass with the speed of lightning and that leaves you chilled, dumbfounded, and nearly stupefied with astonishment—to the point where you question whether you ever heard it."[67] The off-stage chorus is accompanied by a small orchestra consisting of cymbals, triangle, piccolo, four trumpets, four horns, three trombones, and an ophicleide. There is direct imitation and reinterpretation of several elements from Weber's score: chords in the brasses punctuated by the cymbals; "fireworks" in the piccolo; disjointed dotted rhythms; tremolos; and more. "In this infernal sabbath," wrote Castil-Blaze in a description that is more poetically evocative than strictly accurate vis-à-vis the orchestration, "the instruments swirl round in full voice, the reeds pipe in their high register..., and all the while one hears the roar of the timpani, the cymbals and the triangle, the shrill cry of the oboes and the piccolo, and the moan of the chalumeau. Then, all the whirlwinds of the cavern attack a massive G, and the orchestra lays harrowing chords over these cries from Hell."[68]

It was the finale of act 3 (no. 15) that had the greatest impact in this sphere. (Its components will be identified when we discuss the emotional aesthetic of *grand opéra*.) Other works already cited also demonstrate the spread of the fantastic style through French scores. First, there is the well-known church scene from *Faust,* in which, by combining it with formulas associated with the religious style, Gounod manipulates the vocabulary we have just identified: tremolo, chromatic elements, disjointed rhythms, diminished sevenths, monotone declamation, and repetitive figures and contrasts of various kinds—the most striking being the juxtaposition of the religious style with organ, sometimes combined with a chorus of the faithful, and the dramatic fantastic writing that depicts Marguerite's anguish and the presence of evil, as embodied in the chorus of demons and in the character of Méphistophélès. In the opening measures of the Val d'Enfer scene in *Mireille,* the composer sketches a scene influenced by the same techniques, with flashing figures in the strings and flutes, tremolos, and rhythmic woodwind playing. But Weber's influence seems less direct; what we hear are details imitating Berlioz or the Mendelssohn of *A Midsummer Night's Dream*. With the character of the ferryman in the scene set at the bridge at Trinquetaille, the score contains another "fantastic sonic image," this one based on the scene with the Commendatore in Mozart's *Don Giovanni*, of which Gounod was a fervent admirer. The same original, considerably modified, probably served as a model for Lalo in composing the end of act 2 of *Le Roi d'Ys* (1888). There, Karnac and Margaret are terrified by the apparition of Saint Corentin (bass), who calls on them to repent. His words and his "sonic envelope"—especially on the words "Prince sans diadème, / Chef sans armée, / Avare sans trésor"—"Prince without a diadem, / General without an army, / Miser without a treasure"—consistently recall the declamation of the Commendatore, whose influence is to be heard in many operas. But this very French scene is quite different from its Mozartian model; it makes greater use of theatrical effects, with its organ and its celestial chorus of soprano and contralto voices from on high. Well before then, Hérold had composed a work, *Zampa* (1831), that directly imitated *Don Giovanni* both in its libretto and in its score. This is exemplified by the final scene in which the statue of Alice draws Zampa into the flames ("O Dieu cette main glacée"—"Oh, God, that icy hand"). Chromatic scales, brass sonorities including trombones, and drum and timpani rolls contribute their own effects, yet this is far from the horror of Don Giovanni condemned to Hell, and from the genuine existential catastrophe painted by Mozart.

Ambroise Thomas's *Hamlet* provides a final example of this dark poetry, and one of the most convincing, both dramatically and musically. At the first performance, the esplanade scene (act 1, scene 2) made a great impression on Ernest Reyer, who wrote, "Loving phrases and expressions of terror; imitative effects in the orchestra; combinations of timbres; harmonic progressions; poignant melody and plaintive lament: all of this is grippingly real and of undoubted originality.... Clearly it was on his own palette that M. Ambroise Thomas found these dark colors, these fantastic hues, these dissimilarities and these contrasts."[69] Paul Bernard used similar language to describe his own feelings: "The mixed rhythms, the coupling of timbres, the use of new instruments, the poetry of the orchestra: this becomes a whole world in his skillful hands."[70] The orchestra speaks, continued Bernard, "chanting on a single note, and on this lingering note follow a series of magnificent and striking orchestral effects. Hear the English horn and the clarinet, which make us think of the depths of the tomb; hear the flickering thirds in the muted violins heralding the dawn that is about to break; hear the distant fanfares and the cannon that accompany the festivities in the palace." Nestor Roqueplan stressed the dominant emotion, "a feeling of the fantastic that has rarely been encountered since the death of Weber."[71]

Horatio's disquiet is depicted in a chromatic motif, and his description of the ghost is accompanied by a figure that moves between the clarinets and the flute, joined by the bassoon, sustained by a tremolo in the strings on Hamlet's words, "O prodige terrible! O sinistre présage!"—"O dreadful wonder! O evil omen!" Also present is the characteristic sound of low flutes combined with tremolos or rapid figures in the strings. Hamlet sings, "Ici, l'ombre et le deuil"—"Here is shadow and mourning" over repeated notes in the low violins, while midnight strikes with a combination of horn and bell. When he encounters the ghost, the wretched hero is enveloped by a breathless motif that recalls the casting of the magic bullets in *Der Freischütz*, as do the silent gestures of his father's spirit. When the ghost speaks, he declaims on a monotone D simply accompanied by a motif in long note values whose unreal sonority results from the pairing of English horn and baritone saxophone.

## SPECIFIC MUSICAL TECHNIQUES FOR EXPRESSIVE ENDS AND FOR DEPICTING SITUATIONS

Musical figures are not mere "witticisms in music" that make an impression on the listener, like the rhythmic horn motif in the lovely aria "Du pouls le fréquent battement"—"The rapid beat of the pulse" from Hérold's *Le Muletier* (1823)—of which Gounod may have been thinking when he wrote the act 2 sextet (no. 8) in *Le Médecin malgré lui* (1858), in which Sganarelle is seen and heard taking the pulse of Géronte's daughter. They can constitute a perfect musical trompe l'oeil. In no. 9 of act 2 of *Le Prophète,* Meyerbeer creates an "absolutely new effect with the cross-rhythms of two bassoons imitating hurried footsteps and the galloping of horses over a moderato march tempo in the clarinets, horns, violins, violas, and basses. This effect depicts the hasty flight of Berthe and the running of the soldiers who are following her; it creates a real illusion."[72] Indeed, figures such as those we have seen in Gounod, when combined with typical, sometimes very long-standing, compositional techniques and with effects of harmony and modulation, can result in the sonic equivalents of emotions and sensations, represent images, and depict a wide variety of situations. A few examples from this repertory will serve as illustrations.

Counterpoint—traditionally proscribed because it was viewed as complicated and heavy—was associated with seriousness and obscurity. When

Gaveston calls for the law to be read out in the act 2 finale of *La Dame blanche*, Boieldieu expresses the gravity of this moment in a few measures of imitative orchestral writing. At the beginning of *Faust*, Gounod wove a tight musical fabric to evoke the hero's somber meditation. Similarly, he indicated the austerity of Frère Laurent's monastic cell (*Roméo et Juliette*, act 3, no. 10) by means of a fugal introduction. Meyerbeer used counterpoint as a technique of coloration. To sketch the musical framework of the action of *Les Huguenots*, he introduced the drama with the technique of chorale variation, evoking the distant past and, combined with the Lutheran chorale "Ein feste Burg ist unser Gott" and with orchestration that imitated the sound of the organ, lending what contemporary commentators called a "Protestant color" to his musical picture.

With *Samson et Dalila*—originally conceived as an oratorio—Saint-Saëns saw in its biblical subject an opportunity to use choral polyphony and to show off his enormous compositional mastery; he was so skillful at integrating choral writing with dramatic musical forms that he virtually created a new genre, the choral opera. The score is thus marked by a breadth of style unusual among the French, and by uncommon density of writing. These were undoubtedly among the reasons for the difficulty of securing a Paris premiere, which took place—more than a decade after the first German performance in 1877—at the Théâtre Eden on October 31, 1890; the Opéra premiere took place only on November 23, 1892. The Handelian inspiration of the choral sections, blended with completely assimilated Wagnerian elements, has often been noted. Johann Sebastian Bach is another source, especially of the vast choral prelude that constitutes the first scene. The lamentations of the Jews rise out of the depths of the orchestra, which over a tonic pedal bolstered by sforzandos plays a motif in the manner of Bach's preludes. Is this not the structural principle of the celebrated opening chorus of the *Saint Matthew Passion*? The grief-filled text "Kommt, ihr Töchter, helf mir klagen"—"Come daughters, share my mourning" justifies the parallel with the entreaty "Dieu d'Israël! écoute la prière/De tes enfants t'implorant à genoux"—"God of Israel, hear the prayer/Of thy children beseeching thee on their knees." The theme of the dejection of Israel ("Un jour, de nous tu détournas ta face"—"Once, thou turned thy face from us"), stated by the women, then taken up by the full chorus ("Nous avons vu nos cités renversées"—"We have seen our cities destroyed"), is treated in a fugato, which underscores the importance of contrapuntal language in this work.

Any style associated with church music or with an ancient musical language made it possible to add both color and meaning to the score. Vocal polyphony with suspensions (see also the chorus "Brahma, divin Brahma" in act 3 of *Les Pêcheurs de perles*) and either hieratic or archaically simple rhythms invariably figure in collective prayers, along with refined neo-Gregorian inflections or monotone declamation in individual or indeed in choral prayers. The organ was quickly brought into operatic scoring to add its inimitable color to religious ceremonies. As the contemporary press noted, it made a novel effect in act 5 of *Robert le Diable:* "The struggle in Robert's heart between Bertram and his own religious feelings, reawakened by the sound of the organ, ecclesiastical chanting, and the memory of his mother, are rendered with a poignant power that is beyond praise."[73]

Modal writing—as imagined in the nineteenth century in a kind of fantasy re-creation of a medieval or Renaissance language—was also part of this stylistic apparatus, whose effectiveness was enhanced by its linkage to a clearly defined space. This was no genuine reproduction of an older technique; it was an allusion by which the composer aimed at creating the effect of a style while using his own musical language. That was Grétry's explanation: toward the end of the eighteenth century, in his *Richard Coeur de Lion* (1784), having been unable to find period music for the melody played by Blondel, which is repeated several times, he said that he had written the *romance* "Une fièvre brûlante" in "the old style."

In its own dramatic context, Berlioz likened the men's chorus "C'est une croix qui de l'enfer nous garde" from Gounod's *Faust* (act 2, no. 5) to a religious piece "whose theme opportunely and aptly takes the form of a chorale." The modification of the major and minor scales, which gives them the appearance of ecclesiastical modes, could add an antique air to *chansons, ballades,* and laments. That is certainly the case of the "Chanson du roi de Thulé" sung by Marguerite, "written in the tones of plainchant…, which give it a well justified Gothic cast."[74] Lowering the leading tones in minor and exploiting the modal degrees (III and VI) of the key are ever-effective recipes for creating a modal sound; there are good examples in *Les Pêcheurs de perles:* Nadir's *romance* (discussed below) and the duet for Nadir and Zurga. This technique seems to have spanned the entire second half of the nineteenth century, culminating in Mélisande's *chanson* in act 3, scene 1, of Debussy's *Pelléas et Mélisande* (1902). In the midst of all the emotional turmoil, the pure a cappella melodic line in aeolian (A) mode transposed to B projects the heroine into timelessness—or, more precisely, back into the idealized past of childhood.

Certain vocal styles inherited from the typology of the eighteenth century could help depict a character's psychological state. In act 3 of *La Dame blanche,* Boieldieu differentiates the contrasting emotions in the duet (no.

13) by using an opera seria style (broad declamation and a wide range and intervals) for Anna ("O souffrance cruelle!"—"O cruel torment!") and an opera buffa style (lively little eighth-note motifs with a narrow range) for Marguerite ("Quelle bonne nouvelle!"—"What good news!"). When Gounod wished to depict Marguerite's preening in *Faust*, he used a coloratura aria (the Jewel Song), while to express her withdrawal, he wrote a sort of syllabic *romance* in her spinning scene. Old-fashioned dramatic recitative, almost like that of Rameau, was seen as apt for the suffering and grandeur of Zurga, chief of the pearl fishers, at the beginning of act 3 of *Les Pêcheurs de perles*. Other such examples abound. Early in the 1810s, Nicolò sought to use such musical characterization. In *Cendrillon* (1810), the frivolity of the two vain sisters was evoked with a melismatic melodic style ("Ma soeur le bal sera charmant"—"Sister, the ball will be delightful"), while the simple and natural emotions of Cendrillon and Alidor are rendered in syllabic declamation ("pauvre vielliard il est transi"—"the poor old man is chilled"). Along the same lines, the heroine's song in popular style, "Il était un p'tit homme"—"Once there was a little man," is associated with her natural character.

Nearly eighty years later, Lalo was still using the same principle in *Le Roi d'Ys* (1888), but now taking advantage of far greater stylistic potential and of the possibilities afforded by a more sophisticated tonal language. He was able to create sudden changes to heighten the dramatic and psychological contrasts. In act 1, the chorus in popular style, "Venez, l'heure presse!"—"Come, time is wasting!" which cheers the coming marriage of Margared, is contrasted with that character's gloomy thoughts ("Un époux détesté va m'attendre à l'autel"—"A hated husband will be awaiting me at the altar"), which are conveyed in a halting declamatory style and an abrupt change in orchestral texture. In act 2, scene 2, as described by Joël-Marie Fauquet, the effervescence of the chorus celebrating Mylio's victory "is quickly clouded by the gloomy atmosphere relating to Karnac's defeat. The voice of the vanquished emerges from a harmonic substrate marked by unstable and chromatic modulations given a dark color by the low registers of the orchestra."[75]

The palette of the poet-musician included funeral marches, military music, popular styles (with faux-bourdon, pedals, and rustic woodwind sounds), and descriptive scenes, such as storms. The composer also made use of the varied resources of his harmonic language to expressive and dramatic ends. Consistent tonality and consonance signified dramatic stability, while the juxtaposition of different keys, successive modulations, and dissonance indicated trouble and disorder.[76] The introduction of chromaticism went hand in hand with the advent of continuous music drama. As traditional forms broke down, consonance and strong tonal linkages also gave way. But few French musicians took that path, as we see in the works of the most popular composer of the late nineteenth and early twentieth centuries, Jules Massenet. Generally speaking, musical languages, styles, and forms were subsumed into the idea of drama, expression, and coloration. While the possibilities of the language increased in the course of the nineteenth century in terms of such elements as chromaticism, dissonance, and modulation, these were very often viewed merely as enriching the expressive palette, which, however, continued to contain the simpler colors of the first half of the century. Hence, many scores of the period are marred by unfortunate disparities in their language. This may be seen in Saint-Saëns's *Déjanire*, originally composed in 1898 as theater music for the arena at Béziers and recast as an opera in 1911. Saint-Saëns made use of the modal degrees of the key and wrote entire passages in clearly defined modes—basically dorian (D) and aeolian (A)—in response to the uncluttered antique style and the peacefulness of a number of the work's scenes. On the other hand, the composer employed a complex, extremely dissonant, and explicitly chromatic tonal language, using harmonies of the seventh and the ninth and series of modulations, to signify agitation and to express the forces that motivated the characters. At times, certain phrases that are conventional in declamation and language recall the old *recitativo secco* of Mozart.

## FROM STYLISTIC COLORATION TO NEOCLASSICISM

The increasingly precise re-creation of antique styles, involving the use of direct quotations, resulted from an aesthetic of eclecticism that was seen also in other arts and that in its architectural manifestation belatedly gave rise to the Palais Garnier itself. French composers of the second half of the nineteenth century studied the music of past centuries and various contemporary styles as elements[77] that could contribute to the coloration (in a very broad sense) of the opera and to conveying the drama—sometimes with a certain ironic distance. In a frequently quoted interview with *Le Figaro* at the time of the premiere of *Manon* in 1884, Massenet said: "Every [scene] has its own tonality and its own atmosphere. Each has the exact color of the locale it represents at its exact time period. As for the human, impassioned, and timelessly modern note, this is provided by Manon and Des Grieux. And this intentional contrast between the feelings of time and place and human feelings is among the effects on which I feel most able to rely."[78] The difficulty lies in retaining a sense of continuity and unity of language throughout the work. Recurring motifs have a role in achieving this.

In *Le Médecin malgré lui*, Gounod achieved a "seventeenth-century coloration" by using several period styles, in refurbished form. In the over-ture, the march that closes act 2—drawn in fact from Gounod's own 1851 arrangement of Lully's theater music for *Le Bourgeois gentilhomme*—captures the quality of a Grand Siècle style, with its harmonic pomp. On the other hand, Léandre's serenade performed at the beginning of act 2, mandolin in hand ("Est-on sage dans le bel âge"), re-creates the finesse of the gallantry of a classical period in which the seventeenth and eighteenth centuries are muddled together. It is delicately accompanied by pizzicato strings, and traces an elegant melodic curve lightly adorned with orna-ments. In 1858, what Léon Durocher heard was a melody full of grace and tenderness "written in Lully's finest style" to an accompaniment that had "far more elegance than Lully would have been able to give it."[79] For, as Durocher went on to note, Gounod "took from the seventeenth century only what he needed to take." The serenade had no vital dramatic function, any more than did the *fabliau* sung by the same character (act 2, no. 9 *bis*);[80] indeed, it is somewhat inopportune in terms of the unfolding of the plot. Its function is quite different: it is poetic or coloristic.

The Cours-la-Reine scene in act 3 of *Manon* is at the apex of this genre; it is constructed on the basis of a pastiche of eighteenth-century dance music.[81] The *couplets* of the gavotte added for the London premiere even reused a melody, "Sérénade de Molière" (1880), that Massenet had written on the basis of an eighteenth-century theme and had subtitled "Musique du temps" (Music of the period). In the final version, the minuet that is played off-stage during Manon's dialogue with the Comte Des Grieux was inserted at the beginning of the Cours-la-Reine scene with the title "Entracte-Menuet," in place of the original prelude.[82] The arrival of the ballet company from the Opéra is announced musically in a few measures that imitate the double-dotted French overture style of the old *tragédies en musique.* This is especially effective because it is part of an overall concep-tion that aims at reproducing an epoch, in a stylized fashion, both in the score and in the staging. The critic Moreno liked both the "ingenious restoration of an old ballet" and Carvalho's 1884 production, a "complete restoration of the period," which he dubbed a "mise-en-scène *à la* Viollet-le-Duc."[83] Only the previous year, Parisians had witnessed the production of Saint-Saëns's *Henry VIII* (1883), another work that reflected a keen in-terest in achieving local color in both music and decor.

Moreover, the spread of antique styles as re-created by nineteenth-century composers opened the way for genuine neoclassicism. In that connection, it is well to recall the first meaning of that term: a revival of classicism (or, more generally, of any past style) in a renewed form. Music of the past was no longer one among many ingredients in the composition of an opera; it had become a model for entire works. Yet Massenet—who in some of his scores gave great attention to "period color," the equivalent of local color, by which a time rather than a place was depicted—remained devoted to expressive diversity in style and language and thus would sometimes break the relationship he had established between his score and a past era. In *Manon,* as Gérard Condé has noted, "the main motivation of the drama is thus firmly established in the music itself, depending on whether it sounds true or false, modern or antique, free or formal, sincere or artificial."[84]

This movement of a return to the past, which also inspired Fauré and Debussy, was accompanied by revivals of late-eighteenth-century works such as those of Grétry, Gluck, and Mozart, and by more general study of old music, both sacred and secular. Renaissance music, Gregorian chant, and the works of Rameau (which Saint-Saëns edited) were studied, performed, and even published. When Nicolò's *Cendrillon* was revived at the Opéra-Comique in 1877, "the great hit of the evening was the archaic ballet inserted into the score,"[85] arranged by Mlle Marquet using numbers chosen by Théodore de Lajarte, who headed the Opéra's music library between 1873 and 1890. Entitled the "Ballet des Saisons," this *intermède* borrowed its music from Lully, Henry Desmarest, Charles Louis Mion, and André Cardinal Destouches—composers far earlier than Nicolò. Too often, things nearer in time resembled familiar things and were thus seen as less interesting: "One must absolutely set aside works from the beginning of this century and go a little further back," concluded Victor Wilder, "if one wants to give us interesting surprises and to acquaint us with scores whose style will seem to us the less outmoded the more sharply it contrasts with our own."[86]

This revision of *Cendrillon,* which was originally composed in 1810, belongs to three periods. The audiences of the late nineteenth century were rediscovering a score from the beginning of the century, in which music from the period we now call the Baroque had been included with a view to creating, after the event, "period color" for a plot modeled on a fairy tale out of the *Contes de ma mère l'oye* of Charles Perrault (1628–1703).

## POETIC ATMOSPHERES

In an opera, some themes are expressed largely through the libretto and the staging—through lighting effects and scenery, for instance—while others occupy a more important place in the work, owing more to the atmosphere created by the composer than to the evocative nature of the text.

Through evocative strokes, impressionistic choral writing could make an original contribution to the creation of a poetic atmosphere. At the end of Léïla's act 1 aria (no. 5b), the men's chorus, humming, accompanies the short dialogue between Nadir and Léïla, then provides a sonic backdrop for the heroine's vocalises. The chorus's placement off-stage makes for a sense of space and creates an impression of open air. Paul Scudo maintained that the first use of humming was in 1847, citing a barcarole for two voices in the first act of Auber's *Haydée* (1847), which was accompanied by humming in the chorus, a "curious effect that has been much imitated since then" and that much later would be used by composers such as Debussy.[87]

At the beginning of the act 1 finale, just before Léïla's aria, it falls again to the chorus to set a poetic atmosphere with the two lines "Le ciel est bleu / La mer est immobile et claire"—"The sky is blue / The sea is still and limpid." A simple a cappella motif sung off-stage is echoed in the woodwinds and the horn, on an initially unchanging tonic chord; the ensuing harmonic motion thus stands out all the more. Over this, the harp traces an arpeggio, like an utterance from the vast reaches of the sea.

To create a special atmosphere for the prologue of *Les Troyens à Carthage*, Berlioz had a spoken voice summarize the first part of his operatic epic over off-stage music. This sonic veil in the background of the scene evokes the past to perfection. This might have been inspired by the overture to *Dinorah, ou le Pardon de Ploërmel* (1859), which Berlioz held in high regard.[88] There, Meyerbeer had "devised a way to recount...the whole of the scene that precedes the action of the piece: the religious march of the betrothed couple going to the altar with their friends; the canticle they sing; the storm that scatters the procession and brings devastation and fire to the township; and finally the madness of Dinorah running after her goat."[89] On-stage voices from behind the closed curtain are part of this true descriptive symphony. One columnist wrote, "There should be a double curtain so that the sound of the chorus will seem very far away and very weakened."[90] The wings were but another dramatic tool enabling the composer, by manipulating space and time and taking advantage of their acoustic effects, to create a suitable framework for poetic evocation. The beginning of no. 6 in act 2 of *Les Pêcheurs de perles* bears this out: the depths of night, the starry sky, the ruins of a temple, and Léïla's isolation create an initial impression that the off-stage chorus ("L'ombre descend des cieux"—"Shadow descends from the heavens") intensifies.

In large part, Cormon's and Carré's libretto is a nocturnal drama. Night exercises its charms through poetic evocation, but it is not the subject of any descriptive musical passages, apart from the chorus we have just cited, which is set at the beginning of the second act when the pearl fishers sing verses describing the twilight: "La nuit ouvre ses voiles, / Et les blanches étoiles / Se baignent dans l'azur des flots silencieux!"—"Night spreads its sails / And the pale stars / Bathe in the blue of the silent waves." Ambroise Thomas and his librettists Barbier and Carré reproduced the same circumstances at the beginning of act 3 of *Mignon,* with an unaccompanied off-stage chorus, introduced by a harp prelude, singing lines cut from the same cloth.

The mystery of the night, its unfathomable depths, and the play of the lights that illuminate it could be frightening. The lightning and the ensuing fire stand out violently against the darkness. The calm night with its star-spangled sky provides a peaceful setting for the work of the pearl fishers. The darkness seems to isolate each individual and inspire internal monologue. Night is conducive to secrecy and fosters clandestine acts. It is a starry setting for love before shrouding the drama in its sinister veil.

Berlioz—too often viewed solely as a composer of great symphonic frescos—was at the apex of his artistry as a poet-musician in poetic night-time scenes. He gave form to the cosmic shiver of Orpheus's lyre abandoned in the countryside and emitting a "vestige of harmony" mingled with the distant echoes of a happy song interspersed with silences (*Lélio,* no. 5, "La Harpe éolienne," drawn from the cantata *La Mort d'Orphée*). And at the heart of his dramas, he depicted the transient fusion of the night with feelings of poetic fulfillment or of love, sometimes tinged with melancholy: in the recitative and septet of *Les Troyens* (no. 36, "Nuit splendide et charmante!"), in the duet from the same work (no. 39, "Nuit d'ivresse et d'extase infinie"), and in the inspired duet from *Béatrice et Bénédict,* set at night (no. 8, "Nuit paisible et sereine").

Among the multitude of operatic scenes that are centered around the creation of a poetic atmosphere, the Claire de Lune in act 1 of Massenet's *Werther*—whose central motif is recalled in the final scene, when Charlotte confesses the love she had felt from the very day she had met Werther ("Oui...du jour même où tu parus devant mes yeux"—"Yes...from the very day you appeared before me")—has become particularly famous, clearly due to the simplicity of the melodic raw material,[91] which, repeated and developed, pervades the memory of the listener, and to its superb orchestral treatment, which adorns it with delicate nuances. That musical unit, which is enhanced by textural contrasts, tightly unifies this touching depiction of the love of Werther and Charlotte. This scene is as much criticized as admired; it combines the very qualities (evocative power, expressive orchestration, and structural clarity) and defects (mawkishness and a paucity of material) that are associated with French music. But if you immerse yourself in the scenery, listen to the flickering light in the orchestration and surrender yourself to the sentimental tone that is so apt for these two characters, who are hardly more than children, you cannot but acknowledge that this scene is a success. Let us now try to identify some of its components.

"The moon gradually illuminates the house."[92] Over a dominant (C) pedal in the cellos, the first violins play the motif of the ball, which is now but a fading memory, played "as softly and lightly as possible—*sul tasto*," interrupted by a motif with a steady rhythm in the harp; this will soon turn into the moonlight motif itself, as though the light were gradually becoming steadier. "Slow, very calm and contemplative," this eight-measure motif has a classical melodic structure, with a dominant cadence at the end of the antecedent period and a perfect cadence at the end of the consequent period. The harmonies are extremely simple, with a "tonal pallor" at the beginning of the consequent caused by the sequence mediant-tonic-submediant (III-I-VI). Played by solo cello doubled by the left hand of the harp, the melody is echoed off the beat in the high solo flute doubled by the right hand of the harp, creating the impression of a reflection or a luminous resonance; it is punctuated by a chord in the second violins and clarinets. The consequent period retains this instrumentation with small variations.

Massenet continued with this manner of orchestration and constantly renewed its colors, thus creating a beautifully calculated monotint of timbres that could depict the intangible and fleeting nuances of the moonlight. Yet, impelled by passion, the delicacy of this chamber-music orchestration changes at times to powerful waves of sound, thus linking the poetic atmosphere of nature with the emotions that govern Charlotte and Werther. When these arise, the reprise of the antecedent of the melody is divided between the left hand of the harp and solo clarinet; the reply is in the right hand of the harp and solo violin. The more ample consequent period is enlivened by some eighth-note motion, and seems to render the emotion that grips the lovers and that then fades with Charlotte's words, "Il faut nous séparer"—"We must part." A development stage follows in which harmonic alterations underscore the still-suppressed excitement with which

Werther speaks of Charlotte: "pourvu que je voie ces yeux toujours ouverts, ces yeux: mon horizon"—"so long as I see those ever-open eyes, those eyes: my horizon." The language of sonority thus plays an important role here; it emphasizes a word, magnifies an emotion, or demarcates the successive stages of the scene.

## THE POETRY OF MEMORY—NADIR'S ROMANCE

The spellbinding charm of this piece has aroused the admiration of listeners from the opera's premiere to this day. "I am not ashamed to rank Nadir's *romance* among what are for me the few original pieces of music," Joël-Marie Fauquet confesses. "I have long viewed it as a model of genuine melody, and I know of few that equal it in its perfection both of melodic line and of accompaniment."[93] It may be heard as a key example of the French genre of the *romance*,[94] which is part of the poetics of French lyric theater (essentially in the context of *opéra-comique*); it is characterized by simplicity, delicacy, or naiveté (sometimes bordering on sickly sweet), syllabic declamation, and flowing, regular melody. Generally strophic in form, the *romance* most often expresses love or melancholy. Berlioz saw the origin of his own musical sensibility in the *romance* in Nicolas Dalayrac's *Nina, ou la Folle par amour* (1786), "Quand le bien-aimé reviendra." I shall take Nadir's *romance* as the basis for a detailed consideration of the musical depiction of a poetic moment.

Evocation of the past is combined with the theme of a starlit night to produce a reverie:

I
Je crois entendre encore,
Caché sous les palmiers,
Sa voix tendre et sonore
Comme un chant de ramiers.

II
Aux clartés des étoiles
Je crois encore la voir
Entr'ouvrir ses longs voiles
Aux vents tièdes du soir.

*Refrain*
O nuit enchanteresse,
Divin ravissement.
O souvenir charmant,
Doux rêve, folle ivresse.

I
Still I seem to hear,
Concealed beneath the palm trees,
Her gentle, resounding voice
Like the call of the woodpigeon.

II
By the light of the stars
I seem still to see her
Half opening her long veils
To the warm evening breezes.

*Refrain*
O enchanting night,
Divine rapture.
O delightful memory,
Sweet dream, mad exhilaration.

During the recitative preceding this *romance,* the remorse-stricken tenor, in keeping with theatrical convention, thinks aloud. His brief description of his actions is made in the past tense ("J'ai voulu la revoir"—"I wanted to see her again"). This leads to the memory triggered by the voice of Léïla, which becomes the link between past and present. This dissolution of time is like the dispersion of sounds into open space ("J'écoutais ses doux chants emportés dans l'espace"—"I heard her sweet songs carried off into space"). Memory becomes vision; time is eradicated. The mirage comes to an end as the hero falls asleep.

Bizet wrote this *romance* on a barcarole rhythm. Here let us recall how aware he was of the need to control the expressive power of his works by working on their structure. Correcting a composition exercise by his pupil Paul Lacombe—in fact, a *rêverie*—he commented, "It is lifeless, dull! The idea is meager. Its poetry is not exquisite enough for the dreamy tone you are attempting. To be sure, there is a certain languor, a certain charm—but not enough.... I am afraid of things that smack of improvisation. Look at Beethoven; take the vaguest, the most ethereal of his works: it is always *intentional,* always *tidy.* He dreams, and yet his idea has body. You can touch it."[95]

The first twelve measures, which constitute the introduction, are divided into three phrase elements. The first establishes the accompaniment figure, which is constructed of two measures in quarter-note–eighth-note rhythm. It may be divided into an impetus (the initial bass note), an ascending motion (the first measure), and a descending motion of two dotted quarter notes (the second measure). This is divided among several instruments, which strengthens the impression of swaying motion through the interplay of timbres. Above, the English horn plays a second motif, two measures in length, which introduces the first hints of melody. The second phrase element compresses the two motifs, and the third returns to the first element, simplified and transposed into the tonic, as the English horn stands on the dominant (E).

The voice hovers around a constant E; it seems to be suspended between the tenor's high and mid ranges, between dream and reality. It continues the undulation established in the introduction with an inversion of the motif first played by the English horn, which falls silent. Instrument and voice are thus structurally linked, which is borne out by the end of the *romance:* the tenor is doubled by the muted violins in parallel thirds an octave above the voice, supported by subdued basses (with a light pizzicato pulse in the low strings). This is intended to heighten the "detached" nature of the piece. Two solo cellos alone play the principal accompaniment figure.

The second stanza, with its rhythmic repetition and melodic motifs, has a hypnotic quality. The highly evocative atmosphere to which this gives rise is bolstered by a slightly more substantial orchestration and a new motif in the high violins, sparkling like stars or fireflies in the night that Nadir is describing. This time, the voice is doubled by the flute and the English horn: an unusual timbre.

The melodic form reflects the overall feeling of the *romance.* Bizet used the traditional mold of the classical period, but elongates the two symmetrical phrases. The antecedent and the consequent are each sixteen measures in length, and there is a two-measure gap between the stanzas. The continuously repetitive rhythm in long note values adds an obsessive quality to the melody. One measure alone is an exception: the renegade measure containing the words "folle ivresse," generating tension with its leap of a tritone (F to B natural), which is immediately relieved by the sudden pianissimo and the final descent. Harmonically, the melody falls within the normal pattern, with a half-cadence on the dominant then a perfect cadence at the end. But in the orchestral introduction, several measures go by before the key of A minor is clearly established through the appearance of the leading tone, G-sharp; it is as though the evocation ("Je crois entendre encore") is gradually taking form. In the consequent, Bizet created an area of blurred tonality by using the modal degrees of the key. Note that this tonal haziness appears at the very moment that the word *souvenir* (memory) is mentioned, with the fermata on "folle ivresse," over a harmony that

can be analyzed either as the mediant of C or as the fifth degree of the aeolian (A) mode with its lack of a G-sharp leading tone. This strangeness is
accentuated by the parallel fifths between the bass and the vocal line at the
fermata.

In conclusion, note again the combining of many concomitant elements:
the languid rhythms; the tonal ambiguity with its modal coloration; the
swaying orchestral figures; the spinning of a long, floating melodic line; the
use of subtle vocal writing—a sort of high-note introversion with that pianissimo high B-natural; and the repetitive character of the piece. Moreover, throughout the *romance,* sustained notes (mostly Es) in the horns
create a distant color. The emphasis of the dominant (E), which by definition creates a sense of deferral, is underscored in the concluding section
that follows the second stanza: Nadir, doubled by the flute, repeats the
phrase "charmant souvenir," then falls asleep, overcome by the dream he
has created, on a long unresolved E. The English horn, which had begun the
dream, responds by resolving the phrase with an affirmation of the tonic.
The listener has the impression that the English horn is singing; Bizet's use
of the instrument is strikingly in keeping with Berlioz's description in his
treatise on orchestration: "This is a melancholy, dreamy, rather noble voice
whose sound has something of the faded, the *distant* about it, which makes
it superior to any other when the aim is to move [the listener] by reawak-
ening images and emotions from the past, and when the composer wants to
strike the secret string of tender memories."[96]

The counterpart of this *romance* is Léïla's act 2 *cavatine,* "Comme
autrefois dans la nuit sombre." In this aria, Bizet exploits the expressive typology of the instruments, especially the horn, which Berlioz describes as
"noble and melancholy."[97] It is an instrument that resonates in the memory like a fanfare lost in the distant forest: a "timbre of space," as some
modern analysts put it. The main theme is introduced by two horns over a
figure in the cellos. When the voice enters, it replaces the first horn, whose
characteristic sound it seems to continue.

The act 1 duet for Nadir and Zurga is the most highly developed poetic
scene in the opera (too much so for an analysis here). Bizet found sonic
equivalents for the friends' reverie, and gives form to the poetry of the moment when Léïla appears as a goddess, while simultaneously rendering it in
time. It is as though the verses had undergone a metamorphosis; they
gleam with a radiance that one would never have suspected in merely reading them. The job of the librettists was certainly to sketch the form of the
work, but it was also to be evocative for the composer, to stimulate his
imagination, and to provide dramatic and expressive potential through a

set of images. Some critics duly saw this, assessing the libretto of *Les Pêcheurs de perles* as "a good canvas from whose background emerge musical situations and effects of passion, emotion, and color."[98]

Librettists often drew the colorful images so beloved of audiences from exotic subjects; these lent themselves well to performance and contained many ideas for plots. Even better, by depicting a world very different from daily life in Paris—indeed, in France or anywhere else in Europe—authors could revive the lost sense of wonder that was found in operas of earlier centuries and that felicitously gave rise to their spellbinding sounds.

Exoticism is a dominant element of French opera, used by composers of both *grand opéra* and *opéra-comique* and surviving through the end of the nineteenth century—and beyond, as seen in Henri Rabaud's beautiful *Marouf Savetier du Caire* (1914), the first performance of which was remarked on by Gabriel Fauré.[99] By tracing its development and trying to identify its outlines, we can understand an important aspect of the nineteenth-century sensibility, more closely consider the development of the relationship among scenographic, literary, and musical expression, and analyze the process by which a poetic space was created.

### THE HISTORICAL BACKGROUND OF EXOTICISM— PERCEPTIONS OF THE EXOTIC WORLD

Strictly speaking, we should draw a distinction between exoticism in general and its offshoot, orientalism. But this distinction is of no interest in our present context. The important thing is the creation of an exotic world on the basis of a generalized image of a colorful, highly distinctive "elsewhere." The geographical limits of what was called the Orient are hard to pin down. "The Orient meant first of all the Levant," Lynne Thornton observes. "It then included Egypt, Syria, Lebanon, Palestine, and the North African coast. Spain, because of its Arab past, and Venice, because of its historical connections with Constantinople, were viewed by many as the gateway to the Orient."[100]

The growth of exoticism in the nineteenth century was connected to political, commercial, and scientific interest in foreign countries. Colonization, exploration, and proposals by scholars for great studies of distant civilizations were all part of the general infatuation.[101] Europeans saw the boundaries of their universe expanding, as reflected in the titles of two literary reviews founded in Paris in the nineteenth century: *La Revue des*

*Deux Mondes* and *Le Globe*. In general, the press was quick to publish articles on distant lands; and the illustrated papers were important in disseminating the visual images of exoticism. In 1849, *L'Illustration* published a series of "Letters on India" embellished with attractive drawings, including street scenes, architectural monuments, exotic characters, Brahmins, and fakirs, and, as usual, poking fun at the English, always an easy target: "The parallel with the prosaic civilization of England transplanted smack onto Indian soil brings out marvelously well the poetry of unchanging customs that seem to be impervious to man and time."[102] But there were already complaints about the Europeanization that was contaminating those places: "Even with all imaginable money and effort, one could not today see what the author of the 'Lettres sur l'Inde' saw," wrote the editors of *L'Illustration* in 1849. "In 1841, Lahore still existed in all its magical splendor. Since then, what we in Europe commonly call civilization, represented by the English, has applied its dreary norms to this *Arabian Nights* poetry."[103] This apparently pessimistic observation had the two advantages of enhancing the value of the writings of earlier travelers and of using a vanished reality to provoke imagination and dreaming.

The Empire style is a striking example of the direct influence that politics could have on Parisian style. Especially at the outset, it was marked by Egyptian motifs: lotus capitals, sphinxes, obelisks, and pyramids. The infatuation was so great that it gave rise to new words: decades after Napoleon's Egyptian campaign, journalists still delighted in using the adjective *pyramidal*, rather than "gigantic" or "grandiose." It was in May 1798 that Bonaparte embarked at Toulon for his famous expedition to Egypt, along with (in addition to a large army) more than 150 engineers, scientists, scholars, and artists, who were there to study pharaonic civilization. Egyptian art had always been an object of fascination, but Napoleon's expedition to Egypt "added a new dimension by replacing the archeologically faulty work of the eighteenth century with [true] copies."[104] Works published in the wake of that campaign as accounts of Egyptian art were used as references for decoration, furniture, and sculpture. The rendering of Mozart's *Die Zauberflöte* as *Les Mystères d'Isis* (1801) was part of this trend, whose culmination may be seen in Verdi's *Aida* (Cairo, 1871), the plot of which was developed by the librettist and theater director Camille Du Locle, with the help of the Egyptologist Auguste Mariette. This work became a true part of the French repertory with its first performance at the Paris Opéra in 1880.

Advances in botany led to fresh interest in painting or describing exotic plants. "The fashion for distant lands was encouraged by the Jardin des

Plantes…where the young Potaveri, a 'savage' brought back by [the explorer Louis-Antoine de] Bougainville [1729–1811], tearfully embraced a tree that, like him, had been born in Tahiti."[105] The theme of the luxuriant exotic forest (see fig. 21) surfaced in many librettos, and provided an excuse for beautiful stage settings, some of them highly imaginative.

Artists who had traveled or lived in distant countries played a key role in the history of exoticism, leading the way in the eighteenth century. In his *Voyage à l'île de France* (1773) and *Paul et Virginie* (1787), for example, Jacques-Henri Bernardin de Saint-Pierre, who had lived on the Île de France (Mauritius) between 1768 and 1770, had a considerable success by capitalizing on its nearly virgin wealth of luxuriant vegetation, its different customs, and its ever-changing light and skies. Chateaubriand took these strong points and greatly increased their scope. The themes of voluptuous melancholy, solitude, losing oneself in nature, and the role of nature in the emotional life of the individual: all these were combined with more picturesque and exotic scenes. With his sharp descriptive gifts, Chateaubriand raised the presentation of the faraway to the level of inspired poetry. We could cite almost all his work, but we must at least mention *Atala* (1801), *Itinéraire de Paris à Jérusalem* (1811), *Les Natchez* (1826), and *Le Voyage en Amérique* (1827)—a journey Chateaubriand made in 1791—with its poetry of great spaces and deserts. Traveling to the Orient[106] became customary, and even spawned a literary genre to which the greatest writers, such as Alphonse de Lamartine and Gérard de Nerval, contributed. The most up-to-date forms, such as the novels of Flaubert (*Salammbô*, for example), incorporated this exotic material.

It was the same with painting. In 1828, Alexandre Gabriel Decamps departed for Greece and Turkey; Prosper Marilhat visited Egypt between 1831 and 1833; Eugène Fromentin spent six months in Morocco in 1844; Théodore Chassériau lived in Algeria in 1846. Delacroix's 1832 trip to Morocco and Algiers "show[ed] French artists for the first time that North Africa held as much interest as the traditional pilgrimage to Italy."[107] In 1833, Horace Vernet, a highly prominent official painter, made the first of several journeys to Algeria, where he reckoned he would find living biblical scenes.

In the field of music, Louis Moreau Gottschalk (1829–1869), born in New Orleans, composed pieces inspired by the melodies of his native land. The titles are the stuff of daydreams: "La Bamboula" (a type of African drum, or the dance associated with it) and "Le Bananier" ("The Banana Plant"), which enjoyed great popularity at the time. The latter piece, published at Paris in 1850 by the Bureau central de Musique, was subtitled

"Chanson nègre pour piano"; the publisher gave it the stamp of exotic authenticity by printing under the composer's name "de la Louisiane." The following handful of titles only hints at how many exotic pieces Gottschalk composed: "Le Mancenillier" ("The Manchineel"—a poisonous tree native to the Americas) (1851); "Le Banjo: Caprice américain" (1856); "Minuit à Séville" (1859); "Les Yeux créoles: Danse cubaine" (1860); and "Souvenir de Cuba" (1874).

On March 22, 1833, Félicien David (1810–1876) left Marseilles for Constantinople as a missionary of Saint-Simonism (a kind of Christian socialism). His itinerary included Smyrna, Jaffa, Jerusalem, Alexandria, and Cairo, among other destinations. On June 19, 1835, he docked at Marseilles, having stored up a wealth of images, sensations, and melodies, a fertile stock that would bear him abundant fruit—just as a few decades earlier Chateaubriand had fashioned a new literary language by drawing on images and sensations gathered in faraway places. Later, Saint-Saëns, who at one stage in his long life traveled a great deal, would himself collect exotic ingredients for his works, transcribing Egyptian musical scales and popular melodies in a notebook now housed in the Musée de Dieppe.

What was the attitude of French listeners as they discovered this exotic world of music? How was it perceived? In contrast to the visual arts—with their street scenes, costumes, and views of nature, which excited great enthusiasm, and whose images stayed in people's minds—sounds were harder to grasp, especially for writers, who were the main disseminators of orientalism. "The procession moved very slowly to the melancholy sound of instruments that were mimicking the relentless noise of a squeaky door or a cart breaking in a new set of wheels," Gérard de Nerval observed of a Cairo wedding he encountered. "Those guilty of this din were about twenty in number."[108] In his *Roman d'un Spahi* (1881), Pierre Loti speaks of African polyphony condescendingly, but in a way that reveals a perceptive musical ear and—apart from the patent scorn—a keen interest: "In the Sudan, the art of music is entrusted to a caste of special men called 'griots.' ... When a chief feels the need to hear his own glory extolled, he sends for his griots, who sit before him in the sand and instantly compose a long

Figure 21. *Opposite:* Auber's *Le Cheval de bronze,* first performed at the Opéra-Comique on March 28, 1835, and at the Opéra on September 21, 1857. Act 3 set by Charles Cambon (*L'Illustration,* October 3, 1857). "The stage depicts a heavenly palace and gardens in the midst of clouds" (libretto [Paris: Jonas, 1857], p. 24). Seduction scene: young women, along with Delia, attempt to charm Peki with their dances. Choreographic enchantment is combined with the visual enchantment of the scene's lush vegetation.

series of official stanzas in his honor, accompanying their shrill voices with the sounds of a very primitive little guitar whose strings are stretched over snake skins." Of the plaintive ballads of the griots and the songs of the Nubian women, Loti observed: "The melody seems so primitive, so elusive because of its monotony; the rhythm is so difficult and complicated.... The constant off-the-beat playing of those who accompany and the unexpected syncopations, perfectly understood and respected by all the performers, are the most typical characteristics of this art—perhaps inferior to our own, but certainly very different—which our European system does not enable us to understand completely."[109]

Musicians sometimes showed little more understanding. Saint-Saëns, for example, dismissed the music of those who, "owing to their inferior system, are unable to rise to the concept of harmony," such as "ancient peoples," "the Orientals" (although he conceded that these had "taken the pursuit of melody and rhythm very far"), and "the blacks of Africa," who, he said, "possess an infantile and uninteresting music."[110] Nonetheless, he also observed elsewhere: "We often wonder why we do not understand the music of the Orientals and why they do not understand ours. There is no cause for surprise, for they are two different arts.... The great art of antiquity and of the Orient is neither superior nor inferior to ours in absolute terms; it is another art."[111]

For a few rare thinkers, contact with this sonic "elsewhere" gave rise to genuine and disturbing questioning of the concepts of civilization and of evolution. The Other would become a reflection of oneself projected into history. Oscar Comettant realized this at the Universal Exposition of 1867, of which he wrote:

> The savages of Africa and America are poets with dialects of three hundred words; why should they not be musicians with shapeless, even detestable instruments? I do not mean that they are musicians in the way that we are, but that, by being as they are, they are as they should be, so that this art is in keeping with the level of their civilization.... To laugh, to ridicule the barbarous continents that revealed at the Exposition the state of an art that is barbarous but that is relatively full of appealing emotions for those who cannot know or practice any other would be unworthy of even a somewhat thoughtful mind. Ah, how these instruments make us reflect on the origin and destiny of our species![112]

Because they were seen from afar, however, "primitive arts" were jumbled together, in spite of their enormous differences, and with very few exceptions, notions of oriental music remained vague. Gustave Bertrand summed up the view prevalent in 1872: "Oriental music exists only at the folk level, and it is not without difficulty that, in their travels, musicians come to understand that it can contain genuine poetry in the grating, ill-tuned sounds of the instruments or in the guttural vocalizations of the singers of those lands."[113] It was out of the question to accept this music as it was; only certain elements could be retained. This is a subject to which we shall return below.

Literature played a commanding role in the culture of nineteenth-century France, and the exotic experience was chiefly expressed through writing. Even painters by and large took their inspiration from writings that sparked fantasies and dreams. During the Restoration (1815 to 1830), Eugène Delacroix (1798–1863), who was fascinated with Byron, became interested in exotic subjects derived from tales of the Near East. Alexandre Gabriel Decamps (1803–1860) painted oriental subjects before he ever traveled to their sites. Dominique Ingres (1780–1867), who kept to his studio, created several great classics of orientalism, such as *La Grande Odalisque* (1814), *Odalisque et esclave* (1839), and *Le Bain turc* (1862). Reality was quickly reformulated and replaced by imagination. "Travelers and stay-at-homes alike often relied heavily on literary sources for their works," Thornton observes. "These were generally fiction, such as Lord Byron's Turkish epics, Thomas Moore's Indian romance *Lalla Rookh*, Gustave Flaubert's *Salammbô*, Théophile Gautier's *Le Roman de la Momie* and Victor Hugo's *Les Orientales*. In addition, there were the recitals of their journeys by influential writers and poets."[114] Minor writers helped disseminate the vogue for exoticism even more perhaps than those who are today regarded as great. The journalist, poet, playwright, and librettist Joseph Méry (1798–1866) supplied the text for Félicien David's *ode-symphonie Christophe Colomb* (1854) and the libretto for his opera *Herculanum* (1860). Moreover, "a kind of trilogy in which he magnificently depicted the exotic landscapes of India and Africa, countries he had never seen..., was enormously well received [when published in] *La Presse*"[115] between 1843 and 1847. Among his short stories, which were grouped according to their locales, we might note the collection *Les Nuits d'Orient* (1854).

History and the development of thinking, tastes, and literary movements leave great furrows, in which exotic flowers thrive. "The explosion of romanticism," writes Henri Marchal, "began a genuine myth, embellished by a love of travel that was heightened by books of tourism such as the *L'Univers pittoresque* series. We see an imaginary, multifaceted Orient being created, with little care for the facts, one that stressed adventure, enchantment, and dreams."[116] One constantly runs into the notion that realism is fatal to dreaming: exoticism is first and foremost a dream of "elsewhere." Paul Valéry took this idea to its extreme: "For this word [*Orient*] to make its full and complete effect on a person's mind, he must above all other things *never have been* in the poorly defined land to which it refers."[117] To return to Félicien David, Gustave Bertrand considered that "although he had not visited India, ... David was predestined [in his operas] to sing of the land of sapphires and fragrant trees, the loves of the nightingale and the rose, the delights of the valley of Kashmir, the paradise of Hindustan.... In his dreams he must prefer a jungle inhabited by Bengalis to the sandy steppes of Egypt and Asia Minor."[118]

Pierre Jourda defines exoticism as something "not native to [one's] country," saying that it is "first and foremost our ready-made concept of a [foreign] country and its inhabitants" and "a preconceived way of looking at or imagining a country."[119] Broadening the concept of exoticism would soon embrace nearly every opera, apart from a few *opéras-comiques*, however, and the focus here is solely on the sunny exoticism of warm faraway places. It was easy to make Parisians feel as though they were in a faraway land; it is certainly valid to speak of "provincial exoticism," as reflected, for example, in operas on Breton subjects, such as Meyerbeer's *Dinorah, ou le Pardon de Ploërmel* and Lalo's *Le Roi d'Ys*. Travel back to past centuries, too, involves a kind of temporal exoticism.

"*Orient*: this magnetic word, like a magnetic field, 'oriented' nineteenth-century desires toward a magical object weighed down with meaning, which haunted the imagination," Jean-Claude Berchet observes. "It signified, more than a geographic space, a mythic space permeated with contradictory urges."[120] And Jean-Marc Moura stresses that "exotic concepts do not mean a mere change of scene, substituting the charms or horrors of little-known regions for a familiar setting. They imply a certain mental attitude toward what is foreign, a special sensibility." Moura defines exoticism as "a reverie devoted to a distant space and fulfilled in a written work."[121]

The terms "local color" and "picturesque," Moura notes, are often used in speaking of exoticism, and it would be worthwhile to pin down their meanings: "local color," for him, is "the accurate, vivid reproduction of the characteristics of a space and a time," while "picturesque" defines "two different things: the charm, originality or appeal of a landscape or a scene, and, in literature, the quality of a description that vividly and colorfully expresses reality."[122]

## EXOTICISM IN OPERA: STAGE SETTINGS AND LIBRETTOS

Opera combines three different areas that demand special treatment when dealing with an exotic subject: scenic elements such as sets, costumes, and ballet; the libretto; and the music. Poorly understood and misperceived, music made only a modest contribution to exotic writings of the first half of the nineteenth century. External elements—plot and decor—predominated. In an article in *La France musicale* of August 18, 1844, Adolphe Adam wrote of Nicolas Dalayrac's *opéra-comique, Gulistan* (1804):

> The author took no great pains to research local color; he made do with giving the actors turbans by way of hats, wide trousers in place of the tight ones that were then in fashion, and fur-trimmed caftans and dolmans instead of the mouse-gray tail coats in which the dandies of the day decked themselves out. They would say "Seigneur" instead of calling each other "Monsieur"; they swore by Muhammad instead of cursing *morbleu* or *corbleu*; and the show was just as Turkish as [Voltaire's] *Zaïre* [and Racine's] *Bajazet* . . . which passed for models of observation with regard to customs.

This kind of exoticism, seen in costumes, colors, scenery, and subjects inspired by the Orient, gradually helped make opera an entertainment of high visual quality related to the world of pictorial orientalism.[123] When the critic of *L'Illustration* reviewed Auber's *L'Enfant prodigue* (1850), he said that the stage director, François-Hippolyte Leroy, "took care not to draw his documentation solely from the Egypt of [the paleographer Jacques-Joseph] Champollion-Figeac and to interpret the Bible . . . , but . . . he has staged Egyptian customs and biblical traditions as we know them from M. Horace Vernet and the other modern painters who have of late visited Africa and have spent a while on the Delta free from preconceptions, archeological or otherwise."[124]

The Orient makes for dreaming, and it often resembles legend; it thus readily lent itself to the composition of magical entertainments in which designers could show off their skills, such as Scribe's and Auber's *Le Cheval de bronze,* subtitled *Opéra-féerie* (1835), act 3 of which takes place in a celestial palace and its garden, and act 4 inside a splendid pagoda. Scribe's and Saint-Georges's *La Fée aux roses* (1849), with music by Halévy—an *opéra-comique* also subtitled *féerie*—takes place in the kingdom of Caboul, and its cast includes the magician Atalmuc, who is trying to make a love potion. A metal rose that can grant wishes and a magic picture hint at a relationship between this kind of subject and eighteenth-century works such as Grétry's *Zémire et Azor* (1771), a *comédie-féerie* to a text by Jean-François Marmontel. This genre provided a pretext for show-ing off every possible visual marvel; librettists and composers revisited it from time to time until very late in the century. *Esclarmonde* (1889), a fan-tastical opera in eight scenes, with a libretto by Alfred Blau and Louis de Gramont, attracted Massenet precisely because of its dreamlike, magical atmosphere: act 2 begins in the garden of an enchanted island inhabited by spirits.

Rather than purporting to reproduce reality exactly, the scenery in such productions offered a conventional stereotype. "All the sets...are of an ideal perfection, and faithfully reproduce the poetic dreams of the wonders of the Orient that our imagination loves to create," D. A. D. Saint-Yves ob-served of Offenbach's *Barkouf.* [125] But as the century progressed, designs became more specific and sets came to be modeled on authentic images; fantasy was replaced by re-creation. The Paris version of *Aida* (1880) reflected this concern for historical verisimilitude and pictorial accuracy.[126] The costume designer, Eugène Lacoste, turned for advice to the Egyptolo-gists Mariette, Champollion, Beauregard, and Maspéro and studied build-ings, bas-reliefs, sculptures, and colorings in the collections of the Louvre.

On the other hand, choreography lagged far behind the set designers' quest for realism. "Savages" always seemed to dance with the grace of a corps de ballet and to use the most conventional steps. Johannès Weber railed against traditional choreography as inadequate to dramatic truth; this was particularly obvious in the third act of *Les Pêcheurs de perles*, when Nadir is seated before the statue of Brahma: "A charming corps de ballet dances around him in a ring, portraying Indians thrilled at the can-nibal feast that awaits them. Frankly, women who gambol with joy because poor young people who loved each other too much are about to be stabbed could be nothing but appalling shrews. Now I ask you: does any ballerina whatsoever, on any stage, look ferocious or savage? But to demand dra-matic verisimilitude in a ballet would be sheer pedantry!"[127]

It took a long time for librettos to become exotic throughout and not just in a handful of characteristic scenes. Sometimes it would have been enough to change the characters' names for a scene to be as likely to be set in Paris as in Seville or the Indies. F.-J. Fétis complained, for example, that in Scribe's *Le Portefaix* (1835), set to music by José Melchior Gomis, "had it not been for the Spanish costumes the characters were wearing it would have been impossible to say whether the scene took place in Spain or else-where."[128] Librettists gave a brief description of the sets at the beginning of each act or in stage directions. Pagodas, palanquins, mosques, minarets, huts, palm trees, and characteristic landscapes defined the visual outlines of exotic space. Everything relating to a culture was called upon: the natural setting, the flora, buildings, domestic interiors, and furniture and objects, as well as costumes and makeup. In contrast to librettos in which the exotic is fused with the magical were plots that used exoticism in the most prosaic of situations, which gave rise to a sense of foreignness and brought out the theatrical essence of exotic characters: the exoticism itself was the entertainment, as we see from *Le Maçon* (1825) by Scribe and Auber. Madame Bertrand tells Baptiste in act 1, scene 3:

> I promise you a fine show. You know that my house is next to the mansion of that foreign ambassador—that awful Turk who makes all the little neighborhood boys run after his carriage when he goes out. Well, they say that tomorrow he is supposed to be leaving with his Lord High Mamamouchis. The procession will be magnificent; and people have already asked to rent my windows. But, Lord love me, I am above all that: I and my set will enjoy taking a peek.

In many *opéra-comique* librettos, the strange ways and odd customs practiced in exotic countries were contrasted with Western habits. Most often, this provided an opportunity to extol Paris or its fashions and tastes. Scribe and Saint-Georges's *Le Nabab* (1853), with music by Halévy, used such contrasts by setting one act in India and two in England. Saint-Georges employed the same technique in *Le Château de la Barbe-Bleue*, which begins in Madras (acts 1 and 2) and ends in Saint-Germain-en-Laye (act 3).

Besides being a decorative element and a source of dramatic contrast, an exotic theme could also be an effective device for sheer entertainment. The tragic tone of the final act of Scribe's and Auber's *Manon Lescaut* (1856), which takes place in Louisiana, was not typical of the Opéra-Comique, where exoticism was usually viewed as a way to bring in comic characters and comic situations. In *Caïd* (1849), by Thomas Sauvage and Ambroise Thomas, there was a great deal of comedy based on an exotic country—in this case, Algeria—viewed from a European perspective. In *Barkouf* (1860) by Scribe and Boisseaux, with music by Offenbach, the wearing of the veil is explained by the ugliness of the daughter of Grand Vizier Périzade. When she looks at herself in the mirror (in act 2, scene 1), her father orders: "Lower your veil. You know perfectly well that is the only way we in the Orient can marry off our daughters."

The shortcomings associated with given peoples—cruelty, skepticism, primitive character, and so forth—were accentuated. Imitation of a foreigner's faulty pronunciation of French is very rare, but librettists were fond of other stereotypes. In act 3, scene 2, of *Le Château de la Barbe-Bleue* (1851), by Saint-Georges and Limnander, Hercule, who has just returned to France, boasts to a corporal about his glorious status in the Indies: "I was served, Sir, by three hundred slaves of every color....I had millions to spend, a palace that was gilded like a parrot-cage, and outfits covered with diamonds and rubies—to the point where I dazzled the sun." In their *Lalla-Roukh*, Carré and Lucas mocked the conventional exotic spectacle. Mirza laughs at the idyllic picture painted of the Kashmir valley (act 1, scene 5): "It is a marvelous land with its ever-green trees, its ever-blue lake, its ever-blooming flowers! (*Laughing*) If you believe Baskir, nowhere in the whole kingdom is there a nightingale that does not know music or a warbler that cannot sight-read." In a *grand opéra* such as Meyerbeer's *L'Africaine* (1865), the tragic subject added the serious-mindedness needed for a fully developed expression of the exotic, while irony or any kind of comedy created a sense of distance that was hardly conducive to the poetic. With works of various kinds, such as Halévy's *Jaguarita l'Indienne* (1855), and Bizet's *Les Pêcheurs de perles* and *Djamileh* (1872), exoticism was set loose in every theater and in every genre—and not just with lone anecdotes, mere contrasts between Europeans and natives, or a reflection of the author's own society (such as in Montesquieu's *Lettres persanes* of 1722). Operatic exoticism laid the foundations of a complete imaginary world, sometimes derived from history, and provided genuine subjects rather than a mere pretext.

Confined to a single register, exotic writing was heavily influenced by the stereotyped poetic writing of operatic librettos. Still, the locales varied. Although "with few exceptions, the literary exoticism of the nineteenth century before 1870 concerned itself mainly with Old Europe and the Mediterranean basin,"[129] operatic exoticism—undoubtedly more fanciful, and interested above all in the visual possibilities of a subject—wasted no time in transporting the spectator to distant lands. The poetic exoticism of *Les Pêcheurs de perles* is simply a variation on conventional imagery. By playing on stereotypes, authors described an exotic fantasy rather than depicting a faraway reality. "From 1830–1850," writes Jean-Pierre Leduc-Adine, "a genuine code for the representation of orientalism, and hence of exoticism, was gradually laid down. It structured both texts and pictures."[130]

Verses in an opera are like artificial flowers, lacking perfume and the freshness of life. Among these, those on the Orient stood out for a time with a special brilliance; but changing fashion tarnished their golden luster and dulled the perfume of their mystery. The dream described by Selim in Reyer's *La Statue* (1861) was sung—and admired—time and again:

> Mes yeux ont contemplé ce merveilleux empire
> Ce royaume inconnu, ces jardins enchantés,
> Ces palais de cristal, de marbre et de porphyre.

> My eyes have gazed upon this wondrous empire,
> This unknown kingdom, these enchanted gardens
> These palaces of crystal, marble, and porphyry.

The same formulas are to be found in libretto after libretto. Take for example the melody sung by the heroine of Félicien David's *Lalla-Roukh* (1862), most of whose lines could be transferred to Nadir or to Léïla:

> I
> Sous le feuillage sombre,
> Dans le silence et l'ombre
> Il venait chaque soir!

> II
> Sous notre ciel sans voiles,
> Aux clartés des étoiles
> Mes yeux ont pu le voir.

> III
> Dans mon palais, captive,
> Immobile, attentive,
> Et le coeur soucieux,

> IV
> Je crois entendre encore
> Sa voix douce et sonore,
> Ses chants mélodieux!

> *Refrain*
> O souvenir que j'aime,
> Rêves de mes beaux jours,
> Hélas malgré moi-même
> Je vous fuis pour toujours.

> I
> Beneath the dark foliage,
> In silence and shadow
> He came every evening.

II
Under our limpid sky,
By the light of the stars
My eyes could see him.

III
In my palace—captive,
Motionless, watchful,
And anxious of heart—

IV
I seem still to hear
His sweet, sonorous voice,
And his melodious singing!

*Refrain*
O beloved memory,
Dreams of better days,
Alas, reluctantly
I flee you forever.

The wealth of the Orient lavished its poetic images on exotic inspiration. Precious stones, priceless objects, and splendid palaces kept flowing from the pens of the versifiers. The very title of Cormon and Carré's *Pêcheurs* reflects this, and the entire framework of the action is built around the "golden pearl." But we can grant that these librettists did not indulge in a surfeit of this kind of thing; they chose rather to give greater prominence to love and emotions. Nadir's *chanson* in act 2 consolidates the exotic and emotional sides of the drama. In line with the ageless clichés, it depicts the beloved woman as a "sleeping flower...shut up in a palace of gold and azure": an eternal image whose "pure glance" glistens "on the crystal of the dark abyss."

The poetry of exoticism is a poetry of light. Sunlight, firelight, and light in general are constantly invoked. This poetry, in a sense, marks a return to the primitive, and authors gave pride of place to the elements and to the exterior setting. Upward-looking themes such as the sky, light, and purity were contrasted with those of shadow and the depths. This is the other side of exotic poetry: that of brutality and of shadowy, menacing shapes. Between the two extremes lay mystery: perfumed nights, the magical Orient, and tropical forests continued to possess great evocative power. Ralph Locke has rightly observed that exotic passages often combined two conflicting moods, as we can see in depictions of the Orient that accord with the way in which the collective imagination viewed it, as either idyllic or wild and barbaric.[131]

In the second part of *Le Désert* ("La Nuit"), Félicien David and the poet Auguste Colin expressed the charms of the night in a way that would be definitive for spectators of the time:

RÉCITANT:     Comme un voile de fiancée,
              La nuit tombe au front du désert;
              Aux chansons de la nuit notre coeur s'est ouvert[.]

NARRATOR:     Like a bridal veil,
              Night falls over the brow of the desert;
              Our heart opens to the songs of the night[.]

Frequent features of exotic operas were evening reveries and choral supplications to the divinity, along the lines of "Allah, à toi je rends hommage." Oriental fantasies add an additional dimension to the theme of the bewitching voice. It is not so much Léïla as Lakmé—and the Bell Song from act 2 of the opera of the same name (1883)—that the twentieth-century listener thinks of as the archetype of the "operatic Oriental" with her unreal voice. In the bazaar, the young girl, who is accompanied by her father, Nilakanta, agrees to sing the legend of the daughter of the Pariahs. The otherworldly site of the action, as Gérard Condé aptly puts it, is the "Isle of Waning Bel Canto"; this is "a heavenly and fateful song."[132] Here, we are in the world of wonders alluded to earlier in connection with the role of the coloratura aria in nineteenth-century opera, a world that is a perfect expression of the spell of the exotic and that poets long continued to evoke. Here is an example from the novelist Maurice Barrès's *Un Jardin sur l'Oronte* (1922): "Unwearied, the Saracen, sowing her themes in the night, told in her rose garden the rosary of her nocturns. At once chaste and impassioned, she rose from languor to frenzy only to descend again to sighing; and sometimes full of pain like a butterfly in the mesh of a net, at other times warlike and prepared to kill, she made heaven and Earth burst forth with their full measure of voluptuous pathos."[133]

To create an exotic atmosphere, librettists fashioned a *champ lexical* (word field) out of allusions to the customs, objects, and nature of distant lands. Léïla, Zurga, Nadir, Nourabad: the very names of the characters of *Les Pêcheurs de perles*, either borrowed from Arabic or Indian cultures or made up to evoke them by their sounds, are richly evocative. We have already noted the important place of the elements in these librettos; similarly, a whole range of words is used to depict primitive, uncivilized life. In *Les Pêcheurs*, these refer to nature (*palmier, savane, tigre fauve, jaguar, panthère*—palm tree, savanna, tiger-cat, jaguar, panther); to objects (*tente, pirogue, barque, perles, encens*—tent, pirogue, fishing boat, pearls, incense); to customs (*jeux, danses, chef, femme voilée, brasier en feu, sacrifice*—games, dances, chief, veiled woman, fiery brazier, sacrifice); to life among the uncivilized (*coureur des bois*—woodsman); to gods and superstitions (*déesse, brahmines, Brahma, Siva, esprits méchants, sombres divinités*—goddess, Brahmins, Brahma, Siva, evil spirits, dark divinities); and to places (*Candi*—Kandy). The cruel side of the pearl fishers is expressed toward the end of the opera in the chorus with dance: "Nos bras frapperont / Et se plongeront / Dans leur sang infâme"—"Our arms will strike / And will sink / Into their despicable blood." The island theme is evoked by the regular appearance of marine imagery, with words such as *rivage, grève, flot,* and *mer*—shore, strand, tide, and sea. These words do not refer to a specific reality, but rather have an implicit exotic meaning that the spectator immediately grasps. The amassing of words—linguistic "props"—is related to the taste for curios of which Théophile Gautier gives a striking example:

> Laques, ports du Japon, magots et porcelaines,
> Pagodes toutes d'or et de clochettes pleines,
> Beaux éventails de Chine, à décrire trop longs,
> Cuchillos, kriss malais à lames ondulées,
> Kandjiars, yataghans aux gaines ciselées,
> Mille objets, bons à rien, admirables à voir.

> Lacquers brought from Japan, figurines and porcelains,
> Pagodas all of gold and full of little bells,
> Beautiful Chinese fans that would take too long to describe,
> Cuchillos, Malay krises with wavy blades,
> Khandjars, yataghans with engraved sheaths,
> A thousand things, good for nothing, lovely to look at.[134]

### PERCEPTION AND CONSTRUCTION OF AN EXOTIC SPACE IN OPERA

How did nineteenth-century French audiences perceive an exotic opera? What impression did it make on the spectator? And how did composers put the stamp of the exotic on their work? To grasp this process better, we must return to the press accounts of the premiere of *Les Pêcheurs de perles*. One journalist was particularly articulate on this point. Léïla's first-act aria "O dieu Brahma" disappointed the anonymous columnist of *La Revue française,* but he was enthusiastic about her *cavatine* and Nadir's *chanson* in act 2, which apparently corresponded to his own image of the Orient. The beginning of the *chanson,* which includes an oboe solo followed by an effect evoking distance, summoned up visions: "In the distance, a melody is heard, mournful as droning psalmody, which recalls Muslim prayers. During the contemplation of the oriental night, at midnight a shrill, solitary moan soars up: it is the voice of the muezzin calling the believers to prayer. Another heart-rending wail answers from afar."[135]

The composer's evocative powers resonated with the imagination of the listener, who then let his fancy fly on the wings of sonic illusion: "Little by little, the voices become more numerous, the singing swells, and thousands of believers together intone the magnificent prayer. One might say that the half-open tombs have freed their victims, and that the dead run free in the desert uttering long sobs. Suddenly, everything stops, and silence returns." At last the critic stops rambling: "I am surprised that M. Reyer, who has traveled in the Orient at such length, did not take note of this chanting [i.e., Muslim prayers] in all its beautiful originality; I think it would be most effective on stage. Has M. Bizet heard it? I do not know. In any event, his own lament is a distant echo of it."

When he heard David's *Le Désert* again twenty years after its premiere, Léon Gatayes made a similar observation: "I have not seen the oriental sun, but I know it through the music of Félicien David, music whose echoing rays gently warm the heart as they cradle it in dreams of the ideal."[136]

Through the evocative power of his music, the composer became the indirect spokesman for the Orient—indirect because the magic works in the context of a distant echo that is but an "imaginary reality" shared by people of the same culture—or it *should* be shared if the exoticism is to be effective. Victor Hugo experimented with this in *Les Orientales* (1829): "The Orient, either as an image or as an idea, has become, both for the mind and for the imagination, a kind of general preoccupation to which the author of this book may have unwittingly succumbed. Oriental colors have appeared as though by themselves to mark all his ideas and all his daydreams, and his thoughts, nearly without his intending it, have been in turn Hebrew, Turkish, Greek, Persian, Arab—even Spanish."[137]

Another example highlights the persistence in Parisian thought of a certain conservative notion of musical exoticism. When Auber's *La Muette de Portici* was revived thirty-five years after its premiere, the critic of *L'Art musical,* while uncertain about the interest and youthfulness of the work, admired the "local color"...that makes this work charming and that shows here that it is not always obligatory to copy nature; for Auber had never been to Naples, yet this music seems to summarize the entire character of the Neapolitan people with their faults and their merits: carefree, indolent, lazy, dreamy, religious, impassioned, exuberant, noisy, humble, and re-signed—until matters reach a head, when they will be dreadful in their anger, which bursts and thunders like their own volcano. Then, their fury calmed, their vengeance wreaked, they forget yesterday's idol for the glittering splendors of a court that, by dazzling them, enslaves them. Auber's music expresses in succession all these aspects of the highly changeable and exceptional nature of the Neapolitan people.[138]

The composer created local color based on collective psychology, starting with Parisians' shared image of a people or a country, and then translating the actions and character of that image into music. "But," asked Joseph d'Ortigue, writing in *Le Ménestrel*, "does this local color borrow from an overloaded palette? No: it lies in something indefinable, in the bold, fleeting stroke that speaks far more to the imagination than to the senses."[139] The critic Ralph (Léon Escudier) provided some examples: "It is from this warm, perfumed air, from this sapphire air, from this emerald sea that the melodies that the master introduced by the handful into this beautiful score seem to drop, soar, or climb. The barcarole rocks, pliant and carefree; the prayer is solemnly and majestically united to the sound of the basilica organ; the market resounds, cries out, shouts...; the tarantella stamps its feet, nimble and sparkling."[140]

Note the importance of dances and of distinct rhythms. But apart from its exotic rhythmic forms—which, however, had been popularized long before and were well known to and easily identified by Parisian audiences—Auber's music was drawn from no other authentic sources. Now Ralph grew more specific, coming to the defense of the traditional operatic school and berating the advocates of a less Parisian brand of exoticism:

[Auber] managed to remain French while writing Italian music. The barcarole, the prayer, the tarantella are borrowed from no collection of Neapolitan folk songs; their originality is in no doubt; they recall no melody from Sorrento or Posillipo—yet you would think they came directly from those enchanting beaches. It might be said that *La Muette de Portici* is the golden link that unites the French school of music to the Italian.

It is thus and only thus that we understand "local color." Charlatanism and exaggeration have nothing to do with it. It is nearly intuition—or at least it is study so carefully carried out and so skillfully concealed that it is impossible to detect....

> So to create local color there is no need to insert a Spanish or oriental melody into an opera whose subject is of Spain or of the Orient, or to travel to Castille or Andalusia, to Egypt or Persia to study the music of those lands, whatever the local music-makers—and troublemakers—might think.
>
> Those musicians who affect to be "painters in harmony" should really be grouped together with the writers of "imitative music." The schools are not exactly the same, but they have inadequacy in common.[141]

Some composers, including Reyer and Bizet, following in the footsteps of Félicien David, preferred a more boldly defined exoticism, expressed through color, to musical exoticism, which was basically an intellectual exercise that did nothing to adulterate the Parisian style of Auber. Their approach would gradually come to dominate; it would give rise to richly imaginative works based on elements borrowed from the music of other lands. Spectacle, once seen on stage, was now heard in the score. To adopt this approach, composers had to acknowledge the inadequacy of traditional methods; they had to adopt a fresh sensibility and create an exotic musical language.

In his musical criticism for 1862, Paul Scudo noted the emergence in the second half of the eighteenth century of new tastes and a modern sensibility with their roots in a different vision of nature. These grew with the pursuit, first, of the picturesque, then of exoticism in literature. A new language gave rise to this movement: "Rousseau gave French prose a hitherto unknown tone and sonority."[142] Indeed, in 1761, *La Nouvelle Héloïse* was a revelation, for Rousseau used a direct, sensitive vocabulary, full of imagery, that had not been available to his predecessors at the beginning of the century. Then Chateaubriand introduced a prose style with a new kind of phraseology—broad and rich, in keeping with the lands he was describing—and a varied vocabulary, as well as with emotions previously unknown, or unspoken. Chateaubriand used his personal experience of exotic reality and his wealth of impressions of exotic sights to create stylistic ingredients and patterns for scenes. According to his biographer André Maurois, Chateaubriand, on his trip to America,

> observed a great deal in order to return to France with images and colors that no writer before him had been able to set forth.... He meticulously wrote down in his notebooks...the elements of a number of beautiful landscapes, of which he was later to make skillful and repeated use. From that point, his *Nuit chez les sauvages de l'Amérique* [Night among the savages of America] and his *Coucher de soleil sur l'océan* [Sunset over the ocean] would be indispensable aids for setting a scene. He would

often remove them from their portfolios, refresh their colors, simplify them, shorten them, and, according to requirements and circumstances, mix in feelings of despair or happiness.... By blending his own memories and his reading, he would orchestrate a vast symphony; from a few half-forgotten images he would create the estimable opening passages of *Atala*.[143]

Just as words could be inadequate in literature, music too could be incomplete. Cursory *à la turque* numbers, colorful boleros, and so forth were no longer enough. But the problem was a tricky one. It was not until the 1840s that the true spokesman of faraway places made his appearance. Félicien David was an extraordinarily significant figure. He breathed new life into musical exoticism with his *ode-symphonie Le Désert* (1844), which was followed a year later by *Les Brises d'Orient*, based on his *Mélodies orientales* for piano (published privately in 1835), then with his operas, principally *La Perle du Brésil* (1851) and *Lalla-Roukh* (1862). "This delicate and insightful naturalism, this poetry at once intimate and boundless, this vague and idealized sensuality were new to music," noted Gustave Bertrand. "He contributed a hint of genius to which even his most illustrious predecessors were strangers. No one had listened to nature in this way or set down his personal reveries in this manner."[144] According to Scudo, David made use of "rhythmic boldness, stimulating combinations of sonorities, mixtures of timbres and melodic shapes," as found in the works of Berlioz; he "was the first to express in music an entire refined aspect of modern poetry..., [and] to import into his country the strange idioms of Arab melodies, expressed through the creative techniques of European art."[145]

"Two years in the Orient," wrote Félicien David to a friend, "were all I needed to draw the inspiration I had gone there to find. I am returning to sing of the Orient in France." The composer spoke of "those diverse peoples with their splendid, grand dress, their language—sometimes coarse and guttural and sometimes gentle and harmonious—and, then, their simple, original songs," of which he was bringing back "a great number."[146] His *ode-symphonie Le Désert* (see fig. 22), written to a poem by Auguste Colin, was a revelation when it was first heard at the Paris Conservatoire on December 8, 1844. "In a week," exclaimed Théophile Gautier when he left the concert hall, "all France will know this name; in a month, all Europe!... There may never before have been such a triumph!" The eminent critic concluded: "Nothing so powerful has been produced since Beethoven, Rossini, and Meyerbeer."[147] This new genre, so well suited to David's exotic style, combined the poetic dimensions of literature with the expressive power of a symphonic language. Saint-Saëns commented that *Le Désert*

Figure 22.    Félicien David's *Le Désert*. Title page of the first edition ("La Cara-
vane") (Paris: Bureau central de Musique, [1845]).

"pointed the public in a new direction without going over its head, while being a delight for the discerning."[148]

By the combined use of scenery, drama, vocabulary, and poetic style, nineteenth-century French librettists and designers thus created an increasingly specific "exotic space," and when music was added, it made an immediate connection to the exotic imagination. Jean-Pierre Leduc-Adine considers that exoticism is a function of "the intended reader's culture, training, and mental inclination" and wonders whether it "might not be primarily a phenomenon of perception."[149] Composers were hardly seeking precision, but were aiming at best to produce a sense of foreignness, while trying not to become bizarre—and incomprehensible, as, for example, an Arabic poem recited in the original language would be. It was quite a job to translate things viewed as exotic into conventional musical language. Some artist-travelers drew elements from their direct contact with foreign lands, and, once they had been stylized to some degree and adapted to Western expressive forms, used them as devices to evoke the exotic. Operatic music employed such devices to direct the audience's imagination; they were a kind of sonic signal composed of elements that either were, or were considered to be, realistic.[150] Within an "exotic space," a composer could employ a series of devices whose emblematic qualities would color the entire work.

DEVICES TO EVOKE THE EXOTIC

The essence of the musical devices that created local color was melodic inflection. The augmented second is both the simplest and most effective such inflection; it has great evocative power and continued for many years to appeal to many composers. Saint-Saëns used it profusely in the act 3 bacchanale in *Samson et Dalila*; Bizet employed it in his fine opera *Djamileh*, but for Nadir's first words in *Les Pêcheurs de perles* ("Des savanes et des forêts"), he substituted unusual inflections that recalled it.

Exotic melody, composed of fragmented lines and of sequences, could easily be turned in on itself and was conducive to little ornamental motifs, as are found in great number in the muezzin's chant in David's *Le Désert*. Examples in *Les Pêcheurs* are Léïla's invocation "O dieu Brahma" in the act 1 finale and Nadir's act 2 *chanson* "De mon amie fleur endormie," in which every phrase is marked by a florid figure. The oboe introduction to the *chanson* contains the leap of a fifth that is characteristic of instrumental "summonses" like those heard in the opening measures of the overture to *Lalla-Roukh.*

These techniques have little effect on tonality; they merely color it. It took some time for the use of modal inflections, lowered leading tones,[151] mingled major and minor modes, pedals, and open fifths to become widespread and to begin to look like a really distinctive musical language. In 1877, "Voici la nuit," the prayer sung by an off-stage chorus in Massenet's *Le Roi de Lahore,* had a "perfect oriental color"[152] for spectators of the day. Besides featuring a primitive choral melody doubled at the octave or at the fifth, Massenet accentuated the exotic strangeness through the accompaniment: harp, with triangle and tambourine rhythms, in altered aeolian (A) mode with a number of nonfunctional harmonic progressions.

Dances provided a expression of savage or primitive folk culture, as Antoine Reicha observed in his *L'Art du compositeur dramatique.*[153] In opera, it was often the dances that most powerfully embodied musical exoticism. They were constructed with repetitive rhythmic patterns and were thus easily identifiable. Although they were of varied origins, the most popular were Spanish dances—either sung or orchestral, and either taken from authentic sources or invented. *Carmen* stands out here because of the musical quality and dramatic aptness of its habanera, its seguedilla, and its final *entracte*—which is like some hyperrealistic fandango (and strikingly recalls Padre Antonio Soler's fandango, written for the harpsichord a century earlier). Throughout the nineteenth century, plot permitting, these dances were used for their memorable, distinctive rhythms. Two examples are the bolero "Profitez de la vie" from the first scene of Boieldieu's *La Fête du village voisin* (1816), which was cast in the form of simple folklike *couplets* and sung by Mme de Ligneul, and the *Ballade aragonaise* "Par un frais sentier" sung by Maritana in act 1 of *Don César de Bazan* (1872) by Massenet, a composer whose predilection for Spanish subjects also yielded *Le Cid* (1885), *Chérubin* (1903), and *Don Quichotte* (Monte Carlo, 1910).

Dance rhythms aside, composers did not very often seek out new rhythmic ideas. Nadir's act 2 *chanson* contains a novel alternation of triple (9/8) and quadruple (12/8) meters, very likely inspired by the act 2 finale of Reyer's *La Statue,* in which 2/4 alternates with 3/4, or indeed by no. 8 of Halévy's *opéra-comique Jaguarita l'Indienne* (1855), an aria with chorus, where the composer clearly sought an unusual metric treatment to match the evocative text with its internal rhymes:

JAGUARITA

Au sein de la nuit, sans bruit, la tribu s'élance,
Comme le serpent rampant dans l'ombre on s'avance.
Sous le dôme noir du soir marchons avec joie;
Nous allons saisir, tenir, enfin notre proie.

In the night, the tribe hurries noiselessly ahead,
Like the snake creeping in the shadows, we move forward.
Beneath the black vault of the evening, we joyfully stride;
We shall finally capture and hold our prey.

In general, composers kept the accompaniment of exotic melodies simple; they preferred static rhythms and a limited number of harmonies, employing to that end drone and pedal effects, which lent a primitive touch and allowed the melody to stand out clearly from the underlying harmony.

Color was one of the principal elements of the visual imagery of exoticism; its musical equivalent was timbre. Some timbres, such as those of the piccolo and the tambourine, unfailingly created a sense of local color; these were much used by David and by Reyer—for example, in part 4 of David's *Christophe Colomb,* "Danse de sauvages," and the "Fantaisie arabe" from *Le Désert,* and in no. 6 of Reyer's *La Statue.* Although percussion instruments were valued as "signals" of the exotic, they were to be used with a light hand, lest they fatigue European audiences and break the spell—which is what some critics felt when they heard *Carmen:* "This *opéra-comique* should be called *L'Amour à la castagnette,* because the main events unfold to the vulgar sound of that anti-melodious instrument, which is bearable only when used with great moderation."[154]

Woodwinds, especially the double reeds, were essential. In the context of the exotic "space" that we have described, audiences would interpret every melody played on these instruments as an imitation of oriental music, which indeed makes use of many instruments related to the oboe. Similarly, when the harp was given prominence, as in Nadir's *chanson,* it was to imitate the gusla mentioned in the librettos of many exotic operas. Exoticism in fact inspired a search for new instrumental combinations and, in the last quarter of the nineteenth century, provided a justification for expanding the orchestra. Massenet, for example, used a solo saxophone in the ballet divertissement in *Le Roi de Lahore* (1877). "The entire ballet is ... wonderfully orchestrated," we read in *Le Ménestrel,* "and gains vivid local color from the comical sounds of the 'kinnery,' a kind of carillon with metal plates, of the 'tals,' or Indian rattles, with which the bayaderes mark the rhythm of the dance, and of the whole family of percussion instruments that oriental music uses so extravagantly."[155]

In more general terms, composers took pains to use the orchestra to create a picturesque poetic atmosphere on the basis of a given situation. The result is often conventional but, in the exotic context, effective. For instance, the charming *couplets du Mysoli* in act 3 of *La Perle du Brésil* (no. 13), with its bird calls in the obbligato flute, rang out in the virgin forest (see fig. 23) and was heard as the "melodious song" of a "Brazilian Eve," mirroring the "elusive fioriture of our nightingales."[156]

However heroic Nadir's arrival on the scene in *Les Pêcheurs de perles* may be, his character is wreathed in the mystery of the lands he has traveled through. His first words are of the magic of the "savannas and forests whose shadows and mysteries [he has] probed." The strange, sinuous radiance of the vocal line is brought out by the trembling of repeated notes in the strings, flutes, and clarinets, evoking the Orient in its full splendor, bathed in light and in the fragrant air the hero has breathed. The tenor's vocal line is doubled in the violas and the bassoon, the latter in a register that makes it seem like an "instrument of dreams, legend, and fantasy."[157] Meyerbeer created a similar atmosphere in *L'Africaine* (1865) in the very first measures of Vasco's act 4 aria (no. 15), "O paradis sorti de l'onde / Ciel si bleu, ciel si pur dont mes yeux sont ravis"—"O paradise emerging from the waves / A sky so blue, a sky so clear which delights my eyes." The tenor melody, doubled in the English horn, is heard without the basses (as in the Bizet, where they are used only at cadences), sheathed by high violins and flute tremolos. Here we might mention the "reverse exoticism" depicted by Pierre Loti in a scene set in Tahiti in 1872, in his novel *Le Mariage de Loti* (1880):

> I was seated at the piano, and the score of *L'Africaine* was open before me. This piano, which had arrived that morning, was an innovation at the Tahitian court . . . and the music of Meyerbeer was to be heard for the first time in the household of [Queen] Pomare. . . . The chosen piece was the one in which the exhilarated Vasco walks alone on the island he has just discovered and admires the unfamiliar natural surroundings, a piece in which the master so perfectly depicted what he knew by intuition: the distant splendors of that land of verdure and of light.[158]

Limited as we are by our culture, it is only in the imagination (defined by artists) that we are able to find the terms with which to express the faraway.

Maurice Ravel, so adept at transcending his models, used such evocative techniques at the beginning of the spellbinding "Asie" section of *Shéhérazade* (1904). Tremolos in the high muted strings provide a halo for the sinuous line of the two oboes; the voice utters the magical incantation "Asie" (Asia), unlocking exotic regions. Then the English horn varies the

Figure 23.    Félicien David's *La Perle du Brésil,* act 3 (*L'Illustration,* March 20, 1858). "A virgin forest in Brazil illuminated by brilliant sun and shaded by banana plants, cedars, and coconut palms crisscrossed with vines, from which fruits hang. A big tamarind tree is growing in the middle of the stage" (description in the libretto [Paris: Lévy, 1851]). In this exotic setting, Zora sings the "Couplets du Mysoli" at the beginning of the act, then in the finale reprises the act 2 *ballade* in the midst of Europeans and Brazilians, whom she reconciles.

serpentine melody, while the text by Tristan Klingsor appeals to the imagination: "Vieux pays merveilleux des contes de nourrice / Où dort la fantaisie comme une impératrice / En sa forêt toute emplie de mystère"— "Ancient magical land of nursery tales / Where imagination sleeps like an empress / In her forest replete with mystery."

As a daydream about the Other and about Elsewhere, Jean-Marc Moura remarks, French exoticism "expressed through particolored..., enticing elements" a "theatricalization that turned the Other into a spectacle and incorporated it into a style of decoration."[159] I would agree with him that "this initial exotic inspiration existed in the context of a poetics of appearances with a surface connection to distant beings and distant worlds. As a type of writing intended to create spectacle and to depict comical or strange worlds, this style, based on artifice, used a whole range of effects that were known to readers. Its aim was not so much to instill a genuine sense of foreignness as to repeat characteristics that already defined 'foreign.'"[160] In spite of its comic and "Spanish" scenes, *Carmen* was undoubtedly one of the first operas to use exoticism in striving for a profound expression of the Other. Carmen, the Gypsy, proclaims that she is different and leads her life of difference in the midst of, and in spite of, everything around her.

Every formula grows commonplace, and the development of exoticism was accompanied by a proliferation of techniques. In the last quarter of the nineteenth century, borrowed melodies became more numerous and non-Western scales were more frequently used. The visual element, which had been the first to evolve, seemed to be absorbed into the musical scores. New forms of exotic "decor" were to be found in increasingly luxuriant orchestrations. Albert Roussel's lavish opera-ballet *Padmâvatî* (completed in 1918 and first produced in 1923) was without question the end product of exotic opera's long evolution, which progressed through a gradual integration of the various elements we have been discussing. Symphonic lushness, the importance of the chorus, the diversity of the dances, and the enchanting sets and lighting were all combined with the use of ancient and oriental musical modes, with sparkling harmonies, stretched to include chords of the eleventh and the thirteenth, and with melodies borrowed from Hindu folklore.

# PART 3

## FRENCH OPERA: SOCIETY, GENRE, AND AESTHETICS

# Chapter 7    The Parisian Operatic World

The preceding discussion has stressed the decisive role played by theater directors and librettists because of the way opera was organized in Paris. Let us now consider them as members of the curious alliance that produced French opera. As we have seen, owing to the dire conditions of the time, most new productions at the Académie de musique were mediocre, and only highly unusual circumstances enabled the young Bizet to have his work performed at the Théâtre-Lyrique and to get so much attention in the press. Let us look more closely at Bizet's path from prominent student to artist with an audience.

## A THANKLESS CAREER—THE YOUNG COMPOSER— THE INACCESSIBLE PARIS OPÉRA

"The most thankless, arduous and difficult of all careers in France is that of the composer,"[1] was the sweeping judgment of P. A. Fiorentino in 1863. The discontent and the sense that one had reached a dead end were so great that "hardly a day passes without somebody expressing a wish on behalf of young composers; they call for government support, and they request many favors and dispensations for them—without realizing that best of all would be that, when they are given a libretto, it be at least tolerable and not so abysmal as to unfailingly drag them into a disaster."[2] From the outset of his career, the dramatic composer was inevitably doomed to a miserable lot. One needed only to catalogue "the disappointments, humiliations, and anxieties of these poor musicians."[3] And when one of them managed nonetheless to get his music heard, dreadful conditions would doom it to certain failure. Albert Wolff noted:

Theaters normally produce the work of young talents under special circumstances. It is generally introduced to the public on a hot night in July, when the chief hired applauder and the actors' servants are all that's left of *tout Paris*. Around 7 P.M., while the Parisians are dining in the country, the curtain rises on a one-acter performed by the cream of the summer troupe; at 8 P.M., the name of the young artist is announced to the audience, and that's that. The theater director can congratulate himself on having been a patron of the young without damaging the interests of his friends, the old authors.[4]

Already in the 1850s, Adolphe Adam wrote of the nearly insurmountable obstacles facing beginning opera composers. Noting the success that Hérold, Boieldieu, and Auber had enjoyed in Germany, he wondered,

Why, in the light of such success abroad, do we have so few composers at home? It is because there is a lack of opportunities; it is because a young man, left knocking for years on end at the door of our lone Théâtre-Lyrique (the Opéra is and must be for the leading lights alone), realizes that there is no point in continuing to starve to death and takes to giving lessons and to begging for work: a humble life of hard work that rarely leads to wealth, but merely to a comfortable existence. He might have been an artist; perhaps sometimes even a genius.[5]

It was "an extraordinary stroke of good fortune"[6] that Gounod's *Sapho* came to be performed at the Académie de musique in 1850. It took all the leverage of Pauline Viardot, then at the peak of her fame, to get the director to agree to give the young composer something more than one of those little one-act curtain-raisers. The mezzo-soprano even agreed to the renewal of her contract at the Opéra on the explicit condition that a work be commissioned from Gounod and the librettist Emile Augier. Freeing the theaters from government control had not changed this theater or its closed world.

A perfect example is that of Victor Massé (1822–1884), a contemporary of Gounod's. As Steven Huebner tells us, he "received his first performance at the Opéra (*Le Mule de Pedro*, 1863) many years after [his operas] *Galatée* and *Les Noces de Jeannette* had become entrenched in the Opéra-Comique repertoire."[7] *Galatée* (1852) was performed 77 times in less than five years, and *Les Noces de Jeannette* (1853), a straightforward one-act comedy, was given 121 times in less than two years; between 1852 and 1893, not a year passed without it being performed at the Opéra-Comique. Massé's *La Reine Topaze* (1856) was also a great hit at the Théâtre-Lyrique, with 122 performances in a little more than a year. Moreover, Massé had taken the most prestigious of career paths: after winning first prizes in piano (1839), harmony (1840), and fugue (1843) at the Paris Conservatoire and the Prix de Rome (first prize) in 1844, he went on to become chorus master at the Opéra from 1860 to 1875 and professor of composition at the Conservatoire from 1866 to 1880. He was elected to the Institut de France to replace Auber in 1872 and became an Officier of the Légion d'honneur in 1877, after having been made Chevalier in 1856. It did him no good. Having waited until the age of forty-one for the Opéra to perform one of his works—and a mere two-act work at that—the failure of the project (just three performances were given) shut him out of that venerable theater forever. Some of his contemporaries with similar career paths, such as Henri Reber (1807–1880) and François Bazin (1816–1878), never even had the chance to face an Opéra audience—and neither did Bizet, who coveted the opportunity. Opera composers were pigeonholed by genre; it was nearly impossible to change category and even harder to transplant a given genre from one theater to another. Only a few works of genuinely compound genre managed to be transferred to the Opéra, such as *Faust* in 1869 and *Roméo et Juliette* in 1888. Between 1826 and 1892, the works performed at the Académie de musique were mainly new productions or translations.[8] In the version with recitatives by Ernest Guiraud, *Carmen* joined the repertory of the Théâtre national de l'Opéra—the Palais Garnier—only on November 10, 1959, in the presence of President Charles de Gaulle; in the same year, the Opéra-Comique chalked up its 2,942d performance of Bizet's masterpiece.[9] In the French operatic system, each theater retained its own repertory. The twin issues of genres and of institutions are basic to an understanding of that system in the nineteenth century, and we shall be returning to them in due course.

In 1863, G. Dumesnil wrote of the "endless plaint of young composers" heard "outside the Théâtre-Lyrique—[not to] mention inside,"[10] "a most disagreeable music" whose melody he had forgotten but whose text he was able to quote: "Always old music; always masterpieces; always Weber, Gluck, Mozart, and Léo Delibes [*sic*]! And we young people, we the future, when will they perform us?" In his *Ecole buissonière*, Saint-Saëns recalled an 1864 article in which the unnamed author laid the blame at the feet of the young composers themselves: "What is the point of encouraging their efforts when audiences persistently refuse to care about them?...And where are these brilliant young composers anyway? What are their names? Name them!...Let them sit in the auditorium and listen to *The Marriage of Figaro, Oberon, Der Freischütz, Orphée.*...It would do them good to have such models before them." Saint-Saëns then commented that these novices "were, among many others, Bizet and Delibes; they were Massenet; they were the author of these lines."[11]

Massenet is an example of a composer who successfully conducted his career taking full account of the role of political power in the French artistic system and managing to plan his own entry into the various musical institutions as well as his conquest of the public. He wrote a cantata for the Fête de l'Empereur, August 15, 1867, and in the same year had a curtain-raiser, *La Grand'Tante,* produced at the Opéra-Comique. This was followed by a more ambitious work, *Don César de Bazan* (1872), produced in the same theater. Two oratorios—*Marie-Magdeleine* (1873) and *Eve* (1875) —along with some help from Ambroise Thomas, an audience-pleasing style, and carefully chosen subjects in tune with the trends of the moment: all these brought him to the Théâtre de l'Opéra, where his *Le Roi de Lahore* was performed in 1877. He gradually became the leader of the French operatic school.

After devoting a third of his long "Revue musicale" column in the October 5, 1863, issue of *Le Constitutionnel* to the state of new works in France, Nestor Roqueplan wrote of the unknown young composer he had been discussing:

> What is the point of this sad tale ...? I wanted first of all to show how difficult, even impossible, it is for a young composer, a Prix de Rome winner, a beginner, to find a play or a poem that makes any sense; I wanted also to pay tribute to the selflessness of Messieurs Carré and Cormon, who demanded no reward, no sacrifice of dignity or of cash, to give a three-act libretto to M. Georges Bizet—who had, to be sure, written very fine individual pieces, but who was a complete newcomer to the theater and who had a better chance of failure than of success.

The members of the press were all the more amazed because Bizet was being well treated in every respect and was enjoying "princely hospitality," as though *Les Pêcheurs de perles* were the work of a famous master who had the right to enforce his demands.

It was so rare for a young composer's work to be produced that, if he was to believe in the miracle, one writer needed to see this fortunate man with his own eyes, and to gaze upon "the face of this singularly rare being, this modern myth called a 'new author.' "[12] This made Roqueplan cry out, "He is twenty-five years old! The monster! How can anyone be twenty-five years old?! ... In general, a 'young composer' is considered to be any musician who has not yet been performed, even if he is fifty. Beyond that age, he is called a former young composer—and dried fruit."[13] The situation had hardly changed by 1870, and the satirical *Dictionnaire musico-humoristique* defined "Young composer" in a stinging couplet: "Un vieillard que soutient l'espoir de débuter, / Et que mille refus ne peuvent rebuter—An old man sustained by the hope of a debut, / Whom even a thousand rejections cannot discourage."[14]

One journalist used references to characters from Balzac to paint an evocative picture of the typical fate of young composers:

> In general they get the same consideration as the poor relations whom one is obliged to entertain in the country. These Cousin Pons or Cousin Bettes are given a room just beneath the attic, hung with chocolate-brown paper; they are seated at the far end of the table; the best morsels are for the others; and one barely seems to notice their presence. Taking their cue from the attitude of their master, the household servants have only indifference and scorn for these unfortunates; ... with a thousand snubs, they make them feel like intruders, and that they are only putting up with them for a few days because they have no choice.[15]

Gounod described "the poor, unknown musicians who, to earn their daily bread, are reduced to commit real musical crimes, with which their Mephistophelian tempters, the publishers, gull the public and line their own pockets."[16]

WINNERS OF THE PRIX DE ROME—
BERLIOZ: THE EXCEPTION TO THE RULE

Balzac portrayed his Cousin Pons—"the author of the first cantata to take the laurels at the Institut when the Académie de Rome was reestablished"—as a pitiable individual.[17] Sylvain Pons, he wrote, was clearly "one of the many victims of the disastrous system of competitions that still prevails in France, in spite of a century without results.... Try to count on your fingers the geniuses among that century's prizewinners! ... no administrative or educational effort can replace the miracle of fate that produces great men."[18] The works that a stipend holder composed during his time in Rome vanished into obscurity. "France, which strives to produce artists by the hot-house method of the competition, once she has obtained a sculptor, a painter, a engraver, or a musician by this mechanical process pays no more attention to him than the dandy does of an evening to the flower he has worn in his buttonhole."[19] The system against which Balzac railed had hardly changed in 1863. For a long time "submissions from Rome never reached the public," Saint-Saëns noted. "All that would happen was that a report would be

read out at a meeting of the Academy."[20] The composer returning from
Rome "is a legend: his stay in the Eternal City only serves to get him forgotten—assuming that he has ever been known. He himself must work to
make his name, knock on every door, suffer rebuffs, and try on his own to
attract an audience for his works, something that, as everybody knows, is
nearly impossible."[21]

For added rhetorical force, one critic mimicked the exaggerated style of
the tearjerker:

> Has it not been sufficiently trumpeted from the rooftops—of the Opéra-
> Comique and the Théâtre-Lyrique—that the garrets of Paris are crammed
> with Prix de Rome winners? That these unfortunates, carefully fed on il-
> lusions and counterpoint lessons for ten years, are dying in the hospitals
> after wearing out their fingernails clawing at the doors of the theaters?
> That they are sometimes found in the nets at Saint-Cloud, in the morgue,
> or in the sewers? I don't know. All these dark things have been said; they
> have even been written in tear-drenched fiction.[22]

Louis Martinet provided statistics to prove how ineffective the Prix de
Rome had been: "Between 1803, when the Prix de Rome was established,
and 1860, the Institut awarded fifty-four first prizes.... The Government
makes a commitment to the young artist who achieves this victory that it
will see to it that one of his compositions is performed in one of our major
lyric theaters. A clause in the *cahier des charges* of the Opéra-Comique
sets out a formal obligation in that regard."[23] But as the repertory of the
Opéra-Comique began to move toward more ambitious works, that theater
could not "perform young composers, who could hardly, without risk to
the management, make their debuts with lengthy works, which demand
creative powers and practical skills that can be gained only with time and
experience." The end result was "that the Prix de Rome guarantees inevitably turned out to be a dead letter, and that there was no longer any
outlet for young composers." The figures seem to bear him out: "At the
Opéra-Comique, twenty-seven [first-prize winners] had about that number of works performed, and an equal number—twenty-seven—were
never able to make the grade. At the Opéra, out of fifty-four, *eight* were
found worthy of an appearance before the public." Opinion was divided
about what to make of the unexpected production of Bizet's opera. Was it a
rejoinder to those who had criticized the Théâtre-Lyrique for not doing
enough for young composers? Was it an incentive for other Prix de Rome
winners? Or did it give rise to false hopes?

The production of *Les Troyens* in the same theater on November 4—a
work by an experienced musician this time—also caused a stir, despite the

composer's age. Critics such as Johannès Weber summarized the difficult career of the composer of the *Symphonie fantastique,* offering it as a particularly striking example. Weber is revealing about the practices of the closed world of the opera house. He points out that in spite of the promising second and third performances of *Benvenuto Cellini* in 1838 (see fig. 24), the work did not last long at the Opéra (it was given a total of seven times) because "the management had in advance attached no importance to this work; it had classified it among the minor pieces, useful only for diversifying the repertory as a curtain-raiser for a ballet. It claimed practical obstacles; for two months the ritual words 'Expected,' 'Coming soon,' and 'Coming very soon' were rotated on the posters; finally, it settled on 'Expected.' Since that time M. Berlioz has had plenty of time to learn that the obstacles facing a composer have not changed or abated at all."[24]

## OPERA: THE SOLE PATH TO SUCCESS

Roqueplan lamented that "today, whatever the ability of the composer, if he does not want to remain in obscurity he must, willy-nilly, turn out operas."[25] This was because of the particular taste of the French for theater and because of their habit of linking music to some kind of program or of directly connecting it to a text. Early in the twentieth century, Lucien Augé de Lassus, in his convoluted style, described this situation and its consequences for the composer:

> The French—generally speaking, human beings who are indeed from France—completely like music only when it is allied with words. They seek, they demand of this music a drama or a comedy to accompany it, and scenery to frame it. This is no dream of some supreme ideal; it is the way things are. Hence, the obsession with the theater haunts every one of us who thinks and lives amidst the song of notes and sounds. Material profit, resounding glory, popularity: for us, these do not recompense the labors of the musician-composer except when in league with the theater.[26]

An obvious exception was the class of composer-virtuosos, whose success owed more to their verve as performers than to their creative skills.

In a 1913 article on music education, Charles Koechlin stressed that dramatic music was the sole focus of music teaching in the second half of the nineteenth century: "As for composition per se, ... it is fair to say that before 1870 teaching was more theatrical than symphonic. ... The Prix de Rome, for which most students were aiming, was (and still is) awarded for a cantata—a most artificial kind of theatrical exercise. Above all, the climate was

Figure 24.  Anonymous caricature of Berlioz and
his *Benvenuto Cellini* (*L'Album théâtral*, ca. 1838).

not terribly symphonic."[27] A comment on "student exercises" substantiates
the predominance of opera in musical instruction: "Between 1841 and 1862,
...programs were made up almost exclusively of lyric or dramatic works, either complete or in the form of excerpts."[28] Long before Koechlin, Adolphe
Adam conferred primacy on opera by putting "dramatic composers at the
top level of the musical hierarchy."[29] Another mark of the social status of
opera composers was the money they earned for every performance: "Happily, they perform my operas," wrote Saint-Saëns in 1890, "which provides
me with hitherto unknown prosperity."[30]

Bizet's position was part of a social system to which opera composers were answerable for much of the nineteenth century, and that is important to take into account in order to understand the way in which French composers developed and the choices they made. Bizet was greatly affected by the musical customs of the day, and like most of his contemporaries, sought success within that restrictive framework. Berlioz, by contrast, assembled the body of his work very much against the wind of convention. He needed every bit of his moral fiber, his passion, his courage, his strong opinions, and his rebellious nature to stand up against the weight of the establishment and to resist dishonorable compromise:

> For thirty years this bold, courageous man has battled, and he has never given in to his adversaries. His artistic conscience is free of capitulation or weakness. He has always preferred oblivion to owing his success to concessions. He has calmly watched the mediocre and the clever rise to success all around him; he has watched doors that were closed to him open easily to others who certainly lacked his self-respect and his worth. He has struggled, always struggled; all his victories have been won thanks to his unshakable faith and his unflagging perseverance.[31]

### PARIS AND DECENTRALIZATION—MUSICAL PARISIANISM— AUBER, A PARISIAN COMPOSER

The theater was virtually the only path to success for aspiring composers—and their ambitions, moreover, could be realized in one city only. From the public's standpoint, and "throughout the Empire, there will always be a prejudice—and quite a plausible one—against any work that has not gotten its start in Paris, which has not earned the stamp and the approbation of the capital."[32] By and large, the Paris press promoted the idea among composers, singers, and the general public that success could be achieved only in Paris. The capital of good taste was the only place where proper judgments could be made, and where one could reach the artistic summits. As Théophile Gautier wrote, "A poet, a singer, an actor whom Paris has deigned to favor with its supreme approval can go anywhere, head held high, certain of universal applause."[33] Literature generally perpetuated this dual image of provincial mediocrity (in a narrow intellectual sphere, with people embittered by their unrelievedly monotonous lives) and of Parisian genius. This is clearly seen in the novels of Stendhal and Balzac, to name but two.

In his review of A.-L. Mailliot's book *La Musique au théâtre* (1863), "Paul Smith" (Edouard Monnais) unambiguously says that "in anything related to the fine arts or the theater, this dreadful 'decentralization' is nothing but a chimera."[34] For historical reasons, it was impossible. "No power in the world is strong enough to make it happen, because it is impossible to change the course of a river." France, with its centralized system, was contrasted with countries such as Italy and Germany, whose history was completely different: "If a composer cannot get performed in Rome or Naples, he can take his work to Florence, Genoa, Venice, or Milan; if a musician does not succeed in Vienna, he can redeem himself in Prague or Dresden or Weimar or Berlin. A French composer can bank only on Paris."[35] In a lengthy article entitled "On German Music," written in 1840, Wagner reveled in defining the German and French mind-sets in terms of that basic difference, which gave rise to musical ideas suited to the two peoples.[36] In an 1864 essay, Ernest Reyer named Germany as an example worth following. There, he wrote, "the *Kapellmeister,* that learned and modest artist, living far removed from the glittering activities of the great capitals, can see his name and his works spread from town to town and can quickly gain a renown for which he has not had to strive, because it has come to him."[37] But the most ambitious and greatest of foreigners themselves saw Paris as a beacon, as the unique city in which a musician's career could gain endorsement. Gluck, Rossini, Bellini, Donizetti, Meyerbeer, Verdi, and Wagner were all in various ways captivated by the great city and worked to adapt their styles to French tastes.

There was no resolution of the question of decentralization in sight, because it was necessary also to contend with what the Parisians viewed as the appalling state of cultural life in the provinces. Twenty-five drawings by Eustache Lorsay, entitled "Le Théâtre en province" and published in *La Vie parisienne,* June 6, 1863 (fig. 25), sum it up: from the pretentious, second-rate artists, to the petty, coarse audiences, to the local journalists, all the elements of the theatrical world of the provinces were placed under the microscope and their absurdities exposed. On November 1, 1863, Cerfberr pontificated in *Le Théâtre:* "Decentralization is a utopian idea. There is no audience in the provinces—or rather, what there is is worse than an audience. The enterprise is therefore impossible."

A young composer who was determined to succeed had only one option: like the hero of novel after novel, he had to conquer the capital. From the beginning to the end of the nineteenth century, from Rastignac in Balzac's *Le Père Goriot,* issuing his challenge to Paris from the topmost point of Père-Lachaise cemetery, to Saccard in Zola's *La Curée,* up in the heights of Montmartre imagining the rebuilding of that unsettling, fascinating city, ambition brought determined young people to Paris, that "great pharmacy where virtually every element of French civilization is compounded,"[38] that monster that seemed to absorb all the life force of the country, where every hope could be hoped—where "to arrive" really meant something. In Balzac's words, far from that center, where "great minds shine, where the air is heavy with ideas and where everything is in a state of flux, education is outmoded and good taste putrefies like stagnant water."[39]

In the great city itself, people knew they were in a special world, and their life, even their language, was marked by an exclusivity that bordered on self-satisfaction and snobbism. This strict centralization, as we have seen, involved an operatic hierarchy that was closely linked to society's power structure. The opera houses were like sacrosanct temples. To strip Paris of the prestige of its theaters would have been "to diminish it and, in a way, to declare that it has forfeited its primacy in intellectual matters. It is the artistic capital of the entire world; any sacrifice aimed at upholding that primacy is proper."[40] Fashion was everything in this microcosm devoted to the contemplation of its own superiority: "Critics have often pointed out the uniformity of ideas, techniques, and effects in the majority of works written in Paris: the same style of orchestration, of arranging the voices, and of constructing the numbers—all in line with fashion."[41] Young composers did not deviate from these rules and followed a single path; one might think "that they compose in the grip of heaven knows what collection of ideas that they all share in common."[42] Composers who wanted to climb the ladder of success with greater ease had to obey the Law of Parisianism and follow the example of Auber. They also had to accept all the conventions of that world and pay particular attention to etiquette and to the role they were expected to play. In her biography of Verdi, Mary Jane Phillips-Matz contrasts that composer's nature with the social activities necessary for success in the world of French *grand opéra*: "Hating the machinery of the French music business, he said that he would never 'spend the few thousand francs' that he earned on 'publicity, on a claque, and filth like that,' even though he thought they were necessary if one were to have a success in Paris. Equally important were appearances at concerts, operas, receptions, soirees, and banquets; but...Verdi...detested such social events."[43]

Reyer unhesitatingly predicted that Auber would "remain the outstanding personification of French musical genius, as no one else possesses a higher degree of those two eminently French qualities, wit and charm—for which the German masters do not even envy us."[44] And another writer goes even further: "Auber is not merely a Frenchman; he is a pure-bred Parisian. All his works therefore reflect the originality, the elegance, the charm, the high spirits, the grace—indeed, the light, mocking tone—that constitute the Parisian character."[45] That was why "the success enjoyed by

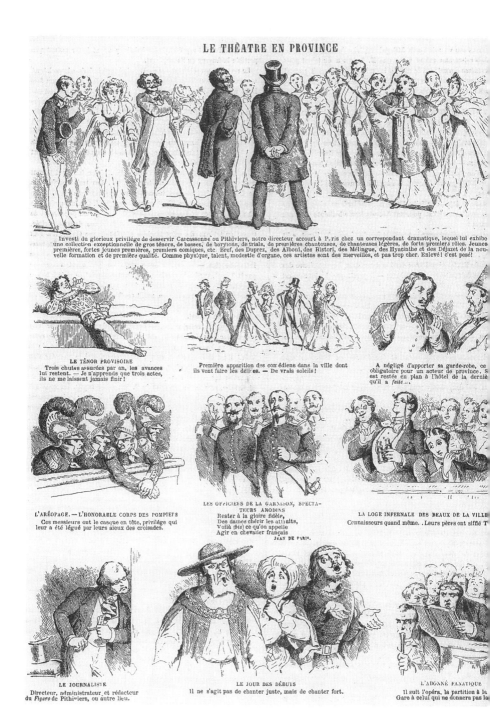

Figure 25.    Eustache Lorsay, "Le Théâtre en province" (Theater in the provinces), *La Vie parisienne*, June 6, 1863.

commencer la danse, on / e ténor; le baryton n'a / long feu. On s'amusera

La basse-taille ayant eu la petitesse
de laisser à la contre-basse le soin de
donner le fameux mi-bémol grave,
Azor donne le sien, — à l'octave. L'artiste s'est trouvé mal dans la cou-
lisse. Parfait! A d'autres!

Cris de la salle: « Le régisseur! le régisseur! » On
n'a rien à réclamer de ce
fonctionnaire, que le plaisir de s'assurer s'il a des
gants et un habit!

Ces messieurs sont en trop
bon train pour ne pas faire tom-
ber la première chanteuse à roulades. Il n'y a plus de sexe, mais
des accusés et des juges.

Quant à la troupe de
drame, on n'en fait qu'une
bouchée. Tous sur le car-
reau, pour ne pas dire sur
le pavé!

eune premier Potinchard, trop *égayé* par
lic, lui a dit: «zut!» A ce moment,
chez Guignol, apparition du commis-

FOYER DU PUBLIC
L'aréopage se félicitant de sa besogne. C'est une leçon de
bon goût donnée aux Parisiens. On en parlera dans Lan-
dernau.

Commission de douze membres, présidée par
l'adjoint au maire, pour l'acceptation ou le refus
de tel ou tel artiste. Douze vilaines boules!

énors tomb s de
les abonnés exi-
ballet! Plus de
pa- de public, donc
gent. Le d recteur
lever le pied. Le-
tre les deux son
ance.

Renfort. Georgeval, le Frédérik Lemaître, le
Mélingue de la province, est dans nos murs.
Tambours, battez! Paysans, payez!

Supplice de l'acteur de province. Cinquante
lignes par jour à se fourrer dans la cervelle, ce
qui lui assurera, à un temps donné, un engagement sérieux... pour Charenton. Il apprend
en marchant, il apprend en mangeant, il apprend
même en dormant — d'un œil!

Le théâtre va mal, Georgeval a fait
long feu; les acteurs, peu payés,
en sont réduits, dans la saison du
carnaval, à louer des costumes pour
vivre. Arrivée d'un célèbre acteur
de Paris Il sera payé sur la recette,
c'est-à-dire qu'il prendra tout
entière.

est vrai que la salle s'emplit parfois de parents
usiciens de l'orchestre, ce qui fait que, ainsi
x, le directeur joue gratis.

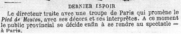

DERNIER ESPOIR
Le directeur traite avec une troupe de Paris qui promène le
*Pied de Mouton*, avec ses décors et ses interprètes. A ce moment
le public provincial se décide enfin à se rendre au spectacle —
à Paris.

MORALE: AU SUJET DU PRÉJUGÉ SUR LES COMÉDIENS
— Louez-moi votre animal, j'en aurais besoin
dans la pièce que je fais répéter. — Mon âne,
monter sur les planches? jamais!

every revival of an Auber piece cannot be explained only by his abilities as a consummate musician, but even more by the perfect consonance between the emotions the composer prefers to depict and those that Parisian audiences are capable of feeling."[46]

## MONOPOLISTIC LIBRETTISTS AND POOR LIBRETTOS

The young composer who wished to succeed in the Parisian operatic world had to abide by the system's rules, and accept its hierarchy and authorities. After harshly criticizing the libretto of *Les Pêcheurs de perles* and discussing what he saw as the appalling overall situation of French opera, Franck-Marie wrote of the monopolies held by certain librettists:

> But it is impossible to believe that such an unbelievable situation is the result of barrenness on the part of our young writers; it is rather the result of the "monopoly" held by a small group, which exists in our musical theaters in fact if not in principle. Anyone who does not belong to a certain category of writers—or, to put it more clearly, to a certain clique—is systematically turned away. Only those who have already succeeded, who have a name and a reputation, whether dazzling or modest, are admitted. Their imagination has run dry; their vein is exhausted; for most of them, the years have chilled the inventiveness that is indispensable for writing any fiction for the theater. But that does not matter; it is only they who must write, it is only they who must overrun every stage and enchant our hours of leisure—and we can see how they do it.[47]

The privileged few were sought after by every composer who wanted a libretto stamped with the guarantee of a famous author; they became inaccessible, to the extent that they aroused murderous feelings in young musicians. To be sure, they were

> very courteous and very friendly, and they welcome young musicians in the manner of the most gracious, cordial circles; but they are so overwhelmed and besieged that a newcomer does not even dare to take the seat that has been offered him for fear of stealing precious moments from the public.... The musician slinks away, despairing of ever getting a scrap of prose or a line of octosyllables from so busy and sought-after a man. He glances longingly at three or four scrolls tied with pink ribbon lying temptingly on the literary man's desk. Just one of these texts, if he were permitted to set it to music, would make his fortune. He feels the beginnings of [murderous] instincts...a cloud of blood passes before his eyes. What if he were to strangle the author and take his plays?[48]

It was high time "for intelligent theater directors to take a stand on retiring these literary compilers, who form a clique that is so harmful to art and to the theaters that continue to work hand-in-glove with it," another critic observed.[49] According to Franck-Marie, "anyone with aspirations to the stage is victimized by a dreadful system of exclusivity, which not only causes unspeakable suffering but sooner or later will inevitably, inescapably, rot the theatrical arts."[50] In his next column, the same critic came to the conclusion that the situation of the playwright was even worse than that of the young composer, who had the option of entering a competition and who could at least hope for a few public performances. On the other hand, the financial circumstances of writers who actually had their works performed were more enviable than that of composers. According to another journalist, "Writers get the lion's share: not only do they hold half the rights, which is fair; not only can they sell their librettos, while the composer sees nothing from this, but they take half the sales price of the score, which . . . seems outrageous."[51]

The situation seems to have been caused by the better playwrights' lack of interest in writing librettos: "Very few authors produce tolerable plays, and they, in general, do not care at all for working in the lyric theaters, where they are performed [only] three times a week. Unless one is working with Meyerbeer or Rossini, this is as unprofitable as writing poetry."[52] Even Verdi came up against the tremendous power of the librettist. When working on *Les Vêpres siciliennes,* he asked Eugène Scribe to make some changes, only to find that composers were by no means in a position to ensure that their wishes were granted: "It is . . . painful and humiliating to me that M. Scribe is not bothering to fix this fifth act, which everyone agrees is uninteresting. I am not unaware that M. Scribe has a thousand other things to do, to which he may be more committed than he is to my opera! But if I could ever have suspected his utter indifference, I would have stayed in my own country, where, to tell the truth, things are not so bad for me."[53]

From his earliest years as a music critic, Berlioz scoffed at the French system. In his inimitable style, he described the various options open to a composer, including that of the lyric theater:

> Does he wish to write for the theater? Then he needs what theater directors are in the habit of calling a "poem." Once he has this "poem"—whether it be detestable, flat, vulgar, passable, or good (for good ones have been heard of )—he must have it read. To secure a reading there are endless steps that have to be taken, every kind of entreaty to every kind of person; ordeals that would ultimately try the patience of a saint. If the libretto is bad, it is rejected; if it is passable, it is still rejected; if it is good, they will advise the author to work with a great libretto-maker who will put his name on it, alter the rhyme in two or three lines and get

it performed. But often, the libretto's author does not want to agree to such a deal; the good "poem" is then conclusively rejected and the frustrated composer is driven to being patient, or changing course, or writing *vaudevilles,* or blowing his brains out.[54]

## THE POWER OF THEATER DIRECTORS—THE HOPES VESTED
## IN FREEING THE THEATERS FROM GOVERNMENT CONTROL

Even more so than librettists, theater directors were all-powerful in the world to which young composers sought access. Since they held the keys to success, they ignored the most elementary rules of courtesy. "You cannot imagine the crudeness and humiliation inflicted on anyone who knocked on a director's door. Nowhere else is there such complete disdain for the most basic propriety, for the most common politeness; if one knew the attitudes—not backstage, but further back still, in the areas between the [doorkeeper's] lodge below and the directorial chambers above—one would not often risk setting foot there."[55] Franck-Marie highlighted the sense of duty that ought to guide these directors as the representatives of institutions under state control, and raised the issue of freedom for the theaters—*la liberté des théâtres:*

> I know perfectly well that generally speaking a director considers himself to be the absolute master of his own domain....He is wrong; every privilege implies a duty, some sort of obligation, and even when he receives no subsidy he is indebted to the state for the advantages that result from the monopoly he has been granted. If we want him to be independent, we should allow competition; otherwise, it is obvious that a small number of individuals can, if they wish, cause mortal damage to artistic interests.

The critic sought more widespread use of the readers' committees that were then limited to the major institutions, and he spoke of the role of the Théâtre de l'Opéra: "Such an organization meets every requirement; unfortunately, it exists only in a single theater, the very one to which inexperienced young authors cannot gain access. The Théâtre-Français and the Grand Opéra are not theatrical testing grounds. Both are devoted to classic works or to authors whose worth is recognized, whose talents are fully developed, whose fame is in hand: in short, veterans of the arts."[56]

Directors were eager above all for strong box-office receipts, and instantly ruled out all risky experiments with young composers. Inevitably, their attention fell on well-known artists and proven works that would guarantee them security. Carvalho, who as we have seen was more interested in creativity than in bookkeeping, stood out in contrast to an otherwise inglorious picture.

From every quarter there were calls for freeing the theaters from government control as the only way to breathe new life into French opera. "Only freedom for the theaters," wrote Charles Desolmes in October 1863, "will silence the moaning and the tooth-gnashing. But will it be instituted, as promised, on January 1st? All the authors whose portfolios are overflowing, all the composers whose scores lie mute, all the privilege seekers who knock in vain at the doors of the Ministry or cool their heels in M. Doucet's antechamber [in the Ministry of Fine Arts], everyone with any sense of adventure, who harbors any illusions, will reply in the affirmative."[57]

After many and repeated petitions, articles, and other requests over the years, the government agreed to loosen the ties that bound the theaters to the state. The astonishing news came during the run of *Les Pêcheurs de perles* and dominated the Paris press: "Freedom for the theaters, a measure...that has long been called for as the best way to encourage the dramatic arts and dramatic literature, has just been adopted through the generous initiative of the emperor, and the Conseil d'Etat is considering a draft decree whose purpose is to endorse this decision."[58]

A few isolated voices qualified the rejoicing unleashed by this reform—a reform needed for the progress of freedom but that was not enough to enable a young composer to get his work performed without encountering problems. One should not, admonished Edouard Monnais, "delight in it excessively or hope for too much from it, as do the authors and composers who do not enjoy great favor, who believe that, thanks to this freedom, [the theaters] will inevitably be obliged and compelled to perform their works."[59]

# Chapter 8   Genre

*Les Pêcheurs de perles* was announced as an *opéra-comique,* but when produced, it turned out to be something quite different. The journalists of the day were hard pressed to grasp this opera, which seemed to be based on a series of paradoxes. As a result, commentary was rife about the matter of genre in French operatic art. The work's ambiguities resulted also from the methods of the young composer, who was drawn to the new sounds of Gounod, was fascinated by *grand opéra* as a model of social success, and was seeking to please his audience with some "easy" numbers.

Genres were by no means mere labels, useful to varying degrees for an understanding of the operatic world and the result of an excessive zeal for classification. Even though it is hard to pin down their exact definitions, they corresponded to a reality. The development of these genres had a decisive effect on the history of French opera in the nineteenth century. The names of genres "are not simply analytic terms that are applied to the history of texts from the outside; to varying degrees, they are part of that history," Jean-Marie Schaeffer observes of literature, and this is just as true of opera.[1]

Bizet's opera—with its lively plot, sung from start to finish, and with its employment of the full power of the orchestra—can be compared only with that higher, more grandiose form of lyric theater, the *grand opéra.* Bizet, as one critic wrote, "succeeded in acquiring a poem by two experienced authors, in composing an opera—a 'grand opéra' in three acts, let me recall—and, even more miraculously, in getting it performed."[2] *Grand opéra,* viewed as the ultimate genre, was thought of as being reserved for well-known composers. Bizet was therefore described as an ambitious young man who was moving ahead by leaps and bounds. Another critic wondered whether this *grand opéra* was appropriate for the Théâtre-

Lyrique: "We were…watching a young composer test his strength…and judging him in a genre entirely new to the Théâtre-Lyrique, *grand opéra*. Will this theater's usual audience like this genre? This is a difficult question to answer."[3] Johannès Weber set about explaining the factors that made Bizet's work belong to that genre: "*Les Pêcheurs de perles* is nothing less than a *grand opéra*, not only because spoken dialogue is replaced throughout by recitative, but also because there is absolutely nothing to laugh at in the piece, not a single comic character, and because the authors of both the text and the music were aiming at grand dramatic effects."[4] Besides the lack of spoken dialogue, other defining elements of *grand opéra* that were constantly mentioned were large dimensions, a serious character, and the use of large-scale effects. So, can the presence or absence of spoken dialogue be viewed as a basis for defining operatic genres?

## THE SPOKEN AND THE SUNG— THE COMPLEXITY OF DEFINING GENRE

It is clear from nineteenth-century theoretical writings that the use of spoken dialogue in a French lyric work was a decisive factor in defining that work's genre. Early in the century, Castil-Blaze wrote, "We have…two genres of lyric performance: drama that is sung from beginning to end, which is commonly called *grand opéra*,…and *opéra-comique*, in which singing is combined with spoken dialogue."[5] A few years later, F.-J. Fétis expressed the same idea: "There are two genres of French opera: *grand opéra*, which is sung from beginning to end, and *opéra-comique*, in which the actors alternately speak and sing."[6] Then, in 1885, Arthur Pougin lamented that in "France, our lyric repertory is divided into two genres defined in a very arbitrary way, not on the basis of the nature of the works, but on the basis of the single fact of whether or not they are interspersed with spoken dialogue."[7] The dichotomy between verse and prose was also connected with this contrast between constant singing and the insertion of speech: "In *grand opéra*, the dialogue, entirely written in verse, is given in music, either through melody or through recitative.…In *opéra-comique*, the dialogue, written partly in prose and partly in verse, is either spoken or sung."[8]

Moreover, the subject had to be suitable for its genre. This was not always the case, and throughout the century, paradoxical situations arose. It would have been terribly simple "if *grand opéra* permitted only serious subjects and if *opéra-comique* always justified its name by the pleasant gaiety of its productions. The magnificent name of *grand opéra*…is given to wretched *vaudevilles*; and, in a most curious turnabout, *Médée, Joseph,* and *Roméo et Juliette* are classed among the *opéras-comiques*."[9] Castil-Blaze concluded that "it is the character of a piece and not the various ways in which its parts are put together that ought to place it in one category or the other."

For the modern observer, who can look back with hindsight over the entire nineteenth century, one problem is that terminology and connotations from different periods of French operatic history tend to become intermingled.[10] For example, *opéra-comique* originated in the eighteenth century; it took a variety of directions and changed a great deal until it became more substantial with Meyerbeer's *L'Etoile du Nord* (1854)—"whose only fault is that it is too big for its venue"[11]—and *Le Pardon de Ploërmel* (1859)—which, according to a conservative critic, was "by no means...*opéra-comique* music,"[12] despite the composer's having lightened his style for the occasion. During the second half of the nineteenth century, operetta, which was originally very circumscribed in style, gradually grew in substance and ultimately replaced traditional *opéra-comique*. For its part, *grand opéra* evolved, especially around 1830, and endured until the end of the century with works such as Massenet's *Le Cid* (1885), in spite of an aesthetic that quickly came to be viewed as archaic. In the 1860s, a new expressive form, sometimes termed *opéra lyrique*, was fashioned, often within the framework of *opéra-comique*, with the works of Ambroise Thomas, Félicien David, and Charles Gounod.

Factors that went into defining genre included the scale of the work; the way in which its text was voiced (in verse or in prose; through singing or through speaking); the subject of its libretto; its overall conception, including the extent of visual elements such as settings and ballet; and its stylistic characteristics. In addition to these internal criteria, there were external ones, such as the work's relationship to its audience. Pierre Larousse explained that "operas continue to be classified by genre according to the kind of impression they seek to create."[13] In a paragraph on comic opera—*opéra bouffe*—Larousse wrote of the relationship between a genre and the way in which that genre responds to the needs of an audience. "The opening of the Théâtre des Bouffes-Parisiens and the success of Offenbach's works prove that this genre responded to a real need."[14] People went to the opera to enjoy a specific type of entertainment. Along the same lines, Albert de Lasalle wrote that operetta "is a genre unto itself, with its own definition, in that it responds to a need."[15] The meager success of Bizet's *Les Pêcheurs de perles* was at least in part because it did not meet the expectations of the Théâtre-Lyrique audience in terms of genre.

## OPÉRA-COMIQUE

This genre was produced mainly at the Théâtre de l'Opéra-Comique, but was seen also at other houses, including in particular the Théâtre-Lyrique. Over the nineteenth century, in its nightly performances, the Opéra-Comique put on a large number of works of varying scale. It would be no exaggeration to suggest that, as a form of sophisticated entertainment, *opéra-comique* was a kind of "artistic commodity"—at least until the 1870s. The Opéra-Comique continued its performances right through the summer up to 1875. Until then, the theater—known also as the Salle Favart—was shut only for exceptional reasons. Between 1840 and 1887, 351 works were performed at the Salle Favart, including 249 world premieres, 25 first performances of works already played in other theaters, 75 pieces from the earlier repertory, and two translations of Mozart operas: *Les Noces de Figaro* in 1872 and *La Flûte enchantée* in 1879.

Despite the numerous exceptions, *opéra-comique*, often called an "eminently French genre," coincided for much of the nineteenth century with a certain notion of French operatic aesthetics. In 1932, Raoul Duhamel could write that this genre had a kind of "affinity...with the outlook of our race."[16] He went on to define the genre by listing its standard characteristics: "So what exactly is French *opéra-comique*? It is basically a comedy or tragi-comedy with a happy ending in which singing alternates with spoken dialogue and is of more or less the same importance; in which the numbers—composed of short phrases of verse that are easy to understand and that are designed for singing—are in traditional forms: *airs, chansons, couplets, romances, cavatines,* duets, trios, quartets, quintets, ensembles, and choruses; in which singing and melody have pride of place; in which melody is always in the form of complete phrases and is 'a clearly shaped, complete progression of sounds' that always has a clear form, a simple and straightforward rhythm, lucid tonality without elaborate chromaticism and with modulations that are few and simple; and in which the harmony is always simple and natural, the counterpoint restrained and subdued and the instrumentation always airy, so that the orchestra will support the voice while never obscuring it."[17]

Well before Duhamel, Wagner had affirmed that in essence *opéra-comique* music was popular and dancelike in its arias and its overall structure, and was characterized by regular melodic periods. He considered that, because of "the essentially French character of his music," Auber provided the perfect model for the genre.[18] And Boileau, in his *Art poétique* ("Chant II"), observed that "the French, born clever, created the *vaudeville.*" Exasperated by that rudimentary form of musical theater (which in expanded form was found in many *opéras-comiques*), Berlioz too would use such turns of phrase in his music criticism to lampoon a French genre that he found laughable when it was too similar to popular song. None of the sometimes successful attempts to expand *opéra-comique* and add greater expressive density to its music made it impossible for audiences to listen with pleasure to the light, catchy numbers of a genre whose golden age was undoubtedly the period between 1830 and 1840. In 1836, one critic expressed his satisfaction at finding Adam's *Le Postillon de Longjumeau* to be a "pure-bred *opéra-comique*" replete with "lucid, straightforward melodies, supported but not overwhelmed by the orchestration."[19] Those were the same ingredients that in another period, enhanced by a more subtle musical language, would ensure the success of a work such as André Messager's *Fortunio,* which had its premiere on June 5, 1907, at the Opéra-Comique, and which happily combined charming melodies, clear orchestration, dramatic effectiveness, colorful scenes, gaiety, and occasional tenderness or melancholy.

In 1841, the critic R. O. Spazier drew an excessively radical distinction between the German and French approaches to opera: "France's *opéras-comiques* are not, as far as we can see, genre operas or musical comedies solely because they contain speaking; it is necessary to speak so much and so wittily that the music becomes a more or less incidental ornament and shares the audience's attention only on terms of equality with the dialogue. That is why tragedy and high passion, which require far greater musical development, are inherently out of the question."[20] Yet the genre evolved, thanks to the increasing importance accorded to the music and to plots that aspired more and more to poignancy. In discussing the repertory of the Opéra-Comique between 1840 and 1887, Albert Soubies and Charles Malherbe noted the extent to which in the *opéras-comiques* of that period "the poem outstripped the score in importance.... One is surprised today at the compositional facility that enabled composers such as Auber, Adam, Halévy, and Ambroise Thomas . . . to provide the theater with its annual allotment of a new work. But it must also be recalled that the role of the music was still rather limited. The slightest operetta today contains more than twenty numbers; [Auber's] *La Sirène* [1844] contained thirteen, only three of them in the first act."[21]

The ratio of speaking to singing was slowly changing, as was the required style of singing. The flexible, light *opéra-comique* tenor was gradually replaced by more of a lyric tenor whose voice could stand up to fuller orchestrations and who was obliged to abandon florid, graceful vocal lines—such as those of Georges Brown in *La Dame blanche*—in favor of broader melodies. The forsaking of spoken dialogue and the changes in singing style were both exemplified by the production at the Opéra-Comique on January 20, 1873, of Gounod's *Roméo et Juliette,* which had first been heard at the Théâtre-Lyrique in 1867. "To some extent," wrote Soubies and Malherbe,

> this was the first "opera" . . . admitted [to the Opéra-Comique], that is, the first score without a spoken element; this innovation was imperceptibly to change the tastes of audiences as well as the nature of vocal performance. [Adolphe] Duchesne had already been the first, at the 1,000th performance of *Le Pré aux clercs,* to sing as a *fort-ténor,* using chest voice in, for example, the *romance* "O ma tendre amie!" where head voice had hitherto been sufficient. Singers such as Couderc and Capoul moved aside for those such as Monjauze and Talazac. Gounod's works more than any others fostered this transition.[22]

Simultaneously, plots became more serious, and purely comedic incidents grew rare. Death, once forbidden in what was supposed to be a pleasant genre, was only warily brought to the stage of the Opéra-Comique. When Louis Ferdinand Hérold's *Zampa* was performed in 1831, the conservatives reacted. A columnist in *Le Messager des Chambres* wrote on May 5 of that year that "in an *opéra-comique,* no matter what, the music does not count for much more than half; the poem does the rest. . . . circumstances dictate that the musical power that they sought to give to this piece must fail, given the requirements of the genre." The orchestra, which conveyed the tragic and poetic dimension of the work; the rich harmonic language; the frequent use of dissonance; the ambitious musical forms; and the serious subject: these aroused concern about the death of this French "national genre."

In 1852, Auber and his librettists Scribe and Delavigne killed off their hero Marco Spada, who found himself in the dire moral dilemma of having to claim that Angela was not his daughter so as not to put her forthcoming marriage in jeopardy. Some journalists railed against such a scene: "Truly, the denouement is too serious, too sad, too tragic for this venue. The final scene . . . has the fault of leaving the spectator with feelings of distress."[23] In 1856, the moving death scene in *Manon Lescaut* by Scribe and Auber marked a new stage in the depiction of death in *opéra-comique.* But in this regard, the work most striking in its violence and its powerful expression of tragedy is obviously *Carmen* (see fig. 26).

The normal compositional forms and techniques, such as *couplets, romances,* standard introductory scenes, and the repetition of words, were dying out. *Opéra-comique* was thus evolving in the direction of drama, and the Théâtre de l'Opéra-Comique was becoming a more experimental

# CARMEN

Opéra-Comique en quatre actes.

Figure 26.  Bizet's *Carmen*, poster for the premiere (1875). The artist-cum-advertising designer captured perfectly the shock that the heroine's sad end would create in the setting of the Opéra-Comique.

house, in which a new sensibility could be expressed. Many works that remain in the twentieth-century repertory premiered there: Bizet's *Carmen* (1875), Offenbach's *Les Contes d'Hoffmann* (1881), Delibes's *Lakmé* (1883), and Massenet's *Manon* (1884), as well as Gounod's *Faust* (1859), which began life at the Théâtre-Lyrique as an *opéra-comique.* Later, the Opéra-Comique became a venue for the avant-garde with productions such as the premiere of *Pelléas et Mélisande* in 1902.

On the other hand, many traditional elements of the genre endured, even in works which in other ways had been freed from older models. Here again, *Carmen* provides a good example. It exhibits a musical density that was unusual for France, yet it originally had spoken dialogue and includes comic scenes and light scenes as well as numbers that are quite ordinary in terms of their form. And *Manon,* structurally similar to a *drame lyrique,* also contains "melodies of varied form, often based on dance rhythms" and "both spoken dialogue and dialogue set as arioso recitative."[24] "Perhaps this flexibility," noted Soubies and Malherbe, "and this willingness to yield to new requirements helped ensure the vitality of a genre in which, however significant the successive changes may have been, the attributes that are the very essence of our race—charm, delicacy, wit, and clarity—are definitively summed up."[25] This is undoubtedly why audiences continued during the second half of the nineteenth century to enjoy works dating from throughout the history of the Opéra-Comique. Just before fire struck the Salle Favart (Théâtre de l'Opéra-Comique) in 1887, the management had announced productions that included Grétry's *L'Epreuve villageoise* (1784), Hérold's *Zampa* (1831), Adam's *Le Chalet* (1834), Félicien David's *Lalla-Roukh* (1862), Ambroise Thomas's *Mignon* (1866), and Chabrier's *Le Roi malgré lui* (1887).

### *GRAND OPÉRA:* ITS ORIGINS AND STAYING POWER

Although it was commonly used in nineteenth-century writings, the term *grand opéra* rarely appeared on scores or librettos, which usually read simply *opéra,* to differentiate the work in question from an *opéra-comique.* And it was not unusual for composers to shift from one term to another. For example, Meyerbeer entitles *Le Prophète* an *opéra* in the score published by Brandus and Troupenas, but specifies in a note that the "role of Jean is for a *premier ténor de grand opéra.*"

There were many assumptions, influences, and trends that affected the creation of the new genre. Gaspare Spontini's *La Vestale* (1807) and especially his *Fernand Cortez* (1809; new version, 1817), each entitled *tragédie lyrique,* sketched the initial outlines of the genre, which took another twenty years to evolve. Other composers, such as Cherubini, other dramatic forms, such as *mélodrame*, and literary movements, such as the vogue for historical novels, might also be named. Also to be mentioned are the resurgence of the crowd scenes found in entertainments of the revolutionary period, changes in stagecraft, and the influence of Rossinian opera seria, among many other factors. It is not the intention here, however, to rehash the entire history of the genre or fully to consider its origins,[26] but rather to identify its basic components and, most important, to clarify the chronology of its development and analyze it as it was when it was first formed and when the public recognized it as a genre.

To understand the extraordinary impact of *grand opéra* in nineteenth-century Europe, we should recall what a fascination it exercised on the majority of composers of the day. Wagner himself published oft-quoted praise of Auber's *La Muette de Portici* and Halévy's *La Reine de Chypre*.[27] Although Auber was one of the first to put forward this new model (with *La Muette de Portici* in 1828, followed the next year by Rossini, with *Guillaume Tell*), his compositional manner cannot be viewed as instituting a new, original "*grand opéra* style." As Wagner noted, "it merely broadened the sphere [of *opéra-comique*] without departing from it."[28] Auber's *Gustave III* (1833)—on which Verdi based his *Un ballo in maschera* (1859)—contributed hardly anything more in this regard. It was Halévy, in *La Juive* (1835) and *La Reine de Chypre* (1841), and to an even greater extent Meyerbeer, in *Robert le Diable* (1831), *Les Huguenots* (1836), *Le Prophète* (1849), and *L'Africaine* (1865), who invented a language and a style appropriate for the new genre.

Nonetheless, 1828 remains a key year in the development of *grand opéra;* this was already clear at the first performances of *La Muette de Portici*, which Castil-Blaze called "a true victory for the newly founded genre, which should bring crowds into this theater, where great effects can be produced thanks to the powerful resources that its administration makes available to authors."[29] The effect on the audience was considerable: "It is impossible to get a complete idea of the power of lyric drama without seeing the third act of *La Muette de Portici*,"[30] the same critic wrote the following day.

Although its language evolved, the form of *grand opéra* was one of the most consistent of all French lyric theater genres, right up to the scores of Saint-Saëns and Massenet. Debussy wrote of a 1903 revival of Saint-Saëns's *Henry VIII* (1883) that "this may be the last of the historical operas!...We can only hope so!" Ironical, as always, Debussy zeros in on Saint-Saëns's deliberate choice to write in the style of *grand opéra* and abide by its rules: "If Henry VIII sings saccharine *cavatines*, believe me it is because M. Saint-Saëns wanted it and conceived it that way.... [He] is uncompromising—in reverse: while others use inflexibility to destroy everything, he sees it only as a way of holding on to everything. His teachers passed on techniques that he considers good, and he is so inherently respectful that he does not want to change any part of them."[31]

Not only did the Académie de musique keep duplicating the formulas of *grand opéra* half a century after that genre's heyday; it continued also to produce the major works of past years. As at the Opéra-Comique, therefore, works and operatic styles from several generations appeared side by side. *La Muette de Portici* was performed 300 times between 1828 and 1851, with performances nearly every season, 20 times between 1854 and 1855, once in 1858, and 134 times between 1863 and 1871; then it was not heard between 1877 and 1882. *Robert le Diable* chalked up 504 performances between 1831 and 1868 and continued to be played regularly, reaching its 600th performance in 1877, its 700th in 1886, and its 750th in 1893. *La Juive* marked its 500th performance in 1886. But *Les Huguenots* was really popular: it reached its 100th performance in 1839 (six years after its premiere), its 500th in 1872, and its 1,000th in 1903. Donizetti's *La Favorite* (1840) was given for the 600th time in 1888, and was also counted among the most successful works—as was *Le Prophète*, which had logged 500 performances by 1899. These figures[32] are particularly astonishing considering that the Académie de musique was obliged to give only a few performances a week (generally three). As a kind of fortress of academic music, the Opéra could be viewed as completely out of step with the tastes and artistic trends of the last quarter of the century. *Grand opéra*, the genre officially associated with that theater, was varied with other forms only at the end of the nineteenth century. Between 1879 and 1884, the official mandate of the Opéra specified that only *grands opéras* and *ballets-pantomimes* could be given at the Palais Garnier. But in the mandates for 1893, 1900, and 1907, the director finally had the option to mount "every kind of lyric drama [opera] and ballet."[33]

Ambrose Thomas's *Hamlet* in 1868 and, above all, Gounod's *Faust* (an émigré from the Théâtre-Lyrique) in 1869 had similar good fortune[34] and brought a subtler brand of expressiveness to a stage famous for grand effects. Thus, genres that were sharply defined at the beginning of our period in the 1830s were evolving toward a blending of styles.

## THE INGREDIENTS OF *GRAND OPÉRA*

A *grand opéra* was distinguished from other lyric works of its time first and foremost in physical ways. It was enormous: consisting of four or five

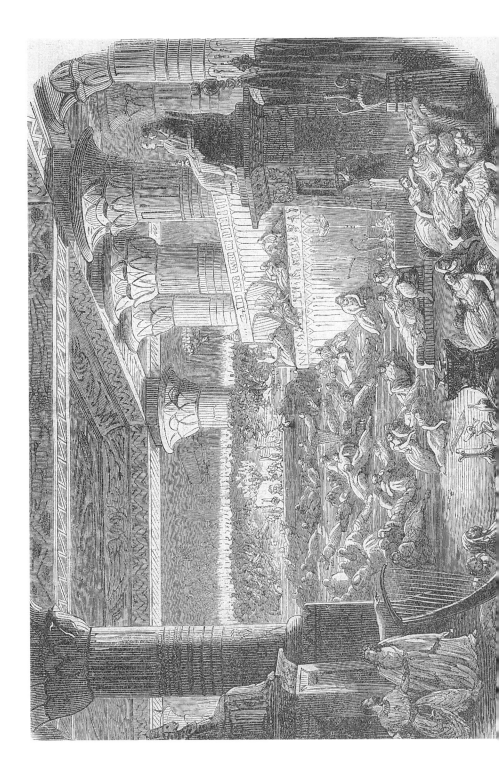

acts, it made for a long evening, to such an extent that Meyerbeer included the following note in his score of *Robert le Diable:* "As the duration of this work exceeds that of the usual performance, the author has marked in the score places that can be shortened as well as passages that can be deleted."[35] That opera demands enormous resources and requires a tremendous budget. The success of Auber's *Gustave III* was due in large part to the sumptuous masked ball in the final act, which involved more than three hundred participants. The mass of performers and supernumeraries constituted an easily malleable raw material that could be fashioned into groupings of every kind in order to shape the on-stage space. In Auber's *L'Enfant prodigue*, the stage director, François-Hippolyte Leroy, "skillfully arranged and harmoniously grouped the masses of choristers, dancers, and extras, all clad in costumes of striking and varied hues,"[36] stunning the 1850 audience. In act 3, the vast number of people enabled Leroy to sculpt the interior space of the Temple of Isis (see fig. 27)."I think this is the least bad thing I have done by way of *grand opéra*, because it combines all the qualities for which I am always striving—often vainly in a work of this kind: a musical, varied subject; pageantry; dance; spectacle; scenery; grand staging," Scribe wrote Auber of his libretto for *L'Enfant prodigue*.[37] Sumptuousness played a twofold role: to impress the audience with richness and magnificence, and to provide raw material for a massive theatrical sculpture. Scribe's libretto for Halévy's *La Juive*, which "lacked neither marches nor countermarches, nor splendid rites, nor crowds coming, going, running, climbing onto roofs, leaning from walls, columns, and windows," was criticized for going too far in this respect in 1835.[38]

The orchestra grew in size and made use of unusual instruments, both to strengthen the highest and lowest registers and the percussion battery, and to provide new color and create remarkable effects. Meyerbeer had no misgivings about using a viola d'amore to accompany Raoul's *romance* "Plus blanche que la blanche hermine," act 1, no. 2, of *Les Huguenots*. In the first scenes of *La Juive*, Halévy depicted Eléazar's work by employing

Figure 27. *Opposite:* Auber's *L'Enfant prodigue*, act 3, the Temple of Isis (*L'Illustration*, December 12, 1850). This was first performed at the Académie de musique on December 6, 1850, with act 3 sets by Charles Cambon. The libretto (Paris: Brandus, n.d.), p. 15, describes the scene as "the innermost place in the temple. The sanctuary reserved for the mysteries of Isis. An immense staircase rises up, on whose steps the initiates of the mysteries are gathered." Scenes 1 and 2: gradually, those present, "overcome with fatigue or drunkenness, have closed their eyes or are beyond seeing and hearing." There is a secret door in the left-hand wall. Nefté appears, followed by Azael.

an anvil—something Wagner later adopted and further developed in *Das Rheingold* to describe the tireless labors of the Nibelungen as they forge their subterranean treasure. The score of *La Muette de Portici* makes great technical demands of the instrumentalists. Wagner admired the "brilliant instrumentation, the meaningful coloration, and the sure-handedness and boldness of the orchestral effects, for example, [Auber's] way, once viewed as so bold, of handling the strings, especially the violins, to the entire section of which he entrusted the most daring passages."[39]

Music played both off-stage and on sometimes required substantial orchestras, adding to the already impressive numbers of players in the pit. The coronation march in act 4 of *Le Prophète* (no. 23) called for twenty-two musicians (saxhorns, trumpets, and field drum) to appear on a lavish set that reproduced Münster cathedral. Members of the chorus and ballet further added to the pageantry and mingled with the numerous soloists, both principal and secondary characters, in musical and theatrical activity that created a powerful effect. Sets, costumes, staging, and lighting were meticulously devised to create a stunning spectacle. Scene changes within an act became more frequent. Dance was of the greatest importance and, as noted, added to the variety of stage effects employed to enhance the expressive power of the performance, using every available resource. The use of dance also met the expectations of regular operagoers who were fond of "protecting" a ballerina; moreover, it served to maintain one of the original sources of French lyric theater. Dance was sometimes well integrated into the action (as in *La Muette de Portici*, whose principal female role is that of a mute and is mimed by a dancer), but was always inserted in the form of substantial divertissements.

It has often been observed that *grand opéra* turned from mythological to historical subjects, which had been in fashion since the vogue for the novels of Sir Walter Scott. In a more general sense, it is worth noting the close relationship between the flourishing of this genre and that of the French romantic movement. In 1865, Blaze de Bury referred to *Robert le Diable* (1831) as the "romantic opera par excellence," appearing "at the finest moment of the blossoming of romanticism."[40] Librettists, notably Scribe, made use of violent and melodramatic situations that had been tested in other genres. They employed high emotions and extremely powerful themes, such as religious intolerance and rebellion against oppression, and based their plots on the contrast between individual action and collective drama. Societal action as used in *grand opéra* takes two forms: the action of society on an individual, and mass action. As Gilles de Van notes, it was in this genre that "opera came closest in spirit to the novel in its efforts to describe a social whole in which collective and individual fates meet and affect each another."[41]

Despite its tangential divertissements, *grand opéra* was characterized by grandeur and pathos. Halévy's talent found its finest outlet in it, according to Wagner, because of "its predominant character of impassioned seriousness" and its basis in "the pathos of high tragedy." The composer of *La Juive* and *La Reine de Chypre*, Wagner thought, had a "deep, inner capacity to be powerfully moved, once and for all turning upside down and enlivening the world of morals."[42] *La Muette de Portici* likewise "immediately surprised [listeners] as something absolutely new; no one had ever seen an operatic subject that was so alive; this was the first true drama in five acts, completely equipped with the attributes of tragedy, especially in its tragic ending."[43]

Wagner clearly saw the new importance given in *La Muette de Portici* to "the choral ensemble, which, for virtually the first time, the master developed as a crowd playing a real part in the action and of serious interest to the audience." The drama found motive force in the use of musical forms that were no longer stereotyped but were adapted to its requirements: "what was new in this music…was this atypical conciseness, this violent concentration of form. The solos seemed to be like lightning flashes, and one moved from solo to choral ensemble as in a storm." "Each of the five acts was an extraordinarily vivid painting, in which one could barely discern the usual operatic arias and duets; in any event, with the exception of one aria for the prima donna in the first act, they no longer produced an effect in that way: with each act, you were always faced with a complete whole that took your breath away and enraptured you." *Grand opéra* was dominated by a pictorial approach to the lyric stage: "One could almost have believed one was seeing real musical pictures," wrote Wagner, who ended his essay with the concept of "theatrical sculpture."

Blending visual, textual, and musical elements, the operatic scene found fertile ground for development in the dramaturgy of *grand opéra*. There were *tableaux scéniques* that had no direct relationship to the main plot, such as the ice-skating scene in *Le Prophète*; *tableaux dramatiques* that developed climactic points of the action and were generally to be found in a finale or in a major ensemble, such as Fidès's repudiation of Jean in the same opera; and *tableaux d'acte*, which constituted an entire act, such as the exotic act 4 of *L'Africaine*.[44] Color and musical characterization unified and invigorated these scenes.[45]

"Slowly, and better to meet modern needs, opera is becoming an enormous machine, a historical epic, a kind of drama incorporating all genres—

Figure 28.    Gounod's *La Reine de Saba*, act 1, scene 2, second setting: view of Jerusalem and the Temple of Solomon designed by Edouard Despléchin, illustration by Godefroy Durand (*L'Illustration*, March 8, 1862). Grandiose staging was an essential element of *grand opéra*.

church music, ballet music, concert pieces, *romances,* and barcaroles," Pierre Larousse noted in his *Grand Dictionnaire universel du XIX^e siècle*.[46] In responding to the tastes of an audience often labeled nouveau riche, *grand opéra* relied on eclecticism, drawing on material from every sphere and every country. It reflected an aesthetic more of the accumulation than of the selection and amalgamation of material. Scores were designed to display a vast palette of forms and styles, from italianate virtuoso arias to comparatively restrained pieces such as *romances*. Solo contributions tended to be integrated into more complex forms. Choruses and ensembles were constructed to make the dramatic action both visible and audible, culminating in spectacular scenes (fig. 28). Yet despite this diversity of resources, *grand opéra* dramaturgy was extremely stereotyped. On November 14, 1863, *La Vie parisienne* published an article with caricature illustrations under the revealing title "Le Parfait Cuisinier dramatique"— "The Perfect Dramatic Cook" (fig. 29).

While in theory limited to the Académie de musique, *grand opéra* was occasionally to be seen on other, less prestigious stages. The Théâtre-Lyrique sought to appropriate the genre: *Les Pêcheurs de perles*, with its blend of various styles, fulfilled some of the defining criteria noted. Its score had moments of abruptness and violence and thus met the emotional requirements of *grand opéra*, and dance contributed spectacle to its impact, although there were no divertissements as extended as those to be seen at the Opéra. Some scenes, such as Léïla's oath, betray a debt to *grand opéra*'s established typology of situations. On the other hand, the drama completely lacks a historical element; there is little affinity between the actions of the tribe of pearl fishers and those of the powerful crowds that drive the works of Auber, Halévy, and Meyerbeer. *Les Troyens* even better reflected the dimensions of *grand opéra*, and it was performed at the Théâtre-Lyrique only because the Académie de musique had persistently rejected it.

OPERATIC INSTITUTIONS AND GENRE—
LEGISLATION AND POLITICAL POWER

As we have seen, the French state controlled the institutional framework within which operas were created. Legislation relating to theaters sustained several of the constituent elements of both *opéra-comique* and *grand opéra*. There are regular references in writings of the time to the relationship between theaters and genres. For much of the nineteenth century, indeed, each theater in Paris had a genre of its own, at least in theory, which was shared with other theaters only to the extent authorized by the government. "Would it not be fairer, more proper, more rational, and at the same time more convenient for *grands opéras* to be performed at the Académie de musique and *opéras-comiques* in the theater that is intended for that genre and bears its name?" a critic asked in 1863.[47] Moreover, it is not as easy as one might think to demarcate the boundary between "straight" theater and lyric theater. Music played a role in most dramatic forms. We forget today that stage music was employed both in popular boulevard theater—especially in *mélodrame*, where it was essential—and at the Comédie-Française. Between a little play with a few insignificant musical interjections or songs and a *grand opéra* sung from start to finish lay a whole gamut of possibilities.

Government played a critical role: "privilege is the key," noted a journalist in 1863, "and it is the state that possesses privilege"—privilege that was renewed with each contract for the theater director. "The state subsidizes the theaters; it issues their mandates; it provides a budgetary credit

# LE PARFAIT CUISINIER DRAMATIQUE

## I

### RECETTE POUR FAIRE UN OPERA

Avant d'en décrire le premier mot, commencez par renier toute idée de poésie : Cette résolution prise vous êtes déjà fort.

Pour le choix du pays et la date de votre action, vous concerter avec le décorateur et le costumier, il faut que ces messieurs trouvent leur vie dans votre *machine*. Ne pas oublier surtout de prendre les *ordres* du maître de ballet, car le ballet est l'âme de ce théâtre.

Quand au s jet de votre *œuvre* voici sur quel ponsif vous devez marcher et duquel vous ne sauriez vous écarter sans imprudence.

Il est de toute nécessité de lever la toile sur un chœur peuple, soldats, seigneurs et dames tous pêle-mêle.

Dans un théâtre de chant ce n'est ni le titre ni la naissance qui règle le rang, mais le caractère de la voix. Sopranos à droite, ténors

Triste exilé de sa belle patrie.

au milieu, contraltos à gauche, les basses derrière. Parfait. Vous leur faites chanter tout ce qui vous passe par la tête. Le vin, la messe, l'amour, voire même l'empereur Sigismond. Arrivé à ce moment, votre héros, — ce sera le premier ténor — brave — *triste exilé de sa belle patrie* (motif de romance, déjà fait et refait mais bon à recommencer encore). Pendant que l'infortuné exhale son désespoir aux échos de la place publique, le chœur se retirera discrètement dans le fond, car il faut qu'il soit là pour faire sa partie à la reprise de l'allegro de Rinaldo-Rinaldi ou d'Edgard. Votre héros aime la fille d'un doge, d'un prince ou d'un duc de Ferrare quelconque. Il est bien entendu qu'il doit avoir un rival — rôle pour le ba-

ryton — rival repoussé s'entend — un baryton n'est jamais c'est dans l'emploi. — Le rival va épouser. Le père qui est *fonde* lui donne sa fille avec le *mi-bémol* toujours en plein vieillard bénira son héritière au premier acte.

Ne pas oublier de la lui faire maudire au cinquième.

Vous baissez la toile sur un défilé. Une rentrée triomphale de l'armée du roi Wenceslas. Première apparition des danseuses qui inondent les soldats de fleurs, et d'entrechats.

Le père, qui est *basse profonde*, lui don avec le *mi bémol*

Deuxième acte. Entrez vite dans l'action. L'hymen va s' chœur dans la chapelle. On traîne déjà la victime à l'au Rinaldo ou Edgard au choix. Patatra à l'orchestre, cymba caisse. Ceci est l'affaire du musicien. La jeune fille forte chanteuse, perd la voix dans un évanouissement gracieux trouve dans son désespoir, le baryton hurle, menace. — Ici naturellement la place d'un solo *allegro furioso* dont le co vous saura gré. Le père qui affec ione la musique gémit sur des notes graves. Le chapelain — deuxième b discrètement s'offrir pour faire un cinquième, quintette. Le et amis des deux rivaux se mêlent de la partie, — car il n'( toujours beaucoup d'amis — à cause des morceaux d'ense

Les deux camps se défient, se provoquent; on tire les ép

Arrogance  Amour  Courons  A la
Vengeance  Toujour (sans s )  Volons  Aux

On traîne déjà la victime à l'autel.

Tout cela r
quante fois
(Ne pas cherc
très rimes, d
luxe qui vous
à jamais da
des musicien
dant, si vous
seulement à l'
Parnasse, vo
vous livrer sur votre manuscrit à une exhibition poétique d

sen tis. Cela sera sans danger, votre maëstro les coupera.
. deuxième acte.

On tire les épées.

vrez le troisième sur un petit décor qui en promet un
eur de dames d'honneur, *Salut à vous, belle princesse!..*
rincesse de n'importe quoi. *Soprano aigü, chanteuse à rou-*
e jeune personne dont l'emploi, ainsi que celui du baryton,
pas avoir de chance en amour, exprime son ennui par un
ussi ennuyeux que sa situation. Le public se passerait bien
es de cette dame, mais c'est une tradition.

ses de la princesse.

Par ses ordres, on lui amène le
ténor Rinoldo, les yeux bandés. —
Ne pas redouter cette inconvenance
féminine, — elle est consacrée par
le succès. On rend le *triste exilé à la
lumière des cieux. — Où suis-je?* La
princesse. *Je t'aime. — Ciel! vous
m'aimez, tu m'aimes, elle m'aime.
— Je t'aime. — Mais je ne vous aime
pas. — Ciel! il ne m'aime pas!* Place
pour deux romances; chacun dit la
sienne. Celle [du jeune homme exprime fort impoliment *qu'il brûle
pour une autre* que la dame. Duo
passionné : c'est bien un peu la situation de Joseph et de Mme Puti-
phar, mais la musique sauve tout.
L'arrivée brusque du baryton fait
du duo un trio...

let, s'il se faisait trop attendre, que diraient MM. les abon-
s il doit être amené par un motif quelconque.—Inutile de se
tête, le duc de
le doge donne une
quelle occasion? —
a préoccuper. Ici,
nférence avec le
allet, dans laquelle
ce qui se fait de-
nte ans : une en
ale de ces demoi-
ses plastiques; un
un pas de 3, un pas
pas tout seul. Et,
re le comble à la

On lui amène le ténor Rinoldo les yeux
bandés.

s grand'mères, le pas de caractère du premier danseur, ce
ndant un grand air de la princesse. Il procure le même
t, mais n'allez pas le faire supprimer. C'est encore une

se termine par un pas de cancan déguisé sous le nom
lle et un tableau vivant, voilà. La danse doit être
e brusquement : c'est plus scénique. — Par quoi? —
uez une idée nouvelle. — Par un tremblement de terre.
le ténor de ce tremblement. — Pour rendre la chose

possible, vous faites passer votre intrigue à l'époque du moyen âge ;
et vous baissez la toile sur un roulement de grosse caisse.

A l'acte suivant, le 1er ténor est dans les fers, la princesse viendra
lui offrir sa liberté s'il
consent à s'enchaîner à
elle. *Plutot la mort! la
mort! la mort!* Apparition
de la jeune fille aimée et
du baryton. Partie carrée
de jalousie et de déses-
poir à tous crins. Entrée
du père... Vous êtes en
plein dans l'action; le reste
est l'affaire de votre imagination ou de votre mé-
moire.

Pourvu que vous placiez
adroitement à la suite une
conjuration, une inonda-
tion, un orage ou un in-
cendie, ce qui ne pourra
que vous attirer la bienveil-
lance du chef machiniste
et l'estime du décorateur,
vous arrivez tout naturellement au cinquième acte.
Mais que ce dernier soit

Le pas de caractère du premier danseur.

court. A ce moment de la soirée, le public est généralement haras-
sé de tant de bonheur pour ses oreilles et pour ses yeux.

On veut la mort du ténor dont la forte chanteuse désire partager
le sort. Faites en mourir au moins un, tous les deux, si le désir vous
en prend. Le spectateur n'y verra pas d'inconvénient, occupé qu'il
est à ce moment avec l'ouvreuse. Les deux amants pleureront l'un
sur l'autre et rendront le dernier soupir sur un *ut* de poitrine, dont
l'un des deux au moins fera un *si* naturel. Le père, à cette vue, expi-
rera à son tour d'une rupture d'ophicléide au cœur. Pour le baryton,
quoi qu'il arrive :

> *Qu'il reste seul*
>
> 1, 2, 3,
>
> Avec son déshonneur.

NOTA. Une fois votre poëme terminé, n'allez pas vous en amou-
racher trop, le compositeur devant vous le faire refaire au moins dix
fois. Encore une tradition.

EUSTACHE.

Tuez-en au moins un ou deux.

for music; it plays a major role in the administration of this art."[48] "Official intervention integrally affected the formation of the genre's artistic traits," Jane Fulcher observes in her study of French *grand opéra*, noting that "for purposes of legal distinction between the theaters," official mandates—the *cahiers des charges*—defined *grand opéra*'s attributes.[49] In this way, magnificence was defined as a primary purpose of the genre. The mandates of the successive directors of what Verdi called "The Big Store" began for the most part with an affirmation of the theater's showcase character in terms of productions and of its representative role. This was true even toward the end of the century, in 1893: "Directors shall be required to manage the Opéra with the dignity and glamour that are proper to the principal national lyric theater. The Opéra must always stand apart from other theaters in the selection and variety of the old and modern works performed there, in the talent of its artists, and in the good taste and artistic merit of its sets, costumes and staging."[50] This was a matter of glorifying, not a Sun King, but a Sun Nation; a very French need literally to display on stage the radiance of France's fortune and culture, and to magnify its power and glory by giving them a new nature.

Every element of a production was painstakingly studied and monitored. The size of the company and its orchestra was set by law; *grand opéra* enjoyed a large contingent of performers. Article 6 of Véron's mandate of 1831, for instance, provides for 79 orchestra players; 2 *chefs de chant* / accompanists; 66 chorus members (plus students from the Conservatoire); a ballet master; 40 male and 30 female supernumeraries (plus children); and a teacher of dance and mime. Article 7 adds that "the students of the Conservatoire shall be at the [director's] disposal."[51]

*Les Pêcheurs de perles* was first performed in a theater that had recently been opened and whose history was sometimes intertwined with the renewal of French opera in the second half of the nineteenth century. "The establishment of the Théâtre-Lyrique was the culmination of a long struggle among musicians, writers, and government to secure the opening of a third lyric theater that would be more open to young composers—Conservatoire and Prix de Rome prize-winners—and that would give a larger and more ordinary audience access to the French repertory, both old and modern."[52] The theater was the beneficiary of special legislation, as noted earlier in this study. Let us now consider this matter in a more general way.

Until 1864, when the decree on the *liberté des théâtres* gave them their freedom, legislation dating back to 1806 had made theaters and their very existence dependent on the government. It was not only the theaters that were controlled; their repertories and the genres they were permitted to perform were also defined by decree of Napoleon I:

> The repertories of the Opéra, of the Comédie-Française, and of the Opéra-Comique shall be determined by the minister of the interior, and no other theater may perform in Paris works included in the repertories of those major theaters without their authorization and without paying them remuneration that shall be determined by mutual agreement and with the authorization of the minister. The minister of the interior may allocate to each theater a genre of production to which it shall be obliged to limit itself.[53]

Censorship and state subsidies—an important financial resource for the major theaters—also played significant roles. "By fixing the genres for each theater by means of granting privileges and monitoring the content of texts through the intermediary of censors, the government held the reins of a still greater power: that of steering the repertories of the Parisian institutions, and hence those of the entire period," Nicole Wild observes.[54] We have already seen how Bizet benefited from a subsidy newly granted to the Théâtre-Lyrique. It is clear that, through controlling subsidies and issuing official mandates, the government retained decisive influence, irrespective of the proclamation of the freedom of the theaters.

It would not be oversimplifying to say that when the Théâtre-Lyrique was established, operatic activity was concentrated in three institutions, which produced three specific kinds of opera: the Opéra ("dedicated specifically to singing and to the dance" and "permitted to perform only plays set completely to music and ballets of a noble and gracious kind"), where *grands opéras* were given in French; the Opéra-Comique ("dedicated specifically to performing every manner of comedy or drama combined with *couplets, ariettes,* and ensemble numbers"), which could present only lyric works in which the music was broken up by spoken dialogue; and the Théâtre-Italien (which "may perform works in Italian only"), where works by Italian composers and a few other works in Italian were produced.[55]

The Théâtre des Bouffes-Parisiens, which Offenbach transformed into a haven of operetta, was authorized only in 1855. It slowly grew in importance, but within the limits of a genre based on comedy and farce. It was the Théâtre-Lyrique that cracked the strict organization of the Parisian operatic world by breaking away from the principle that institution and genre were of one substance. The decree of May 9, 1851, stated:

Article 4: the repertory shall consist of new works in one or several acts, in verse or in prose, combined with new music, with choruses, solos, duets, trios, ensembles, and, in general, all the forms that comprise the lyric genre. [The director of the Théâtre-Lyrique] shall have the right to add choreographic divertissements. He may produce translations of foreign lyric works, on the condition, however, that the number of such works shall not exceed two per year. He may produce the works of living authors belonging to the repertories of other lyric theaters, but only ten years after their first performance at those theaters. The same shall hold true for works of deceased authors that have not yet come into the public domain.[56]

This meant that the Opéra no longer held by right its monopoly on producing works entirely set to music without any limitations in principle on the artistic means to be used. The Théâtre-Lyrique had no traditions or reputation to uphold, and it was not limited to any predefined genre; it therefore became the venue where, even before the theaters were officially liberated, it was possible to try out new concepts of music drama.

Ralph (Léon Escudier) stressed the versatility of the Théâtre-Lyrique and the opportunity for it to produce works that did not fall within the two traditional genres of *grand opéra* and *opéra-comique,* saying: "Would it not be fairer...for the third musical theater, the Théâtre-Lyrique, to produce without distinction the two genres—indeed, the three, for there are pieces intended for the musical stage that are neither opera proper nor *opéra-comique.*"[57] Jules Lovy wrote that "the fusion of light elements with the serious genre, or *demi-caractère,*" as typified by Adam's *Si j'étais roi,* was perfectly suited to the Théâtre-Lyrique.[58]

OLDER GENRES DIE OUT—THE *OPÉRA-COMIQUE HÉROÏQUE*

When Gounod's *La Reine de Saba* was premiered in 1862, Paul Scudo conducted an inventory of the Opéra: "Everything there is worn out, both the repertory and the people who perform it." Like Scudo, the audience seemed "to want something other than these fatally long five-act operas, in which the human voice collapses beneath the weight of excessive sound from the orchestra."[59] *Opéra-comique* was the target of harsh attacks—even more so than *grand opéra,* which continued to appeal to many composers. In his 1863 memoir, Léon Escudier expressed the view that "the model has grown old and must be replaced."[60]

"It has been noted that dialogue was completely excised from the new opera; it is certainly not we who will object to such boldness; this is a step toward the only possible form of opera, that which will replace today's worn-out and poorly defined forms,"[61] wrote A. de Gasperini. Other writers joined him in advocating an operatic renewal. Gaston de Saint-Valry declared that there was "a universal need for innovation and renewal" in dramatic music, and especially in *opéra-comique*. He felt that there was "no doubt that the young composer [Bizet] faced…the insurmountable lassitude that is today at the root of the outmoded banality of present-day *opéra-comique* with the somewhat muddled abundance of means and the confident zeal that characterizes youth. He had to work very hard indeed to avoid stumbling when he took his first steps."[62]

The evolution of operatic genres was in stride with that of the straight theater—which Berlioz seemed to defy with his *Les Troyens:* "At a time when classic tragedy has been deposed by drama, it was certainly a rash venture to give the public a five-act opera about the love of Aeneas and Dido."[63] "Take a look at this long-haired romantic," jeered Louis Roger, "who is exhuming the musty antiques of French theater."[64]

Bizet's work derived from a branch of *opéra-comique* referred to in the nineteenth century as *opéra héroïque;* for the sake of clarity, it is better called *opéra-comique héroïque.* Composers, weary of waiting on the doorstep of the Académie de musique for a nod from the readers' committees or the management, chose instead to fall back on the Opéra-Comique and to adapt their works—sometimes already composed as grand spectacles to fulfill the epic criteria of *grand opéra*—to that theater's requirements. This was nothing new: "Since the beginning of the century, with composers like Méhul, Cherubini, and Le Sueur, the character of [the Opéra-Comique] had changed…[and that theater] rang with the tones of high passion."[65] The young composers of the day left an enduring mark: "after their departure, *opéra-comique* as a genre never had the coherence it had had on the eve of 1789."[66]

In his history of dramatic music in France, the critic and composer Gustave Chouquet stressed the relationship among theatrical and operatic genres, and defined each genre in terms of subject and characters: "A subject appropriate for a tragedy or a serious drama would not be suitable for a *demi-caractère* opera or a *comédie lyrique;* in no event must purely picturesque elements be confused with truly musical ones. Thus, for dance, enchanting scenes and magical spectacles; for *opéra buffon,* liveliness and a casual air; for comedy, wit, sparkling repartee, grace, and touching charm; for genre opera, poetic flights and indescribable tenderness; for drama and for *tragédie lyrique,* solemn and grandiose expression, high emotion, and dark terror."[67]

*OPÉRA POÉTIQUE — OPÉRA LYRIQUE — DRAME LYRIQUE POÉTIQUE*

In his 1891 history of French music, Henri Lavoix *fils* described what he called *opéra-comique poétique,* a description that fit works by Gounod and Thomas; in such mid-century works, a new conception of the libretto emerged, corresponding to an original musical style. Their authors "altered the old genre of *opéra-comique,* made it more colorful and more symphonic, and looked to French and foreign poets for more inspiring subjects, in keeping with their new ideal."[68] We have seen the key role Michel Carré played in the development of a fresh kind of operatic style and, through the flourishing of "operatic poetry," the new expressive richness of the works of Gounod.

Morton Achter defines what he calls *opéra lyrique*—specifically the work of Félicien David and Ambroise Thomas, but including a number of Gounod's operas—as a compound of *grand opéra* and *opéra-comique.* Most of the works he considers were originally composed as *opéras-comiques,* a hybrid genre that he views as a manifestation of the French mind-set, comprising lyricism, refinement, and moderation, combined with entertainment elements such as dance.[69]

The term *opéra lyrique* might seem tautologous if *lyrique* were used in its sense of "intended to be set to music and sung; relating to dramatic music." But it makes perfect sense in terms of modern usage, which goes back to the middle of the eighteenth century: "Used of poetry that expresses intimate feelings by means of rhythms and imagery suited to communicating to the reader the poet's emotions; that which belongs to this type of poetry."[70]

In the first part of the duet between Nadir and Zurga in *Les Pêcheurs de perles,* Saint-Valry found a special dreamy character similar to the new tone of *opéra lyrique:*

> a kind of alternating utterance of admirable expression, contrast and coloration. Here, [Bizet] has been truly original and fresh. This is how I envision the renewal of outmoded musical forms....
>
> One had to be struck by the trend to which our musical theater is increasingly yielding, which is day by day to erase the boundary once so strictly drawn between opera proper and *opéra-comique.* None of the picturesque *opéras-comiques* of Félicien David, such as *Lalla-Roukh,* differ from *grand opéra* except in their dimensions and their inclusion of spoken dialogue that is, to say the least, trivial. M. Gounod has employed the same method: apart from his *Le Médecin malgré lui,* all his works are true operas in which one would indeed like, as in *Faust,* to hear recitative replace the insipid and vulgar dialogue that is included there because of

the remnants of a tradition. That is the trend. M. Bizet, along with the librettists, has followed it boldly.[71]

Gounod's *Sapho* is noteworthy here from the standpoint of its genre. "No other music…was like its music or made it possible to anticipate it when it was first heard," wrote Camille Bellaigue in 1910.

> At that time, three forms, or three genres, had a share in French tastes: Italian opera…, *opéra-comique,* and *grand opéra.*…A musical and dramatic type needed to be created that would be as remote from [grand] opera as from *opéra-comique,* and even more remote from Italian opera. Gounod created it. Open the score of *Sapho* to the right places.…You will find melodic, harmonic, and instrumental novelty, stylistic purity, and something that is simultaneously noble and elegant, tender and passionate, intimate and intense.[72]

Most of the characteristics of *opéra lyrique* are found in Bizet's *Les Pêcheurs de perles.* There is an obvious determination to omit comic elements from the libretto. With its refined sonorities and great musical interest, the orchestra is a strong point of the score. The use of arioso and expressive recitative adds a melodic fluidity that is not invariably broken when the vocal writing moves from one kind of declamation to another. Large-scale scenes are not limited to the usual finales, and generally convey the unfolding of the action in complex musical forms. Finally, Bizet expanded poetic expression by creating atmosphere, by rendering memories, and by evoking the exotic. But unlike for Gounod and Thomas, expressing "indescribable tenderness" (at least its more saccharine variety) was not a key aspect of his artistic approach. In *opéra lyrique,* particular importance was attached to ordinary private life, which tended to foster a middle-class kind of drama, and hence a muted lyricism, even if we limit ourselves to *Faust.* Indeed, in that work, the drama "loses intensity in order to be more intimate; the composer depicts characters, and with charm, elegance, and color renders the emotions that he would invite us to share."[73] There is nothing of the kind in *Les Pêcheurs de perles,* which except in its poetic passages aims at depicting lively scenes, feelings expressed through fiery passion, such as the rage of Zurga, and solemn events, such as Léïla's oath.

The characteristic elements of *opéra lyrique* would be adapted in many scores belonging to the genre that dominated the end of the nineteenth century, the *drame lyrique. Drame lyrique* owed a debt to Wagner; it involved continuous action, symphonic orchestral writing, and a rich harmonic vocabulary. This new French genre could be differentiated from *grand opéra* in its literary subjects and in its abandonment of pomp and spectacle as ends in themselves, in favor of subtler psychological character studies. Gustave Charpentier's *Louise* (1900), subtitled a "musical novel," bears witness to the way in which poetic opera or *opéra lyrique* could be amalgamated with *drame lyrique.* Just as Zola often rose in his descriptive passages to a lyricism that transfigured the most prosaic of realities, Charpentier succeeded in blending naturalism with a sense of color that released the poetry of the mundane. A good example of this is act 2 of *Louise:* "We are . . . in Montmartre, before day has completely broken; through the mist of the late dawn, we see all the little morning tasks being carried out."[74] Charpentier translated into music the poetic emotion of the wakening town. Moreover, the entire work is suffused with a distinctly sentimental atmosphere and revolves around scenes of private life, characteristics readily associated with *opéra lyrique.*

## GENRE: SAFEGUARDING THE BEAUTIFUL

Seen as the highest form of musical expression, a mirror of art in all its diversity, and hence the expression of French civilization, opera was the best, if not the only, road to success for a composer:

> Opera is the musical work par excellence and requires for perfect performance the collaboration of everything that is most exquisite from all the other branches of the fine arts. It requires that music be combined with poetry, which delineates the dramatic action, and with painting, which frames it with scenery; dance is often its necessary complement; and the science of mechanics is manifested in all its sophistication in the marvels of scene changes in full view of the audience and in the optical and other effects that constitute the complex science of the stage crew. Hence, in a way, an opera is the ultimate expression of human creativity at the time it is performed.[75]

Before the collapse of a French operatic system based on institutions, privileges, subsidies, and official mandates, the classification of the various genres established a hierarchy: the Napoleonic legislation of 1807 divided Paris theaters into "major" and "secondary" theaters. This reflected the government's wish to control public events and the image of itself conveyed to the French public and to other civilized nations. Legislation and subsidies were formulated with an artistic and a moral purpose. Arthur Pougin defined these subsidies as "annual grants that the state or the municipalities award to certain major theaters in order to encourage them along the path of high art, to urge them not to be guided by the faulty taste of the majority of the public, and to enable them to retain artistic superiority over those of their counterparts that are limited to their own resources."[76] The imperial regime had taken upon itself nothing less than a civilizing mission. The Académie de musique et de danse was at the glittering summit of the operatic structure, a showcase of French civilization. Its director amounted to the de facto ambassador of Paris.

The term *grand* as applied to opera referred both to quality and to quantity. The problem with the French school was that it tended to confuse the two, making *grand opéra* into a sumptuous display that was made possible by the Académie's large annual subsidy of 800,000 francs. Grandeur and splendor, glamour and luxury pushed more traditional aesthetic values out of the way. Within this genre, the beautiful tended to yield to the magnificent (etymologically, that which makes big—or *grand*—things). The mandate that the government entrusted to the director attached special importance to the dignity and the glamour of the performances, and stressed the Opéra's mission (equivalent to that of the Comédie-Française) of preserving the nation's heritage by designating it as a museum of lyric art.

Any work that did not belong to an "official" category called into question this legislative definition of the genres, whose role was to "protect the beautiful in the musical art on the stage."[77]

# Chapter 9   The Aesthetic Foundations of Nineteenth-Century French Opera

In his 1863 review of *Les Troyens,* Nestor Roqueplan summed up the basic issues facing writers of opera. He spoke of national schools that championed their own melodic and harmonic styles and of the relationship between libretto and music and between sung and spoken declamation; he highlighted the traditional division of an opera into self-contained units intended to establish an emotion or a dramatic incident, and the contrary temptation to supply a continuous flow of music for the steady unfolding of the drama:

> This poses the abiding issues of Italian music and German music, of form and expression, of pattern and color. Is dramatic music a freestanding art form with its own rules, like sculpture or painting, or must it model itself closely on the words with which it is supplied? Should it not be a mere musical echo, imitating the spoken inflections as closely as possible? Is metrical recitative its ideal, its supreme purpose? Should it unfold like the successive figures on a frieze, or should it be intermittently concentrated in clusters of emotions, images, and actions? Yet even a frieze is limited by the features of the building to which it belongs.[1]

Some of the responses of the French to these matters have already been addressed in our discussion of the ways in which nineteenth-century operas were constructed. We must now consider the principles and purposes of the form. It is not my intention, of course, to determine why a given opera is or is not successful in terms of aesthetic criteria such as beauty (which I would then be obliged to define), but rather to try to identify the ideas that formed the basis of French lyric theater in the nineteenth century. These ideas arose within the framework of genre, and by the third quarter of the nineteenth century, they were in a difficult situation; they somehow survived, and attempts were made to modernize them. True disorder reigned in the spheres of thought and taste. Shortly after the first production of Thomas's *Mignon* on November 17, 1866, Théodore de Lajarte wrote indignantly, "We are facing complete musical anarchy; we should have seen it coming. The Rossinian school enjoyed too many sunny days. It flooded the musical world with too bright a light, and we have now been plunged back into darkness."[2] Audiences still believed in the preeminence of melody with accompaniment, as established by the Italian school, but their convictions were being constantly shaken by the rising German school, even though the press mostly held conservative views of opera. Again, in this great debate, Auber and Berlioz were at opposite extremes, and Bizet's *Les Pêcheurs de perles* holds the key. That work and the reactions to it can help us understand the aesthetic choices that faced the author and the relationship of those choices to the predominant tastes of the day.

## DRAMATIC MUSIC AND ENTERTAINMENT

"We do not know," observed the *Revue et Gazette des Théâtres*, "how and why this piece [*Les Pêcheurs de perles*], which, they say, was conceived as an *opéra-comique*, has come to be transformed into a *grand opéra*; this has greatly disappointed those all-too-numerous spectators who want a lyric work above all to entertain them as a *vaudeville* does, or to provide them with the emotions of a drama."[3] Opera was first and foremost theater—especially *opéra-comique*, originally a play supplemented with musical numbers. Opera had to be diverting. *Les Troyens* was criticized for "not being *entertaining*."[4] Boring the public was the cardinal sin that had to be avoided at any cost. The rule applied even to *grand opéra*, where authors were free to roam the expanses of grandeur and raging emotions, but where there was also room for comic elements.[5] The dramatic construction of *grand opéra* needed a few moments of respite to balance the additional tension and fiery expressivity provided by the music. This was also quite simply a way of enhancing the work by giving it greater contrast. "Art lives above all on contrasts: light next to shadow—the one makes the other stand out. It's a question of the *repoussoir* [giving a sense of depth and relief in a painting]."[6] In the same way, the ballets that were a part of *grand opéra* provided an opportunity for creating a contrast with the musical and dramatic narrative, while at the same time being by nature a source of entertainment.

Many observers shared the Rousseau-like view of Oscar Comettant that music is "first and foremost an art that charms, whose purpose is to give pleasure with combinations of sounds that are pleasing to the ear and attractive to the heart."[7] "Since music is an art of pleasure, the only music is pleasant music," cried much of the public.[8] But in the theater, inherently beautiful music was out of the question, which is how A.-C. Bouyer explained the meager success of *Les Troyens*:

> *Les Troyens* has finally been produced on the stage of the Théâtre-Lyrique, delivered up for the judgment of the few music-lovers capable of understanding its beauty; it has thus not been a success there—although M. Carvalho and the composer himself could have expected nothing else, because audiences want to come to the theater above all to be entertained or absorbed.... You should not go to hear *Les Troyens* as you would go to a concert, to listen enraptured to a number of pieces whose masterly beauty stirs all the fibers of your soul.[9]

As early as 1825, Stendhal had felt obliged to remind the dilettanti of the Théâtre-Italien that they had to differentiate between the genres:

> In the theater, I prefer four measures of the cavatina from [Rossini's] *Ermione* as Rubini sang them yesterday to all the symphonies of Haydn. When my spirit feels the need for instrumental music, I go to the Conservatoire on a Sunday; there, I affirm with pleasure, nothing in Europe except perhaps the Dresden orchestra can compare with our players. When will they care to remember that in the theater their glory lies in letting the voices stand out?[10]

Even in 1884, and speaking of pieces that might today seem very slight indeed, the conservative press made use of the antithesis between concert and ballet. Raoul de Saint-Arroman criticized the ballet in the third act of *Manon*, writing, "I would happily listen to its music in the concert hall, but I wish they would omit it in the theater."[11]

French audiences particularly liked music when it ornamented a performance. They liked "to see scenery on stage, in the midst of which costumed characters come and go, and not singers in black evening clothes sitting on benches and holding a book of music in their hands."[12] In France, lamented Louis de Romain,

> outside the theater, music does not exist for a mass of people who barely know the names of Beethoven, Mendelssohn, Schumann, Schubert, and so many other great composers who wrote little or nothing for the stage. To them, it seems, symphonies, concertos, and oratorios belong to a category completely devoid of interest.... This, moreover, is easy to explain. It is not absolutely indispensable to like music in order to like the theater, and opera contains an adequate ration of attractions that are independent of the art of music. The pleasures of the eye mingle with the pleasures of

the ear; the dramatic action itself and the production—to which increasing importance is wrongly attached—can make the spectator completely forget the harmonic and melodic combinations of the composer, who on occasion finds himself relegated to a secondary position.[13]

## AN AESTHETIC OF INTENSE EMOTIONS—
## PLAYING ON THE NERVES OF THE SPECTATOR

Let us look at the *grand opéra* aesthetic in terms of how authors conceived their works with a view to producing particular effects, often intense emotions. This aesthetic was concerned solely with stirring the feelings of the audience, which constituted an end in itself. In that sense, it reached its apex in the works of Meyerbeer.

*Grand opéra* was constructed as a succession of contrasting scenes. With reference to *La Muette de Portici,* Wagner noted that "just as the subject was lacking neither in frightening nor in tender elements, so too Auber made his music express every contrast and every combination with such powerful forms and colors that one could not remember ever before having seen such striking accuracy." He unerringly described the clash of styles and dramatic situations: "in the midst of this frenzied chaos, suddenly [come] the most emphatic calls for calm, or repeated appeals; then more furious wildness and bloody affrays, interrupted by a moving, anguished entreaty or by the murmuring of an entire people in prayer."[14] The primary purpose of these contrasts was to be entertaining and moving, by striving constantly for effect: visual, sonic, and dramatic effect, working on the spectator's entire nervous system.[15] "Meyerbeer operates by cleverly calculating the increasingly powerful blows that, in the course of five hours of wonderment, strike the musical imagination of the listener, whose fatigue-damaged nerves can no longer feel emotion."[16] The two extremes of a contrast were sometimes devised more to cause an emotional shock than for their intrinsic value. What counted was what happened when those extremes met and the resultant explosive effect on the spectator's nervous system. The literary equivalent that comes to mind is Victor Hugo's technique of antithesis.

As Larousse says, *grand opéra* aimed "to express, in their more intense and clamorous aspects, not only individual emotions but the emotions and the experience of peoples, as for example in *La Muette de Portici, Les Huguenots,* and *Le Prophète.*"[17] Shock is an intense and sudden emotion that affects the mind or the sensibilities; it is certainly among the key elements of the aesthetic of *grand opéra.* Meyerbeer was the master of this technique, and played upon the nerves of his audience by using both subtler gradations and sharply contrasting juxtapositions. "The output of this great artist," wrote F.-J. Fétis of the premiere of *Le Prophète*, "will stand as a model of the art of stirring up the emotions, of stimulating them, of interrupting them and of imperceptibly taking them to their limits."[18] Théophile Gautier found an image to convey the intensity of such contrasts when he wrote of an act 2 scene featuring the false messiah Jean: "In the midst of this rage, like a drop of cold water in a boiling cauldron, we hear the psalm of the Anabaptists."[19]

In *Les Huguenots*, Meyerbeer perfected a mechanism for producing effects that propelled the drama toward the violent clash of the final battle, in which fragments of the Lutheran chorale both energize and contrast with the other musical elements.[20] Displacing "The Beautiful," "The Extraordinary," and "The Startling" were new categories—like "The Fantastic" in Weber and Berlioz, or "The Sublime" and "The Grotesque" in the plays of Victor Hugo—that were accessible to everyone. Or, rather, no one could help feeling them, as Berlioz wrote in 1836 of the blessing of the daggers in act 4 of *Les Huguenots:* "Every two measures, in the silences that separate each part of the phrase, the orchestra swells to a fortissimo and, by means of irregular strokes of the timpani doubled by a drum, produces a strange, extraordinary growling that arouses dismay even in the listener most incapable of feeling musical emotions. This 'sublime horror' seems to me better than anything of this kind attempted in the theater for many years."[21] The parallel with attempts in the spoken theater to expose the spectator to a wide range of violently contrasting sensations, from laughter to fright, is clear from act 3, scenes 1 and 2, of Victor Hugo's *Lucrèce Borgia* (1833), where hooded penitents burst in while supper is being served, bearing coffins intended for the guests.

The depiction of violence in all its forms spread to music after having already been reflected in many paintings and in a great number of literary works. The expression of such energy gave rise to what has been called the "frenzied genre," which took its inspiration from the gothic literature of the late eighteenth century and from English novels; its principal merit was undoubtedly that it allowed raw, subconscious forces to be brought out into the open. Sacrilege, the theater of cruelty, macabre stagings, the subversion of moral and aesthetic values: these were among the elements that drove this art, which was sometimes crude but had substantial repercussions.[22] This fascinating interplay among the arts and among theories of aesthetics and dramaturgy was at its most productive between 1820 and 1840. There would be similar abundance during the eras of naturalism and symbolism at the end of the century.

Much of this was connected with the changes in sensibility brought about by the Christianity to which artists now looked for inspiration instead of to the ancient world, with romanticism replacing classicism. Victor Hugo noted this in his preface to *Cromwell,* dated October 1827: "Christianity brings poetry to truth. Like Christianity, the modern Muse will view things from a higher and broader vantage point. It will sense that not everything in creation is beautiful in human terms, but that ugliness exists side by side with beauty, deformity near grace, absurdity as the other face of the sublime, evil with good, shadow with light."[23] It is without question in Berlioz's *Benvenuto Cellini* that we find the most masterly stage and musical setting of the twin notions of the absurd and the sublime. The composer carried off the feat of depicting both concepts in the Roman Carnival, where the audience witnesses a mime show pitting Harlequin against Pasquarello. The sublimity of the first, represented by the fine English horn melody enveloped by the sound of the harp, gives way to the absurdity of the second, depicted by a melody in the ophicleide punctuated every measure by a drumbeat.

In his book *The Urbanization of Opera,* Anselm Gerhard stresses the profound changes in the perceptions and psyches of early nineteenth-century individuals faced with the stress and confusion of large modern cities, with ever more varied impressions and images, and with a transformation in the perception of time.[24]

All means were focused on achieving one end, and the visual aspect of a performance was no less important than the music. One of the best-known examples is the act 3 finale of *Robert le Diable,* discussed in chapter 6 in connection with the fantastic style brought to France by Weber. On a set designed by Pierre Ciceri, depicting a convent—based on that of Montfaur-Lamaury near Paris—with moonlit tombs and vaults, the satanic Bertram calls the wayward nuns to rise up from their biers (see fig. 30). After a procession, they grow livelier and seduce Robert with their dancing. The infernal bacchanal ends with ghosts and demons ascending from underground.

The introduction to Bertram's recitative "Voici donc les débris du monastère antique" (Behold then the ruins of the ancient monastery) begins with string tremolos punctuated by chords in the bassoons and low clarinets. The impression of strangeness is intensified by the alternation of broad declamation based on a tonic arpeggio with less stable harmonic elements, such as parallel keys, diminished seventh chords on the subdominant, and Neapolitan sixths. Trombones and ophicleide, playing in unison, convey the deep, dark atmosphere of the convent. When Bertram has completed his

Figure 30.    Meyerbeer's *Robert le Diable,* act 3 finale, the nuns' bacchanal. The librettists (Eugène Scribe and Germain Delavigne) and the composer collaborated with their designers to heighten the impression a scene would make on the audience. P.-L.-C. Ciceri designed the sets for the first performance, at the Opéra, on November 31, 1831. F.-G.-G. Lepaulle designed the costumes; Philippe Taglioni choreographed the ballet divertissements; and Adolphe Nourrit served as stage director.

invocation, "Will-o'-the-wisps appear and hover over the tombs" and sixteenth-note figures move between the violins and the piccolo and flute. Now the procession of the nuns begins. The tombs open and the nuns emerge, silently moving down stage. They "leave it to the orchestra to depict their feelings," wrote Castil-Blaze, "and to provide a second interpretation of their gestures in uniting with their expressive mime. Only instrumental melody strikes the ear during this long and beautiful scene, and its charm, its picturesque imagery, its varied coloration, and its witty, vigorous details, full of feeling, make a deep impression on the spirit."[25] Note the string-bass pizzicati combined with off-beat chords played *ppp* in the brasses, with a timpani-roll underpinning; the strangeness and darkness of this passage are increased by the oppressive sound of the tam-tam. Then, Castil-Blaze continues, "the nuns arise, and the bassoons play a melody whose ascending line follows the movement of the statues."[26] In utter contrast to the invocation, the bacchanal ensues, its program given in great detail in the printed score.[27]

The woodwinds ("very light") and the triangle add their ethereal sonorities, which grow gradually more substantial.

By basing their dramaturgic approach on effect and spectacle, the authors of *grands opéras* found themselves with an overabundance of resources that could only lead to a dead end. In Halévy's *Le Juif errant* (libretto by Scribe and Saint-Georges after Eugène Sue), it is clear how this massing of means would result in an opera of absurdly exaggerated dimensions that wound up exhausting its mid-nineteenth-century audience. *Le Juif errant* is worth considering as an attempt to create a super *Robert le Diable:* a super *grand opéra.* The production pulled out all the stops: act 3 took place "at Constantinople, in the palace of the eastern emperors.— Huge semicircular room in Byzantine style, opening through extremely high and wide arches upon magnificent gardens."[28] A triumphal march with on-stage musicians added its own touch of grandeur to this setting, with its terrace, fountains, and throne. Fétis described the "march by which the grandees of the empire paid their respects and made their vows to the empress." It was performed by a small sixteen-piece orchestra: one small E-flat saxhorn; two B-flat cornets à pistons; two contralto saxhorns or B-flat bugles; two tenor saxhorns or E-flat horns; two E-flat cylinder trumpets; one B-flat baritone saxhorn; three trombones; one B-flat bass saxhorn; one B-flat ophicleide, and one E-flat contrabass saxhorn. But Fétis observed that those modern instruments were in an "antique form" that had been "borrowed from the figures seen on Trajan's column in Rome."[29]

The two scenes of act 4 obey the law of contrasts: "The second scene of the fourth act," wrote Fétis, "presents dramatic situations quite different in nature from those of the first scene. These give the music priceless opportunities for contrasts. Everything is devised to serve those effects: a picturesque locale, imposing ruins, the shores of the Bosphorus, and the shadows of the night." In the full view of the audience, the scene was changed from the empress's oratory of the first scene to "the ruins of a temple on the banks of the Bosphorus" with moonlight effects, a lustrous night, blue gauze in front of the footlights, rocks, and a nearly destroyed temple, in which wild grasses are growing. As the Wandering Jew contemplates his unhappy lot in this romantic setting, a trombone solo is heard.

But the most powerful impressions are left for the final act. The sleeping Ashvérus, the Wandering Jew, dreams of the resurrection of the dead and the Last Judgment (no. 24). The spectator sees the immense valley of Josaphat strewn with carved tombs and funerary stones. It is night. "Amid this solitude, angels set at the four points of the compass, with the sound of their trumpets, call all the dead to the Last Judgment." Halévy used the sixteen-member orchestra from act 3 (no. 17) for this instrumental introduction. Then, to silent gestures on stage, the same ensemble plays the 54-measure allegro marcato accompaniment, employing a repeated-note motif in a solid unison, punctuated by fortissimo chords in the pit orchestra: "The dead (all of them with long muslin veils on their heads, covering them nearly completely), slowly arrive in groups....The stones covering the tombs...are lifted by the dead they confine. Others enter [from various directions].... Trap doors...then open." A saxophone quartet—one soprano, two tenors, and a bass—accompanies with its unusual and therefore strange timbre[30] the *sotto voce* chorus of the dead: "Qui vient aujourd'hui sous leur froide tombe / Agiter les morts d'ici-bas?" The curtain showing the valley of Josaphat is replaced by a vista of "the entrance to Hell, from which great flames are darting, and a crowd of devils, led by Satan with his trident, swarm over the landscape displaying the wildest joy; one by one they seize the damned souls, whom they hurl into the abyss in spite of their despair." After a scene representing heaven, the setting is once again as it was at the beginning of act 5: a vast expanse of sea, and a dry, wild shore. Ashvérus awakens and finds that he has been dreaming, and that he must resume his trek, as the chorus is heard off stage singing the chilling words, "Marche toujours"— "Walk forever."

Meyerbeer and Scribe were interested above all in startling their audience, and their dramatic approach was at times formed at the expense of stylistic unity. When *Les Huguenots* was first produced, Fétis hailed its "variety, an inexhaustible source of pleasure."[31] Such diversity became an aesthetic principle that the same critic proclaimed in 1830: "Variety in works and in feelings, and eclecticism in opinions are...the future of music.... There will no longer be any preference for one style over another; only genius will prevail."[32] In 1836, the critic of *Le National* agreed: "What the public needs is a kind of music in which all genres will be mixed up, blended, tangled; a completely diversified kind of music. Meyerbeer understands this need of our times and meets it with uncommon adroitness."[33] A German who became a French composer, Meyerbeer sought in his music dramas not to merge a great number of elements, like Weber, then Wagner, but to juxtapose them. Here he was meeting a need that Heine had observed:

> A Frenchman goes to the theater to see a play and in search of emotions. The action makes him forget those who portray it; it has hardly anything to do with them. It is excitement that draws the Frenchman to the theater, and the last thing he wants is calm. If the author leaves him a single moment for contemplation, he would be capable of summoning Azor—

that is, of whistling [in outrage]. The important thing for the dramatic poet in France is to make sure that the audience neither becomes disengaged nor has time to breathe, that emotions come one after the other, that love, hatred, jealousy, ambition, pride, and honor—all the passionate feelings that are already raging in the Frenchman's real life—explode on the boards with even greater intensity![34]

## HISTORY AS AN AESTHETIC POWER

"[T]his may be the last of the historical operas!...We can only hope so!" Debussy declared when Saint-Saëns's *Henry VIII* was revived at the Paris Opéra in 1903 (see also page 234).[35] The genre had become irrelevant. Much of its aesthetic power had come from the fashion for historical subjects that was part of genuine historical movements of the turn of the nineteenth century, and from what Anselm Gerhard calls urbanization:[36] the impact of Parisian life on opera, which is comparable to the great role it plays in Balzac's monumental *La Comédie humaine*. This power diminished toward the end of the 1840s.

At the beginning, *grand opéra* had room for the encroachment of history as a tangible embodiment of social diversity. The major outlines of the French Revolution, of the revolutionary wars, and of the Napoleonic saga (which, György Lukács argues, for the first time made history into something directly experienced by the masses)[37] were given suitable artistic form thanks to a unique element of lyric theater. The modern notion of the proletariat as the motive force of history and of the masses as an active player could be especially well conveyed in music drama, which included a collective character in the form of the chorus. Hence, opera may be viewed as the best expressive form to convey this profound transformation of history through one of its traditional elements, the chorus—which rose from secondary to primary importance. At the first performance of *La Muette de Portici*, the audience rightly detected a new kind of stage action (see chapter 8). The populace was everywhere, and actively participated in moving the drama forward and in expressing it. Among the many scenes that demonstrate this, one might cite the incident in act 2 when Masaniello is joined by the crowd of men responding to his call, "the people must be armed, and the signal given." The appropriation of national feelings by the broader masses is directly reflected in the librettos of the earliest *grands opéras*, which, like the novels of Sir Walter Scott, favored subjects that pitted antagonistic groups against one another, principally in the form of race, clan, religious, or class confrontations. When grafted onto collective drama, individual drama could still be seen, in the violent light of battles or of *grandes journées*,[38] as a version of the new dialectic of the individual and the masses. The diversity, combinations, and vastness of available expressive resources, which ended up petrifying *grand opéra*, initially gained coherence from this historical force.

The scene that initiated this search for effect bolstered by the combining of expressive resources was clearly the act 3 scene from *Robert le Diable* referred to earlier. That famous scene, with its nuns' ballet, would long continue to draw audiences. When the opera was revived at the Palais Garnier in 1876, Raoul de Saint-Arroman marveled: "The convent scenery is utterly beautiful; it is a Rembrandt. The chiaroscuro effect of the vaults of the ancient monastery, contrasted with the calm, gentle light that floods the great pillars of the ruined cloister, and the overall unity and artistic arrangement of this scene make it one of the great achievements of decorative art."[39] In this "galvanic" and "fantastic" process (to use adjectives found in the first reviews), deployed in a tale of the twelfth century, amid ruins and dead bodies brought to life by demiurges in the form of librettists, composers, set designers, and stagehands, it is hard not to see a spectacular theatrical rendition of history as it might have been conceived by some of the Romantics, and as it reached its highest form in the works of the historian Jules Michelet (1798–1874). This scene gave form to a historical force that, as Roland Barthes notes, arose from the notion that the historian must experience death and must engage in a kind of primitive communion with the dead, exchanging with them the signs of life.[40] Michelet, that devourer of the dead, approached the resurrection of the past through a kind of taming of death, like Bertram on the stage of the Opéra. The introduction to volume 4 of his *Histoire de France*, which deals precisely with the Middle Ages, might have been written to describe the convent scene, with the nuns viewed as a sort of allegorical symbol of the Archives de la France:

> When I first entered the [Archives], those catacombs of handwriting, that necropolis of national monuments, I would have willingly said..., "This is the dwelling I have chosen; this is my place of repose for centuries of centuries." Yet I quickly perceived in the seeming silence of those galleries that there was movement there, a murmuring that did not belong to death. Those papers, those parchments long left there, asked nothing more than to see the light of day once more. Those papers are not papers, but the lives of men, of provinces, of peoples.... And as I blew away the dust, I saw them rise up. They drew from the tomb a hand, a head, as in Michelangelo's *Last Judgment* or in a dance of death. The galvanic dance they danced around me is what I have attempted to reproduce in this book.[41]

In *Robert le Diable,* the music is an incantation, a song of death that confers life. But following the trend toward realism that affected all the arts, it would be more than a breath, an emotion, or a spirit; it would become the true material of history. Its vocabulary would color the drama and enhance the characterization of the time and place of the drama's historical framework. For this to work, the composer needed historically distinctive musical material, and had therefore to become something of a musical archaeologist. *Grand opéra* was created at a time of growing interest in old music and in music history. Old styles were investigated; scores were unearthed, studied, and performed; harmonic theory could constitute a history of musical language. As noted earlier, historical material was far more than a mere decorative element; it helped set out the drama and was part of an eclectic aesthetic. Moreover, the abundance and diversity of material was suited to what I have called an aesthetic of intense emotions, which played on the nerves of the audience. The concentration of varied historical material in a single score made for electrifying clashes. In a more general sense, this was false-antique work, in the manner of Viollet-le-Duc.[42] Meyerbeer's successors made good use of his experiments. In his account of a conversation with Queen Victoria, Saint-Saëns discussed his approach in writing *Henry VIII:* "I explained to her how, wishing to give my work the appearance of its period, I ferreted about in the royal library in Buckingham Palace, . . . and how, in a thick manuscript collection dating from the sixteenth century, I found, arranged for harpsichord and buried in a thicket of useless arabesques, the lovely theme that is to some extent the opera's skeleton."[43]

For Meyerbeer, the return to a musical past was based on a concern for realism, for dramatic truth, and for creating effects; it reflected the major nineteenth-century tendency to look to the past to better illuminate the extraordinary progress made during that century and to merge all other periods in order to emphasize the century's domination of history. The composer of *Les Huguenots* viewed historical material as an element of artistic progress: something modern that could enrich his musical language; something very much of his own time. But a few decades later, a very different attitude arose, reflected especially in the work of Saint-Saëns. For a variety of reasons—because of generational and aesthetic changes, as well as for nationalistic reasons, with Wagner representing the Music of the Future—it was as though it were no longer a matter of moving forward, strengthened by the past, but of ignoring the passage of time. Eclecticism turned into a kind of neoclassicism based both on pastiches and on genuine borrowings from music history (see chapter 6). In its changed form, *grand opéra* often served as a preserve for history, a way of denying or avoiding the Music of the Future (from which it could nonetheless draw lessons). This standstill in time may reflect a yearning for an end to history, a delusion that undoubtedly underlies any art that becomes academic. In my view, Saint-Saëns's *Samson et Dalila* (1877) is the masterpiece of that trend.

Basically, *grand opéra* as championed by Meyerbeer and Halévy was too closely linked to historical material, and it lost its aesthetic power relatively early, with the disintegration of the cultural movements and historical forces that had spawned it. This was paralleled by what has been called the "silence of the people," which gradually arose after 1830 and also affected the spoken theater.[44] The transition from collective panoramas and romantic drama to the drama of everyday private life was also seen in the lyric theater, which after the reign of *grand opéra* found a new mode of expression in *opéra lyrique*. Fétis fully understood the close relationship between history and an aesthetic of the extreme, of effect, and of shock in *grand opéra:*

> The revolutionary spirit distorted the feelings of artists. . . . It was this that gradually caused any real notion of the *grand* to disappear from music, and that gave us the exaggerated and the gigantic; it was this that replaced innocent inspiration with manner; it was this, finally, that forced composers, like painters, to seek out the new, making them believe that systematically to do something different from the great men of the past is to possess their genius. . . . Seeking out the new and making an effect are the two constant concerns of our artists. . . . The effect they want to produce is nothing but a physical sensation. Its aim is neither to touch the heart nor to satisfy the mind, but only to rattle the nervous system.[45]

Debussy's irritation at the tenacity of *grand opéra*'s dying embers at the turn of the twentieth century is understandable. *Grand opéra* would soon sink into oblivion, but at that stage it still held its position and constituted a solid obstacle to that composer's ambitions. Debussy's ideas were developed in an aesthetic environment that could not have been farther from the great historic movement that gave rise to *grand opéra*. In 1889, in a conversation with his composition teacher, Ernest Guiraud, Debussy said that in his view "music is written for the inexpressible." To the question of which poet could provide him with the ideal libretto, he replied: "The [poet] who half-says things. Two dreams combined, that is the ideal. No country, no date. No scene to set. No pressure on the composer who executes [the libretto]."[46] No longer reality, but dream; no longer history, but a negation of time; no more local color. In a few words, Debussy was describing the antihistorical opera, a new concept, realized in 1902 with the premiere of *Pelléas et Mélisande*—at the Opéra-Comique, *not* at the museum-theater of the Palais Garnier.

## REASON, COMMON SENSE, AND ACADEMICISM

For conservatives, the successful revival of Félicien David's *La Perle du Brésil* on the heels of what they saw as the musical folly of *Les Troyens* amounted to revenge. A contemporary account of that revival reads like a credo of good taste: "Success was complete, enormous, and as resounding as a protest. Indeed, this music, so tuneful, so natural, so thoroughly bathed in the flowing waters of inspiration; this music, learned, melodic, and human in the feelings it inspires and in the gentle tears it causes to flow; this music, I say, appearing after *Les Troyens* like a ruddy sunrise after a starless night, is a protest by good taste, principles, appropriateness, and true art against the unspeakable attempted misuse of a highly dubious theory."[47]

That was an explicit statement of the canons of an aesthetic that drew upon the old founts of French art. Good taste, principles, appropriateness, and truth are indeed the unalterable pillars of that classical temple. *Les Pêcheurs de perles*, neither entirely faithful to tradition nor completely aberrant like *Les Troyens*, confounded the critics. They could not hand down clear-cut judgments, as they could with *Les Troyens*, depending on whether they sided with the ancients or with the moderns. They occasionally chided Bizet with a view to drawing him back into a more classical mold, typically saying that he lacked "moderation" and "taste."[48] Another critic sought to demonstrate how excessive harmonic flexibility damaged the clarity of discourse required by classical rigor: "We have only praise for M. Bizet. Yet we still criticize him for a certain diffuseness in his score's tonality. It is vital to give the audience an idea of the key. The composer wrongly lets us hear six or eight in a single piece—at the expense, obviously, of the clarity of his ideas."[49]

At least in the theater, French audiences required that a musical innovation be justified by a nonmusical purpose; it had to meet a dramatic or literary need. Bizet sometimes evaded this rule and thus incurred the wrath of at least one well-informed listener: "Some sixteenth-note figures in the violins, violas, and violoncellos evoke a sort of completely unmusical squealing sound that is difficult to justify in terms of the action. Moreover, the use of three trombones, which descend through a chromatic scale and form a minor second, a major second, a common chord, and an augmented

fifth chord to end in an enharmonic modulation—although very effective—does not seem to us to be called for by the situation."[50]

Omnipotent reason ever dominated the arts; that is why common
sense—a cardinal value that one dares not define as middle-class[51]—was
seen as an essential quality in a creative artist. Comettant wrote in 1862
that genius "comprises more than one precious element," among which
"the most precious of all is undoubtedly common sense," which was exactly what was "lacking in the ineffectual reformers of the art of
Beethoven and of Rossini." He added that "the strangeness of the human
mind knows no limits when that mind is not restricted to truth by common
sense, that supreme attribute of genius and that indispensable corollary of
the creative faculties, without which imagination amounts to nothing
more than brain fever."[52] This is why Eugène Scribe is so closely identified
with the tastes of his contemporaries. His "literary good fortune," wrote a
journalist in 1877, "was nothing other than clever, bold common sense."[53]

By age-old tradition, France is strongly devoted to reason, the "light of
the world," which Saint-Saëns would champion until the turn of the twentieth century. In a curious reversal, this would go against a large majority
of music-lovers and critics who were stricken with a Wagnerism that had
to be fought against. It ran counter to the fashion of proclaiming
unashamedly, in the very land of Descartes, that "to understand is so terribly middle-class."[54] In the mid nineteenth century, the press was guilty of
the opposite kind of excesses. To enable values to survive when times were
changing, it wound up with a paralyzing observance of tradition; by re-
stricting the language to a predictable set of rules, permitting innovations
only when they were very obvious or were easily justified on rational
grounds, it irretrievably lapsed into academicism. The only option was to
repeat models that had been adjudged perfect and eternal. Many critics demanded nothing of the theaters but that they reproduce ready-made formulas, as Henri Vignaud called upon the director of the Théâtre-Lyrique to
do in 1863:

> The Théâtre-Lyrique has been open only two months, and it has already
> given two works belonging to the ultra-romantic school [*Les Pêcheurs de
> perles* and *Les Troyens*]; it has even announced a third, M. Gounod's
> *Mireille*. M. Carvalho should dispense some of his favors to a few com-
> posers of the old school; he should let us hear a few scores written by
> young authors in the pure traditional style. I venture to assure him that
> his theater would gain in reputation, his box office in money, and the au-
> dience in healthy, enduring pleasure.[55]

French opera was the victim of this firmly rooted tendency toward conservatism. Few composers were independent-minded enough to fight this "force of habit that degenerates into a mentality of the routine."[56] In this environment, melody was the supreme operatic value. "I believe that the same regard will always be enjoyed by divine melody and by the true accents of the heart, and that this is an unchanging value, like that of diamonds," a writer avowed in *L'Univers musical* in 1863.[57] When *La Muette de Portici* was revived in the same year, one critic pointed out that Auber's melodies had remained intact "because melody is the soul of music, and the soul is immortal and thus eternally young."[58]

## THE REIGN OF MELODY—THE ITALIAN MODEL

"What is melody?" asked Nestor Roqueplan. "This is a nearly unanswerable question, because it is first of all a matter of feeling and intuition that eludes analysis, like those common-sense truths for which we turn to Scottish philosophy."[59] Along the lines of Rousseau, he suggested a hypothetical origin for this musical mystery: "Perhaps it could be defined in principle [as] a musical phrase that is naturally emitted from the mind or the heart in given moral circumstances or upon encountering a given external phenomenon." He still stressed the essential role of this jewel, which is both the substance and an ornament of music: "It is of these basic phrases, of these sounds, of these tonalities, of these instinctive rhythms—it is of these gems, not yet polished, cut or set, that music makes its language and its finery." One reviewer of *Les Pêcheurs de perles* took the opportunity to reaffirm the basic principle of opera: "We have already tried to explain how in the theater, because everything takes on a defined form, dramatic music has to be essentially melodic; in other words, it must not disappear in pointless meanderings and must grip the listener's spirit in the most concise way possible."[60]

There was a clear hierarchy between melody, "the soul of music," and harmony, which must merely "serve as its body," Xavier Aubryet declared in *Le Nain jaune*. "To have a musical idea is not to lay down a learned, dense, and solid framework; it is to use that excellent basis to enable what I shall call intellectual flora to grow."[61] Inveighing against antiquated formulas and popular triumphs to which repetition had made people deaf, the writer surprisingly proposed as a model Louis Ferdinand Hérold, who at the time of his success with *Zampa* (1831) had been criticized for succumbing to German influences, and who as a French melodist had profited from the examples of Rossini among many others, including Auber and Meyerbeer.

A brief survey of performances at the Théâtre-Italien[62] reveals that after 1817, the repertory of that theater was overrun by the works of Rossini. *L'Italiana in Algeri* was performed 11 times in 1817, 18 times in 1821–22, and 63 times between 1824 and 1834—a pattern that was to continue. Then *Il Barbiere di Siviglia* arrived, and between 1819 and 1823 chalked up 91 performances, its popularity never abating. Apart from a few works such as *L'Inganno felice* and *Elisabetta regina d'Inghilterra*, most of Rossini's operas remained in the repertory. *Tancredi*, for example, was given 108 times between 1822 and 1832, and in the twenty years between 1821 and 1841, *Otello* was heard 247 times. Adding up the performances of all the Rossini works given in a year yields impressive statistics: in 1825, for instance, there were no less than 142 performances of his *opere serie* and *opere buffe* combined.

Rossini moved to Paris in 1824 and held official positions there, such as his post at the Théâtre-Italien. This was the heyday of the dilettanti, hedonistic amateurs who loved Italian music, and who were opposed by the antidilettanti, the enemies of this "Italian vandalism." Plunging into the aesthetic battle enlivening the Paris press and Parisian society, Berlioz scoffed at the dilettanti:

> They are men of taste...who go only to the Théâtre-Italien, who never read scores (for a good reason that is easily divined), and who, as a court of final resort, rule on the merits of operas, singers, and orchestras. Their sensitivity is such that breath fails them when they hear that moving passage from *La Gazza ladra* where the servant girl is condemned to death; it is such that they are better able to maintain their composure at performances of operas such as [Gluck's] *Iphigénie* and [Salieri's] *Danaïdes*.[63]

Although this mad infatuation for Rossini was a fashion at times deserving of criticism, the fact remains that the composer's technique—vocal melody, the form of the individual numbers, the construction of ensembles and finales, and so forth—was a breath of fresh air that French opera badly needed. The establishment of Rossini's works in France was successful also because the Théâtre-Italien managed to attract great performers: Giovanni-Battista Viotti, director from 1819 to 1821, sent Hérold (who served as accompanist at the theater between 1818 and 1826) to Italy to negotiate an engagement for Giuditta Pasta, and to recruit other singers as well.

A balance between French tradition and the Italian aesthetic was struck in 1825 with Boieldieu's *La Dame blanche*, although many critics of the time refused to understand this and tried to set the French composer up as the champion of anti-Rossinianism. That score employs the simple expressive means valued by eighteenth-century composers of *opéra-comique*, such as strophic forms, *couplets*, and the kind of martial aria typical of the genre (Georges's "Ah! quel plaisir d'être soldat!"—"Oh, what a pleasure to be a soldier!"—in act 1). At the same time, the orchestra has been filled out and the score's vocal requirements call for real singers. There is a small-scale Rossinian crescendo in the overture, but it is in the vocal parts and the form that we see the Italian composer's most substantial influence. Most vocal lines are ornamented, to the extent that it is sometimes possible to think that one is hearing a work by Rossini. The act 1 duet for Georges and Jenny (no. 4) is an entirely successful example of the merging of Italian and French style. The situation is an amorous one (a soldier wooing a farm girl) and contains a reference to one of those spineless characters typical of French *opéra-comique* (in this case Dickson, Jenny's husband). Boieldieu here composed a number in which *couplets* alternate with refrain, a musical form that conveys the playfulness of the meeting of the two characters and their interplay, whereby they keep moving closer together, only to dodge each other. The first phrases sketch the gallant outlines of a minuet, then Jenny injects a syllabic melody in a style similar to that of Neapolitan *dramma giocoso;* finally, the two voices unite in a common style with flowery ornamentation that could easily come from Rossini's *Le Comte Ory* (premiered at the Opéra in 1828, three years after *La Dame blanche*). Other examples of Italian influence are the *cantabile-cabaletta* structure of arias for Georges (no. 8) and for Anna (no. 12); and the manner in which the *concertati* (no. 5, "Je n'y puis rien comprendre," no. 7, "A la douce espérance," and no. 10, "O ciel! quel est ce mystère") are written.[64]

In the 1830s, much music by Bellini and Donizetti began to be heard at the Théâtre-Italien. Verdi was added to the repertory in 1845 with *Nabucco,* followed by *Ernani* and *I due Foscari* in 1846, *Il Trovatore* in 1854, *La Traviata* in 1856, and *Rigoletto* in 1857, all of which were very popular. But none of this compared with the Rossini fever of the 1820s.

"The Italian school is characterized first and foremost by simplicity of means and melody, by a focus on rhythm, by brilliance and light," Roqueplan observed.[65] And in spite of the considerable changes in Italian vocal writing and the Italian operatic aesthetic brought about by Bellini, Donizetti, and, above all, Verdi, the dramaturgy of Italian opera continued to be based on the supremacy of singing.

However skillfully implemented, effect could never replace living melody. Traditionalists could only see the trend toward increasing instrumental participation and toward augmenting the sonic resources of the orchestra as a clumsy attempt to disseminate a sterile idea. Paul Scudo wrote of Berlioz: "If the composer's ideas were stripped of the noisy sonorities that enwrap them, they would most often be discovered to be a body without youthfulness or grace. M. Berlioz…thinks he is performing a miracle when he has ten trombones strike up an extremely mediocre pattern. If one set sixty instruments to playing the tune 'J'ai du bon tabac,' one would achieve the very effects of which M. Berlioz is so fond."[66] It remained only to identify the culprits of this aberration: "Readers should know," wrote a critic before the opening of *Les Troyens,*

> that the absence of melody was instituted as a system in recent times (or at least the attempt was made). M. Wagner in Germany and M. Gounod in France have tried to push back the boundaries of music by seeming to despise specific forms and the normal elements of style that until they came along had sufficed for expressing all the emotions involved in a theatrical performance, however varied its effects might be. These self-styled reformers have done nothing but transfer the techniques of symphonic writing to the stage.[67]

Bizet earned praise for the ballet music and the choruses of *Les Pêcheurs,* "which play a large part in his score" and were written in a "manner full of delicacy and skill." These were precisely the parts of the opera that had to fit into a rigid framework and that would almost automatically avoid the danger of vagueness and of excessively complex writing: "Dance music must be very rhythmic, lest it be impossible to dance to it; a chorus will not be singable if feats of counterpoint are indulged in."[68]

The "old claim that [Wagner's music] lacked melody meant that [the melody] was set out and employed in a previously unknown way," Reynaldo Hahn comments. The old operatic norm had been accompaniments that were neutral and without significance:

> Audiences were thus accustomed to these passive styles of accompaniment. They knew that the melody belonged in the voice; they looked for it there, and there they found it. They were therefore disconcerted when one day it emerged from everywhere at once, gushing, bursting, pouring in a thousand different ways and, in countless opposing and harmonious currents, complementing and combating one another to form an indivisible whole. The ears of the listener, beckoned from every direction, were at first disconcerted and panic-stricken by this multidimensional flood of melody; they no longer knew where to turn to take it in. Audiences thus thought for years that melody was absent from this music, whereas in fact it abounded there in inexhaustible supply.[69]

Saint-Saëns recalled that early in the century, with Rossini, Italian melody had conquered all French resistance. Stendhal became a disciple of the Italian school, and his *Les Vies de Haydn, de Mozart et de Métastase* (*Metastasio*) was henceforth "the breviary of most of the critics." Unfortunately, its "astonishing basic triviality was concealed by a semblance of musical erudition that foisted itself on the ignorant." Stendhal's "disastrous influence," continued Saint-Saëns, "is still felt today both in society and in the press, even though the book itself is long forgotten." Hence, undoubtedly, the fact that "for 150 years," as Saint-Saëns wrote in 1876, " 'melody' has been the facile catchword of musical criticism."[70] And in another article, he wondered, like Roqueplan, "So what was melody? We were never able to know; the Italians alone had the secret."[71]

### VOCATION AND INSPIRATION—TECHNIQUE AS THE ENEMY OF ART

Among the writings that supported a traditional understanding of French opera, the columns of the critic Louis Roger reveal the paradox at the core of the crisis of French opera. He explained that there was "one point on which serious critics agree: the misuse and affectation of technique in the works of M. Bizet. There will also be willing agreement that these are lacking in originality. This is perhaps less serious: a young author may be forgiven for imitating his favorite masters. It is almost unheard of for a beginner not to imitate someone." This implied dividing the creative process into two separate areas: vocation and tradition on the one hand, and personal inspiration on the other. But matters were more complicated than that, for although Bizet was seen as an unimaginative imitator, some felt that he displayed a dreadful eccentricity, which arose, paradoxically, from the excessive technicality of his writing. "This need for something to be heard that has never been heard before made him tinker with a heap of bad techniques that good taste can only disown," Roger wrote. He then listed the composer's "unpleasant quirks": "He labors his modulations; he changes key or mode at least five or six times in the course of a piece; he writes crazy music for the trombones; he makes the violins squeak like a door on rusty hinges; he forces the singers to shout; he is so immoderate in his sonic effects that pieces of unquestionable brilliance are drowned in the noise that is being produced all around them." Roger thereupon raised the specter of arid technicality and let fly with a diatribe against modernity as the murderer of sacrosanct inspiration: "It is necessary to protest against these deplorable trends. This is a question not only of M. Bizet's future…but…that of the entire present generation of musicians, who have embarked on a disastrous path. I have often said it here: art is not a cold calculation of notes subject to stupid, immutable rules. To try to substitute the demands of near-sighted academicism for free, spontaneous, innocent inspiration is to be doomed to failure."[72]

A technical approach both destroyed the freshness of inspiration and disfigured melody. Excessive craftsmanship and the strictness needed for studied composition ran counter to musical emotion. A work had to be built on a foundation of melody; only this could arouse such emotion in the listener and accommodate a range of feelings.

Bizet followed the trend toward shifting the importance of the vocal line to the orchestral structure that had previously supported it and that now would envelop it. As we have already seen, general observations now began to turn to the specific question of Wagnerian influences. There was a distinct conflict between the school in which melody reigned and that of the technicians, just as *musique savante* had vied with *musique chantante* at the end of the eighteenth century: "A large part of the public, which was unwilling to give up hearing pleasant, easy musical phrases at the Salle Favart or the Salle Feydeau," writes Jean Mongrédien, "called this repertory [Méhul and Cherubini] *savant*—learned—although naturally it had nothing to do with learned or academic music in the modern sense. At that time, the lovers of melody, of the *chantant*, rallied around Paisiello at the Théâtre-Italien, then later, just before the Revolution, around Cimarosa and Mozart."[73] By a curious twist of fate, we can recognize here the conflict depicted in Wagner's *Die Meistersinger von Nürnberg*. The bold, inventive young Walther, with his free inspiration, symbolizes musical renewal, while Beckmesser, attached to strict rules, represents conservatism.

Along with Wagner, Berlioz was conjured up to describe a style of music that broke the rules (see fig. 31). "When they want to criticize a composer for certain kinds of harmonic boldness, when they think they detect the mildest inclination to break with routine or with scholastic tradition, they say indiscriminately, 'You are writing like Wagner' or 'You are writing like Berlioz: watch out!'"[74] Another critic worried, "If one day this music wins out, we shall go to the theater, not to read the logarithmic tables, but rather to discover that they have been translated into sounds and chords."[75] Louis Roger waxed oxymoronic in suggesting that in the hands of reckless composers, technique posed a threat to art: "Now that there seems to be a willingness to open the theaters to [young composers], they must not manifest their ignorance in *frivolous technical displays*."[76] That juxtaposition of words expressed a paradox. In some numbers, such as the Nadir-Zurga duet and Léïla's *cavatine*, Bizet managed to skirt the issue, respecting the primacy of

Le Tannhauser demandant à voir son petit frère.

Figure 31. "Tannhäuser Asking to See His Little
Brother," caricature of Berlioz and *Les Troyens* (*Le
Charivari,* November 25, 1863). Berlioz was pigeon-
holed as an intellectual composer who made noise
rather than charming his audience with melodies.
He was thus linked with Wagner.

melody while modernizing the coloration, especially through his orchestration. Those pieces, Roger wrote, were admired because they displayed "nothing that could subvert the customary laws of musical composition." Such notions come from an aesthetic that saw a work of art in terms of models and
that viewed simplicity as the key to the beautiful—or at least to the pleasant.
"The most delightful [of Bizet's] phrases flow transparent from the well-
spring, like everything that is beautiful," the *Revue française* declared.[77]

## THE NEED FOR RENEWAL AND THE FEAR OF CHANGE

One critic, Xavier Aubryet, spoke out against a situation that most other
journalists seemed to accept:

> We have such a thirst for original music that we would nearly abandon
> the veteran composers in order to open the doors to the newcomers. To
> grow old while still hearing *Les Mousquetaires de la Reine* in 1863 is to

grow old twice. To run into people who will still tell you, "How inspired *The Barber of Seville* is!" and who will sing you a ritornello that has been around the world sixteen billion times, is to be horrified by something of which you were once supremely fond. And *Le Trouvère [Il Trovatore]*, with which you are bludgeoned at the entrance to every summer restaurant![78]

Music-lovers were so familiar with standard music that they could predict in advance the shape of new melodies: "And," continued Aubryet, "one is so weary of the musical idioms! There is such a need to renew them! Is it not true that, three-quarters of the time, a composer's phrases complete themselves automatically as you hear them?" He then described some of the clichés: recitative as "monotonous as the whine of a tethered dog"; echoes; syncopations "that give the musical discourse the appearance of a woman who does nothing but faint"; and cadenzas that are "so easy to perform and still earn the prima donna swooning 'bravas' from stupid dilettanti." Despite his pique, he could not agree with the advocates of radical change, and inveighed against "this fine modern theory that is being inflicted on us in the name of His Majesty King Progress—a real monarch of fantasy: melody must be indeterminate; music must be as vague as the sound of the sea or of the wind."

"When I earnestly call for renewal of the forms of our *opéra-comique*," wrote Gaston de Saint-Valry,

> God save me from wanting a collective art form to replace the personal, vivid melody that must always be the foundation of the true meaning of theater. What I demand is that the trite, outdated mold that shapes all pieces should be inventively and imaginatively renewed, and that we escape the monotonous formulas that burden every tenor aria, every love duet, and every comic aria. But I would never agree to having the tenor, the baritone, the bass, and the soprano reduced to the diminished and nearly passive role of organ pipes or instruments in some sort of newfangled symphony.... I am convinced that just as Rossini, by respecting all the established artistic rules, created with his flights of genius all the forms that still survive in Italian music, so too a new inventor will restore our *opéra-comique* and enable it to rise from the triviality and repetitiousness in which it threatens to founder.[79]

The critic's hopes must be seen in the light of the self-contradictory phrase "conservative reform." It was toward this that Bizet was moving when he poured the original language of *Carmen* into the traditional mold of *opéra-comique*. It was toward this that the composers of *opéras lyriques* seem to have been inclining in the 1850s.

It was only in the 1870s and 1880s that the press as a whole acknowledged that there was a crisis and unequivocally stated the need for renewal in all genres. But it still had to be done gently, as the critics wrote when Massenet's *Le Roi de Lahore*—by no means a revolutionary work—was premiered at the Opéra in 1877. Jules Ruelle wrote of the libretto, "Our generation is looking for a new ideal completely different from that of the masters who have been acclaimed for the past half a century."[80] And Paul Bernard stressed:

> The present musical period, especially in the theater, is a transitional period. As in every sphere, there is a need for progress that would shatter the old molds, even though these seem to have been hallowed by the masterpieces of the past.... Gradually, styles fall from fashion and wear out. As they become more refined, dramatic sensibilities reject conventional techniques and aim for more accurate modes of expression. That is why stereotyped pieces are very gradually disappearing to make room for musical diction that is more in keeping with the situation at hand.... [Some people] are very willing to share these goals; others are set in their ways and want nothing to change. Between these two disparate trends...the poor composer today is very confused; he dares not give way completely to the trite ideas that will please the crowds but will put off the more sophisticated, yet he does not want to make a complete break and replace them with an abstruse approach that might be purer but that would certainly be more tiresome.[81]

There is no doubt about the influence of audiences on the creative process, about the conflict between an aspiration to lofty expression and the tendency to retain a conventional framework, or about the fact that the need to entertain eclipsed the desire to express more elevated musical ideas. And it is clear that a composer who wanted to succeed had to hedge— had to find a middle road.

## NORTH VERSUS SOUTH—THE AESTHETIC OF THE HAPPY MEDIUM

*Opéra lyrique* was an initial response to the call for the renewal of French opera, and it came about without breaking any of the basic rules. Composers aimed at adding intensity to their expressive forms and greater density to their scores. Let us recall that Gounod was often viewed as a symphonic technician, and that the beauties of his *Faust* were sometimes spoken of as classical and austere. Even his little *opéra-comique Le Médecin malgré lui* (1858), in which he lavished equal care on vocal melody and instrumental writing, was classified as a technical work, or at least one with a studied style: "M. Gounod seems to be in the habit of

Figure 32. *Left:* Engraving by Aristide Louis after Ary Scheffer's painting *Mignon Longing for Her Homeland* (1835; final version, 1839). *Right:* Engraving by Aristide Louis after Scheffer's painting *Mignon Yearning for Heaven* (1838). Goethe's heroine was stripped of all violence, all passion, and all pain, and was idealized as a dreamy character. These two images of Mignon, which Louis showed at the 1844 Salon, were very popular.

thinking of the instruments before he thinks of the voice," affirmed Léon Durocher; he was "more German than Italian."[82]

Ambroise Thomas, too, was an expert composer, and the publisher-journalist Marie Escudier worried that *Mignon* would be criticized for "being too well written, not to say too classical."[83] It is important to remember that these scores, which many people today regard as facile and sentimental, broke with the *opéra-comique* tradition in terms of their subtlety and their rather elevated musical ideas. Listeners were struck by the handling of the orchestra and by the expressive role it played. The most conservative of the critics were horrified by the score of *Faust*, which seemed to them to reject melody, that precious Italian legacy, in favor of "the triumph of orchestration" and the clamor "of extravagant and noisy chords"[84] that were attributed to German influence.[85] Clearly, national styles had become the battleground of this debate.

The French image of German art, culture, and thought yielded two of the most important scores in the sphere of *opéra lyrique: Faust* and *Mignon*. Both were adapted from works by the personification of German genius, Goethe: *Faust* and *Wilhelm Meister*, respectively.[86] Even the most chauvinistic of journalists were fond of the German master's characters, at least in the new, stripped-down form they were given in French works, and as they were seen in the many paintings of Ary Scheffer (1795–1858), engravings of which were widely distributed, depicting Marguerite and Mignon in ethereal poses (see figs. 32 and 34). Recalling statements by the authors of the operatic version of *Mignon*, Georges Loiseau reported that "the question of her costume was long debated, and it was only after great hesitation that it was decided to opt for the costume chosen for Mignon, and popularized, by Ary Scheffer"[87] (see fig. 33).

In the view of Gustave Chaudeuil, types such as Marguerite and Mignon, as disseminated in every artistic form, had become more authentic than Goethe's originals, which is why he searched *Wilhelm Meister* in vain for Mignon as he knew her: "This was perhaps because there are too many digressions in the book that constantly lose us in the world of aesthetics, of the abstruse, of the nebulous—indeed, of the incomprehensible—and because we often get thoroughly bogged down in them."[88] In 1859, the same journalist derided those "who see all manner of things in Goethe's *Faust*,"[89] a play that was simultaneously philosophical, religious, didactic, poetic, idealistic, and naive. For the rabid defenders of French national art, this was a true struggle between French thought, based on clear-mindedness, and German thought, mired in vague profundity; a rivalry between the concrete and the abstract. *Opéra lyrique* might be seen as the acclimatization of the German aesthetic to France—or as a German renewal of French opera.[90] But Germanic profundity arrived only by a circuitous route. It was only a reflection of German art that could be seen in French works, not its real language or ideas. Albert Soubies and Charles Malherbe said that the subject of *Mignon* was treated, "like that of *Faust*, in the French manner, that is, with a blend of pleasant grace and a somewhat middle-class approach."[91]

A critic in *Le Ménestrel* could write that in *Mignon* "the composer discovered the secret of writing two operas in one: one of them essentially French, of the Opéra-Comique vintage, and the other eminently lofty, in the German manner."[92] Théophile Gautier had a very different view: that

Figure 33. Célestine Galli-Marié, who created the role of Mignon in Thomas's opera of the same name, photographed in her costume (probably in 1866). This image amounts to an amalgam of the two Aristide Louis engravings after Scheffer's paintings (see fig. 32).

a fundamental antagonism was in play. He saw Mignon, a young girl "with a pale complexion and big, dark eyes, her mouth painfully tensed," as the "personification of southern poetry that has strayed North."[93] He went on to write, "Mignon's love—which is a yearning for light in the depths of shadow—ought to shine like a ray of sunlight through a background of dreamy German mist." This indeed is a basic principle in Goethe, who is well known to have been fascinated by Italy, a country that had a decisive influence on the development of his imagination and his thinking. But Gautier does not seem to have grasped the contribution of these two extremes to the 1866 work. In Thomas's opera, the contrasts we have noted

Figure 34. Ary Scheffer's painting *Marguerite at Her Spinning Wheel* (1848). This interpretation of Goethe's Margarete was characterized by intimacy, gentleness, and reverie.

may still be viewed in the watered-down, pre-Nietzschean form of a North-South confrontation, personified in the pairing of the introspective, dreamy Mignon and the happy, extroverted Philine.

Rather than juxtaposing the two stylistic languages, French composers softened German boldness by putting it through the filter of *opéra lyrique*. The antagonisms between German thought and French thought, between serious style and light style, between profundity and superficiality, were smoothed over in *Faust* and *Mignon* by means of a stylistic hybrid. This genre reflected the concept of an operatic temperate zone and an aesthetic happy medium: the characteristic of French art. "The German school is noted for cleverly wrought harmonies combined with powerful, expressive melodies, and the Italian school for sweet melodies and elegant craftsmanship; the French school has adopted a mixed genre that draws upon German rigor and Italian grace."[94] As in the other arts, France played "a role for understanding and conciliation," Nestor Roqueplan argued.[95] "Since excess in anything is an error and since the extremes of idealism and materialism can degenerate into madness or brutishness, it follows that the correct and generous cosmopolitan school of 'absolute beauty' should exist in an environment in which conflicting qualities come together harmoniously," Charles Poisot explained. He concluded that this could be called a "harmonious union of opposites." France was the ideal country for such an aesthetic, because "through its geographical position, through the reason, wit and genius of its language, and through the influence of its varied and noble ideas, [it] tends to appropriate what it sees as the best of every school."[96] In fact, according to Poisot, it would be wise to avoid the conflicting qualities that go to make up the beautiful in favor of a happy medium that plays down the extremes. "French melody has more meaning but is smaller in scale than Italian melody; it is more human but less lofty and penetrating than German melody,"[97] Roqueplan wrote perceptively.

In approving new modes of expression once they had grown accustomed to them, French academic critics long recurred to this "ideal of mildness." At the start of our period, in *Zampa* (1831), Hérold attempted just such a difficult blend of styles. While many initially saw a dominant Germanic influence (that of Mozart and Weber), there was gradual recognition of the importance of Italian models. "To my mind, *Zampa* is the very definition of what is known as the modern French school—I would even say the Parisian school," Joseph d'Ortigue wrote in *Le Ménestrel* on June 14, 1863. "Hérold had a wonderful grasp of the level of his audience, which would accept a little bit of German inspiration and a little bit of Italian inspiration, all toned down and gallicized."

In 1884, Raoul de Saint-Arroman, who was closely associated with the old styles, ended his article about the premiere of *Manon* by expressing the hope that he would soon discover a new champion of the happy medium—without realizing that he had just heard him: "The French school can only be proud of this new work by one of its leaders. But it still awaits the man who by integrating the musical achievements of all countries, including Germany, will write a genuinely French masterpiece, truly distinctive and the equal of *Le Pré aux clercs, Faust,* or *Les Huguenots.*"[98] But this was just the thinking of an old-fashioned columnist. Audiences got the point, and were applauding, along with that part of the press that was not so fanatically committed to tradition. Between 1880 and 1910, Massenet would update the "conservative reform" carried out by Thomas and Gounod, but condemned by the progressive Marcel Rémy, who preferred a more clearcut idiom: "All in all, *Werther* is a score that marks the exhaustion of a genre: the false-modern genre that consists of concessions and pseudoboldness."[99] *Manon* and, later, *Werther* reflected an evolution of *opéra lyrique* to *drame lyrique*. Writers who were less categorical than Rémy and Saint-Arroman dredged up phrases long used to describe the genre—poetry and melancholy, delicacy and charm, sentimentality and compassion—and stressed the preeminent role of the orchestra as an expressive and poetic factor. One of them, for example, was pleased that the librettists of *Werther* had managed to retain "the delightful romantic color and the intimate, sentimental, and charming aspects of the narrative."[100]

Massenet himself described his commitment to the aesthetic of the happy medium:

> Let us make a distinction. The Italian masters are too exclusively concerned with the phrase; they sacrifice too much to the voice without giving enough attention to what has been called the underpinnings—what I myself call the dramatic atmosphere. The result is that the characters live only in a world of their own—a somewhat artificial world—and not enough in the real world around us. It is the opposite with the German master. To my mind he is closer to absolute truth. The ideal would be a harmonious fusion of the two systems in the proper proportions. And that is the ideal for which I am aiming.[101]

## EXPRESSIVE PROFUNDITY AND *L'ESPRIT FRANÇAIS*

It was obviously not profundity that was looked for in musical discourse in a Paris where, in Balzac's still-valid words, "witticisms slaughter the greatest of ideas."[102] E. T. A. Hoffmann's apt comment in 1814 on the *esprit français* (made apropos of Boieldieu's opera *Le Nouveau Seigneur du village*) remained true during Bizet's lifetime:

> The theater of the French comes from the bedrock of their character, their lives, and the way in which they converse. By polishing every detail, they make sure that everything will be easy in ordinary society; but the distinguishing mark of the individual disappears from it. It is thus in theater, in which the poet aims for a pattern that is uncomplicated and consistent, but by no means for the profundity of ideas and meanings on the basis of which the entire play and individual features may be developed....
>
> Music, which is not a vital element but a mere arbitrary ornament to the dialogue, follows the same trend. It could be called unassuming, for here too the only expectation is that everything should be arranged in a simple and pleasant way, that nothing should be out of place, and that the end result should be entertaining in a conventional way: that it should be understood and savored without effort and without any particular attention.[103]

Once again contrasting Berlioz and Auber, Louis de Romain did a good job of summing up the situation, and covered much of the subject matter we have discussed, beginning with the social standing of the Parisian artist and ending with French attitudes toward music. In the days of Berlioz, he wrote,

> there could be no popularity for a composer outside the theater, and when Berlioz arrived on the scene, the theater was inhabited by the pleasant, uncomplicated Muse of composers such as Boieldieu, Adam, and Auber, as well as by the Italian repertory. Although he gave greater importance to the orchestra, Meyerbeer himself did not reform or change anything. Neither *Robert [le Diable]* nor *Les Huguenots,* nor even *Le Prophète,* blazed new trails; the mold remained the old mold, although it had been enlarged by a powerful hand. These works required no intellectual effort to be understood; they never had to face the ordeal that is so often beyond our powers: the need to think.[104]

Wagner's description of *opéra-comique* referred to its "air of charming elegance that delights and pleases the senses without furnishing truly profound pleasure and without very powerfully moving our sensibilities."[105] Auber's *Le Domino noir* (1837), which is nothing but disguises and mistaken identity, perfectly embodied this aesthetic. Its music is elegant and thoroughly well suited to pleasant, witty entertainment. In the same vein, one might also note *Fra Diavolo* (1830), which throughout the rest of the nineteenth century was performed at the Opéra-Comique almost without interruption. Its nonchalant tone and lively rhythms, and the hint of local color with which the composer tinged the entire score, effectively brought to life Scribe's light, spirited, and impeccably constructed libretto. When there was an attempt in *opéra lyrique* to add depth to the expressive qualities and density to the musical writing, the traditionalist critics were terrified. Astonishingly, act 1 of Gounod's *Faust* would seem "too abstruse."

The weightiness of the musical discourse and the density of ideas, which needed time to be appreciated, ran counter to the principle of immediacy that in opera oriented the French mind toward seeking an immediate sensory and emotional return. According to one shrewd columnist, Berlioz—who knew what audiences liked—should have abandoned some of his pretensions and should instead have developed his ability to express emotions, while freeing his melodies from the fabric of sound that enwrapped them: "If he wrote ... for the present and not for the future (whose judgment he cannot know), he would take his place among our premier theater composers."[106] To succeed in France, adaptations of German works had to omit abstract thoughts and symbolic figures: "The translation of *Faust* by Messieurs Michel Carré and Jules Barbier," wrote the critic for *Le Figaro,* "follows the original as closely as permitted by the requirements of music and the dramatic inclinations of the spectators for whom the opera was intended. Here, we want to get the point of things, ideas, passions, and feelings clearly and quickly."[107]

The *esprit français*—a concept that encompasses such characteristics as wit and lively intelligence—seems by its nature to have put a brake on musical progress. Even a confirmed Wagnerian like Louis de Romain remained under its influence as late as the 1890s; referring to symphonic music, he explained that in the works of many of the German masters of the day, such as Brahms and Max Bruch, "erudition abounds; thought is lofty and sometimes obscurely poetic; and the style seems to be of irreproachable purity. But we seek in vain for the easy wit and delicate cleverness that mark so many charming works by our countrymen."[108] It is therefore easy to understand the difficulty that the works of Wagner had in being performed in France. Ernest Reyer, who in 1857 heard *Tannhäuser* at Wiesbaden, wrote, "In the music of *Tannhäuser* there are magnificent solos, ample melodies laden with very great dramatic feeling, admirably well devised instrumentation, beauties of the first order; but there is nothing pretty, nothing light, nothing graceful, no fioriture, no cadenzas, no roulades: that is why...I see problems for the success of this kind of music in Paris."[109] Any history of opera in nineteenth-century France must take note of the aesthetic categories that were typically scorned and that Reyer stressed. The pretty, the graceful, the light were central, but they were hard to define because they related both to purely artistic factors and to the history of taste and of thinking. What Auber wanted to capture amounted to one side of the human character to which little value is accorded today in "serious" art: the je ne sais quoi that talent can add to the ordinary to make it special or to reveal its essence; that little something that reveals more than it says; that little something that lends things a particular character that the French were always pleased to find. Auber, one columnist wrote in 1862,

> will earn a name in music and a fine place in the sun for as long as we live in a world of sunshine, gaiety, light, and that elusive and indefinable French quality known as *esprit*. . . . I like that clarity, that craft, that skill, and that frothy sparkle that delight the mind. In those aspects of our deepest being, I see the very soul of my country: clarity, light, gaiety, delicacy, and good taste. Man does not live by Beethoven, Schumann, and Wagner alone, but also by a lovely ray of sunlight, by a ruby glitter in the crimson of a glass of wine, by the exciting little face of a blonde beauty, by resounding laughter, by the brightness of the morning light;

and our French composers possess the clarity, the beauty and the joy of our homeland.[110]

In 1913 or 1914, when Wagner had become a model for many musicians, Reynaldo Hahn, the "prince of operetta," gave a lecture on singing and on ways of using music to move the listener in which he protested that too much attention was being given to the pursuit of powerful, clamorous emotions; people were unaware, he said, of "the value of graduated sensations, the sometimes great worth of a light, fleeting emotion, the sad pleasure of tears, the sweetness of a sigh, the exquisite, bitter charm of melancholy."[111] All this was precisely what the French valued so highly in opera in the nineteenth century, never suspecting that their children would get rid of the very things that had so largely dominated their music.

In 1922, Fauré paid tribute to the memory of Saint-Saëns, highlighting this aspect of the French character: "In Saint-Saëns, of course, thought seems sometimes to have dwelled in those serene precincts...where violence and outbursts are unknown, where seriousness, wit, charm, and cheerful tenderness together reign. That atmosphere arouses feelings that could perhaps be called ordinary. But for him they were enough to inspire many passages that are both delightful and enduring."[112]

Composers touched on things lightly rather than flourishing them; they had to know how to conceal the loftier and more serious elements in a pleasant guise: "This *esprit français*—which is basically nothing other than a well-honed mind—is able through common sense and good will to give clear and practical meaning to the ideal and a subtly familiar cast to poetic thought," Henri Delaborde wrote.[113] This balanced and light-handed approach was not devoid of delicacy or even subtlety—as called for and regulated by good taste. Specifically, at the Opéra-Comique, the goal, Saint-Saëns said, was to realize "the ideal of those who, fearful of growing exhausted listening to music that is hard to understand, wish nonetheless to experience artistic and refined pleasures not unworthy of people of taste."[114] Hence the success of Auber, whose "popularity managed to remain refined and distinguished."[115] In a manifestation of the continuity of the *esprit français*, Louis de Romain described the music of Massenet in similar terms:

> The world is full of learned contrapuntists who, loaded with fugues and drudgery, would happily trade a year of their lives for an hour's inspiration. For Massenet, that hour lasted a lifetime. Here is the secret of his charm, the reason for his successes, the source of his talent. His melodies go straight to the heart; they delight us, move us, and embrace us. Vigor

abounds to overflowing. Dazzled by the constantly refreshed brilliance of youthfulness and love, we never dream of probing the depths of the idea. His lightness is enough, for it consists of smiles, tenderness, and grace.[116]

When Massenet died in 1912, Debussy, although very critical of his music, wrote essentially in the same vein of "that ability to please, which is a true gift," and of the "delightful glory" of hearing one's music hummed.[117] "Nothing will prevent Massenet from being one of the most glittering diamonds in our musical jewel-box," Saint-Saëns wrote. "No other musician enjoyed the favor of the public as much as he did, apart from Auber—whom he did not like any more than he liked his school, yet whom he strangely resembled: they shared fluency, extraordinary inventiveness, wit, grace and popularity, and both wrote the right music for their times."[118]

Moreover, the fact that composers touched on emotions rather than expressing them in depth or belaboring them reflects a French approach to art that was grounded in understatement. Linked with this is a sense of familiarity and the special attention that some composers, such as Massenet, paid to the little things, and to the minor matters of daily life, using "Realist" symbols to portray ordinary surroundings. These are the *piccole cose* so dear to Puccini, who was similar to Massenet in so many respects. "Adieu notre petite table" from act 2 of *Manon* expresses both the melancholy of a memory focused on a single detail and the heroine's distress linked with an object as a symbol of the happy times when the lovers, united in simplicity, shared the ordinary things of life. The same holds true for act 3 of *Werther*, when the hero returns to his friends and recalls the old days. The house and the things in it are unchanged, and hold timeless feelings and memories—in contrast to the people: "Oui, je vois…ici…rien n'a changé…que les coeurs!…/Toute chose est encore à la place connue./Voici le clavecin qui chantait mes bonheurs/Ou qui tressaillait de ma peine,/Alors que votre voix accompagnait la mienne!…/Ces livres!… sur qui tant de fois nous avons incliné nos têtes rapprochées!"—"Yes, I can see that nothing has changed here, except hearts./Everything is in its accustomed place./Here is the harpsichord that sang my happiness/Or shivered at my grief/When your voice accompanied mine./These books, over which we bent our heads, close to one another."

This reflects a romanticism that Victor Hugo described in his *Voyage aux Pyrénées:*

> What a mystery the past is, and how true it is that we leave something of ourselves in the objects that surround us. We think them inanimate, but they are alive, for they live the mysterious existence that we have given

them. At every stage in our lives, we cast aside our whole being and lose ourselves in some corner of the world. This whole assemblage of inexpressible things that was "us" lies there in the shadows, just one among the objects on which we have unknowingly imprinted ourselves. Then one day, by chance, we see these things once again; they suddenly appear before us, and instantly, with the omnipotence of reality, they restore our past.[119]

### THE AUBER MODEL: AN AESTHETIC OF CONVERSATION

Let us try to understand this rejection of profundity and identify the meaning of the French operatic style by setting out the basic elements of a musical aesthetic of conversation that was embodied in the works of Auber. Again, it is in Paris that we must seek the origins of this art of the ephemeral, which reached its apex in the *salons* of the seventeenth and eighteenth centuries. Even though the spirit of those past times was well and truly gone, its legacy was influential through much of the nineteenth century. In his *Autre étude de femme*, Balzac took pains to portray this extremely subtle social routine in describing the *salon* of Mlle des Touches, "the last refuge of the *esprit français* of old." He recounts an unforgettable soirée:

> Ingenious repartee, penetrating observations, superb jibes, and pictures sketched with brilliant clarity all sparkled and tumbled out unaffectedly, and flowed lavishly, effortlessly, and uncontemptuously. It was all delightfully to the point and was savored with delicacy. Members of society were notable above all for their charm and their utterly artistic gusto. Elsewhere in Europe you find elegant manners, cordiality, geniality, and learning, but only in Paris, in this *salon* and in the others of which I have just spoken, do you find in plenty that special *esprit* that gives all the social graces a pleasant and unpredictable aspect, an indefinable air that lets this profusion of thoughts, turns of phrase, tales, and historic documents meander easily, like a river. Only Paris, the capital of good taste, understands this skill, which turns a conversation into a joust in which every kind of wit is delivered in a single stroke; in which everyone says his say and casts his experience in a neat phrase; in which everyone has fun, relaxes, and flexes his mind.[120]

There was nothing immoderate; no bombast or pedantry: only delicacy, nuance, and restraint. Stendhal, that subtle observer of French society, noted in 1826 that "good Parisian society makes very few gestures; indeed, perfection resides…in making none, in not indulging in any vocal inflections, and in speaking as though one were reading. The Italians are still far removed from this *beau idéal* of conversation."[121] The great literary historian Marc Fumaroli has shown how conversation was a truly French institution.[122] In its quest for naturalness rather than uniqueness and for clear, graceful language, conversation aimed for felicitous turns of phrase, speed, liveliness, flashes of inspiration, and taunts and witticisms that would remain in the memory, entertain the mind, and cause a mild feeling of intoxication.

Let us compare those ideas with a scene that Benoît Jouvin devised to illustrate Auber's genius:

> When he arrives at a great soirée where the guests are crowded in, hurrying to and fro, and stifling, a wit will not demand silence and calm in order to deposit a fine morsel of eloquence. He will let the crowd rush about in the ballrooms and, finding a room where it is possible to move about without difficulty, will seat himself comfortably, speak without raising his voice, engage in discreet chit-chat, and, without thinking it beneath him, will adopt the superficial tone of the black-coated, ball-gowned audience listening to him. In the confused action of a very complicated plot, M. Auber's music is that wit, in the midst of a ball, who does not raise his voice above the sound of the violins, and who makes lovely remarks rather than long speeches.[123]

Auber's muse was a musical incarnation of the intellectual environment of Paris as described by Balzac. It was a "pleasant, smiling, discreet, conversational voice accustomed to shining in the salons of elegant society."[124] The extraordinary success of the composer of *Le Maçon* and *Le Domino noir* was due to his ability to make music as pleasant and entertaining as conversation. In this connection, it is worth rereading Hoffmann's comments (see page 281) on the French rejection of profundity.

In writing of Auber's operas, critics were fond of praising "this delicacy of feeling and of taste, . . . this spirit of moderation both in terms of expression and in the creation of musical ideas."[125] The qualities of his music went beyond technique. It was "clever"; it had "wit" and "elegance."[126] In writing about the premiere of *Le Domino noir*, Berlioz accurately observed that his "style is light, brilliant and gay, often full of piquant flashes of wit and touches of elegance."[127] The attributes of good conversation were recognized in Auber's musical style, and came to be fused with the composer's own vivacious talents. He possessed "keen, quick repartee, a sharp tongue, and hearty good humor,"[128] and his works contained to a supreme degree "the clarity that constitutes the civility of the French spirit."[129] His music combined "all the characteristics, all the qualities of the French language."[130] It was therefore no surprise that he should have been compared to a great writer: "In his sparkling mind, in the marvelous clarity of his style, in his gift of unfailingly understanding everything while taking care not to try too hard—as though he were at play—Auber closely resembled the quintessential writer of wit [Voltaire]; one would seek in vain a mind that is more naturally akin to his in any other artistic sphere."[131] Even going beyond the French repertory, there was a literary outlook on music, and it was symptomatic that Saint-Saëns "compared our trinity—Corneille, Racine, and Molière—with the no less glorious trinity of Haydn, Mozart, and Beethoven."[132]

The art of conversation safeguarded the *esprit français* against the more profound powers of memory and dreams, which were so important for the Germans; it is seen in *Les Pêcheurs de perles* through the prism of romance, and more generally in *opéra lyrique* in the form of reverie and melancholy recollection of the past. Here again Heine was most perceptive in comparing the characteristics of German, English, and French styles of speech:

> French speech has a grace and smoothness that are completely foreign to—and would indeed be impossible in—English speech. In France, language has been so thoroughly filtered, over three centuries, through the informal conversational habits of society that it has permanently lost every contemptible expression, every obscure locution, everything that is murky or coarse—but also all the flavor, all the beneficent qualities, all the secret magic charms that well up and flow in uncultivated speech. The French language, like French speech, like the French themselves, is suited only to the present moment, to the needs of the day. The hazy regions of memory and premonition are forbidden that language. It thrives only in the bright sunlight, and this is the source of its beautiful clarity and warmth. The night, with its pale moonlight, its mysterious stars, its sweet dreams, and its fearsome specters, is foreign to it and virtually beyond its grasp.[133]

This taste for subtlety and nuanced declamation, which was perfectly in line with the characteristics of the language, was one of the most important reasons for the continuity of the French school of opera; it formed a link between Gounod and Ambroise Thomas, on the one hand, and Massenet, then Debussy, on the other.

## THE MOTIF

"Auber was above all a wit. His melodies smiled, chattered, and hummed. Just as he fashioned delightful remarks—*mots*—in his conversation, he fashioned *motifs* in his music. The motif: something that remains more French than Italian; a clever and precise melody, the smaller the more perfect."[134] Victor Massé, writing about *La Fiancée* and *Fra Diavolo,* was "struck first of all by the extraordinary abundance of popular motifs. You hum all of this music; you sing it; and you don't even think about judging it. There would be as much point in analyzing the literary merits of a proverb."[135] Motifs have the qualities of witticisms: they are striking and easy to remember:

> The pleasure of an audience on its way out of the theater, and the hope of an audience on its way in, is to hum a motif from a brand-new work. After the first performance of *Les Troyens,* no one sang even the tiniest phrase from Berlioz's opera, and the audience—too arrogant to blame itself—blamed the composer. It reproached Berlioz for lacking melody: the easy melody that needs no accompaniment, that spurns harmony; the snatches that are appropriated for every barrel organ.[136]

But on his way out of *Le Domino noir,* one critic recalled "a series of delightful motifs; a most original bolero; charming trios; *couplets* full of grace and elegance," and made special note of the ensemble and chorus (act 3, no. 12), which featured "prattling nuns: a real masterpiece of *opéra-comique.*"[137] In the 1840s, 1850s, 1860s, and 1870s, it was always clear and pleasant melodies that made the success of an *opéra-comique* and even of an *opéra.* Adolphe Adam owed his success to his talent for melody. The music of his *Le Toréador* (1849) is indeed "scattered with delightful motifs" that pleased the audience. After the premiere of Auber's *L'Enfant prodigue* (1850) at the Académie de musique, the *Revue et Gazette musicale* wrote, "It is ever the same profusion of elegant and easy ideas with lively and catchy rhythms that seize the ear and lodge as a matter of course in the memory."[138]

Massé went into more detail about this notion, using the example of his predecessor at the Opéra, Auber, whose melodies "did not consist of phrases subjected to successful or less successful development; they were short, and their merit lay above all in the beginning of the melodic idea, which is almost always prominent. In a word, his key ability was to find themes—or motifs, to use the word that he seems to have invented."[139] Wagner summarized Auber's style as harnessing the spirit of song, and he stressed that the essence of *opéra-comique* motifs was dancelike. He commented that it was in the "Parisian *contredanse* that we must look for the defining feature of the Parisian character."[140]

Larousse's *Grand Dictionnaire universel,* whose contributors were rather conservative when it came to music, observed that "despite all the aberrations of certain schools, especially that of the so-called music of the future, it will be necessary to use motifs so long as there is a desire that music should have common sense."[141] That view—which was shared by the entire mid-nineteenth-century critical community—will be easier to understand if we remember that, unlike Wagner, who linked motifs to meanings, gave them a dramatic dimension, and included them in a powerful and varied musical flow, French composers assigned only an entertainment function to their motifs; they liked them to be striking and clearly distinguishable from the general musical fabric. Although abuse of the motif deserved censure, its absence was viewed as the negation of music. It remained only for the scholarly lexicographer to provide a few examples that will astound the modern reader:

> The tunes of "Au clair de la lune," "Le Roi Dagobert," and "Malbrough s'en va-t-en guerre" may be coarse motifs, but those of the serenade from *Don Giovanni,* Berthe's *romance* from *Le Prophète,* and Isabelle's aria from *Le Pré aux clercs* are motifs too, and are certainly not to be looked down upon. Is the melody of "La Marseillaise" not a wonderful motif? And in his whole life did M. Wagner—with all his nebulous theories and his rabid aesthetic—ever have a more sublime, more grandiose or more stirring inspiration?[142]

By giving the impression of having musical ideas burst from all sides in an uninterrupted stream, as we have noted, Wagner's style ran counter to the economy of means prized by French critics, who viewed it as a guarantee of clear musical discourse: "What is essential in music is not to constantly have ideas…but rather to know how to use them. The composer who ceaselessly introduces new melodic phrases and unremittingly follows one musical period with another will quickly sate his listeners, however felicitous his ideas may be."[143]

According to the press of 1863, Bizet would occasionally drown his melodies in orchestral richness and lose the listener in an excessively powerful dramatic flow. But he understood the fundamental role of simple melodic elements, when well formed and given prominence in the sonic fabric, in winning over an audience. He wrote to his mother in 1859 that the best French musicians of the time lacked "the composer's only means of making today's audiences understand him: motifs, which have very wrongly been called 'ideas.' One can be a great artist without having motifs, but one must then renounce money and popular success. But one can also be outstanding and possess that precious gift. Think of Rossini. Rossini was the greatest of all because, like Mozart, he had everything: high-mindedness, style, and, finally…motifs."[144] Writing of a comic opera he had just finished, *Don Procopio,* he returned to this basic issue: "I have finally found that much-sought-after magic key: in my opera, I have a dozen motifs—real ones, rhythmic and easy to remember—and yet have not compromised my taste....Next year I shall try to achieve the motif in *grand opéra,* which is far more difficult. But it is already something to have found it in *opéra-comique.*" A few months later, he wrote, "I have followed Father Auber's advice: I have a little book, and I have already taken many musical notes. This may work."[145]

## THE INFLUENCE OF SOCIETY
## ON THE AESTHETICS OF FRENCH OPERA

The French style, portrayed as a conversation, was the musical version of an aesthetic shaped by good manners. Stereotypes, whose operation we have analyzed, were among the clichés described by Max d'Ollone and "corresponded to the gestures laid down by etiquette and to the polite forms used in letters and dedications."[146] Generally speaking, composers, "in part because of their environment" and "in spite of sometimes rising up and taking wing," retained "in their works the politeness of their 'well-brought-up' childhoods: politeness to the audience and to the artists, as well as to the very sounds, which in their hands avoid vulgar clashes and efface themselves with elegance."[147] Once again, the exemplar of this musical world was Auber, who "considered it both unseemly and pointless to rebel against social convention, whatever it might be; nor did he refuse to accommodate—at least by all appearances—other people's opinions or prejudices, or to accept with prompt resignation the changing demands of fashion or the no less varied repercussions of political revolutions."[148]

Dramatic music, charged Saint-Valry in 1863, was little by little becoming "a collective art, a symphony to which the human voice contributes its part, which is perhaps a little smaller than that of the instruments. Individuality is gradually dwindling, to end up melting into a kind of huge, very powerful, very complete system. This trend may be viewed as the transferal of democratic values into art, and, frankly, seems to me highly regrettable and doomed to grow quickly barren."[149] The fear that democratic thinking would intrude into the aesthetic sphere was symptomatic of a weariness resulting from the turmoil that had disrupted the nineteenth century. That fear reflected the wishes of a public that, when it came to the arts, wanted to enjoy itself in the company of its own habits. French opera wavered between the heroic world that was breathing its last in the form of *grand opéra* and the world of realism, which was having a hard time getting a foothold. It hesitated among a number of trends, one of which—poetic expression—was to be dominant for a while in the sometimes watered-down form of *opéra lyrique*. In his *Französische Zustände*—successfully republished during the Second Empire under the title *De la France*—Heine immediately caricatured the middle-class essence of this interregnum, when there was considerable mediocrity among the contemporaries of Berlioz, Gounod, and Bizet: "This shrinking of all grandeur and this complete annihilation of heroism are above all the work of the middle class that attained power in France with the fall of the hereditary aristocracy and triumphantly imposed its rigid, cold shopkeeper's ideas in every sphere of life."[150] As understood by the members of the Jeunes-France movement, the middle class "expressed the domination of the real over the ideal."[151] Revitalized by legend and Wagnerian myth, the heroic world was resurrected at the end of the century in the operas of Reyer, Chausson, Chabrier, and d'Indy.

The decline of French opera was caused by the public's exclusive fondness for values that at times had nothing to do with lofty aesthetic considerations. "It is clear," wrote Louis Roger in 1863, "that the present generation is descending toward materialism. Art is no major factor for it."[152] Saint-Saëns denounced the incompetence and narrow-mindedness of music critics: "They do not tell musicians, 'Be great, be powerful, be sublime!' but 'Be easy to understand; be accessible to the common people.' "[153] In the arts, he explained, powerful inertia gives rise to serious errors of judgment. In any given era, convention is the basis of creation. But "great artists...quickly wear out their tools...; they soon see through the convention they are using to express their ideas, and they create another that meets their needs. They change art before the public has felt the need for this—which leads to furious resistance."[154] There was also a certain sense of being disgusted by art, which "works tirelessly for the triumph of the middle-class, shopkeeper's spirit over the artistic spirit; for the victory of small ideas over great feelings."[155]

Writing of Gounod and other French composers of the 1860s through the 1880s, Max d'Ollone observed that "the conformist and conventional elements in their works related not only to the aesthetic of the time but also to their human nature, which had been shaped by an anti-revolutionary education."[156] This middle-class mentality existed in every social class, and, as d'Ollone put it, took on the reassuring form of traditional values: "Their common characteristic was a desire for order and a fear of anarchy. Common sense and rules were set against 'unhealthy' metaphysical and moral anxiety. There was room for a certain taste for romanticism, so long as it was restricted to its picturesque elements."[157] Compared to Berlioz the revolutionary, Auber, as Hahn bluntly put it, was a talented "apologist for middle-class love, middle-class picturesqueness, middle-class poetry, and middle-class mischievousness....He embodied the operatic ideal of the French middle classes, and was the Paul le Kock of music."[158] A writer in *La France musicale* in 1855 expressed the same idea in more favorable terms:

> Rather than drawing us into imaginary or invisible worlds, Auber's music anchors us to real life, to family life, to tender, happy, pleasant life. One loves this music as one loves a sister who enjoys all one's friend- ship: it is nice to be with it and to hear it at any time of the day. The emotions it evokes do us good....If the musical phrase is melancholy, we weep gently, without emotion painfully upsetting our nerves. The phys- iognomy of a melody by Auber, even when it is weeping, is never con- torted or aged by tears; it quickly regains its habitual pleasantness with a serene expression that delights the heart.[159]

Bizet's arrival on the Parisian operatic scene put a new face on the ancient-versus-modern argument, and posed the problem of the relation- ship between composers, who wished to exploit their own creativity, and the society in which their works were performed. The creative artist had to fit his style into an official framework. "Composers," wrote Roger, "are faced with three powers with which they are obliged to contend: the audi- ence, the state, and the prerogatives of the theaters."[160]

Those who desired only to create an ideal object, a work of art, had hardly any chance of being performed, while those who designed an "ef- fective product" could hope for success. Both playwrights and composers, so to speak, traded aesthetic for social aspirations. Jules Barbier wrote about the change made at the end of the libretto for *Mignon,* where to be faith- ful to the novel, the heroine ought to have died: "But by retaining the death of Mignon, which is barely sketched in Goethe's novel, we would have capriciously deprived ourselves of seven or eight hundred perfor- mances. It was far better to marry them off like decent middle-class people and leave the way open for their numerous offspring."[161] The tastes of the audience were thus a factor even during the creative process.

Simply put, two divergent paths emerged in French theater: that of au- thors such as Victor Hugo and Hector Berlioz, and that of others such as Scribe and Auber.[162] The first tended to be based on theory (on ideas) and aimed at creating an ideal theater, sometimes abstract or unperformable. The second was generally based on practice (on formulas) and aimed at presenting concrete, "pragmatic" theater—pragmatic in the sense of prac- tical, and grounded in experience rather than in theory. The first looked down on the philistine public ("O vulgar ignoramuses! O jaded crowd who have never experienced any feelings! Penguin-winged imaginations! Yet today it is before you that one has to grovel in the theater!" Berlioz raged);[163] the others were concerned only with indulging it.

Among playwrights, Scribe blazed his own path to success with the greatest aplomb. His motto (and Auber's) might have been "To please is to succeed." As the historian Jean-Claude Yon has explained: "Scribe clearly understood that besides the intellectuals and the critics, the public was now a force on which he could if necessary rely in order to do without the support of the others.... It is clear that [he] saw himself first and foremost as a member of the middle class, and that his theater, intended to entertain and not to educate, expressed a middle-class view of society."[164]

Success meant accepting the musical Parisianism that was the legacy of the Second Empire; before being able to tackle *grand opéra* and its theater, which were the preserve of recognized masters, composers had to give their work the subtle but outmoded—compared with the musical "progress" of mid-century—character of a conversation. Abandonment of the model exemplified by Auber was seen as a break with the central concept of French opera, which united music, language, and society. France had never seen a composer who was more likable than Auber—"more inspired by a pleasant, gay and rebellious spirit, and better qualified to express in music, not deep feelings of love or mighty human passions, which are hardly part of his nature, but the flower of chivalry that has bloomed in our language and our nation since the establishment of polite society," Paul Scudo wrote.[165]

GERMAN SOUL AND FRENCH SOCIETY

As a form of entertainment, French opera displayed a certain traditionalism that tended to become petrified and academic, a tendency exacerbated by what might be called musical Parisianism. There was a fear, due perhaps to inadequate education or to some national cultural failing, of becoming lost in the abstract arcana of a musical discourse—and of no longer having a good time. In France, observed Reyer, "our musical education still leaves a great deal to be desired.... By no means do we like to subject ourselves to excessively lengthy efforts of the imagination to grasp the meaning of an idea that has been set before us in unfamiliar form and that it seems simpler to condemn than to think through. For the Germans, music is a form of study; for us, it is most often nothing but a source of entertainment."[166] In 1835, François Stroepel felt the need to explain to the French how different German art was from Parisian musical practice by publishing an

"Essay to Help Appreciate German Music": "In Germany, music is not a mere fashionable amusement; it is the most beautiful and most widespread of all the arts, the one that provides a sensitive people with the purest delight; for that people it is the constant companion of its prayers and its religious and national celebrations; it is an inexhaustible source of pious and elevated poetry."[167] For the Germans, music was a matter of soul, of the inner life; for the French, it was a social matter, a matter of entertainment.

It was common for writers to make much of German seriousness about music. Germans "do not always understand, but they always want to understand, and the abstract nature of certain works does not frighten them," Reyer observed. "That is not how it is with us. We want to grasp the meaning of what we hear without ever taking the trouble to think or to make an effort; we insist on being entertained, and we avoid the heights of brilliant art, which stops being charming the minute it demands the least brainwork."[168] This cast of mind may explain a certain French resistance to romanticism, whose aims were to develop matters that lay outside the norms or merely within the sphere of the inner life and to harness the deepest forces of existence and of the beyond. When *grand opéra* portrayed romantic themes, it looked to the (often magnificent) effects it could draw from them, and not to opening a door on the world of ideas or to any disturbing or mysterious evocation of the human being and the universe—a world that was depicted in German opera of the nineteenth century from Beethoven through Weber to Wagner. The exteriority of spectacle was preferred to Germanic interiority; image to idea. " 'If the French have understood this music [of Meyerbeer's *Robert le Diable* ... ],' " exclaims Gambara in Balzac's novel of the same name. " 'It is because it presents ideas,' said the Count. 'No, it is because it authoritatively presents the *image* of battles in which so many men are killed, and because all their individual lifetimes can be linked through memory.' "[169]

In this respect, Meyerbeer was a truly French composer. His *grands opéras* were based, of course, on ideas: the struggle between good and evil in *Robert le Diable*, for example. But the principle was deflected; the impact of the spectacular elements relegated ideas to a secondary role. So good and evil principally appear only as vehicles for grandiose feelings that generated spectacular scenes. Marie d'Agoult transcribed in her journal a conversation between George Sand and Franz Liszt that has something to add to this comment: "George said to Franz, 'Meyerbeer's music creates nothing but images. Beethoven's arouses feelings and ideas. Meyerbeer shows you a magnificent spectacle; he sets his characters before you. Beethoven draws you into the most intimate depths of the self.' "[170]

Schumann, the personification of the German romantic soul, as Marcel Brion puts it so well,[171] was on target with his provocative articles in his new musical journal, *Die Neue Zeitschrift für Musik:* "To astound or to titillate is the byword dearest to Meyerbeer's heart, and he succeeds extremely well among the rabble. He is simultaneously contemplative and hollow, superficial and profound."[172]

Offenbach's *Les Contes d'Hoffmann* is particularly interesting in this connection. The composer and his librettists portray on stage a man's (Hoffman/Offenbach's?) inner torments: they dramatize the soul, so to speak. As already noted (see page 116 and page 367, note 48), this idea is carried out principally through the theatrical depiction of song. The broken song of the automaton Olympia symbolizes the broken, or absent, soul. Hopeless love is symbolized by the fatal song so finely embodied in the trio for Dr. Miracle, the voice of Antonia's mother, and Antonia herself, who dies surrendering herself to the "desire to sing." The authors also depict clichés that to the French connoted the German mentality: vacillation between dream (or nightmare) and reality, the ordinariness of the German students' choruses, the intervention of an evil genius, and so on. Note that this aesthetic approach achieved success only very late in France, and that Offenbach's music, apart from some splendid numbers, remained very conventional and at times technically rudimentary.

Fantastic and horrific themes were used on the French stage far earlier than one might think, but they were stripped of their metaphysical role and were limited to physical effects. This is found also in literature, as Paul Bénichou has stressed in pointing out Charles Nodier's contribution in this sphere:

> Beginning in 1830, Nodier developed a doctrine of the fantastic, which was already scattered through his earlier work. As we know, the fantastic was then in fashion owing to the influence of Hoffmann and his tales, which had just become known in France; these were usually seen as a storehouse of tales belonging to a new genre. In his article on the fantastic, Nodier turned this notion to a solemn philosophical purpose.[173]

In the second half of the eighteenth century, there were a few advocates of the gloomy style and of terrifying stage settings. At the beginning of the nineteenth century, *mélodrame* showed how the most tragic of plays would be judged only by their potential for effects and how only the external, often horrific, elements of the supernatural world were retained. *Hamlet* was transformed into a magic show or into a pantomime mixed with dancing, with an infernal denouement. The visual eclipsed the spiritual, as reflected in the title of Jean-Baptiste-Augustin Hapdé's *Les Visions de Macbeth, ou les Sorcières d'Ecosse,* a blockbuster three-act *mélodrame* modeled on Shakespeare's tragedy and its genre.[174] In 1828, *Le Chasseur noir* by Benjamin Antier and Théodore Nézel[175] featured the famous Frédérick Lemaître and a mysterious individual in the title role who wore a mask throughout, until it was ripped off in the final scene: "Everyone cried out in horror when they saw beneath the mask a skull." In the same year, Lemaître was also seen at the Théâtre de la Porte-Saint-Martin as Méphistophélès in *Faust,* a "Drama in three acts, modeled on Goethe," by Antony Béraud and Jean-Toussaint Merle.[176] All that remained of Goethe's drama was a phantasmagoric framework. In scene 2, Faust sees a "dreadful phantom." Scene 5 is set in the hut ("a cluttered jumble of bizarre figures") of Bembo, "the most renowned sorcerer of the Brocken." Scene 10 takes place in a "fearsome setting," similar to that of the Wolf Glen in *Der Freischütz,* and ends with a vision of utter horror: "Mothers holding...their children, their throats slit, flee the hordes of murderers...; men holding their own heads in their arms move, swaying, along the mountain. Executioners bring a corrupt judge before the sorcerers and slit his throat to cries of rage and vengeance from all who witness the horrific scene." The play ends with a Dantesque image: "The stage is divided in two. Below is Hell, with Faust tormented by demons; above is heaven, with all the angels gathered around Marguerite."

It is indicative that *Robin des bois* (*Der Freischütz*) was billed at the Théâtre de l'Odéon as a special New Year's "spectacle." As announced in *Le Corsaire,* it was performed on January 1, 1826, "modernized and considerably expanded with magical effects. There will be new scenery, and an entirely new spectacle in the incantation scene. It is said that M. Ciceri has expended all the resources of his brilliant imagination on inventing the devils, monsters, specters, ghosts, phantoms, demons, goblins, etc., that appear in this phantasmagoria."[177] In Weber's original, the spectacle lies in the score; the music amplifies the effects that shake the listener to the core. But it was a while before the French would understand this idea and turn away from spectacle. Their conception of lyric theater was quite different, and the influence of the Italian model remained far too strong. In 1829, when performances were given by a German company, *La Revue musicale* made this observation in connection with a performance of *Fidelio:* "We acknowledge that nothing could be more dissimilar to the mellow periods of the Italians—so utterly rounded and so independent— than the melodic phrases that are often jerky and are always treated as slaves by the domineering genius of Beethoven. Impatient and impulsive people, who want music to provide easy relaxation, where thinking plays no role, will not find that this suits them." Contrasted with the clear course of Italian melody are "German inventions, which one minute appear, immediately vanish, reappear in another form, and undergo a never-ending mass of transformations." "Southern cantilena" was also contrasted with music born of "the dreamy and contemplative imagination of the peoples of the North."[178] Italy lay at the opposite pole to the Germanic world.

At the time when Rossini represented the music of the sun and Mozart that of northern climes, Stendhal wrote: "The primary characteristic of Rossini's music is a quickness that banishes from the spirit all the dark emotions that are so powerfully drawn from the depths of our soul by the slow notes of Mozart. I also detect a freshness that in every measure evokes a smile of pleasure. Every other score therefore seems heavy and tiresome after those of Rossini."[179]

Once again, France lay somewhere between north and south, and was the arena of a struggle for influence. This was recognized in 1824 by one of the era's few French partisans of German opera:

> The triumph at the Odéon of operas belonging to the German school will strike a devastating blow to fanaticism for things from south of the Alps. We shall learn . . . to know authors whom fashion has by no means imposed upon us; the Rhine will no longer be a barrier to our operatic enthusiasm; and just as we once sought our idols in the villages of degenerate Italy, we shall henceforth forge a glorious alliance with the Orpheuses of a land that was the birthplace of Gluck and Mozart.[180]

Roqueplan contrasted Italian music, which shone in the vocal realm, with German music, founded on instrumental and symphonic styles.[181] The relationship between voice and orchestra should be viewed as a musical version of that between exteriority and interiority—or between Italy and Germany. Describing new writings by the German author Johann Paul (Jean-Paul) Friedrich (1763–1825), and contrasting the solitary act of reading with theatrical production, Alfred de Musset described the opposing feelings that this literature inspired among the French, who viewed it as interesting in intimate surroundings but ridiculous in company: "There is not one of his thoughts that, read in one's study, is not in some way pleasing and charming; there is not one that, spoken by an actor, would not be laughed at by the audience." And Jean-Paul, continued de Musset, "speaks to meditation, to the silence of the night, to the lover, to the philosopher, to the artist; he speaks to all who have souls and who use them rather than their minds to form judgments."[182]

As noted above, the opposition of France/exteriority to Germany/interiority was connected with those countries' political structures. In 1840, Wagner explained how Germany "became musical," as Marcel Beaufils put it over a century later.[183] A fragmented Germany was conducive to a chamber-music approach aiming for inner contentment and profound truth in emotions and ideas, and unconcerned with the tastes of the public. France was strictly centralized and was fond of protocol and performance; as we have noted, it made music into a social event. It used every artifice to achieve immediate success. A German "loves the art of music for art's sake and for its divine essence, and not as a vulgar way to excite his passions or as a means of achieving wealth and admiration." Wagner explained that the "lack of centralization greatly contributed to the retention of the intimate and familiar character of our music."[184] A few weeks before the performance of *Der Freischütz* at the Opéra, Wagner tried to help the French public understand the Germanic essence of the work and of the legend behind it:

> The tradition of the *Freischütz* bears…the deep imprint of the German nationality. For any other people, the devil would probably have been involved, for we find the devil anywhere that misfortune occurs. But it was only among the Germans that this demonic element could have appeared in such mystical forms, with this character of dreamy melancholy, and that external appearances could have been so intimately merged with the human soul, producing such innocent and moving emotions.[185]

As an educator, the future author of *Tristan und Isolde* did a good job of describing the forces buried deep in the soul and deep in the world, which well up in his predecessor's score:

> Ah, if you could—if you wanted to—see and hear the real German *Freischütz*, perhaps you would be drawn into the intimate, meditative life of the spirit possessed by the German nation; you would come to know the sweet, innocent emotions that would gradually make you yearn for the presence of your beloved and for the solitude of the woods; perhaps you would understand the mysterious horror, the indefinable sensations for which your language has no word and which you try in vain to render with splendid scenery and diabolical masks.[186]

It was therefore nonsensical to alter *Der Freischütz* to fit French *grand opéra* conventions: "the *external system* that they sought to adapt to

Weber's work" stood against the "dreamy enthusiasm" that "the original work inspires in the Germans."[187]

### GERMANIC FERTILIZATION—FRENCH IDENTITY

The incursion by the German repertory and spirit into French lyric theater was launched in three waves, successively bearing the operas of Mozart, of Weber, then of Wagner.[188] The first, originating in the eighteenth century and rich in the finery of Italian opera,[189] had no trouble infiltrating the Parisian operatic structure. The second, initially repulsed by the defenses of the Italianate aesthetic, would enrich French soil in the middle of the nineteenth century by contributing the new sonic raw materials needed to create what we have called "operatic poetry," which can be simply described as lying between the physical and the metaphysical. At the same time, however, French translations of literary works such as Goethe's *Faust* were beginning to bear fruit and to provide a creative impetus. Then, despite those, like Massenet, who continued to practice it splendidly, *opéra lyrique* was in turn engulfed by the wave of Wagnerism. French critics' habit of basing their judgments on nothing but appearances meant that they condemned as Wagnerian some scores that merely had the "flaw" of setting a libretto that borrowed substantially from Wagnerian themes.[190] Among these was Chabrier's splendid *Gwendoline* (1886), in which Saxon legend, the "Ehayo!" cries of the hordes of Danish warriors, Gwendoline's offering of a crown of flowers to the dreadful Harald, the theme of union in death, and the final pyre recall scenes from *Tristan*, the *Ring*, and *Parsifal*. Apart from some ringing sonorities and a few harmonies that might be considered Wagnerian, however, Chabrier's music was highly original, and in many ways, it paved the way for operatic impressionism.

Other works besides operas influenced French composers, such as piano, chamber, and symphonic music, either through performance or publication in France, or during French composers' travels abroad. Haydn at the end of the eighteenth century, then Beethoven, Mendelssohn, and Schumann, among others, each fertilized French music with Germanic artistry. Think, for instance, of Bizet's love for Schumann, which must not be ignored if we are to understand his rich harmonic language, as in *Carmen*.

Although French opera was in need of it, such German influence became overwhelming in the final decades of the nineteenth century, and some French musicians fought to reassert essentially French values and "break away from Germany" ("s'évader d'Allemagne")—as Debussy put it, no longer to compose after Wagner, but post-Wagner.[191] We know too how between the two world wars, young French composers, picking their way be-tween the schools of Wagner and of Debussy, and encouraged by Jean Cocteau, aimed for simplicity rather than for vagueness and indistinctness: "We must not get lost in a Debussy mist any more than in a Wagner fog, lest we catch cold," Cocteau said.[192]

In such reactions—sometimes violent, sometimes beneficial—there was fear that the last wave of Germanic influence would cause a loss of French identity. In conversation with Edouard Lalo, Delibes expressed his dismay:

> "Wagnerism is invading us; swamping us. In my composition class at the Conservatoire, my pupils are constantly thinking about this, talking about it among themselves, and talking about it to me. What should we do, we musicians of another generation? Remain indifferent, dead to this universal movement? Or rather evolve with the times, change our ideas, our style—our art?" "Delibes," replied Lalo, "I admire Wagner enor-mously. But I have nothing to do with him."[193]

Lalo explained this in a letter dated May 19, 1888, addressed to Adolphe Jullien following the premiere of *Le Roy d'Ys*. He confessed to having wanted to write a true music drama and to having shrunk from the task:

> So far, only that colossus Wagner, the inventor of true music drama, has had the stature to bear such a burden; all who have strived to follow in his footsteps, whether in Germany or elsewhere, have failed. . . . To fight on Wagner's territory and gain the upper hand, it is necessary to overtake him; and such a combatant has not yet appeared. As for me, I have come to be aware of my powerlessness, and I have written a plain opera . . . ; that accommodating form still lets one write *music* without creating a pastiche of one's predecessors.[194]

# Conclusion

Commencing with the tangible factors of performance and production, this book has sought to uncover the abstract underpinnings of nineteenth-century French opera, an art that was simultaneously literary, musical, and scenic.[1] Opera is inconceivable without all three of those dimensions—not individually, but combined. Libretto, score, scenery, costumes, production, and choreography: each involves one or more individuals, who together define an opera's shape.

Whom should we think of as the true parent of a work with such an extended family? Here, too, we must not forget the performers, who sometimes persuaded the composer to rewrite his music, or the audiences, whose reactions may have resulted in the jettisoning of whole scenes. How do we measure the effectiveness (the criteria for which may change over time) of a work viewed first and foremost as something intended to give pleasure? Both performers and the editors of critical editions must ask this question. Like the Italian opera to which Rossini was heir, French opera was alive, not petrified; it was an art in motion. In more general terms, the history of opera in the nineteenth century may be studied as a gradual honing of the work into a perfect, untouchable artifact, defined by an increasingly autonomous, solitary creator.[2] Operas had hitherto belonged to a distinct musical family, and had met known criteria, which in large part determined their form, if only in terms of genre; now they were sui generis.[3]

An opera is theater, but it is not merely a sung play. Rather, it is a reformulated play, guided by principles of its own that do not apply to ordinary theater, which require a special conception of space, time, verisimilitude, and poetry. In opera, emotion and evocativeness arise from the music, rather than from the librettist's verses, which are not necessarily very poetic. The effective fusion of poetic and musical writing gave rise to what I have called "operatic poetry," which was freshly reformulated in France by Gounod and championed by Berlioz. The spectator perceived the text and the staging as a body of signs indicating a meaning or a type of emotion. The music would then fill the listener's imagination with sensations and images, both through its own powers and through its ability to create an atmosphere by means of clichés such as evocative figures and the use of instruments in accordance with a specific typology. This may be seen in Debussy's *Pelléas et Mélisande* (1902), an opera that many critics say cannot be classified, which undoubtedly marked the end point of a branch of the French operatic school that was associated with such operatic poetry. According to Debussy himself, the Maeterlinck text contains "evocative language whose sensibility could be extended through music and through orchestral decor."[4]

Apart from certain aspects of the *grand opéra* of the 1830s and 1840s, French opera was antirevolutionary. It long remained immune to the romanticism that sought to destroy the various frameworks within which individuals, and artists in particular, felt they were imprisoned. French opera was a social art, opposed to the notion of omnipotent creative individuality and total freedom of expression. Yet, as *opéra lyrique*, it achieved the seemingly impossible union of two antithetical aspects of romanticism: the taste for theatricality and the desire for intimacy.

The interiority so dear to the Germans was reflected in their literature as dream, analysis, and introspection, and sometimes also as an exploration of the domestic world. The house—that intimate focus of a life composed of simple actions and inhabited by familiar objects—is at the heart of a kind of romanticism that is also seen among a few French authors,[5] and that was perhaps best expressed in opera by Gounod and later by Massenet, often drawing upon key German works, from which they cleansed the harshness and retained, or even developed, the gently subtle elements to which I have referred. Using those elements, opera depicted private space, achieved a poetics of trusting intimacy, and revealed the close ties that bind individuals and their environment.[6] Moreover, by referring spectators to their own experience of the tangible world, operatic poetry is one of the main aspects of opera's expressive realism.

The interest in realism that marked the development of nineteenth-century opera was filtered through a stereotyped style of writing. Philippe-Joseph Salazar observes that from Rossini on, there was "a tripartite system that limited what was possible in opera: a precise vocal typology based on the middle-class fantasy that gender in opera was the same as it was in real life; a typology of dramatic usage that made it possible to leave nothing to chance and to incorporate dramatic triangulation into opera;...[and] a classification of the scenes to be played."[7] The display on stage of a sort of unrefined mode of expression running counter to conversational good form was first seen in the *grand opéra* aesthetic of effect and shock. But unusual situations and highly stylized emotions, magnified by the impressive movements of the collective entities of the chorus, did not come close to examining the genuine human feelings of individuals. It is not until *Carmen* (1875), a precursor of verismo, that we find a real portrayal of raw human feelings.[8]

Just as religious themes could be a substitute for the supernatural, musical exoticism made it possible to reconcile realism and the supernatural. By clinging to a notion of the "beauties of nature" built upon an Orient— or an Elsewhere—dreamed up by the French, exoticism spurned authenticity and convincingly offered vocal enchantment in the form of female characters who cast a melodic spell. But by gradually incorporating foreign elements in the form of evocative figures and by wandering away from conventional portrayals, it referred more and more precisely to a specific, real world. Still, it remained impossible to insert the musical material that composers brought back from their travels without altering it; this would have shattered the Western scale and tonal systems. "Elsewhere" could thus not be directly expressed through its own sonic image. Exotic characters remained figurines sculpted by the French imagination. French operatic exoticism did not portray Otherness itself, but a French sense of that Otherness. For much of the nineteenth century, the Other was nothing more than an image. Later, in a stylized and poeticized form, exotic material pervaded the musical idiom and became an element of fertilization and renewal; this was an embryonic form of a phenomenon whose extraordinary potential would be realized only in the twentieth century, as, for example, in compositions inspired by African polyrhythm, such as the piano etudes of the Hungarian composer György Ligeti (1923– ). It is no longer in opera but in "pure" sonic designs that we see these endeavors to renew or to broaden the range of music. To choose an exotic subject for an opera was to turn the Other and the Elsewhere into a spectacle.

Realism came gradually to affect all areas of operatic writing. Number opera, which divided time into segments, yielded to music drama with its continuous motion; syllabic writing came to be preferred to melismatic writing; ensembles—the purest operatic artifice—were reduced in number; local and period color contributed a sense of authenticity. This approach, which dominated the end of the nineteenth century and the beginning of the twentieth, had its dangers and limitations. For one thing, composers relinquished coloratura and the richness of vocal polyphony, and for another, local and period color could result in a loss of identity and reduce the creative act to the assembly of a pastiche. Finally, there could be a sense of discontinuity between extremely mundane, realistic description, as found in the naturalistic operas of composers such as Alfred Bruneau, and the artificial nature of sung discourse.

We have seen how in the first half of the nineteenth century, and indeed beyond, much French opera was burdened by a duty to entertain and to abide by a conversational aesthetic, for which Auber's output provides a model. This measured style was perceived as reflecting the French language, which, like the French school of music, lay between the more well-defined sounds of German and Italian, between north and south. The taste for conversation and the conversational ideal, it was held, were especially French. Drawing on Montesquieu's theory of climates,[9] Victor Hugo articulated this idea as follows:

> There is a balance of consonants and vowels in intermediate languages—those that arise in temperate climates. This is one of the reasons for the dominance of French.... French ..., supported by consonants without bristling with them [like German], and softened by vowels without being made insipid by them [like Italian], is such that every human tongue can accommodate it. Hence, I have said and shall repeat here that it is not only France that speaks French, it is civilization.[10]

The notion of the universality of the French language as that best suited for conversation, as the softest and clearest, and as the most appropriate for harmonizing opposites, was repeatedly advanced.[11] This helped form the aesthetic basis for much French opera in the nineteenth century, in the third quarter of which the level-headed French style was given a boost when it shook off the influence of Rossini and moved closer to Germany—but without yet giving way to the Germanic aesthetic, as it would in the era of Wagnerism.

There was also a happy medium in terms of time. We have seen how the repertory was enriched during the nineteenth century by revivals of eighteenth-century operas, and how contemporary works absorbed stylistic elements drawn from those operas in order to create period color. This neoclassicism may be seen also as the pursuit of balance. Using music of the past could, within a given work, offset the bold innovations that the Music of the Future had instilled into the music of the present. It also responded to the romantic quest for an idealized ancient world, or indeed to a need to flee the real world of the present.

In the early nineteenth century, French taste would accept only blunted romanticism and cautious artistic reform that sought to unite past and present, tradition and cosmopolitanism. This goal of "conservative reform," which deeply affected operatic output, is reflected in a manifesto published in *Le Globe* on September 15, 1824: "We shall not extol the Germanic and English schools, which pose a threat even to the language of Racine and Voltaire; nor shall we yield to the academic anathema of an old-fashioned school that responds to boldness only with worn-out admiration [of the old days], that constantly invokes the glories of the past in order to conceal the destitution of the present, and that can conceive of only timid remarks about the achievements of the great masters."

France's centralized system and the cultural hegemony of Paris heightened the pressure to fall willy-nilly into line and follow the example of one's elders. "In France, the recollection of social propriety haunts talent, even in its most personal emotions; the fear of ridicule is a sword of Damocles that no flight of the imagination can make you forget," Madame de Staël wrote in 1810, a comment still valid at mid-century and beyond.[12] "But how can one be original in France?" Alfred de Musset asked in *Le Temps* on May 17, 1831. "This is made impossible by the Parisians' invariable habit of walking with their faces to windward, continuously watching their neighbors. To see and to be seen: those are the two phrases that have killed originality and tormented it on the anvil of propriety. The words on every idiot's lips are, 'One must do as everybody does.'" And Stendhal, with his inordinate love of Italian music, observed that the French "are very pleasant in society, but *society* has become their primary concern. They are the wittiest and most agreeable of peoples, and, so far, the world's least musical."[13] First and foremost, the artist had to respect the canons of taste handed down by society; understanding them "helped above all to know what to avoid."[14] The relative failure of French opera in the view of posterity is undoubtedly explained in part by the confusion of principles of good taste and principles "that depend on the relationships of society."[15] Much of France's operatic output was marked by the confusion of social with aesthetic success. Proper form in society was equated with proper taste in the arts. Just as the first "helped hide our shortcomings,"[16] the second could lead to superficiality.

We cannot get to the heart of French operatic style without reconstructing the social, and indeed the political, conditions that controlled a work's creation, performance, and reception. An opera resulted from an interplay of varied forces. Composers had to maneuver and haggle within this sphere of influences, attractions, and repulsions. They had to negotiate with the practices of the society they wanted to win over and with the figures who dominated it. For it was these men and women who defined the frameworks within which the act of aesthetic creation was possible. The burden of the constraints on Parisian creative artists was great, leading to a kind of aesthetic determinism that tended to minimize the role of originality and personality in favor of academicism. The range of aesthetic action was defined by the various proprieties to which composers were subject. It was in the face of this appalling situation that opera composers had to choose an approach, depending on their artistic and social ambitions as well as on their talent. Even Debussy was tempted to "fall back into line"[17] and write a *grand opéra* (*Rodrigue et Chimène,* begun in 1890 and abandoned two years later), with the sole purpose of achieving a success—that is, making money and gaining recognition.

The coded nature of French opera enables us to use genre as an approach to understanding the form. The critic Arthur Pougin's comments about the premiere of *Carmen,* a work that was clearly in the form of an *opéra-comique,* are illustrative:

> Everyone knows that M. Bizet has on many occasions vaunted his utter contempt for the *opéra-comique* genre and for the talents of its most brilliant past exponent, Boieldieu. So one was somewhat anxious to know whether the author of *Les Pêcheurs de perles,* violently breaking with the traditions of more than a century, would try to impose a new and incomprehensible poetics upon a stage that had been graced by so many pleasing masterpieces, or whether, bursting away from the little clique of which he has thus far been a part, he too would make "concessions to the audience" and embark on a fertile path, and one rich in prospects for him.[18]

At the end of the nineteenth century, Massenet succeeded by selecting subjects that combined most of the literary trends that had arisen in the course of the century and that also matched the sensibilities of his fin-de-siècle audience. His music brought together the basic components of the French aesthetic in a framework that was less rigorous than those of the now-archaic traditional genres, and to which spectators had had time to become accustomed since Gounod's experiments. Paul Landormy, who was among those who noted the French public's rejection, in the early twentieth century, of too much expressive depth in music, and its taste for middle-of-the-road sentiments and clearly defined motifs, noted bluntly:

> To be sure, the music of Massenet is not "great music." It does not ordinarily express feelings that are very noble, or very profound, or very varied; or if it tries to express them, it does so badly. And it uses techniques that are often a little perfunctory and that are unchanging. But

isn't there anything besides "great music"? Within its limited sphere, the music of Massenet is charming. It has its own personal, original character. A phrase by Massenet can be recognized from its first notes.[19]

In an 1871 letter to the widow of Fromental Halévy, Bizet admitted that "what makes for success [in art] is *talent,* not *ideas.* Audiences…only understand ideas later on. To get to that 'later on,' the artist's talent, by means of a pleasing form, must make his path an easy one and must not immediately discourage him." And he went on to compare the musician most representative of Parisian art with the least typical French composer of the century: "Auber, who had so much talent and so few ideas, was almost always understood, while Berlioz, who had genius but no talent, hardly ever was."[20]

# Appendix 1    The Sources of Bizet's
## *Les Pêcheurs de perles*

This opera is a particularly indicative example of the kinds of problems that arise with respect to sources and versions.

### THE LITERARY SOURCES

Lesley A. Wright was the first to study the three sources housed in the Archives nationales (AN).[1] It is easy to establish the chronology of the three manuscript librettos: L1, intended solely to be read by the censors, is completely unaltered. L2, the prompter's libretto, was certainly copied at the same time as L1; its text is identical, but marked with additions and cuts. L3 is obviously a copy of L2 or of another libretto that had undergone the same editorial process: some words that are crossed out in the prompter's libretto do not appear at all in L3.

> L1    Manuscript libretto. AN F/18/737; libretto submitted to the censorship office by L. Carvalho on August 11, 1863.
>
> L2    Manuscript libretto. AN AJ/13/1158; prompter's libretto.
>
> L3    Manuscript libretto. AN AJ/13/1158; libretto for the stage production.
>
> L4    Published libretto. Paris, Michel Lévy Frères [late 1863 or 1864]; BN [Bibliothèque nationale] Impr. 8° Yth 13 689.

### THE MUSICAL SOURCES

In addition to the published piano-vocal score (P1), we have the manuscript short score prepared for the violinist-conductor of the premiere (C), which is

housed in the collection of the Opéra-Comique, as well as scores published
after Bizet's death, which reflect new versions of the work (P2, P3, and P4).

C   Manuscript conducting score, 1863. Orchestration reduced to six
    staves.

P1  Piano-vocal score. Paris, Choudens [October–November 1863].
    A.C. 992, 211 p. BN mus [Vm2—671].

P2  Piano-vocal score. Paris, Choudens Père et Fils [1887–88]. A.C.
    992, 204 p. BN mus [Vmb 28].

P3  Piano-vocal score. "Nouvelle édition." Paris, Choudens [1893]. No
    catalogue number apart from pp. 36, 40, 185 and 188: A.C. 992,
    202 p. BN mus [Vmb 1667].

P4  Orchestral score (corresponding to P3). Paris, Choudens [1893].
    A.C. 7283 [pp. 1–310] and A.C. 7283 $N^{vlle}$ $V^{on}$ [pp. 312–20] 320 p.
    BN mus [Vma 412].

The passages deleted in the course of the various revisions of the opera
have until now been found only in the 1863 piano-vocal score, P1. In the
1970s, Arthur Hammond wrote a free orchestration of those passages. By
studying the conducting score (C), I have been able to reconstruct a complete orchestration that for the first time since 1863 enables us to hear *Les
Pêcheurs de perles* in its original form.[2] The restored passages, in five parts
of the work, total 350 measures. Act 1: (1) the second part of no. 2, duet for
Nadir and Zurga; act 3: (2) two portions of no. 12, duet for Léila and Zurga
("Quoi? innocent, lui?" and "tu demandais sa vie"); (3) a fragment of no.
13, chorus with dance ("Hélas, qu'ont-ils fait de Léila?"); (4) no. 14, duet
for Léila and Nadir ("O lumière sainte"); and (5) a fragment of the finale
("Par ce passage resté libre fuyez!").

SELF-QUOTATION

There is no doubt that Bizet drew upon several of his own works.[3] *Ivan IV*
provided material for three passages in *Les Pêcheurs de perles:* the prelude (*Ivan IV,* Ivan's aria "Sur une pente ardue"); act 1, "Et nul ne doit la
voir" (*Ivan IV,* act 4, duet for Marie and Igor); act 3, duet "O lumière sainte"
(*Ivan IV,* act 5, duet "Adieu, fière Circassie," also heard in act 1 in Marie's
aria "Quand il fait jour sur la Caucase"). The act 1 chorus "Brahma, divin
Brahma" was borrowed from the "Pleni sunt coeli" of Bizet's *Te Deum,* and
the act 2 chorus "Ah! chante, chante encore" from the chorus "Cheti
piano" in *Don Procopio.* In act 2, the theme "O courageuse enfant" comes

from no. 4 of the Prix de Rome cantata *Clovis et Clotilde*. In the final act, the funeral march accompanying Léïla's entrance is similar to the symphonic *Marche funèbre* of 1860–61. Most of these borrowings are connected with the expression of situations: a religious chorus is reused for the pearl fishers' song to their god, and the funeral march accompanies Léïla's arrival for her execution.

# Appendix 2    The Versions of
## *Les Pêcheurs de perles*

The slow rediscovery of the work may be traced through six revivals: August 7, 1886, Cercle d'Aix-les-Bains (in Italian, as *I pescatori di perle*); December 7, 1887, Théâtre municipal de Nice (in Italian); February 19, 1889, Théâtre de Monte-Carlo (possibly in Italian); April 20, 1889, Paris, Théâtre de la Gaîté (in Italian); April 24, 1893, Paris, Opéra-Comique (in French); and March 17, 1932, Paris, Opéra-Comique (in French).

### THE 1863 CHANGES

Compared with the published piano-vocal score, which constitutes a "stable" state of the opera at a given moment, the manuscript conducting score (C) used for the rehearsals reflects a work in progress, combining several states of the opera. As with modern techniques for analyzing paintings, it is possible by studying the various layers in the manuscript, as well as the librettos, to reconstruct the successive states of the opera in 1863, from the initial draft libretto to the stage production, through the process of setting the text to music and the work carried out during the rehearsals and possibly even during the first performances. Victorin Joncières wrote in 1889 that the third act "had been redone several times in the course of rehearsals"[1] at the time of the premiere.

The chorus "L'ombre descend des cieux," which opens act 2, is not found in the manuscript librettos. Bizet had undoubtedly requested it from the librettists, at the time when they were putting the recitatives into verse, in order to create a poetic atmosphere for Léïla and to depict her isolation through the distancing effect of the off-stage chorus. Nadir's act 1 passage "Des savanes et des forêts" was originally conceived as a brief aria in two stanzas, but was shortened to a single stanza. In no. 3, a reprise of the chorus "Soyez la bienvenue" was replaced by the chorus "Brahma, divin

Brahma," which had already been composed as the conclusion of act 2. The entire second part of the act 2 love duet for Léïla and Nadir was cut. The final reprise of no. 14, the love duet "O lumière sainte," supplied by the librettists, was replaced by a recollection of the goddess motif from the act 1 duet for Nadir and Zurga.

THE THREE VERSIONS OF THE SCORE: P1, P2, AND P3

Librettos subsequent to 1863 were put together indiscriminately, and combine various versions. They provide little essential information. On the other hand, scores published well after Bizet's death enable us to follow the major stages in the opera's process of change.

Comparison of Three Versions of the Score: P1, P2, and P3

The figures correspond to the number of measures in each number. This table indicates only the main musical changes.

| | P1 | P2 | P3 |
|---|---|---|---|
| | | *Act 1* | |
| Prélude | 43 | Same | Same |
| No. 1, Introduction | | | |
| A–Choeur | 165 | Same | Same |
| B–Scène et choeur | 118 | Same | Same |
| C–Récit et reprise . . . | 112 | Same | Same |
| No. 2, Récit et duo | | | |
| A–Récit | 46 | Same | Same |
| B–Duo | 177 | 1–75 same 76–79 changed Reprised 30–46, 3 new measures | 1–75 same 76–79 changed Reprised 30–46, 3 new measures |
| No. 3, Récit, choeur et scène | | | |
| A–Récit | 85 | Same | Same |
| B–Choeur | 59 | Same | Same |
| C–Scène et choeur | 167 | Same | Same |
| No. 4, Récit et romance | | | |
| A–Récit | 26 | Same | Same |
| B–Romance | 88 | Same | Same |
| No. 5, Finale | | | |
| A–Scène et choeur | 95 | Same | Same |
| B–Air et choeur | 128 | Same | Same |

*(Continued on next page)*

Comparison of Three Versions of the Score: P1, P2, and P3 *(Continued)*

|  | P1 | P2 | P3 |
|---|---|---|---|
| | | *Act 2* | |
| No. 6, Entr'acte, choeur et scène | 216 | Same | Same, with cut marked for performance (mm. 185–216) |
| No. 7, Récit et cavatine | 107 | Same | Same |
| No. 8, Chanson | 26 | Same | Same |
| No. 9, Duo | 239 | Same | Same |
| No. 10, Finale | 347 | Same | Same |
| | | *Act 3, scene 1* | |
| No. 11, Entr'acte, récit et air | 146 | Same | Same |
| No. 12, Scène et duo | | | |
| A–Récit | 23 | Same | Same |
| B–Duo | 275 | Same | Same |
| | | 1–49 same | 1–49 same |
| | | 50 and 126 cut | 50 and 126 cut |
| | | 2 new measures | 2 new measures |
| | | 127–199 same | 127–199 same |
| | | 200–216 cut | 200–216 cut |
| | | 217–275 same | 217–275 same |
| C–Scène | 41 | 200–216 same | 200–216 same |
| | | 217–275 same | 217–275 same |
| | | *Act 3, scene 2* | |
| No. 13, Choeur dansé | 265 | 1–136 same | 1–136 same |
| | | 137–253 cut | 137–253 cut |
| | | 253–265 same | 253–265 same |
| No. 14, Scène et duo | | | |
| A–Scène | 23 | 1–18 same | 1–18 same |
| | | 19–23 cut | 19–23 cut |
| | | 7 new measures | 7 new measures |
| B–Duo | 71 | Cut | Cut |
| | | No. 14 (cont.) | No. 14 (cont.) |

Comparison of Three Versions of the Score: P1, P2, and P3 *(Continued)*

| | P1 | P2 | P3 |
|---|---|---|---|
| | | *Act 3, scene 2* | |
| No. 15, Finale | 81 | 1–45 same | 1–45 same |
| | | 46–48 moved | 46–48 moved |
| | | 49–81 cut | 49–81 cut |
| | | No. 15, Trio | No. 15, Trio |
| | | 83 new measures | 83 new measures, with cut marked for performance (mm. 2–55) |
| | | No. 16, Finale | No. 16, Finale |
| | | 1–50 new | 1–24 same |
| | | | 25–40 same, but without Léïla |
| | | | 41–42 same |
| | | | 43–161 cut |
| | | 51–70 moved from theme of No. 13 | |
| | | 71–159 [=177–265 of No. 13 (P1)] | |
| | | 160–161 new | |
| | | | 43–59 new |
| | | | 60–78 = 63–81 of No. 15 of P1 |

# Appendix 3  Several States of the Beginning of the Act 2 Finale

The passage in which the lovers are discovered posed major problems for the authors. We can trace their uncertainty in the various sources dating from 1863. These uncertainties may be tabulated in five main stages, from the first manuscript libretto to the published libretto, preceding the final versions as reflected in the conducting score (C) and in the published piano-vocal score (P1).

L1 - - - - - - - - - - - - - - - - - - - - - - - - - - - - - - - - - - - - - - - - - - L4

| Stage 1 | Stage 2 | Stage 3 | Stage 4 | Stage 5 |
|---------|---------|---------|---------|---------|
| ZURGA<br>Un homme dans ces lieux | X | ZURGA<br>Un homme en ces lieux, ô trahison! | NOURABAD<br>Same | NOURABAD<br>Un homme dans ces lieux,<br>trahison! trahison! |
| NADIR<br>Zurga! . . . tout est perdu | X | X | X | X |
| ZURGA<br>Venez tous! . . . Venez tous! | ZURGA<br>Same | X | X | X |
|  |  | LÉÏLA<br>Partez maintenant!<br>Partez! je tremble | LÉÏLA<br>Same | LÉÏLA<br>Ah! revenez à la maison<br>Partez! Partez vite!<br>je tremble |
|  |  | Ils sont là . . .<br>ils peuvent venir!<br>Je tremble. Partez!<br>partez! | X | X |

| Stage 1 | Stage 2 | Stage 3 | Stage 4 | Stage 5 |
|---------|---------|---------|---------|---------|
| | | NADIR<br>Oui, mais chaque soir, ici<br>Léïla je te reverrai | NADIR<br>Same | NADIR<br>Que l'amour chaque soir dans<br>l'ombre nous rassemble |
| | | LÉÏLA<br>Oui! mais adieu! | LÉÏLA<br>Oui! adieu! | LÉÏLA<br>Oui! oui, demain je t'attendrai |
| | | NADIR<br>Adieu | NADIR<br>Same | NADIR<br>Oui, demain je te reverrai |
| | | | | NOURABAD<br>Malheur sur lui! Malheur sur nous! Accourez, venez tous! |
| CHORUS<br>Quelle viox nous appelle | CHORUS<br>Same | CHORUS<br>Same | CHORUS<br>Same | CHORUS<br>Same |

# Appendix 4 Passages Cut in the Course of Performance

There are cuts in the conducting score (C) that are not reflected in the published piano-vocal score (P1) and that were therefore made later, either during the run of performances, or at the time of revivals. The latter is unlikely because the conducting score contains none of the added passages found in P2 and P3. These fairly numerous cuts were made to passages already heard or to developmental passages, as well as to passages whose musical material is completely eliminated by the cut. On October 8, 1863, Jules Ruelle, who attentively followed the performances, explicitly noted that "some skillfully made cuts trimmed the work perceptibly."[1]

Passages Cut from the Conducting Score (C) That Appear in the Published Score (P1)

| Cut Passage | Details |
|---|---|
| 1. No. 1 A (mm. 46–104) | Cut of 59 measures, removing the men's chorus "Voilà notre domaine." Some press accounts refer to this chorus, which must thus have been sung at the first performances. |
| 2. No. 1 C (mm. 70–83) | Cut of 14 measures, shortening the reprise of the chorus with dance. |
| 3. No. 2 B (mm. 152–66) | Cut of 15 measures, truncating the stretta of the duet "Amitié sainte." |
| 4. No. 3 C (mm. 125–32) | Cut of 8 measures, shortening the chorus "Brahma, divin Brahma." |
| 5. No. 6 (mm. 33–60) | Cut of 28 measures, shortening the chorus "L'ombre descend des cieux." |

Passages Cut from the Conducting Score (C) That Appear
in the Published Score (P1) *(Continued)*

| *Cut Passage* | *Details* |
|---|---|
| 6. No. 10 (mm. 84–112) | Cut of 29 measures, shortening the chorus "O nuit d'épouvante." |
| 7. No. 10 (mm. 170–97) | Cut of 28 measures, shortening the reprise of the chorus "Pour eux point de grâce!" |
| 8. No. 10 (mm. 239–54) | Cut of 16 measures, removing the crescendo achieved by a buildup of voices, on the words "Ni pitié, ni merci," perhaps because it was considered too dissonant. |
| 9. No. 10 (mm. 417–24) | Cut of 8 measures, shortening the chorus "Brahma, divin Brahma" (as cut 4 above). |
| 10. No. 12 B (mm. 50–103) | Cut of 54 measures, removing an entire section of the duet for Zurga and Léïla ("Quoi! innocent, lui"). |
| 11. No. 13 (mm. 101–36) | Cut of 36 measures, removing an entire section of the chorus "Dès que le soleil, dans le ciel vermeil." |
| 12. No. 13 (mm. 217–52) | Cut of 36 measures, identical to cut 11 above. |
| 13. No. 14 B (mm. 59–67) | Cut of 9 measures, shortening the stretta of the duet for Nadir and Léïla. |

# Appendix 5 Performances and Daily Box-Office Receipts of the Théâtre-Lyrique, September 27– November 28, 1863

The box-office figures are based on (1) the material in the Bibliothèque-Musée de l'Opéra (TH 42/270), which contains the receipts from the Théâtre-Lyrique and the Opéra-Comique for the period April 1862 to September 1869; and (2) statements of the daily receipts of the theaters of Paris for the period 1858 to 1867, now in the Archives nationales (F/21/1042). In the rare cases where these two sources differ, I have used the second. The number in parentheses following the name of a work indicates how many times it had been performed at the Théâtre-Lyrique.

| Date | Opera | Receipts (francs) |
|------|-------|-------------------|
| Sunday, Sept. 27 | *Joseph*<br>Méhul<br>*L'Epreuve villageoise*<br>Grétry | 3,002.50 |
| Monday, Sept. 28 | *Les Noces de Figaro* (158)<br>Mozart (Carré and Barbier) | 3,452.50 |
| Tuesday, Sept. 29 | *Les Noces* (159) | 3,703.00 |
| Wednesday, Sept. 30 | *Les Pêcheurs de perles* (1)<br>Bizet | 1,267.00 |
| Thursday, Oct. 1 | *Les Noces* (160) | 4,793.00 |
| Friday, Oct. 2 | *Les Pêcheurs* (2) | 3,136.00 |
| Saturday, Oct. 3 | *Les Noces* (161) | 4,527.50 |
| Sunday, Oct. 4 | *Joseph* | 2,883.00 |
| Monday, Oct. 5 | *Les Pêcheurs* (3) | 3,007.50 |
| Tuesday, Oct. 6 | *Les Noces* (162) | 4,194.50 |
| Wednesday, Oct. 7 | *Les Pêcheurs* (4) | 2,198.50 |

| Date | Opera | Receipts (francs) |
|------|-------|-------------------|
| Thursday, Oct. 8 | *Les Noces* (163) | 3,882.50 |
| Friday, Oct. 9 | *Les Pêcheurs* (5) | 2,037.50 |
| Saturday, Oct. 10 | *Les Noces* (164) | 4,297.00 |
| | | |
| Sunday, Oct. 11 | *Les Noces* (165) | 4,837.50 |
| Monday, Oct. 12 | *L'Epreuve villageoise* | 2,355.00 |
| | *Les Pêcheurs* (6) | |
| Tuesday, Oct. 13 | *Les Noces* (166) | 3,804.00 |
| Wednesday, Oct. 14 | *L'Epreuve villageoise* | 2,296.00 |
| | *Les Pêcheurs* (7) | |
| Thursday, Oct. 15 | *Les Noces* (167) | 2,658.50 |
| Friday, Oct. 16 | *L'Epreuve villageoise* | 2,046.00 |
| | *Les Pêcheurs* (8) | |
| Saturday, Oct. 17 | *Les Noces* (168) | 3,793.00 |
| | | |
| Sunday, Oct. 18 | *Les Noces* (169) | 4,952.00 |
| Monday, Oct. 19 | *L'Epreuve villageoise* | 1,928.00 |
| | *Les Pêcheurs* (9) | |
| Tuesday, Oct. 20 | *Les Noces* (170) | 3,104.00 |
| Wednesday, Oct. 21 | *L'Epreuve villageoise* | 1,616.00 |
| | *Les Pêcheurs* (10) | |
| Thursday, Oct. 22 | *Les Noces* (171) | 3,266.50 |
| Friday, Oct. 23 | *L'Epreuve villageoise* | 1,888.50 |
| | *Les Pêcheurs* (11) | |
| Saturday, Oct. 24 | *Les Noces* (172) | 3,708.00 |
| | | |
| Sunday, Oct. 25 | *Les Noces* (173) | 3,606.00 |
| Monday, Oct. 26 | *L'Epreuve villageoise* | 1,667.00 |
| | *Les Pêcheurs* (12) | |
| Tuesday, Oct. 27 | *Les Noces* (174) | 2,778.50 |
| Wednesday, Oct. 28 | *L'Epreuve villageoise* | 1,256.50 |
| | *Les Pêcheurs* (13) | |
| Thursday, Oct. 29 | *Les Noces* (175) | 3,035.50 |
| Friday, Oct. 30 | *L'Epreuve villageoise* | 986.50 |
| | *Les Pêcheurs* (14) | |
| Saturday, Oct. 31 | *Les Noces* (176) | 3,387.50 |
| | | |
| Sunday, Nov. 1 | *L'Epreuve villageoise* | 3,305.00 |
| | *Les Pêcheurs* (15) | |
| Monday, Nov. 2 | House dark for dress rehearsals of | |
| | *Les Troyens* | |
| Tuesday, Nov. 3 | *Les Noces* (177) | 2,122.00 |

*(Continued next page)*

| Date | Opera | Receipts (francs) |
|---|---|---|
| Wednesday, Nov. 4 | *Les Troyens* (premiere)<br>Berlioz | 729.50 |
| Thursday, Nov. 5 | *Les Noces* (178) | 3,578.00 |
| Friday, Nov. 6 | *Les Troyens* (2) | 2,644.50 |
| Saturday, Nov. 7 | *L'Epreuve villageoise*<br>*Les Pêcheurs* (16) | 1,204.50 |
| Sunday, Nov. 8 | *Les Noces* (179) | 5,683.00 |
| Monday, Nov. 9 | *Les Troyens* (3) | 3,408.50 |
| Tuesday, Nov. 10 | *Les Noces* (180) | 2,426.50 |
| Wednesday, Nov. 11 | *Les Troyens* (4) | 2,661.50 |
| Thursday, Nov. 12 | *Les Noces* (181) | 2,664.00 |
| Friday, Nov. 13 | *Les Troyens* (5) | 4,623.50 |
| Saturday, Nov. 14 | *Obéron* (revival / 97)<br>Weber (Nuitter, Beaumont, De Chazot)<br>*Le Jardinier et son seigneur*<br>Leo Delibes | 1,701.00 |
| Sunday, Nov. 15 | *L'Epreuve villageoise*<br>*Les Noces* (182) | 4,923.50 |
| Monday, Nov. 16 | *Les Troyens* (6) | 3,776.50 |
| Tuesday, Nov. 17 | *Obéron* (98) | 1,312.50 |
| Wednesday, Nov. 18 | *Les Troyens* (7) | 3,765.50 |
| Thursday, Nov. 19 | *Obéron* (99) | 1,302.50 |
| Friday, Nov. 20 | *Les Troyens* (8) | 3,443.50 |
| Saturday, Nov. 21 | *Les Pêcheurs* (17) | 1,076.50 |
| Sunday, Nov. 22 | *L'Epreuve villageoise*<br>*Les Noces* (183) | 4,456.50 |
| Monday, Nov. 23 | *Les Troyens* (9) | 2,826.00 |
| Tuesday, Nov. 24 | *Les Pêcheurs* (18) | 674.00 |
| Wednesday, Nov. 25 | *Les Troyens* (10) | 3,223.50 |
| Thursday, Nov. 26 | *La Perle du Brésil* (revival / 117)<br>Félicien David | |
| Friday, Nov. 27 | *Les Troyens* (11) | 2,446.50 |
| Saturday, Nov. 28 | *La Perle du Brésil* (118) | 307.50 |

# Appendix 6    The Staging of
## *Les Pêcheurs de perles*

Léon Durocher described the main elements of the opening scene in the following passage: "The ocean extends across the backdrop, bounded on the right by a sheer cliff, which overlooks it. On the steepest summit of this cliff is a pagoda of massive and strange construction, as seen in Hindustan."[1] The 1863 poster, which is reproduced with minor differences on the cover of the most recent edition of the piano-vocal score (1975), in part confirms that description. It matches the 1863 libretto's description of the scenery, although for want of space, we do not see the wild and barren beach, or the sea, or the huts. We see palm trees, cacti, and the ruined temple. To help us reconstruct a more complete mental picture of the scenery, we can turn also to three illustrations published in the Italian periodical *Il Teatro illustrato*, which were drawn at the time of the opera's La Scala premiere, as *I Pescatori di perle*, in 1886. These illustrations enable us to visualize a setting that matches the descriptions we read in the press accounts of 1863 and in the librettos. The first illustration is similar to the 1863 poster, and depicts the last scene of act 1, when Nadir, nearing the rock, recognizes Léila, who parts her veil.

In act 2, "Léila is sighing in a sort of temple with heavy columns, with fierce idols crouching everywhere and with broken walls, from which the eye is cast into the vastness of the sky and the sea."[2] These "idols" are none other than "sphinxes crouching on the rocks of the crypt."[3] The Milan illustration retains the general layout described in the libretto, with "upstage, a raised terrace with several steps, overlooking the sea," and "palm trees." We can also make out those "fierce idols crouching." But rather than depicting ruins overgrown with vegetation (a scene marking the end of a civilization), it shows a temple in perfect condition. The poor pearl fishers temporarily occupying an abandoned site have been supplanted by a tribe that is clearly prospering.

Press accounts are silent about the first scene of act 3. The libretto says only that it depicts "an Indian tent closed by a hanging" and that "a lamp is burning on a small rattan table." The third illustration of the La Scala production depicts the duet for Léïla and Zurga. The scene is the interior of a sumptuous tent with a table and a lamp upstage. It is important that this intimate scene, in which Zurga's personal drama comes to the fore, should be played as indicated in the libretto and not outdoors, as it is in some modern productions.

Johannès Weber was hard on the final scene, in the middle of which "there is a grotesque cardboard image of the god Brahma," which "nods its head...at the least movement made nearby."[4] For the change of scene in act 3, "a front-cloth was lowered, and when it was raised again, the scene depicted a sacred wood."[5] This corresponds to the stage direction in the libretto, which describes Nadir as "seated at the foot of the statue of Brahma, on a pyre that has been built in the middle of the stage." The final picture in *Il Teatro illustrato* completely omits the statue, but clearly depicts the "furious dances" called for by the libretto.[6]

The scenery depicts three kinds of space: nature, including the sea, the beach, the rock, and the vegetation; architecture, comprising temples and ruins; and the interior of Zurga's tent. The 1863 poster and the Italian illustrations of 1886 hint at the splendor of the costumes, mentioned in the press, which were intended with their wealth of accessories, fabrics, and colors to delight the spectator rather than to reproduce in a realistic way the traditions of this group of Singhalese, who would in reality have been dressed more simply.

In keeping with convention, the curtain went up after the orchestral prelude. Nadir's act 1 *romance* was less conventional, and even angered one columnist. The tenor Morini, he wrote, was obliged "to perform a real feat: he sings his piece in a nearly horizontal position; he lies on the ground, and the authors at most permit him occasionally to raise himself up on his elbow. That is an innovation that does not seem to me at all successful. Now, for the sake of a stage effect, they are making the tenors lie down."[7]

Johannès Weber complained in turn about the poor conditions for Léïla: "It is...a clumsy idea to have someone sing an aria upstage, on a platform. The voice will be lost in the scenery; it will reach the listener only in a weakened and muffled state. Without sensing any support from the resonance of the auditorium, the artist will certainly become exhausted. Rather than singing like this, I would sooner play the violin while holding the instrument behind my back." He then compared this innovation to a similar experiment in the staging of a Meyerbeer work premiered in Paris at the Opéra-Comique on February 16, 1854: "A mistake of this kind had earlier been made in *L'Etoile du Nord,* and it was possible to see the resulting problems. *Les Pêcheurs de perles* even outdoes Meyerbeer's opera, because Léïla is raised several meters above the stage floor."[8] H.L. d'Aubel was more specific: "Fifteen feet above the floor!"[9]

In the fourth scene, Nadir is "tied, not on top of, but against a little pyre atop the statue of Brahma. A crowd of women enter and dance around him in a ring."[10]

In addition to press accounts,[11] a study of the sources gives a good idea of the placement of the main characters on stage. The libretto for the stage production (L3: see Appendix 1) contains many such directions. Little letters—*d* for *droite* (right); *g* for *gauche* (left)—follow the placement of the characters; the lighting used to enhance events is specified. The opera climaxes in the final scene: "The glow of the fire spreads over the stage.—The Indians rush into the forest. The women fall on their knees. Zurga remains standing stage center. Tableau.—Curtain."

With its conventional nature, undermined here and there by unusual and disturbing elements, the 1863 production reflected an aesthetic that was solidly rooted in tradition but was already affected by the onslaught of realism.

# Appendix 7 Symmetrical Versification and Reformulation of the Text

*Symmetrical versification of a duet with shared sentiments: excerpt from the act 2 duet of Nadir and Léïla (no. 9)*

| LEÏLA | NADIR |
|---|---|
| Ainsi que toi je me souviens! | Ton coeur avait compris le mien! |
| Au sein de la nuit parfumée, | Au sein de la nuit parfumée, |
| Mon âme alors libre et charmée, | Quand j'écoutais, l'âme charmée, |
| A l'amour n'était pas fermée! | Les accents de ta voix aimée, |
| Ainsi que toi je me souviens! | Ton coeur avait compris le mien! |

*Symmetrical versification of a duet with opposing sentiments: the act 3 duet of Zurga and Léïla (no. 12); text as in libretto*

| LEÏLA | ZURGA |
|---|---|
| Va prends aussi ma vie, | Tu demandais sa vie, |
| Mais ta rage assouvie, | Mais de ma jalousie |
| Le remords, l'infamie | Ranimant la furie, |
| Te poursuivront toujours! | Tu le perds pour toujours! |
| Que l'arrêt s'accomplisse | Que l'arrêt s'accomplisse |
| Et qu'un même supplice | Et qu'un même supplice |
| Dans les cieux réunisse | Me venge et réunisse |
| A jamais nos amours! | Vos coupables amours! |

When setting this duet expressing opposing sentiments, Bizet proceeded to destroy its symmetrical structure completely. Here are the two voices as they appear in the score:

*Duet with opposing sentiments: the act 3 duet of Zurga and Léïla (no. 12); text as in score (the final text)*

| LEÏLA | ZURGA |
|---|---|
| Va prends aussi ma vie, | O rage! |
| Mais ta rage assouvie, | O fureur! |
| Le remords, l'infamie | O tourment affreux! |
| Te poursuivront toujours! | O jalousie! Tremble! |
| Que l'arrêt s'accomplisse | Ah crains ma fureur! |
| Et qu'un même supplice | Oui, crains ma vengeance! |
| Dans les cieux réunisse | O fureur! |
| A jamais nos tendres amours! | O jalousie! |
| Va prends ma vie, | Que l'arrêt s'accomplisse. |
| Je te défie! | Point de grâce, |
| Oui, l'infamie | Point de pitié, |
| Te poursuivra toujours! | Tu vas périr avec lui! |
| Va! barbare! cruel! | Pour tous deux, oui, la mort! |
| Les remords te poursuivront toujours! | Point de grâce! |

There are symmetrical structures at two levels. The rhythm and meter of the verses must follow regular patterns corresponding to a rhythmic or melodic motif and to the regular phrase structure of the music; and, especially in numbers for more than one singer, the rhymes and what might be called the "semantic symmetries" must make it possible to superimpose melodic lines—and therefore words—and must lead all the vocal parts to the same rhyme or the same refrain.

The well-known but rarely analyzed relationship between music and libretto in terms of symmetry deserves a thorough study of its own. It is worth reading what Steven Huebner has to say in his *The Operas of Charles Gounod* (New York: Oxford University Press, 1990), especially in his chapter on melody. The matter must be considered also in the light of declamation, accents, and rhythms that are specific to French. In this connection, see Gottfried R. Marschall's *Massenet et la fixation de la forme mélodique française* (Saarbrücken: Musik-Edition Lucie Galland, 1988).

# Biographical Notes on Composers

These brief notes are intended merely to sketch the careers of the main composers mentioned in the text (who range chronologically from Boieldieu to Massenet) and to provide additional information about some of the works to which reference has been made. For composers of the generation of Massenet's pupils, such as Bruneau, Charpentier, and Chausson, only those whose works were heard in the nineteenth century are included.

ADAM, ADOLPHE CHARLES (BORN PARIS, JULY 24, 1803; DIED PARIS, MAY 3, 1856)

Adam composed more than eighty lyric works, some of which, written in large part for the Opéra-Comique, earned great and lasting success. At the Conservatoire, he studied organ with François Benoist (1794–1878), counterpoint with Antoine-Joseph Reicha (1770–1836), and composition with Boieldieu (q.v.). He assisted with the preparation of the latter composer's *La Dame blanche*. Adam composed songs, little theatrical pieces for secondary theaters, and ballet music, including *Giselle*, written in 1841 for the Opéra. *Le Chalet* (*opéra-comique* in one act, libretto by Eugène Scribe and Mélesville [Joseph Duveyrier] after Goethe's *Jery und Bätley*, first performed at the Opéra-Comique on September 25, 1834) made his name as a master of the classic *opéra-comique;* its 1,000th performance took place in 1873 and its 1,500th in 1922. *Le Postillon de Longjumeau* (*opéra-comique* in three acts, libretto by Aldolphe de Leuven and Léon Brunswick, first performed at the Opéra-Comique on October 13, 1836) confirmed him as the successor to Boieldieu. *Si j'étais roi* (*opéra-comique* in three acts, libretto by Adolphe Philippe d'Ennery and Jules Brésil, first performed at the Théâtre-Lyrique on September 4, 1852) was among his most famous works, but many would prefer *Le Toréador* (*opéra-comique* in two acts, libretto by Thomas Sauvage, first performed at the Opéra-Comique on May 18, 1849), which in some respects is a perfect example of its kind. Adam played an important role in the rediscovery of the late-eighteenth-century repertory, reorchestrating or arranging Grétry's *Richard Coeur de Lion* and *Zémire et Azor,* Pierre Alexandre de Monsigny's *Aline* and *Le Déserteur,* and Nicolas Dalayrac's *Gulistan.*

AUBER, DANIEL FRANÇOIS ESPRIT (BORN CAEN, JANUARY 29, 1782; DIED PARIS, MAY 12 OR 13, 1871)

A pupil of Cherubini's, Auber, with his nearly fifty scores, formed a link between the *opéra-comique* of the beginning of the century—that of Nicolas Isouard (Nicolò) and Boieldieu—and the *opéra lyrique* of the 1850s and 1860s. His position as the master of *"l'esprit français* in music," was made official with his election to the Institut de France in 1829 and with his appointment to the directorship of the Conservatoire in 1842, a post he held until 1870. Auber found an ideal collaborator in Eugène Scribe for works built around contrasting situations and complicated plots that were sometimes implausible but almost always effective. In the 1820s, Auber was strongly influenced by Rossini; he balanced this influence with French practice, as we see in *Le Maçon* (*opéra-comique* in three acts, libretto by Eugène Scribe and Germain Delavigne, first performed at the Opéra-Comique on May 3, 1825), *Fra Diavolo* (*opéra-comique* in three acts, libretto by Eugène Scribe, first performed at the Opéra-Comique on January 28, 1830), and *Le Domino noir* (*opéra-comique* in three acts, libretto by Eugène Scribe, first performed at the Opéra-Comique on December 2, 1837), which reached its 1,000th performance in 1881. After 1840, Auber's *opéras-comiques* grew more serious and lyrical, as in *Haydée* (*opéra-comique* in three acts, libretto by Eugène Scribe after Prosper Mérimée, first performed at the Opéra-Comique on December 28, 1847) and *Manon Lescaut* (*opéra-comique* in three acts, libretto by Eugène Scribe, first performed at the Opéra-Comique on February 23, 1856). Although Auber launched the age of *grand opéra* with *La Muette de Portici* (*opéra* in five acts, libretto by Eugène Scribe and Germain Delavigne, first performed at the Opéra on February 29, 1828), which enjoyed a resounding success, his talents really flourished in *opéra-comique.* Neither the moderately successful *Gustave III* (*opéra* in five acts, libretto by Eugène Scribe, first performed at the Opéra on February 27, 1833) nor *L'Enfant prodigue* (*opéra* in five acts, libretto by Eugène Scribe, first performed at the Opéra on December 6, 1850) were ever viewed as real jewels of *grand opéra*, which quickly came to be dominated by the style of Meyerbeer. Other works mentioned include: *Le Cheval de bronze* (*opéra-comique* in three acts, libretto by Eugène Scribe, first performed at the Opéra-Comique on March 23, 1835, and transformed into an opera-ballet for the Opéra, September 21, 1857); *Le Duc d'Ollone* (*opéra-comique* in three acts, libretto by Eugène Scribe and Joseph-Xavier Boniface, called Saintine, first performed at the Opéra-Comique on February 4, 1842); *Marco Spada* (*opéra-comique* in three acts, libretto by Eugène Scribe and Germain Delavigne, first performed at the Opéra-Comique on December 21, 1852); and *La Sirène* (*opéra-comique* in three acts, libretto by Eugène Scribe, first performed at the Opéra-Comique on March 26, 1844).

BERLIOZ, HECTOR (BORN LA CÔTE-SAINT-ANDRÉ, DECEMBER 11, 1803; DIED PARIS, MARCH 8, 1869)

During his lifetime, Berlioz, who has often been called the most genuinely romantic of French composers, entirely failed to make a career as an opera composer, because of his style, which was viewed as too personal and un-usual, and because of his refusal to follow the rules of the traditional gen-res. *Benvenuto Cellini* (*opéra* in two acts, libretto by Auguste Barbier and Léon de Wailly, first performed at the Opéra on September 10, 1838) was performed only three times in 1838 and four times in 1839. *Les Troyens* (*opéra* in five acts, libretto by Berlioz after Virgil, conceived as a vast lyric structure and intended for the Opéra, was finally produced at the Théâtre-Lyrique on November 4, 1863, under the title *Les Troyens à Carthage,* with its entire first part deleted [*La Prise de Troie,* whose content was summa-rized in a prologue]). After twenty-two performances, the work was dropped from the schedule, then was played twice in concert form in 1879. It was not until 1890 that it was performed in its entirety, over two evenings, at Karlsruhe. The experience of *Béatrice et Bénédict,* a remark-able two-act *opéra-comique,* with libretto by Berlioz after Shakespeare, is indicative of the composer's banishment from the French operatic world of the nineteenth century: it was first performed in Baden-Baden on August 9, 1862, and received its first French performance, at the Théâtre de l'Odéon, only on June 4, 1890. *La Damnation de Faust* (*légende drama-tique* in four parts, libretto by Berlioz and Almire Gandonnière after Goethe's *Faust* as translated by Gérard de Nerval) defies classification. It was first performed, in concert version, at the Opéra-Comique on Decem-ber 6, 1846. It was as a columnist in the *Journal des débats* that Berlioz par-ticipated in the Parisian operatic milieu of the day.

BIZET, GEORGES (BORN PARIS, OCTOBER 25, 1838;
DIED BOUGIVAL, JUNE 3, 1875)

Bizet's initial success was as a gifted student, winning prizes at the Conservatoire and, in 1857, the first prize in the Prix de Rome competition. In 1856, he had shared first prize with Charles Lecocq in a competition organized by Offenbach to inaugurate the Théâtre des Bouffes-Parisiens with *Docteur Miracle* (*opéra-comique* in one act, libretto by Léon Battu and Ludovic Halévy, first performed at the Bouffes-Parisiens on April 9, 1857). After this brilliant beginning, Bizet, who considered himself destined for the lyric stage, faced major difficulties: his style, rich in color and harmony, was disconcerting, and his aesthetic vision, inherited from Gounod, resulted in an "operatic poetry" and depth of expression that the French were slow to understand. *Les Pêcheurs de perles* (*opéra* in three acts, libretto by Eugène Cormon and Albert Carré, first performed at the Théâtre-Lyrique on September 30, 1863) perplexed audiences. While acknowledging the young composer's skill, they were unable to pigeonhole the work in any of the usual categories. In the press, the work gave rise to debate on French opera in general. *La Jolie Fille de Perth* (*opéra* in four acts, libretto by Jules Henri Vernoy de Saint-Georges and Jules Adenis, first performed at the Théâtre-Lyrique on December 26, 1867) was no more successful; nor was *Djamileh* (*opéra-comique* in one act, first performed at the Opéra-Comique on May 22, 1872), one of the most polished works of the French repertory and still little known today. *Carmen* (*opéra-comique* in four acts, libretto by Henri Meilhac and Ludovic Halévy, first performed at the Opéra-Comique on March 3, 1875) brought together a great number of trends in the guise of a traditional *opéra-comique*. After being performed all around the world, the work was revived at the Opéra-Comique in 1883 with unqualified success.

BOIELDIEU, ADRIEN (BORN ROUEN, DECEMBER 16, 1775;
DIED JARCY, OCTOBER 8, 1834)

Boieldieu left his mark on the transitional period between two eras of *opéra-comique:* the late eighteenth century and the first signs of gallicized romanticism. He was quickly recognized as a master of traditional *opéra-comique* and was invited to Saint Petersburg, where he headed the French opera company. On his return to Paris in 1811, he continued to compose unsurprising but brisk, fresh works, such as *Le Nouveau Seigneur de village* (*opéra-comique* in one act, libretto by Auguste François Creuzé de

Lesser and Edme-Guillaume-François de Favières, first performed at the Opéra-Comique on June 28, 1813), with a plot that was in the spirit of an eighteenth-century *divertissement*, and *Les Voitures versées* (*opéra-comique* in two acts, libretto by Vedel after Dupaty, first performed at Saint Petersburg in 1808, then revised for the Opéra-Comique, April 29, 1820), a simple and cheerful work that contains duet variations on "Au clair de la lune," which were extremely popular. Just as he was elected to the Institut de France, in 1817, his countrymen were discovering the music of Rossini, which had a profound influence on a great many musicians. To some degree, *La Dame blanche* (*opéra-comique* in three acts, libretto by Eugène Scribe after Sir Walter Scott, first performed at the Opéra-Comique on December 10, 1825) merges the *opéra-comique* genre, Rossinian influences, and some aspects of the romantic movement (such as a taste for colorful locales such as Scotland, for Gothic and other troubadour styles, and for the fantastic), watered down and adapted to simple expressive forms that do a good job of conveying the drama. The 1,000th performance of *La Dame blanche* was given in 1862 and the 1,675th in 1914. Other work mentioned: *La Fête du village voisin* (*opéra-comique* in three acts, libretto by Charles-Augustin Sewrin, first performed at the Opéra-Comique on March 5, 1816).

BRUNEAU, ALFRED (BORN PARIS, MARCH 3, 1857; DIED PARIS, JUNE 15, 1934)

A pupil of Massenet's at the Conservatoire, Bruneau won second prize in the 1881 Prix de Rome competition. A decisive influence was that of Zola, who became his librettist. He practised musical naturalism in music dramas inspired by Wagner, such as *Le Rêve* (*drame lyrique* in four acts, libretto by Louis Gallet after Emile Zola, first performed at the Opéra-Comique on June 18, 1891). That work is not divided into numbers, and the vocal lines are woven into the score's symphonic development. On the other hand, in *L'Attaque du moulin* (*drame lyrique* in four acts, libretto by Louis Gallet after Emile Zola, first performed at the Opéra-Comique on November 23, 1893), it is easy to see the importance of traditional models, such as *airs, romances,* ensembles, and recitatives. In *Messidor* (*drame lyrique* in four acts, libretto by Emile Zola, first performed at the Opéra on February 19, 1897), verse gives way to prose, and the composer adds a symbolic dimension to his naturalism, as he does in *L'Ouragan* (*drame lyrique* in four acts, libretto by Emile Zola, first performed at the Opéra-Comique on April 19, 1901), which achieved only a succès d'estime.

CHABRIER, EMMANUEL (BORN AMBERT, PUY-DE-DÔME,
JANUARY 18, 1841; DIED PARIS, SEPTEMBER 13, 1894)

Forced by his father to pursue an administrative career, Chabrier was unable to devote himself entirely to music, which undoubtedly delayed his arrival on the Parisian scene. He was well known as a composer of orchestral and piano music, but never made his mark in any of the operatic genres. Yet some of his works are wonderful, such as *L'Etoile*, classified as an *opéra bouffe* in three acts and first performed at the Bouffes-Parisiens on November 28, 1877, but displaying workmanship and musical richness that are worthy of the best *opéras-comiques* (with added farce); it was first performed at the Opéra-Comique in 1941. Although a "genuine pearl" according to Stravinsky and a treasure of the *esprit français* according to Reynaldo Hahn, *Le Roi malgré lui* (*opéra-comique* in three acts, libretto by Emile de Najac, Paul Burani, and Jean Richepin, first performed at the Opéra-Comique on May 8, 1887) was no more successful in finding a niche on the lyric stage. Nor was *Gwendoline* (*opéra* in two acts, libretto by Catulle Mendès, first performed in Brussels, at the Théâtre de la Monnaie, on April 10, 1886, and revived in Lyon in April 1893, then in Paris on December 27, 1893). Historically speaking, although this was one of the most original and French of operas, and although it was rich in its melodies and varied in its rhythms, harmony, and orchestration, it remained beyond the boundaries of the French operatic world, and still awaits recognition.

CHARPENTIER, GUSTAVE (BORN DIEUZE, JUNE 25, 1860;
DIED PARIS, FEBRUARY 18, 1956)

Charpentier enrolled in the Conservatoire in 1881, joined Massenet's class in 1885, and took first prize in the 1887 Prix de Rome competition. In *Louise* (*roman musical* in four acts, libretto by the composer, first performed at the Opéra-Comique on February 2, 1900), he followed Wagner's example by writing his own libretto. He combined a naturalistic style with themes of bohemian life, conflict between the generations, free love, and city life: Paris was a central character in this work. Over a sometimes raw background of realism, his music created an atmosphere and evinced a lyricism that won audience support from the outset.

CLAPISSON, ANTOINE-LOUIS (BORN NAPLES, SEPTEMBER 15, 1808; DIED PARIS, MARCH 19, 1866)

As reflected in the splendor of his "official" career—he was made chevalier of the Légion d'honneur in 1847, a member of the Institut de France in 1854, and professor of harmony at the Conservatoire in 1862—and in a number of successful *opéras-comiques,* Clapisson exemplified the composer lacking in genius but possessing a certain talent in the conventional forms. Bizet, who loathed his music, nicknamed him Glapisson—*glapissement* is the yelping of a dog—and would entertain his friends with improvisations combining Clapisson's melodies with themes from Beethoven. The composer's greatest success, *La Fanchonnette* (*opéra-comique* in three acts, libretto by Jules Henri Vernoy de Saint-Georges and Adolphe de Leuven, first performed at the Théâtre-Lyrique on March 1, 1856), owed much to the gifts of its star, Caroline Miolan-Carvalho. Other work mentioned: *La Perruche* (*opéra-comique* in one act, libretto by Dupin and Dumanoir, first performed at the Opéra-Comique on April 28, 1840).

DAVID, FÉLICIEN (BORN CADENET, APRIL 13, 1810; DIED SAINT-GERMAIN-EN-LAYE, AUGUST 29, 1876)

After musical studies that won him no recognition in the form of prizes, David joined the Saint-Simonians (see Ralph P. Locke, *Music, Musicians, and the Saint-Simonians* [Chicago: University of Chicago Press, 1985]) and composed music for them. When the government disbanded that community in 1832, he departed, along with other members, for the Orient. He returned to France in 1835 bearing a wealth of visual and sonic impressions that would mark his work and make him a key proponent of the oriental exoticism that would have such a great influence on the mid-nineteenth-century French repertory. On December 8, 1844, his *Le Désert* won a great success and opened the way for a more intensely colored musical exoticism. It made use of simple but effective techniques that he would transfer to the stage in works whose titles are indicative: *La Perle du Brésil* (*opéra-comique* in three acts, libretto by J. Gabriel and Sylvain Saint-Etienne, first performed at the Théâtre-Lyrique on November 22, 1851) and *Lalla-Roukh* (*opéra-comique* in two acts, libretto by Michel Carré and Hippolyte Lucas after Thomas Moore, first performed at the Opéra-Comique on May 12, 1862).

DELIBES, LÉO (BORN SAINT-GERMAIN DU VAL, FEBRUARY 21,
1836; DIED PARIS, JANUARY 16, 1891)

After less than brilliant studies at the Conservatoire, including in Adolphe
Adam's composition class, Delibes failed to win a Prix de Rome. His revenge came in 1881, when he followed Henri Reber (1807–1880) as professor of composition at the Conservatoire, and in 1884, when he was
elected to the Institut de France. In the meantime, he kept his hand in by
composing operettas. Following his unsuccessful *Le Roi l'a dit* (*opéra-
comique* in three acts, libretto by Edmond Gondinet, first performed at the
Opéra-Comique on May 24, 1873)—a bright score that reflects the taste
for classical-period pastiches—Delibes finally won over the audience of a
major theater with *Lakmé* (*opéra* in three acts, libretto by Edmond
Gondinet and Philippe Gille after Pierre Loti, first performed at the Opéra-
Comique on April 14, 1883), a work in conventional form and entirely
given over to the fashion for exoticism. Its pleasant style, delicate orchestration, effective coloratura aria, and melodic richness testify to how well
the traditional French models would survive through the end of the century: the work was performed 179 times at the Opéra-Comique between
1888 and 1893.

DONIZETTI, GAETANO (BORN BERGAMO, NOVEMBER 29,
1797; DIED BERGAMO, APRIL 8, 1848)

After a musical education dominated by Johannes Simon (Giovanni Si-
mone) Mayr, Donizetti's first major success was *Zoraida di Granata* (*opéra*
in two acts, libretto by Bartolomeo Merelli, first performed at the Teatro
Argentina, Rome, on January 28, 1822). After a career in Italy, during
which he conformed to the Rossinian model and was also influenced by
Bellini, he gained international fame with the triumphant success of *Anna
Bolena* (opera in two acts, libretto by Felice Romani, first performed at the
Teatro Carcano, Milan, on December 26, 1830). In 1835, on Rossini's invitation, he visited Paris to produce his *opera seria Marino Faliero* (opera in
three acts, libretto by E. Bidera after Byron, first performed at the Théâtre-
Italien on March 12, 1835). During this first contact with the French capi-
tal, he discovered the *grands opéras* of Meyerbeer and Halévy; he was critical of several aspects of these works, but they influenced him nonetheless.
He admitted to the French style of *L'Assedio di Calais* (*opera seria* in three
acts, libretto by Salvatore Cammarano, first performed at the Teatro San
Carlo, Naples, on November 19, 1836). For a variety of professional and

personal reasons, he left for Paris in 1838. *Les Martyres* (*opéra* in four acts, libretto by Eugène Scribe, first performed at the Opéra on April 10, 1840) was a true *grand opéra,* but after eighteen performances in 1840 and two in 1843, it disappeared from the repertory of that theater, to reappear in Italian, as *Poliuto,* at the Théâtre-Italien in 1859. Still in 1840, Donizetti composed *La Fille du régiment* (*opéra-comique* in two acts, libretto by Jules Henri Vernoy de Saint-Georges and J.-F.-A. Bayard, first performed at the Opéra-Comique on February 11, 1840), which remained popular throughout the century. He also gave the *grand opéra La Favorite* (*opéra* in four acts, libretto by Alphonse Royer and Gustave Vaëz, first performed at the Opéra on December 2, 1840), which remained in the repertory there until 1904. Donizetti traveled a great deal and often produced works abroad, but still wrote another popular work for the Théâtre-Italien: *Don Pasquale* (opera buffa in three acts, libretto by Donizetti and G. Ruffini based on A. Anelli's 1810 libretto *Ser Marc'Antonio,* first performed at the Théâtre-Italien, January 3, 1843). *Dom Sébastien du Portugal* (*opéra* in five acts, libretto by Eugène Scribe, first performed at the Opéra on November 13, 1843) was heard only 31 times between 1843 and 1845 and twice in 1849. On February 20, 1846, a French version of the romantic opera *Lucia di Lammermoor* was produced at the Opéra, and remained in the repertory until the mid 1860s; during the same period, it was also given in its original language at the Théâtre-Italien, along with many other works by Donizetti, whose operas, in French, were produced also at the Théâtre-Lyrique (for example, *Elisabeth* in 1853–54 and *Don Pasquale* in 1864–65).

GOUNOD, CHARLES (BORN PARIS, JUNE 18, 1818;
DIED SAINT-CLOUD, OCTOBER 18, 1893)

After an outstanding student career at the Conservatoire, Gounod won first prize in the 1839 Prix de Rome competition. In Rome, he discovered the music of Palestrina. Fanny Mendelssohn introduced him to the music of her brother Felix, as well as to that of Bach and of Beethoven. All these influences, together with his passion for Mozart, would result in a depth and an attention to painstaking composition that were crucial in the appearance of a new expressive form in French opera. In *Sapho* (*opéra* in three acts, often revised, libretto by Emile Augier, first performed at the Opéra on April 16, 1851)—which was "forced" upon the Académie de musique by Pauline Viardot—Gounod (in spite of a few bombastic, rather uninteresting choruses and recitatives that are sometimes ordinary) displayed a keen sense of declamation and spurned *grand opéra* effects in favor of a more delicate form of musical expression that reached its peak in the last act. In *Le Médecin malgré lui* (*opéra-comique* in three acts, libretto by Jules Barbier and Michel Carré after Molière, first performed at the Théâtre-Lyrique on June 15, 1858), he developed a stylistic synthesis of a kind of neoclassicism, Mozartian influences, and the *opéra-comique* tradition. In *Philémon et Baucis* (*opéra* in three acts, with a two-act version as well, libretto by Jules Barbier and Michel Carré, first performed at the Théâtre-Lyrique on February 18, 1860) and, perhaps even more so, in *La Colombe* (*opéra-comique* in two acts, libretto by Jules Barbier and Michel Carré, first performed at Baden-Baden on August 3, 1860), he adopted the approach of composing charming and elegant music that gave the orchestra an important part while still based on apt declamation, melodic simplicity, and suppleness in its recitatives, qualities that were uncommon at the time.

Gounod was a Catholic and was drawn to the religious life, but he was also a man of great sensuality, and the romantic dualism (notable also in Liszt, for example) between body and spirit, profane love and sacred love, thus deeply marked his work. His dramatic masterpiece, *Faust* (*opéra* in five acts, libretto by Jules Barbier and Michel Carré, first performed with spoken dialogue at the Théâtre-Lyrique on March 19, 1859), achieved the seemingly impossible integration of his dual personality by depicting this internal conflict in the title character's questioning and sins, as well as in Marguerite's Christian yearnings. The work had already been given 300 times by 1868 before it was revived at the Opéra with recitatives and ballets on March 3, 1869, where it was performed nearly without interruption through the remainder of the century. *Faust* introduced a new genre in France, which harmoniously blended a certain French tradition born of *opéra-comique* and *grand opéra* with an interpretation of German romanticism, and whose new approach to lyric theater focused on intimacy, on conveying atmosphere, and on poetry. That approach was to be seen also in *Mireille* (*opéra* in five acts, existing in many versions, libretto by Michel Carré after Frédéric Mistral, first performed at the Théâtre-Lyrique on March 19, 1864) and, in a different way, in *Roméo et Juliette* (*opéra* in five acts, libretto by Jules Barbier and Michel Carré after Shakespeare, first performed at the Théâtre-Lyrique on April 27, 1867). At the same time, Gounod wanted a hit at the grandest of Paris theaters, and tried unsuccessfully to adapt to the true *grand opéra* style: works such as *La Nonne sanglante* (*opéra* in five acts, libretto by Eugène Scribe and Germain Delavigne after Matthew Lewis, first performed at the Opéra on October 18, 1854) and *La Reine de Saba* (*opéra* in four acts, libretto by Jules Barbier and Michel Carré, first performed at the Opéra on February 28, 1862) were short-lived. Other work mentioned: *Polyeucte* (*opéra* in five acts, libretto by Jules Barbier and Michel Carré, first performed at the Opéra on October 7, 1878).

HALÉVY, FROMENTAL-ÉLIE (BORN PARIS, MAY 27, 1799; DIED NICE, MARCH 17, 1862)

Halévy enrolled in the Conservatoire at the age of nine; he became a pupil of Cherubini's and took first prize in the 1819 Prix de Rome competition. At the Conservatoire he was appointed professor of harmony and accompaniment in 1827, then of counterpoint and fugue in 1833, and of composition in 1840. He soon became a prominent teacher: Gounod, Massé, Bizet, Lecocq, and Saint-Saëns all joined his class. He was elected to the Institut de France in 1836 and to the very prestigious post of its secretary in 1854. He reached his artistic peak with *La Juive* (*opéra* in five acts, libretto by Eugène Scribe, first performed at the Opéra on February 23, 1835), a work that was played nearly uninterruptedly throughout the remainder of the century and that helped define *grand opéra* in the wake of Auber's *La Muette de Portici* (1828) and Meyerbeer's *Robert le Diable* (1831). After an initially resounding success, *La Reine de Chypre* (*opéra* in five acts, libretto by Jules Henri Vernoy de Saint-Georges, first performed at the Opéra on December 22, 1841) saw its popularity decline over the next decade. Despite the esteem in which he was held during his lifetime, Halévy never again managed to achieve the great success that Wagner, in his famous articles in the *Revue et Gazette musicale*, considered to be justified. *L'Eclair* (*opéra-comique* in three acts, libretto by Jules Henri Vernoy de Saint-Georges and François Antoine Eugène de Planard, first performed at the Opéra-Comique on December 16, 1835) and *Les Mousquetaires de la reine* (*opéra-comique* in three acts, libretto by Jules Henri Vernoy de Saint-Georges, first performed at the Opéra-Comique on February 3, 1846) testify to Halévy's skill in the more modest genre of *opéra-comique*. Other works mentioned: *Le Juif errant* (*opéra* in five acts, libretto by Eugène Scribe and Jules Henri Vernoy de Saint-Georges, first performed at the Opéra on April 23, 1852); *Jaguarita l'Indienne* (*opéra-comique* in three acts, libretto by Jules Henry Vernoy de Saint-Georges and Adolphe de Leuven, first performed at the Théâtre-Lyrique on May 14, 1855); and *La Magicienne* (*opéra* in five acts, libretto by Jules Henry Vernoy de Saint-Georges, first performed at the Opéra on March 17, 1858).

HÉROLD, LOUIS JOSEPH FERDINAND (BORN PARIS, JANUARY
28, 1791; DIED PARIS, JANUARY 19, 1833)

At the Conservatoire, Hérold was a pupil of Louis Adam's in piano,
Rodolphe Kreutzer's in violin, Charles-Simon Catel's in harmony, and
Etienne Méhul's in composition, and took first prize in the 1812 Prix de
Rome competition.

After the spirited little one-acter *Le Muletier* (*opéra-comique* in one
act, libretto by Paul de Kock after La Fontaine, first performed at the
Opéra-Comique on May 12, 1823), Hérold triumphed with the sentimental idyll *Marie* (*opéra-comique* in three acts, libretto by Eugène de
Planard, first performed at the Opéra-Comique on August 12, 1826),
which was performed more than 400 times in less than a decade and in
which the expression of the libretto's drama and that of its emotions are
nicely balanced. The composer's approach was now to try to bring together in the very French context of *opéra-comique* the influences of
Mozart, Rossini, and Weber, mixing conventional forms with great
scenes of pathos or tragedy. Hérold benefited also from his position as
*chef de chant* at the Opéra, which enabled him to work with Rossini and
Meyerbeer. Tragic, comic, and fantastic elements were combined in
*Zampa, ou la Fiancée de marbre* (*opéra-comique* in three acts, libretto by
Mélesville [Joseph Duveyrier], first performed at the Opéra-Comique on
May 3, 1831), in which the composer approached *grand opéra*—to the
great displeasure of the conservatives. *Le Pré aux clercs* (*opéra-comique*
in three acts, libretto by Eugène de Planard after Prosper Mérimée, first
performed at the Opéra-Comique on December 15, 1832) marked a return to more traditional *opéra-comique*, although its vivid scenes with a
wealth of delightful melodies also contained picturesque coloration and
atmosphere in the orchestral writing and several more serious incidents.
It enjoyed immediate success and logged its 1,000th performance in
1871.

INDY, VINCENT D' (BORN PARIS, MARCH 27, 1851;
DIED PARIS, DECEMBER 2, 1931)

D'Indy was a pupil of César Franck's and an active member of the Société
nationale de musique. His *Fervaal* (*action musicale* in a prologue and three
acts, libretto by d'Indy after Esaias Tégner, first performed at Brussels,
Théâtre royal de la Monnaie, on May 12, 1897, and at the Opéra-Comique
on May 10, 1898) is often referred to as "the French *Parsifal*."

LALO, ÉDOUARD VICTOIRE ANTOINE (BORN LILLE, JANUARY
27, 1823; DIED PARIS, APRIL 22, 1892)

Lalo composed chamber music and, as violinist in a string quartet, was involved in disseminating a repertory previously held in rather low regard in
France. Although he was well known from the 1870s on for his orchestral
music, it was hard for him to make his name as a dramatic composer. Lalo
composed *Le Roi d'Ys* (*opéra* in three acts, libretto by Edouard Blau, first
performed at the Opéra-Comique on May 7, 1888) between 1875 and 1877,
then revised and completed it in 1887. In order to avoid any comparison
with Wagnerian works, and to inject life into the drama through the use of
concise forms and a rejection of musical development, *Le Roi d'Ys* was constructed as a traditional opera. Some of its scenes are typical of French
*grand opéra*, but there are also certain Germanic literary and musical
themes. The inclusion of Breton folk tunes adds a hint of local color and is
part of a growing trend toward drawing on folklore or on past times for
vivid melodic material. *Le Roi d'Ys* was very successful: it was performed
153 times at the Opéra between 1888 and 1892.

MASSÉ, VICTOR (BORN LORIENT, MARCH 7, 1822;
DIED PARIS, JULY 5, 1884)

Massé enrolled in the Conservatoire in October 1834 and took first prizes
in piano, harmony, and fugue. Then, after attending Halévy's composition
class, he won first prize in the 1844 Prix de Rome competition. He was
fairly successful in the genre of conventional, light *opéra-comique*, but had
an outstanding "official" career: appointed professor of composition at the
Conservatoire in 1866; elected to the Institut de France in place of Auber in
1872; named chevalier of the Légion d'honneur in 1856 and officier in
1877. His *Les Noces de Jeannette* (*opéra-comique* in one act, libretto by
Michel Carré and Jules Barbier, first performed at the Opéra-Comique on
February 4, 1853) was a big hit, and was given every year between 1856
and 1893.

Massé's *La Reine Topaze* (*opéra-comique* in three acts, libretto by Joseph
Philippe Simon [Lockroy] and Léon Battu, first performed at the Théâtre-
Lyrique on December 27, 1856) enjoyed a huge vogue, logging about 100
performances in its first year, thanks in good part to the variations on "Car-
naval de Venise" sung by the soprano who had created the title role in *Les
Noces de Jeannette*, Caroline Miolan-Carvalho, the wife of the director of the
Théâtre-Lyrique, Léon Carvalho. Other work mentioned: *La Mule de Pedro*

(*opéra* in two acts, libretto by Philippe-François Pinel Dumanoir, first performed at the Opéra on March 6, 1863).

MASSENET, JULES (BORN MONTAUD NEAR SAINT-ETIENNE,
MAY 12, 1842; DIED PARIS, AUGUST 13, 1912)

Massenet enrolled in the Conservatoire at the age of eleven; he left in 1863, having studied composition with Ambroise Thomas and having won first prize in that year's Prix de Rome competition. After the Franco-Prussian War of 1870, the success of *Don César de Bazan* (*opéra-comique* in four acts, libretto by Adolphe d'Ennery, Philippe-François Pinel Dumanoir, and Jules Chantepie after Victor Hugo, first performed at the Opéra-Comique on November 30, 1872) was followed by that of the oratorio *Marie-Magdeleine* (*drame sacré* in three acts, libretto by Louis Gallet, first performed on April 11, 1873), whose title character was the first of Massenet's many heroines tormented in mind and in body, and torn between the sacred and the profane. A year following the successful *Le Roi de Lahore* (*opéra* in five acts, libretto by Louis Gallet, first performed at the Opéra on April 27, 1877), he was appointed professor of composition at the Conservatoire, and most of the great French opera composers of the late nineteenth and early twentieth centuries attended his classes. *Manon* (*opéra-comique* in five acts, libretto by Henri Meilhac and Philippe Gille after the abbé Prévost, first performed at the Opéra-Comique on January 19, 1884) confirmed his position as the most popular opera composer in France.

Massenet's style combines a great number of elements and influences, and swings among a variety of aesthetics because of the composer's interest in exploration and reform, and probably even more so because of his eagerness to use any form that would help him achieve success. He wanted to please, and he sometimes erred in the direction of superficial writing. He composed a great number of works—more than twenty—which always showed great technical skill. His success was founded on bountiful melodic inventiveness, and on the way in which he combined, in a more or less different way for each opera, French conventions—for instance, those of *grand opéra* in *Hérodiade* (*opéra* in four acts, libretto by Paul Milliet and Henri Grémont [pseudonym of Georges Hartmann] after Flaubert, first performed in Brussels, in Italian, on December 19, 1881, in Nantes on March 29, 1883, and in Paris, at the Théâtre-Italien, on February 1, 1884)—and innovations from Wagner—especially in *Esclarmonde* (*opéra romanesque* in four acts with prologue and epilogue, libretto by Alfred Blau and Louis de Gramont, first performed at the Opéra-Comique on May 14, 1889)—and even, at the end of his life, from Debussy. Massenet sought to strike a balance between the Italian and German schools and an expressive style based on proper declamation of the French language. To an extent, he succeeded in striking this balance in *Werther* (*drame lyrique* in four acts, libretto by Edouard Blau, Paul Milliet, and Georges Hartmann after Goethe, first performed at Vienna on February 16, 1892, and at the Opéra-Comique on January 16, 1893). Other works mentioned: *La Grand'Tante* (*opéra-comique* in one act, libretto by Jules Adenis and Charles Grandvallet, first performed at the Opéra-Comique on April 3, 1867); *Le Cid* (*opéra* in four acts, libretto by Adolphe d'Ennery, Edouard Blau, and Louis Gallet after Corneille, first performed at the Opéra on November 30, 1885); *Thaïs* (*comédie lyrique* in three acts, libretto by Louis Gallet after Anatole France, first performed at the Opéra on March 16, 1894, and in a different version on April 13, 1898); *Chérubin* (*comédie chantée* in three acts, libretto by Francis de Croisset and Henri Cain, first performed in Monte Carlo on February 14, 1903); *Don Quichotte* (*comédie héroïque* in five acts, libretto by Henri Cain after Cervantes and Jacques Le Lorrain, first performed in Monte Carlo on February 19, 1910, and in Paris, at the Théâtre de la Gaîté-Lyrique, on December 29, 1910).

MESSAGER, CHARLES PROSPER ANDRÉ (BORN MONTLUÇON, DECEMBER 30, 1853; DIED PARIS, FEBRUARY 24, 1929)

Messager enrolled in the Ecole Niedermeyer, Paris, in 1869, where he met Saint-Saëns and Fauré. In 1876, his symphony took first prize in a competition organized by the Société des Auteurs et Compositeurs de Musique. Along with being an organist, conductor, administrator, and critic, he became a masterful composer of operettas. He displayed great talent in melody, harmony, and orchestration, which gave his few *opéras-comiques* great charm and stylistic elegance. These include: *La Basoche* (*opéra-comique* in three acts, libretto by Albert Carré, first performed at the Opéra-Comique on May 30, 1890), *Le Chevalier d'Harmental* (*opéra-comique* in five acts, libretto by P. Ferrier after Alexandre Dumas and Auguste Maquet, first performed at the Opéra-Comique on May 5, 1896), and *Fortunio* (*opéra-comique* in five acts, libretto by Gaston Arman de Caillavet and Robert de Flers after Alfred de Musset, first performed at the Opéra-Comique on June 5, 1907).

MEYERBEER, GIACOMO [JACOB LIEBMANN MEYER BEER]
(BORN VOGLESDORF, GERMANY, SEPTEMBER 5, 1791;
DIED PARIS, MAY 2, 1864)

After a few inconclusive attempts in Germany, Meyerbeer went to Italy, where he composed Italian operas that made him an international celebrity. Paris opened its doors to him after the success of his final Italian opera, *Il Crociato in Egitto* (opera in two acts, libretto by G. Rossi, first performed in Venice on March 7, 1824), and after his pivotal meeting with the librettist Eugène Scribe, he was to become one of the masters of the *grand opéra* style, in which he composed what are among the best known and most influential works of the time: *Robert le Diable* (*opéra* in five acts, libretto by Scribe and Germain Delavigne, first performed at the Opéra on November 21, 1831), *Les Huguenots* (*opéra* in five acts, libretto by Scribe and Emile Deschamps, first performed at the Opéra on February 29, 1836), *Le Prophète* (*opéra* in five acts, libretto by Scribe, first performed at the Opéra on April 16, 1849), and *L'Africaine* (*opéra* in five acts, libretto by Scribe, first performed at the Opéra on April 28, 1865). Meyerbeer also contributed to the history of *opéra-comique* by expanding its framework and its style in two works that were, however, less frequently performed than his *grands opéras: L'Etoile du Nord* (*opéra-comique* in three acts, libretto by Scribe, first performed at the Opéra-Comique on February 16, 1854), and *Dinorah, ou le Pardon de Ploërmel* (*opéra-comique* in three acts, libretto by Jules Barbier and Michel Carré, first performed at the Opéra-Comique on April 4, 1859).

OFFENBACH, JACQUES [JACOB] (BORN COLOGNE, GERMANY,
JUNE 20, 1819; DIED PARIS, OCTOBER 5, 1880)

Having arrived in Paris in 1833, Offenbach gained access to musical circles and to salons, where he played the cello. But he found it harder to get his lyric works produced. During the 1855 Exposition, he opened his little theater, the Bouffes-Parisiens, where operetta was to rule. In 1856, to gain official recognition, he organized a competition in which Bizet and Lecocq were jointly awarded first prize for their respective settings of *Le Docteur Miracle*. Initially constrained by the rights officially granted to his theater, he gradually enlarged its instrumental and vocal forces, and composed larger-scale operettas. *Orphée aux enfers* (*opéra bouffe* in two acts, libretto by Hector Crémieux and Ludovic Halévy, first performed at the Théâtre des Bouffes-Parisiens on October 21, 1858) marked the beginning of the composer's stunningly successful career. But he still wanted to be "taken seriously," and sought to conquer one of the major "official" theaters. But the failure of *Barkouf* (*opéra-comique* in three acts, libretto by Henri Boisseaux, first performed at the Opéra-Comique on December 24, 1860) was a stinging defeat. No more successful were *Robinson Crusoé* (*opéra-comique* in three acts, libretto by Eugène Cormon and Hector Crémieux after Daniel Defoe, first performed at the Opéra-Comique on November 23, 1867) or *Fantasio* (*opéra-comique* in three acts, libretto by P. de Musset, first performed at the Opéra-Comique on January 18, 1872). *Vert-Vert* (*opéra-comique* in three acts, libretto by Henri Meillhac and Charles Etienne Louis Nuitter, first performed at the Opéra-Comique on March 10, 1869) was played 58 times before being dropped from the schedule. *Les Contes d'Hoffmann* (*opéra fantastique* in a prologue and three acts, libretto by Jules Barbier and Michel Carré, first performed posthumously, revised by Léon Carvalho, at the Opéra-Comique on February 10, 1881), whose fantasy conceals a certain tragic expressiveness, achieved a stylistic balance that finally hit the mark. The work quickly reached its 100th performance, then went on to become one of the most-performed French operas in the world.

REYER, ERNEST [LOUIS ÉTIENNE ERNEST REY]
(BORN MARSEILLES, DECEMBER 1, 1823;
DIED LE LAVANDOU, JANUARY 15, 1909)

Reyer first achieved success in 1850 with *Le Sélam*, an "oriental symphony" to a text by Théophile Gautier, which identified him as a follower of Félicien David and an exponent of musical exoticism. This was confirmed with *Sacountalâ* (ballet, performed at the Opéra in 1858) and with *La Statue* (*opéra-comique* in three acts, libretto by Michel Carré and Jules Barbier after *The Thousand and One Nights*, first performed at the Théâtre-Lyrique on April 11, 1861). The influences of Gluck, Weber, Berlioz, and Wagner are clearer in subsequent works. *Sigurd* (*opéra* in three acts, libretto by Camille Du Locle and Alfred Blau, first performed in Brussels on January 7, 1884, in Lyons on January 15, 1885, and at the Opéra on June 12, 1885), to a libretto inspired by Norse sagas, was not very Wagnerian at all in its style, despite what one might have expected given the subject. Mnemonic motifs and arioso replace aria, but this cannot conceal a certain harmonic monotony, a scarcity of counterpoint, and sometimes heavy orchestration. Yet the work was very popular: it offered music of great spontaneity that was easy for audiences to follow despite its more original elements. *Salammbô* (*opéra* in five acts, libretto by Camille Du Locle after Gustave Flaubert, first performed in Brussels on February 10, 1890, in Rouen on November 23, 1890, and at the Opéra on May 16, 1892) is related to *drame lyrique* in terms of its continuous succession of musical numbers, but falls far short of the melodic expression and orchestral writing of the French masters of the day. Reyer would be important as a critic in various publications, especially in the *Journal des débats* from 1866 to 1898. He was elected to the Institut de France in 1876.

ROSSINI, GIOACCHINO (BORN PESARO, FEBRUARY 29, 1792;
DIED PASSY, NOVEMBER 13, 1868)

After a dazzling career that made him Italy's most famous composer, after having reformed Italian opera seria during his years in Naples, and after traveling in Europe, Rossini moved to Paris in 1824, first serving as the director of the Théâtre-Italien. For the coronation of Charles X, he composed *Il Viaggio a Reims* (*dramma giocoso* in one act, libretto by Luigi Balocchi, first performed as a *cantate scénique* at the Théâtre-Italien on June 19, 1825). The popularity of Rossini's Italian music became nearly frenzied toward the end of the 1810s, and its influence on French operatic music was among the most important of the nineteenth century. He then turned to *grand opéra.* He began by translating and adapting earlier works: *Maometto secondo* (1820) became *Le Siège de Corinthe* (*tragédie lyrique* in three acts, libretto by Alexandre Soumet and Luigi Balocchi, first performed at the Opéra on October 9, 1826), and *Mosè in Egitto* (1818) became *Moïse* (*opéra* in four acts, libretto by Luigi Balocchi and Etienne de Jouy, first performed at the Opéra on March 26, 1827). He ended his career as a composer with *Guillaume Tell* (*opéra* in four acts, libretto by Victor Etienne Jouy and Hippolyte Bis after Schiller, first performed at the Opéra on August 3, 1829), which was one of the first true *grands opéras;* its second act would be acknowledged as a masterpiece by many French composers.

SAINT-SAËNS, CAMILLE (BORN PARIS, OCTOBER 9, 1835;
DIED ALGIERS, DECEMBER 16, 1921)

The amazingly precocious Saint-Saëns made his solo piano debut at the Salle Pleyel at the age of ten. He enrolled in the Conservatoire in 1848, but, despite having been a brilliant student, did not win first prize in the Prix de

Rome competition. He was an extremely gifted organist and pianist, and enjoyed a successful career in instrumental music both as composer and as performer. He taught for a while at the Ecole Niedermeyer and was involved in the founding of the Société nationale de Musique in 1871. In his operas, Saint-Saëns was more interested in purity of form than in dramatic expression, and he was late to gain recognition. *La Princesse jaune* (*opéracomique* in one act, libretto by Louis Gallet, first performed at the Opéra-Comique on June 12, 1872) failed miserably. Saint-Saëns would succeed in this light genre with *Phyrné* (*opéra-comique* in two acts, libretto by Lucien Augé de Lassus, first performed at the Opéra-Comique on May 24, 1893). *Henry VIII* (*opéra* in four acts, libretto by Léonce Détroyat and Armand Silvestre, first performed at the Opéra on March 5, 1883), which fell into the category of historical *grand opéra*, gained success both at home and abroad. *Samson et Dalila* (*opéra* in three acts, libretto by Ferdinand Lemaire, first performed in Weimar on December 2, 1877, in Rouen on March 3, 1890, and in Paris, at the Théâtre-Lyrique de l'Eden on October 31, 1890) was not "officially" sanctioned by a performance at the Opéra until November 23, 1892. This work was slow to become entrenched at the Académie de musique; the writing is of high quality and is indebted more to oratorio and to the English and German traditions than to French opera. The work's history exemplifies the difficulty the French had in shaking off their own national models. Saint-Saëns was also a talented writer with an insatiably curious mind, and left a number of prose works, including collections of musical criticism that are of great interest; in these we can see how he began early on by admiring the music of Wagner, but without succumbing to idol worship. Other work mentioned: *Déjanire* (music for the four-act tragedy by Louis Gallet, first performed in the arena at Béziers on August 28, 1898; recast as a *tragédie lyrique* in four acts, libretto by Louis Gallet, first performed in Monte Carlo on March 14, 1911, and at the Opéra on November 22, 1911).

THOMAS, AMBROISE (BORN METZ, AUGUST 5, 1811;
DIED PARIS, FEBRUARY 12, 1896)

Thomas enrolled in the Conservatoire in 1828, and took first prizes in piano and in harmony; he then joined Jean-François Lesueur's composition class and won first prize in the 1832 Prix de Rome competition. Upon his return to Paris, he began his career in *opéra-comique* with *La Double Echelle* (*opéra-comique* in one act, libretto by François Antoine Eugène de

Planard, first performed at the Opéra-Comique on August 23, 1837). This enjoyed a good success, which was reaffirmed by the enormous popularity of *Caïd* (*opéra-comique* in two acts, libretto by Thomas Sauvage, first performed at the Opéra-Comique on January 3, 1849). Thomas conformed to the model of his day, as represented by Auber. Despite a few scenes that foreshadow the composer's future style, *Le Songe d'une nuit d'été* (*opéra-comique* in three acts, libretto by J. B. Rosier and Adolphe de Leuven, first performed at the Opéra-Comique on April 20, 1850) demonstrates how the French could retain only the amusing elements of a foreign source, in this case Shakespeare, who is in fact a character in this opera. Thomas's success gained him admission to the Institut de France in 1851, and to the Conservatoire in 1856, as professor of composition. Following the production of Gounod's *Faust* in 1859 and his own failure with *Le Roman d'Elvire* (*opéra-comique* in three acts, libretto by Alexandre Dumas *père* and Adolphe de Leuven, first performed at the Opéra-Comique on February 4, 1860), it was six years before Thomas produced another operatic work. Taking up Gounod's ideas and writing scenes of an intimate lyricism, Thomas—collaborating with the librettists of *Faust*—composed *Mignon* (*opéra-comique* in three acts, libretto by Jules Barbier and Michel Carré after Goethe, first performed at the Opéra-Comique on November 17, 1866), which achieved considerable popularity and reached its 1,000th performance on May 13, 1894. He broadened the framework and the tragic expressivity of *opéra lyrique*, a genre that he and Gounod helped to establish, with *Hamlet* (*opéra* in five acts, libretto by Jules Barbier and Michel Carré after Shakespeare, first performed at the Opéra on March 9, 1868).

VERDI, GIUSEPPE (BORN LE RONCOLE, ITALY, OCTOBER 9 OR 10, 1813; DIED MILAN, JANUARY 27, 1901)

Verdi's works were performed both in Italian, at the Théâtre-Italien, and in translation, at the Opéra and at the Théâtre-Lyrique. He very quickly rose to fame in France, and collaborated in adapting *I Lombardi* (1843) as the much-altered *Jérusalem* (*opéra* in four acts, libretto by Alphonse Royer and Gustave Vaëz, first performed at the Opéra on November 26, 1847), before writing any French works from scratch: *Les Vêpres siciliennes* (*grand opéra* in five acts, libretto by Eugène Scribe and Charles Duveyrier, first performed at the Opéra on June 13, 1855) and, later, *Don Carlos* (*grand opéra* in five acts, libretto by Joseph Méry and Camille Du Locle after Schiller, first performed at the Opéra on March 11, 1867). These works testify to the fascination that *grand opéra* could hold for European musicians in the nineteenth century. Yet we should note that Verdi's French works were failures in France, whereas his Italian works (sometimes in translation) enjoyed great success—not, however, to be compared with that of Rossini a few decades earlier, and not resulting in any defining influence on French composers.

# Notes

INTRODUCTION

1. Georges Duby and Guy Lardreau, *Dialogues* (Paris: Flammarion, 1980), p. 63.

2. Depending on the regime, it was known as the Académie impériale, the Académie royale, or the Académie nationale de musique, and also as the Opéra, the Théâtre de l'Opéra, the Grand Opéra, and so forth, but I shall simply call it the Académie de musique for purposes of this book. Capitalized names such as Opéra, Opéra-Comique, Théâtre-Lyrique, Théâtre-Italien, and Odéon are those of theaters and institutions, while the terms *opéra*, *grand opéra*, and *opéra-comique* refer to genres.

3. The year in parentheses following the title of a work is that of its first production in France.

4. "Théâtre impérial de l'Opéra," *Revue et Gazette musicale*, January 25, 1863, p. 25.

1. THE GENESIS OF AN OPERA

1. Charles Malherbe, "Du théâtre musical," in *Encyclopédie de la musique et dictionnaire du Conservatoire...*, ed. Albert Lavignac and Lionel de La Laurencie, pt. 2, vol. 5 (Paris: Delagrave, 1930), p. 3238.

2. Letter from Charles Gounod to Georges Bizet dated May 24, 1858, quoted in Mina Curtiss, *Bizet and His World* (New York: Knopf, 1958), p. 240.

3. Reynaldo Hahn, "La Musique au théâtre sous le Second Empire," *Conférencia*, February 15, 1925, p. 239.

4. See Albert Soubies, *Le Théâtre-Italien de 1800 à 1913* (Paris: Fischbacher, 1913). *Rigoletto* was first performed at the Théâtre-Italien in 1854, and *La Traviata* in 1856.

5. Verdi's *Louise Miller* (1853), a translation for the Opéra of *Luisa Miller*, is not the equivalent of these works, which were completely new or greatly

reworked for the French stage by Verdi himself. The composer in fact made known his dissatisfaction at the translation of *Luisa Miller.* See Mary Jane Phillips-Matz, *Verdi: A Biography* (New York: Oxford University Press, 1993), pp. 335–36.

6. Gustave Chadeuil, "Revue musicale," *Le Siècle,* January 20, 1863.

7. Paul Smith [Edouard Monnais], "Revue de l'année 1863," *Revue et Gazette musicale,* January 3, 1864, p. 1.

8. Hector Berlioz, "Feuilleton," *Journal des Débats,* October 8, 1863.

9. Dr. Aldo [A. Azevedo], *Dictionnaire musico-humoristique* (Paris: Gérard, 1870), p. 5.

10. Hahn, "La Musique au théâtre..." (cited n. 3 above), p. 246.

11. Undated letter from Bizet to Choudens, manuscript copy in the Bibliothèque-musée de l'Opéra.

12. Hector Berlioz, "Feuilleton," *Journal des Débats,* April 22, 1852.

13. Camille Bellaigue, *Gounod* (Paris: Félix Alcan, 1910), p. 79.

14. Nestor Roqueplan, "Théâtres," *Le Constitutionnel,* November 9, 1863.

15. The Théâtre-Italien, founded in 1801, closed for good in 1878, and the handful of performances of Italian opera given subsequently in other Paris theaters failed to give rise to any similar ongoing venture. See Nicole Wild, *Dictionnaire des théâtres parisiens au XIXᵉ siècle* (Paris: Aux Amateurs de Livres [Klincksieck], 1989), pp. 194–201.

16. Ibid., pp. 37–38.

17. Gustave du Taillys, "Revue musicale," *Revue de l'Empire,* October 10, 1863.

18. Gaston de Saint-Valry, "Revue dramatique," *Le Pays,* October 5, 1863.

19. Albert Soubies, *Histoire du Théâtre-Lyrique (1851–1870)* (Paris: Fischbacher, 1899), p. 26.

20. Prior to moving to the Place du Châtelet, the Théâtre-Lyrique occupied the former auditorium of the Théâtre-Historique at 72 boulevard du Temple, which was expropriated for reasons of city planning in June 1862. See Wild, *Dictionnaire des théâtres...* (cited n. 15 above), pp. 237–38. It closed for good in 1872.

21. Soubies, *Histoire du Théâtre-Lyrique,* pp. 37–38.

22. Ernest Reyer, *Notes de musique,* 2d ed. (Paris: Charpentier, 1875), p. 24.

23. Henri Maréchal, *Paris: Souvenirs d'un musicien* (Paris: Hachette, 1907), p. 2.

24. Ibid., p. 11.

25. Frédéric Soulié, *Deux séjours: Province et Paris* (Paris: Hippolyte Souverain, 1836), 2: 255, quoted in Nicole Wild, "Le Spectacle lyrique," in *La Musique en France à l'époque romantique (1830–1870)* (Paris: Flammarion, 1991), p. 44.

26. Maréchal, *Paris...,* pp. 13–14.

27. See Joël-Marie Fauquet, *Les Sociétés de musique de chambre à Paris de la Restauration à 1870* (Paris: Aux Amateurs de Livres, 1986); id., "Les Sociétés de musique de chambre," in *La Musique en France à l'époque romantique* (cited n. 25 above).

28. From *L'Exposé de la situation de l'Empire,* in "Nouvelles," *L'Entr'acte,* November 14, 1863.

29. "Corps législatif," *Le Moniteur universel,* April 19, 1863, p. 597. This matter was debated at the meeting held on Friday, April 24. See "Corps législatif. Extrait du compte rendu de la séance du vendredi 24 avril," *Journal des Débats,* April 25, 1863.

30. Decree of the minister of state, A. [Count Alexandre] Walewski, dated June 5, 1863 (Arch. nat., F/21/1121). Emphasis added.

31. Léon Carvalho's *cahier des charges.* Decree of A. Walewski dated November 10, 1862 (Bibliothèque-musée de l'Opéra, Archives Théâtre-Lyrique, pièce 3). Emphasis added.

32. Unpublished letter from Gounod to Jules Barbier, undated. Bibliothèque nationale, Dép. de la musique, N.L.a. 24, I.

33. See Odile Krakovitch, *Les Pièces de théâtre soumises à la censure (1800–1830)* (Paris: Archives nationales, 1982), and id., *Hugo censuré: La Liberté au théâtre au XIXe siècle* (Paris: Calmann-Lévy, 1985).

34. See Appendix 1, "The Sources of Bizet's *Les Pêcheurs de Perles.*"

35. Steven Huebner, *The Operas of Charles Gounod* (New York: Oxford University Press, 1990), p. 31.

36. See Wild, *Dictionnaire des théâtres*...(cited n. 15 above), pp. 239, 330.

37. "Opéra-Comique," *Le Ménestrel,* May 3, 1840.

38. J.-L. Heugel, "Causeries musicales: *L'Enfant prodigue,*" *Le Ménestrel,* December 15, 1850.

39. Georges Loiseau, "La Millième de *Mignon,*" *Le Figaro,* March 13, 1894.

40. Nicolo Isouard, *Aladin, ou La Lampe merveilleuse, opéra féerie en cinq actes.* Libretto by Etienne (Paris: Roullet, 1825).

41. "Académie royale de musique," *Le Ménestrel,* March 1, 1835.

42. Gustave Chadeuil, "Revue musicale," *Le Siècle,* March 22, 1859.

43. Gustave Chadeuil, "Revue musicale," *Le Siècle,* April 5, 1859.

44. Unpublished letter from Gounod to Jules Barbier, undated. Bibliothèque nationale, Dép. de la musique, N.L.a. 24, I (39).

45. Letter from Scribe to Auber dated September 4, 1843, in *Correspondance d'Eugène Scribe et de Daniel-François-Esprit Auber,* ed. Herbert Schneider (Liège: Mardaga, 1998).

46. Reyer, *Notes de musique* (cited n. 22 above), pp. 60–61.

47. Ibid., p. 285.

48. Quoted in G. Loiseau, "La Millième de *Mignon,*" *Le Figaro,* March 13, 1894.

49. L. Blondeau, "Comment se font les opéras en Italie," *La France musicale,* July 18, 1841, p. 254.

50. *Les Troyens* was performed in 1863 at the Théâtre-Lyrique in a version that omitted the first part, "La Prise de Troie," which was summarized in the form of a prologue.

51. Act 4, sc. 2, of the complete version of *Les Troyens.* The "Chasse et Orage" was cut after the 1863 premiere.

52. Act 4, sc. 2, nos. 30 and 31, of the complete version of *Les Troyens*.

53. Act 4, sc. 2, no. 34, of the complete version of *Les Troyens*.

54. Act 5, no. 40, of the complete version of *Les Troyens*.

55. The French texts of all these quotations come from Hugh Macdonald's excellent critical edition of *Les Troyens*, in Hector Berlioz, *Les Troyens*, new edition of the complete works (Kassel: Bärenreiter, 1970).

56. Alfred Bruneau, *A l'ombre d'un grand coeur: Souvenirs d'une collaboration* (Paris, 1931; reprinted Geneva: Slatkine, 1980), pp. 89–90.

57. Camille Saint-Saëns, *Harmonie et mélodie* (Paris: Calmann-Lévy, 1885), p. 176. This quotation comes from an article first published in September 1879.

58. Letter from Camille Saint-Saëns to Gabriel Fauré dated July 1, 1917, in Saint-Saëns and Fauré, *Correspondance (1862–1920)*, ed. Jean-Michel Nectoux (Paris: Société française de musicologie, 1994), p. 125.

59. Edmond Galabert, Preface, in *Georges Bizet: Lettres à un ami (1865–1872)* (Paris: Calmann-Lévy, 1909), p. 42.

60. Interview with Galli-Marié, quoted in G. Loiseau, "La Millième de *Mignon*," *Le Figaro*, May 13, 1894. The journalist tells us that, according to Ritt (associate director along with Leuven), the first four lines of one melody were chosen and the last four lines of the other.

61. Letter from Scribe to Auber dated August 25, 1845, in *Correspondance* (cited n. 45 above).

62. Giacomo Meyerbeer, *Le Prophète* (Paris: Brandus, Troupenas [1849]).

63. See Belinda Cannone, *La Réception des opéras de Mozart dans la presse parisienne (1793–1829)* (Paris: Klincksieck, 1991), pp. 62–63.

64. "Chronique musicale," *Journal des Débats*, December 21, 1824.

65. A. S., "Théâtre royal italien," *Revue musicale*, ed. F.-J. Fétis, 3, no. 5 (1829): 403.

66. "Chronique musicale," *Le Corsaire*, December 19, 1824.

67. *Le Chasseur noir. Freischütz: Opéra romantique en trois actes* (Paris: M. Schlesinger [1824]), Coll. des chefs-d'oeuvre dramatiques modernes des Ecoles italienne, française et allemande. "The work has been published as we heard it in Germany," the same journalist noted ("Chronique musicale," *Le Corsaire*, December 19, 1824).

68. *Robin des bois, ou les Trois Balles: Opéra en trois actes, imité de Der Freischütz* (Paris: Chez Castil-Blaze [1824]).

69. William Shakespeare, *Théâtre complet*, trans. François-Victor Hugo (1859; reprint in 3 vols., Paris: Garnier, 1961–64). *Oeuvres complètes de Shakespeare*, trans. Félicien Letourneur, ed. François Guizot and A. P. 13 vols. (Paris: Chez Ladvocat, 1821).

70. B. de Grimm, "Académie royale de musique," *La France musicale*, June 13, 1841, p. 209.

71. Richard Wagner, "Le Freischütz," *Revue et Gazette musicale*, pt. 1, May 23, 1841; pt. 2, May 30, 1841.

72. Camille Saint-Saëns, July 1876 article for the revival of *Der Freischütz* on July 3, 1876, at the Palais Garnier, reprinted in *Harmonie et mélodie* (cited n. 57 above), pp. 107–13.

73. Soubies, *Histoire du Théâtre-Lyrique* (cited n. 19 above), p. 26. The piano-vocal score in question is *Orphée: Opéra en quatre actes, représenté au Théâtre-Lyrique,* "seule édition conforme à la représentation," réduction au piano par Théodore Ritter, 131 pp. (Paris: Léon Escudier, [1859]).

74. Franz Liszt, "De la situation des artistes et de leur condition dans la société," a series of six articles published in *La Gazette musicale* in 1835, reprinted in *Pages romantiques,* ed. Jean Chantavoine (1912; reprint, Plan de La Tour: Editions d'aujourd'hui, 1985), p. 47.

75. Théophile Gautier, article dated July 5, 1843, reprinted in *Histoire de l'art dramatique en France depuis vingt-cinq ans,* vol. 3 (Paris: Hetzel, 1859), p. 72.

76. Théophile Gautier, article dated November 7, 1843, in ibid., p. 125.

77. F.-J. Fétis, "Nouvelles de Paris: Concert historique de la musique du XVI$^e$ siècle, donné par M. Fétis," *Revue musicale,* ed. F.-J. Fétis, December 22, 1832, p. 372.

78. See Ulrich Drüner, "La Version du *Tannhäuser* de Richard Wagner...," in *Le Théâtre lyrique en France au XIX$^e$ siècle,* ed. P. Prévost (Metz: Editions Serpenoise, 1995), pp. 163 ff.

79. One might venture an exaggerated portrait: the social-climbing bourgeois Wagner who by adapting to its conventions had sought instant success on the stage of the most prestigious theater (the Académie de musique) in the world's most prominent capital (Paris) later became Wagner the aristocratic prophet, who constructed for the future an ideal work beyond the scope of any traditional genre.

### 2. PERFORMANCE

1. Alfred Bruneau, *A l'ombre d'un grand coeur: Souvenirs d'une collaboration* (Paris, 1931; reprint, Geneva: Slatkine, 1980), pp. 28–29.

2. Unpublished letter from Gounod to Jules Barbier dated September 11, 1861. Bibliothèque nationale, Dép. de la musique, N.L.a. 24, I (32).

3. Letter from Scribe to Auber dated November 2, 1847, in *Correspondance d'Eugène Scribe et de Daniel-François-Esprit Auber,* ed. Herbert Schneider (Liège: Mardaga, 1998).

4. See Hector Berlioz, "Feuilleton," *Journal des Débats,* October 8, 1863.

5. Jules Ruelle, "France," *Guide musical,* October 1, 1863, p. 4.

6. Marie Escudier, "Théâtre Lyrique Impérial," *La France musicale,* October 4, 1863.

7. "Actualités," *La France musicale,* October 18, 1863, p. 330. In addition to these three, the first cast of *Les Pêcheurs de perles* also included M. Guyot (Nourabad, bass).

8. Frédéric Soulié, *Deux séjours: Province et Paris* (Paris: Hippolyte Souverain, 1836), 2: 250, quoted in Nicole Wild, "Le Spectacle lyrique," in *La Musique en France à l'époque romantique (1830–1870)* (Paris: Flammarion, 1991), p. 26.

9. Johannès Weber, "Critique musicale," *Le Temps*, October 6, 1863.

10. Emmanuel Chabrier, "Chronique musicale," *Le Parisien*, October 2, 1863.

11. Nestor Roqueplan, "Théâtres," *Le Constitutionnel*, October 5, 1863.

12. Littré's dictionary defines *paletot* as a "garment of a soft, warm fabric that men wear either by itself or, more commonly, over another garment." Antoine Elwart speaks of the "Conservatoire subscriber's *paletot*" (*Histoire des concerts populaires de musique classique*, 3d ed. [Paris: Castel, 1864], p. 19).

13. Albert Wolff, "Chronique théâtrale," *Le Journal amusant*, October 10, 1863.

14. G. Bertrand, "Semaine théâtrale," *Le Ménestrel*, October 4, 1863. Patrick Barbier writes the opposite in *Opera in Paris, 1800–1850: A Lively History*, trans. Robert Luoma (Portland, Oreg.: Amadeus Press, 1995), p. 123. Presumably, the custom of calling for authors changed during the period 1840 to 1850.

15. Emile Cardon, "Chronique théâtrale," *Le Monde artiste*, October 3, 1863.

16. The Jockey Club, founded in 1834, brought together members of the Parisian aristocracy and the *grande bourgeoisie*.

17. Paul Smith [Edouard Monnais], "Théâtre-impérial de l'Opéra: Seconde représentation de *Tannhäuser*," *Revue et Gazette musicale*, March 24, 1861, p. 89.

18. "Actualités," *La France musicale*, March 31, 1861, p. 102.

19. Letter from Count Alexandre Walewski to Richard Wagner dated March 8, 1861, quoted in Georges Servières, *Tannhäuser à l'Opéra en 1861* (Paris: Fischbacher, 1895), p. 40.

20. Ernest Reyer, *Quarante ans de musique*, ed. Emile Henriot (Paris: Calmann-Lévy, [1909]), p. 262.

21. J. Lovy, "Semaine théâtrale," *Le Ménestrel*, December 28, 1856.

22. August Vitu, article in *Le Figaro*, May 16, 1889, quoted in Patrick Gillis, "Genèse d'*Esclarmonde*," *L'Avant-scène opéra: Esclarmonde, Grisélidis*, no. 148 (September–October 1992): 27. The Eiffel Tower was a highlight of the 1889 Exposition.

23. Franz Liszt, "De la situation des artistes et de leur condition dans la société," in *Pages romantiques*, ed. Jean Chantavoine (1912; reprint, Plan de La Tour: Editions d'aujourd'hui, 1985), p. 46.

24. Ibid., p. 48.

25. Marietta Alboni (1826–1894), a genuine Rossini contralto, whose voice covered the whole range from low G to high C, made her debut at the Théâtre-Italien in Paris on December 2, 1847.

26. Théophile Gautier, article dated January 15, 1849, reprinted in *Histoire de l'art dramatique en France depuis vingt-cinq ans,* vol. 6 (Paris: Hetzel, 1859), p. 42.

27. Théophile Gautier, article dated December 27, 1847, ibid., vol. 5 (1859), p. 208.

28. Théophile Gautier, article dated January 29, 1849, ibid., vol. 6 (1859), p. 46. The writer had just heard *L'Italiana in Algeri.*

29. Théophile Gautier, article dated December 27, 1847, ibid., vol. 5 (1859), p. 207.

30. Stendhal in the *Journal de Paris,* September 13, 1824, on a performance at the Théâtre-Italien of Rossini's *La Donna del lago.*

31. Hector Berlioz, column in *Le Journal des Débats,* January 10, 1841, reprinted in *Les Soirées de l'orchestre* (1852), republished in *Oeuvres littéraires,* ed. Léon Guichard (Paris: Gründ, 1968–71).

32. See Rodolfo Celletti, *Storia del belcanto* (Fiesole: Discanto, 1983), trans. Frederick Fuller as *A History of Bel Canto* (New York: Oxford University Press, 1991).

33. The Opéra occupied the auditorium at 10 rue Le Peletier from August 16, 1821, to the night of October 28–29, 1873, when it was destroyed by fire. See Nicole Wild, *Dictionnaire des théâtres parisiens au XIX$^e$ siècle* (Paris: Aux Amateurs de Livres [Klincksieck], 1989), p. 227.

34. Théophile Gautier, article dated January 4, 1847, reprinted in *Histoire de l'art dramatique en France...,* vol. 5 (1859), p. 6.

35. Hector Berlioz, article in *Le Journal des Débats,* May 17, 1837, reprinted in id., *Cauchemars et passions,* ed. Gérard Condé (Paris: J. C. Lattès, 1981), p. 260.

36. An allusion to an epigram attributed to Napoleon I: "Tout soldat français porte dans sa giberne la bâton de maréchal de France."

37. "Le Bilan lyrique de 1858," *Le Ménestrel,* January 9, 1859, p. 42.

38. *Le Ménestrel,* July 3, 1859, p. 243.

39. J. Lovy, "Semaine théâtrale," *Le Ménestrel,* April 5, 1863, p. 141.

40. Jean-Jacques Rousseau had complained about this French trait as early as the 1760s: "No one goes to a performance to enjoy the performance, but rather to see the assembled company, to be seen among it and to pick up something to chatter about after the play; and no one gives any thought to what he is seeing except in order to figure out what to say about it" (*La Nouvelle Eloïse,* pt. 2, letter 16).

41. Hector Berlioz, "Feuilleton," *Journal des Débats,* April 22, 1851. This was a general comment in a column on the first performance of Gounod's *Sapho* at the Opéra.

42. P. A. Fiorentino, "Théâtres," *La France,* November 9, 1863.

43. Reynaldo Hahn, "La Musique au théâtre sous le Second Empire," *Conférencia,* February 15, 1925, p. 240.

44. Barbier, *Opera in Paris,* p. 119–20.

45. Théophile Gautier, article dated October 9, 1841, reprinted in *Histoire de l'art dramatique en France...,* vol. 2 (1858), p. 163.

46. *Grand Dictionnaire universel du XIX$^e$ siècle,* ed. Pierre Larousse (15 vols., Paris: Administration du Grand Dictionnaire universel, 1866–76; vol. 16 [first supplement], 1877, vol. 17 [second supplement], [1879]), s.v. "Claque."

47. Ibid.

48. Honoré de Balzac, *Les Illusions perdues* (1837–43; Paris: Gallimard, 1976), 2: 387, 389.

49. See Barbier, *Opera in Paris,* pp. 126–28; Arthur Pougin, *Dictionnaire historique et pittoresque du théâtre et des arts qui s'y rattachent* (Paris: Firmin-Didot, 1885), s.v. "Claque"; John Rosselli, in *The New Grove Dictionary of Opera,* ed. Stanley Sadie (London: Macmillan, 1992), s.v. "Claque."

50. Letter from Bizet to Gallet quoted in Mina Curtiss, *Bizet and His World* (New York: Knopf, 1958), p. 325.

51. "Académie royale de musique," *Gazette musicale de Paris,* March 8, 1835, p. 82. Note also this remark concerning Auber's *L'Enfant prodigue:* "The entire show, from beginning to end, is of unbelievable magnificence, and one's eyes are so busy from start to finish that, on a first evening, one's ears have genuine trouble in playing their part in the enjoyment" (Georges Bousquet, "Chronique musicale," *L'Illustration,* December 13, 1850, p. 373).

52. "Semaine théâtrale," *Le Ménestrel,* April 29, 1877, p. 170.

53. Letter from Zola to Bruneau dated July 22, 1896, quoted in Bruneau, *A l'ombre d'un grand coeur* (cited n. 1 above), p. 89.

54. Marie-Antoinette Allévy, *La Mise en scène en France, dans la première moitié du dix-neuvième siècle* (Paris: Droz, 1938), p. 7. This section was largely inspired by Allévy's book, which remains outstanding today.

55. *Mélodrame* here refers to the theatrical genre caricaturally opposing good and evil in the context of *les sentiments forts,* i.e., hatred, love, blood ties, and so on (see also chapter 9, n. 15, below).

56. Allévy, *La Mise en scène en France,* p. 55.

57. Ibid., p. 82.

58. Quoted in G. Loiseau, "La Millième de *Mignon,*" *Le Figaro,* March 13, 1894. It should be noted that scenic realism and accuracy had their opponents, who viewed them as a constraint on imagination.

59. Allévy, *La Mise en scène en France...,* pp. 108–9.

60. G[eorges] B[ousquet], "Chronique musicale," *L'Illustration,* December 4, 1847, p. 218.

61. See Nicole Wild, *Décors et costumes du XIX$^e$ siècle,* vol. 1: *Opéra de Paris,* Bibliothèque-Musée de l'Opéra, Catalogues de la Bibliothèque de l'Opéra, 3 (Paris: Bibliothèque nationale, Dép. de la musique, 1987), p. 102.

62. Allévy, *La Mise en scène en France...,* pp. 101–2.

63. Pougin, *Dictionnaire historique et pittoresque du théâtre et des arts* (cited n. 49 above), s.v. "Mise en scène."

64. *Collection de mises en scène de grands opéras et d'opéras rédigés et publiés par L. Palianti* (Paris).

65. In addition to vol. 1 of Nicole Wild's *Décors et costumes du XIX$^e$ siècle* (cited n. 61 above), see also vol. 2: *Théâtres et décorateurs* (Paris: Bibliothèque

nationale, 1993), and id., *Les Arts du spectacle en France: Affiches illustrées (1850–1950). Catalogue* (Paris: Bibliothèque nationale, 1976). See, too, Catherine Join-Dieterle, *Les Décors de scène de l'Opéra de Paris à l'époque romantique* (Paris: Picard, 1988), and H. Robert Cohen and Marie-Odile Gigou, *Cent ans de mise en scène lyrique en France* (One hundred years of operatic staging in France) *(env. 1830–1930),* Catalogue descriptif des livrets de mise en scène, des libretti annotés et des partitions annotées dans la Bibliothèque de l'Association de la régie théâtrale (Paris) (New York: Pendragon Press, 1986).

66. See H. Robert Cohen, *Les Gravures musicales dans l'illustration, 1843–1899,* 3 vols. (Québec: Presses de l'Université Laval, 1982–83).

67. Jules Ruelle, "Chronique musicale," *Le Messager des théâtres et des arts,* October 4, 1863.

68. See Wild, *Décors et costumes du XIXᵉ siècle,* 1: 251.

69. See Join-Dieterle, *Les Décors de scène de l'Opéra de Paris à l'époque romantique,* pp. 13 and 137.

70. A. de Rovray [P. A. Fiorentino], "Revue musicale," *Le Moniteur universel,* October 7, 1863.

71. Claude Debussy, article in *Gil Blas,* May 19, 1903, in id., *Monsieur Croche, antidilettante,* reprinted in *Monsieur Croche et autres écrits,* ed. François Lesure (Paris: Gallimard, 1987), p. 174.

72. See Alfred Loewenberg, *Annals of Opera, 1597–1940* (1943; rev. 3d ed., Totowa, N.J.: Rowman & Littlefield, 1978).

73. Adrien Barbusse, "Les Premières," *Le Siècle,* April 21, 1889, p. 3.

74. Arthur Pougin, "Semaine théâtrale," *Le Ménestrel,* April 28, 1889, p. 131.

75. Arthur Pougin, "Semaine théâtrale," *Le Ménestrel,* April 21, 1889, p. 123.

76. Victor Roger, "Chronique musicale," *La France,* April 22, 1889, p. 2.

77. See Hervé Lacombe, "La Réception de l'oeuvre dramatique de Bizet en Italie: Un Exemple du rapport culturel France/Italie," *Mélanges de l'Ecole française de Rome: Italie-Méditerranée* 1 (1996): 171–201.

78. A. Jullien, "Revue musicale," *Le Moniteur universel,* May 6, 1889.

79. Letter from Lalo to Blau dated September 22, 1886, in Edouard Lalo, *Correspondance,* ed. Joël-Marie Fauquet (Paris: Aux Amateurs de Livres, 1989), pp. 273–74. *Les Pêcheurs de perles* was performed at Berlin (in German) only in June 1893, but it had been put on at Coburg (also in German) in November 1886.

80. See A. Jullien, "Revue musicale," *Le Moniteur universel,* May 8, 1893.

81. See John W. Klein, "The Centenary of Bizet's *The Pearl Fishers,*" *Music Review* 26, no. 4 (November 1964): 302, 305.

## 3. RECEPTION

1. *Le Sport,* founded in 1854 by Eugène Chapus (1802–1877), covered horse racing in particular, but unlike other French papers, it also concerned

itself with other sports, in response to new tastes acquired from the English. Chapus also published a paper entitled *Paris et Chantilly: Bulletin des arts, de la littérature et des chasses.* (Chantilly was and is the site of a major race course.) Such publications were aimed principally at the higher classes, as indicated by *Le Sport's* first subtitle, *Journal des gens du monde.* In that sense, they have no equivalent today. But *Le Sport's* subtitle evolved, and its coverage of pigeon shooting, fencing, boating, swimming, fishing, dancing, and billiards, among other amusements, reflected a desire to reach a wider readership.

2. See Belinda Cannone, "La Presse parisienne entre 1793 et 1829," in id., *La Réception des opéras de Mozart dans la presse parisienne (1793–1829)* (Paris: Klincksieck, 1991), pp. 39–43; and Patrick Barbier, *Opera in Paris, 1800–1850: A Lively History,* trans. Robert Luoma (Portland, Oreg.: Amadeus Press, 1995), pp. 205 ff.

3. See H. Robert Cohen, "La Presse française du XIX^e siècle et l'histoire de la musique," and J.-M. Bailbé, "La Critique musicale au *Journal des Débats,*" in *La Musique en France à l'époque romantique (1830–1870)* (Paris: Flammarion, 1991); Christian Goubault, *La Critique musicale dans la presse française de 1870 à 1914* (Paris: Slatkine, 1984).

4. F.-J. Fétis, "Le Prophète," *Revue et Gazette musicale,* April 22, 1849, p. 121.

5. Ch. Desolme, "Théâtre-Lyrique impérial," *L'Europe artiste* (weekly), October 11, 1863.

6. "Mouvement théâtral," *Le Théâtre,* August 30, 1863.

7. H. L. D'Aubel, "Théâtre-Lyrique impérial," *L'Europe artiste* (weekly), October 11, 1863.

8. Letter from Hérold to Charles-Martin Charles ("Chaulieu"), dated Naples, January 26, 1815, quoted in "Hérold," *Le Pianiste,* May 5, 1835.

9. Geoffroy taught rhetoric and was editor in chief of *L'Année littéraire* before becoming a columnist for the *Journal de l'Empire* in 1800.

10. Cannone, *Réception des opéras de Mozart,* p. 43.

11. Jules Ruelle, "France," *Guide musical,* October 15, 1863, p. 4.

12. Benoît Jouvin, "Théâtres," *Le Figaro,* October 8, 1863.

13. Henri Vignaud, "Revue musicale," *Le Mémorial diplomatique,* October 11, 1863.

14. S. Saint-Etienne, "Chronique musicale," *L'Illustrateur des dames...,* October 10, 1863.

15. Ralph [Léon Escudier], "Théâtre-Lyrique," *L'Art musical,* November 12, 1863.

16. Paul Scudo, article in *La Revue indépendante* (ca. 1850), quoted in id., "Courrier musical," *L'Art musical,* November 12, 1863.

17. E. Mathieu de Monter, "Musical Criticism," *La Revue et Gazette musicale,* September 13, 1868. See also F.-J. Fétis, "Musical Genius and Criticism," ibid., February 16, 1862.

18. G. du Taillys, "Revue musicale," *Revue de l'Empire,* October 10, 1863.

19. Hector Berlioz, column in *Le Rénovateur* of July 27, 1834.

20. Arthur Pougin, "Premières représentations," *Le Théâtre,* October 4, 1863.

21. A. de Rovray [P. A. Fiorentino], "Revue musicale," *Le Moniteur universel*, October 7, 1863.

22. Nestor Roqueplan, "Théâtres," *Le Constitutionnel*, November 9, 1863.

23. P. Lacome, "The Language of Criticism," *L'Art musical*, June 2, 1870.

24. Johannès Weber, "Critique musicale," *Le Temps*, January 23, 1893.

25. Benoît Jouvin, "Théâtres," *Le Figaro*, November 8, 1863.

26. G. Bertrand, "Semaine théâtrale," *Le Ménestrel*, October 4, 1863.

27. Dr. Aldo [A. Azevedo], *Dictionnaire musico-humoristique* (Paris: Gérard, 1870), s.vv. "Bruit" and "Cacophanie."

28. Marie Escudier, "Théâtre-Lyrique impérial," *La France musicale*, October 4, 1863.

29. Sigismund Neukomm, "Théâtre-Lyrique impérial," *L'Art musical*, October 8, 1863.

30. Richard Wagner, *Quatre poèmes d'opéras traduits en prose française, précédés d'une lettre sur la musique* (Paris: Bourdillat, 1861).

31. Richard Wagner, "Lettre sur la musique," in ibid., p. lxiv, reprinted in *Oeuvres en prose de Richard Wagner*, trans. J.-G. Prod'homme and F. Caillé (Paris: Delagrave, 1910; reprint, Editions d'aujourd'hui, 1976), 6: 240. In English, see *Richard Wagner's Prose Works*, trans. William Ashton Ellis (1897; reprint, New York: Broude Brothers, 1966).

32. See "Oeuvres wagnériennes au programme des concerts parisiens, 1841–1914," in Martine Kahane and Nicole Wild, *Wagner et la France* (Paris: Bibliothèque nationale, Herscher, 1983), p. 158. In 1861, Wagner's music was heard at the Salle Herz on January 3 and February 3 and 17, and at the Casino Cadet on March 19, 21, and 23.

33. Baudelaire eventually published an article about Wagner in the *Revue européene* of April 1, 1861. See Martin Gregor-Dellin, *Richard Wagner* (Paris: Fayard, 1981), pp. 448–64. Originally published as *Richard Wagner: Sein Leben, sein Werk, sein Jahrhundert* (Munich: R. Piper, 1980); also translated into English by J. Maxwell Brownjohn under the title *Richard Wagner: His Life, His Work, His Century* (London: Collins, 1983). And see also Léon Guichard, *La Musique et les lettres en France au temps du wagnérisme* (Paris: Presses universitaires de France, 1963).

34. Champfleury, *Richard Wagner* (Paris: Bourdillat, 1860; reprinted, with the addition of a chapter entitled "Après la bataille," in the series Grandes figures d'hier et d'aujourd'hui [Paris: Poulet-Malassis, 1861]). In fact, this simply described the author's impressions during the first concert performances of excerpts from Wagner's works in Paris, but it used imagery that effectively described the composer's art and its evocative power.

35. See, e.g., Franz Liszt, *Artiste et société*, edited from the French texts by R. Stricker (Paris: Flammarion, 1995), article on *Tannhäuser* in the *Journal des Débats*, May 18, 1848. Liszt conducted *Tannhäuser* at Weimar in 1849.

36. Hector Berlioz, "Richard Wagner's Concerts: The Music of the Future," *Journal des débats*, February 9, 1860.

37. See Gregor-Dellin, *Richard Wagner*, p. 852 n. 5.

38. "Nachrichten," *Berliner musikalische Zeitung,* June 12, 1847.

39. Ruelle, "France," *Guide musical,* October 15, 1863.

40. Ernest Reyer, "Revue musicale," *Journal des Débats,* January 22, 1893.

41. Victorin Joncières, "Revue musicale," *La Liberté,* January 23, 1893.

42. H. Vignaud, "Revue musicale," *Le Mémorial diplomatique,* October 11, 1863.

43. Alexis Azevedo, "Musique," *L'Opinion nationale,* October 6, 1863.

44. Benoît Jouvin, "Théâtres," *Le Figaro,* October 8, 1863.

45. Oscar Comettant, "Théâtre impérial de l'Opéra-Comique," *L'Art musical,* December 27, 1860, p. 29.

46. Camille Saint-Saëns, "Préface," in id., *Germanophilie* (Paris: Dorbon-Aîné, 1916), pp. 9–10.

47. Wagner sketched *Eine Kapitulation* in November 1870 during the Franco-Prussian War. Not finding a publisher for it, he suggested to Hans Richter that he set it to music in the form of a parody of Offenbach, which Richter felt unable to do. In 1873, it was included in vol. 9 of Wagner's collected works, and it also evidently appeared in French as *Richard Wagner et les Parisiens,* Traduction complète de la comédie de M. Richard Wagner contre Paris assiégé avec une préf. et un portrait de l'auteur (Paris, 1874?). An English translation by William Ashton Ellis is to be found in *Richard Wagner's Prose Works* (cited n. 31 above), 5: 3–33. See further Martin Gregor-Dellin, *Richard Wagner* (Paris: Fayard, 1981), pp. 623–24.

48. See Guichard, *La Musique et les lettres en France au temps du wagnérisme,* pp. 55–71.

49. Camille Saint-Saëns, "*L'Anneau du Niebelung* et les représentations de Bayreuth (août 1876)," article reprinted in id., *Harmonie et mélodie* (Paris: Calmann-Lévy, 1885), p. 41.

50. Letter from Guiraud to Mme Chabrier dated July 31, 1882. Bibliothèque nationale, Dép. de la musique, L.a. 12 (17).

51. Albert Lavignac, "Avertissement," in *Le Voyage à Bayreuth* (Paris: Delagrave, 1897).

52. Letter from Théophile Gautier *fils* dated January 17, 1886, quoted in *Catalogue vente Drouot (22–23 mai 1997)* (Paris), Thierry Bodin, expert.

53. Emile Zola, article in *Le Journal* of 1893, quoted in Alfred Bruneau, *A l'ombre d'un grand coeur: Souvenirs d'une collaboration* (Paris, 1931; reprinted Geneva: Slatkine, 1980), p. 64.

54. Camille Mauclair, *Servitude et grandeur littéraires: Souvenirs d'arts et de lettres de 1890 à 1900,* 4th ed. (Paris: Ollendorff, 1922), p. 222.

PART 2: DRAMA, POETRY, AND MUSIC

1. Catherine Kintzler, *Poétique de l'opéra français de Corneille à Rousseau* (Paris: Minerve, 1991), p. 13.

2. Ibid., p. 16. The poetic function is defined as the "ordering of facts, seen in a theoretical manner."

## 4. THE CONSTRUCTION OF A DRAMA

1. Richard Wagner, "Halévy et *La Reine de Chypre*," pt. 3, *Revue et Gazette musicale*, April 24, 1842, p. 179.

2. Arthur Pougin, "Boieldieu...," *L'Art musical*, April 7, 1870, p. 145.

3. Gottfried R. Marschall, "Werther," in *Dictionnaire des oeuvres de l'art vocal*, ed. M. Honegger and P. Prévost, 3 vols. (Paris: Bordas, 1991–92).

4. Jean-François Le Sueur, *La Caverne: Drame lyrique en trois actes* [music score] (Paris: Naderman, [1793?]; reprint with introduction by Jean Mongrédien (New York: Pendragon Press, 1985).

5. We should also mention the final scene of act 3 of Auber's *Marco Spada* (1857), and the entrance to the subterranean reaches in act 5, sc. 1, of Reyer's *La Statue* (1861). Boulevard theaters used a similar technique—for example, in *Mandrin* (1827) by Benjamin and A. Arago, which depicts the underground cavern of Mandrin with a forest above it.

6. See Klaus Wolfgang Niemöller, "Die kirchliche Szene," in *Die "couleur locale" in der Oper des 19. Jahrhunderts*, ed. Heinz Becker (Regensburg: Bosse, 1976).

7. See the persuasive article by P. Prévost, "De l'église des Missions étrangères à la cathédrale de *Faust:* Notes sur la pensée et le style de Charles Gounod," in *Le théâtre lyrique en France au XIXᵉ siècle*, ed. P. Prévost (Metz: Serpenoise, 1995), pp. 137–61.

8. "La Juive," *L'Artiste* 9, no. 1 (1835). Quoted in Karl Leich-Galland, *La Juive: Dossier de presse parisienne (1835)* (Saarbrücken: Musik-Edition Lucie Galland, 1987).

9. See François-René Chateaubriand, *Essai sur les révolutions; Génie du christianisme*, ed. Maurice Regard, Bibliothèque de la Pléiade, 272 (Paris: Gallimard, 1978); and *The Genius of Christianity: or, The Spirit and Beauty of the Christian Religion*, trans. and ed. Charles I. White (New York: H. Fertig, 1976).

10. Théophile Gautier, article dated April 23, 1849, reprinted in *Histoire de l'art dramatique en France depuis vingt-cinq ans*, vol. 6 (Paris: Hetzel, 1859), p. 82.

11. Jules Janin, *Un Hiver à Paris* (1842), 3d. ed (Paris: Veuve Louis Janet, 1846), p. 179.

12. Ibid., p. 181.

13. Ibid., p. 187.

14. Letter from Jacques Rouché addressed to the minister of fine arts, quoted in Patrick Gillis, "Genèse d'*Esclarmonde*," in *L'Avant-scène opéra: Esclarmonde, Grisélidis*, no. 148 (October 1992): 29.

15. H. Moreno, "Semaine théâtrale," *Le Ménestrel*, February 10, 1884, p. 83.

16. G. Condé, "Commentaire musical et littéraire," in *L'Avant-scène opéra: Manon*, no. 123 (September 1989): 89.

17. See Nicole Wild, "Eugène Lacoste et la création de *Henry VIII* à l'Opéra de Paris en 1883," in *Echos de France et d'Italie: Liber amicorum Yves Gérard*, ed. M.-C. Mussat, Jean Mongrédien, and J.-M. Nectoux (Paris: Buchet/Chastel, 1997), pp. 213–32.

18. See the already classic study by Jacques Scherer, *La Dramaturgie classique en France* (Paris: Nizet, 1986).

19. Wilhelm [Edouard Monnais], "Revue musicale," *Revue contemporaine,* September–October 1863.

20. Johannès Weber, "Critique musicale," *Le Temps,* October 6, 1863.

21. Nestor Roqueplan, "Théâtres," *Le Constitutionnel,* October 5, 1863.

22. G. de Saint-Valry, "Revue dramatique," *Le Pays,* October 5, 1863.

23. Charles-Augustin Sainte-Beuve, "De la littérature industrielle," *Revue des Deux Mondes,* September 1, 1839, pp. 675–91.

24. Patrick Berthier, *Le Théâtre au XIXᵉ siècle* (Paris: Presses universitaires de France, 1986), pp. 4 and 24.

25. J.-P. Ryngaert, *Introduction à l'analyse du théâtre* (Paris: Bordas, 1991), p. 7

26. Ferdinand Brunetière, *Les Epoques du théâtre français* (Paris: Hachette, 1892), p. 377, quoted in Berthier, *Le Théâtre au XIXᵉ siècle,* p. 81.

27. Emmanuel Mathieu de Monter, "Eugène Scribe: Ses oeuvres complètes," *Revue et Gazette musicale,* pt. 1, September 2, 1877, p. 275.

28. See Gilles de Van, "Le Grand Opéra entre tragédie lyrique et drame romantique," *Il saggiatore musicale* 3 (1996–92): 325–60; "Teatralità francese e senso scenico italiano nell'opera dell'Ottocento," in *La realizzazione scenica dello spettacolo verdiano,* Atti del Congresso internazionale di studi, ed. P. Petrobelli and F. Della Seta (Parma: Istituto nazionale di studi verdiani, 1996), pp. 167–86.

29. Lintilhac, *Histoire du théâtre,* quoted in Berthier, *Le Théâtre au XIXᵉ siècle,* p. 81. In the 1950s, Rey Morgan Longyear analyzed the stereotypes in *opéra-comique* librettos and studied Scribe's dramaturgy in his thesis "Daniel-François-Esprit Auber (1782–1871): A Chapter in French Opéra-Comique" (High Wycombe, Bucks: University Microfilms, 1957). See also Karin Pendle's thesis "Eugène Scribe and French Opera of the Nineteenth Century" (Ann Arbor, Mich.: University Microfilms International, 1970).

30. Octave Sachot, *L'Île de Ceylan et ses curiosités naturelles* (Paris: Victor Sarlit, 1863).

31. Gaspare Spontini, *La Vestale* (Paris: Roullet, 1807).

32. F. B., "Les Nouvelles de Paris," *Revue musicale,* September 22, 1834, p. 310.

33. See Pendle, "Eugène Scribe...," p. 91, and Steven Huebner, *The Operas of Charles Gounod* (New York: Oxford University Press, 1990), pp. 266–67.

34. De Marcoux, "Causerie théâtrale," *Les Coulisses du monde,* October 15, 1863.

35. See Hervé Lacombe, "The Writing of Exoticism in the Libretti of the Opéra-Comique, 1825–1862," *Cambridge Opera Journal* 11, no. 2 (1999): 135–58.

36. Scherer, *La Dramaturgie classique en France,* p. 128.

37. Ibid., pp. 130–31. At revivals of *Les Pêcheurs de perles,* there was an attempt to address the questions of Zurga's fate and of the religious conflict with

the death or suicide of the chief. The king would pay with his life for the betrayal of those nearest him and would die to expiate the sacrilege of Nadir and Léïla.

38. Jean-Marie Thomasseau, *Le Mélodrame* (Paris: Presses universitaires de France, 1984), p. 8. See also id., *Le Mélodrame sur les scènes parisiennes de Coelina (1800) à L'Auberge des Adrets (1823)* (Lille: Service de reproduction des thèses, Université de Lille III, 1974).

39. Quoted in Thomasseau, *Le Mélodrame*, p. 19.

40. Ibid., p. 22.

41. Ibid., p. 76.

42. Marie Escudier, "Théâtre-Lyrique impérial," *La France musicale*, October 4, 1863. We can get a sense of what an extraordinary cultural phenomenon and font of dramaturgic experimentation *mélodrame* was from the important book by Emilio Sala, *L'opera senza canto: Il mélo romantico e l'invenzione della colonna sonora* (Venice: Marsilio Editori, 1995).

43. Guzla: a one-stringed bowed instrument found in the Balkans. Prosper Mérimée [Joseph L'Estrange, 1803–1870] had used the word as the title of a collection of poetry, *La Guzla, ou Choix de poésies illyriques, recueillies dans la Dalmatie, la Bosnie, la Croatie et l'Herzégovine* (Paris: F.-G. Levrault, 1827).

44. It is worth reading what Steven Huebner has to say in *The Operas of Charles Gounod* (cited n. 33 above), especially in his chapter on melody. The matter must be considered also in the light of declamation, accents, and rhythms that are specific to French. In this connection, see Gottfried R. Marschall, *Massenet et la fixation de la forme mélodique française* (Saarbrücken: Musik-Edition Lucie Galland, 1988).

45. In the same way, Rossini borrowed the overture of *Elisabetta, Regina d'Inghilterra* (1815) for *Il Barbiere di Siviglia* (1816); this came in turn from *Aureliano in Palmira* (1813). Rossini also drew a portion of Don Basilio's calumny aria from *Sigismondo* (1814), among other borrowings.

46. L. Blondeau, "Comment se font les opéras en Italie," *La France musicale*, July 18, 1841, p. 253.

47. H. Moreno, "Semaine théâtrale," *Le Ménestrel*, January 27, 1884.

48. Indeed, *Les Contes d'Hoffmann* may be seen as being entirely about singing. The story is focused on a singer, Stella, and reflects the relationship between various vocal techniques and various characters. The preternatural vocalizations of a soulless creature yield to increasingly ample, lyrical singing. That is one of the difficult aspects of the score: the different incarnations of Woman, intended to be performed by a single singer, shift from a light coloratura soprano to a lyric soprano and finally to a dramatic soprano; since World War II, the roles have increasingly been assigned to different singers. Offenbach also toys with singing when Franz emits "Quacks" as he tries to sing beautifully.

49. Letter from Gounod to Barbier dated August 21, 1860. Bibliothèque nationale, Dép. de la musique, N.L.a. 24, I (27).

50. Louis Roger, "Théâtre-Lyrique impérial," *La Réforme musicale*, November 15, 1863.

51. H. Vignaud, "Revue musicale," *Le Mémorial diplomatique*, November 15, 1863.

52. Huebner, *Operas of Charles Gounod*, p. 267.

53. A. Durand, "Revue musicale," *L'Esprit public*, November 13, 1863, quoted in Frank Heidlberger, *Les Troyens à Carthage: Dossier de presse parisienne (1863)* (Heilbronn: Musik-Edition Lucie Galland, 1995).

54. Johannès Weber, "Critiques musicales," *Le Temps*, January 23, 1893.

55. V. Joncières, "Revue musicale," *La Liberté*, January 23, 1893.

56. E. Reyer, "Revue musicale," *Journal des Débats*, January 22, 1893.

57. M. Rémy, "Chronique de la semaine," *Le Guide musical*, January 22, 1893, p. 42.

58. H. Moreno, "Semaine théâtrale," *Le Ménestrel*, January 27, 1884, p. 67.

59. Raoul de Saint-Arroman, "Théâtre National de l'Opéra-Comique," *L'Art musical*, January 1884, p. 1.

## 5. SPACE AND TIME

1. Claude Lévi-Strauss, *The Raw and the Cooked*, trans. John Weightman and Doreen Weightman (1969; Chicago: University of Chicago Press, 1983), p. 15. Originally published as *Le Cru et le cuit* (Paris: Plon, 1964).

2. Ibid., pp. 15–16.

3. Carl Dahlhaus, *Richard Wagner's Music Dramas* (1971), trans. Mary Whittall (Cambridge: Cambridge University Press, 1979), p. 42.

4. Alfred de Musset, maiden speech to the Académie française, May 27, 1852, in *Oeuvres complètes*, ed. Philippe van Tieghem, vol. 1 (Paris: Seuil, 1963), p. 429.

5. In *Les Pêcheurs de perles*, see nos. 5 (chorus), 6 (chorus), 8 (Nadir), and 15 (Nadir-Léïla).

6. *Zémire et Azor* was revived at the Opéra-Comique in the nineteenth century. There were a number of performances in the 1820s and 1830s, then 40 between 1846 and 1848, and 27 in 1862.

7. See nos. 6 and 15 of *Les Pêcheurs de perles*.

8. See no. 8 of *Les Pêcheurs de perles*.

9. See Gottfried R. Marschall, *Massenet et la fixation de la forme mélodique française* (Saarbrücken: Musik-Edition Lucie Galland, 1988), pp. 46–47.

10. Charles Gounod, "Préface à *Georges Dandin*," in *Autobiographie de Charles Gounod et articles sur la routine en matière d'art*, ed. Georgina Weldon (London: Mrs. Weldon [1875]), p. 88.

11. Regarding all these problems, see Marschall's careful analysis in *Massenet et la fixation de la forme mélodique française*.

12. Antoine Reicha, *Art du compositeur dramatique, ou Cours complet de composition vocale . . . accompagné d'un volume de planches* (Paris: A. Farrenc, 1833), 1: 14.

13. During the first part of the opening number of act 1, the pearl fishers dance, drink, and sing to celebrate their arrival on the island and to drive out evil spirits. This is a collective song of rejoicing and superstition—realistic for a primitive tribe. It is unexpectedly interrupted by a middle section that is followed by a descriptive recitative ("Voilà notre domaine"). Concurrent utterance by the pearl fishers is not demanded by the situation; the men are indeed expressing a common thought, but there is nothing to explain why every member of the group should simultaneously merge into a choral mass.

14. Steven Huebner's *The Operas of Charles Gounod* (New York: Oxford University Press, 1990) provides a very good introduction to the subject of the musical form of arias and ensembles in French opera, specifically as it relates to the duet in the works of Meyerbeer, which Huebner cites as a model.

15. Dahlhaus, *Richard Wagner's Music Dramas*, trans. Whittal, p. 13.

16. Jean-Marie Thomasseau, *Le Mélodrame* (Paris: Presses universitaires de France, 1984), p. 32.

17. "It was because he was constantly moving from one genre to another that Scribe could be such an innovator in each sphere," Jean-Claude Yon stresses ("Eugène Scribe: La Fortune et la liberté" [thesis, Department of History, Université de Paris I, 1993], p. 14). Let us recall that the single exception to this assertion is *mélodrame*, which Scribe wrote only occasionally.

18. See David Charlton, *Grétry and the Growth of Opéra-Comique* (Cambridge: Cambridge University Press, 1986).

19. See Michael D. Grace, "Méhul's *Ariodante* and the Early Leitmotiv," in *A Festschrift for Albert Seay*, ed. id. (Colorado Springs: Colorado College, 1982), pp. 173–94.

20. See Anselm Gerhard, "Giacomo Meyerbeer et le thriller avant la lettre," in *Le Théâtre lyrique en France au XIX$^e$ siècle*, ed. P. Prévost (Metz: Serpenoise, 1995), pp. 107–35.

21. Franz Liszt, article in *Le Journal des Débats*, May 18, 1849, reprinted in id., *Artiste et société*, edited from the French texts by R. Stricker (Paris: Flammarion, 1995), p. 354.

22. See chs. 11 and 12 of Manfred Kelkel, *Naturalisme, vérisme et réalisme dans l'opéra* (Paris: Librairie J. Vrin, 1984), and the articles on Bruneau's operas in *Dictionnaire des oeuvres de l'art vocal*, ed. M. Honneger and P. Prévost, 3 vols. (Paris: Bordas, 1991–92).

23. See G. Condé, introductions to *L'Avant-scène opéra: Esclarmonde, Grisélidis*, no. 148 (September–October 1992): 36–37, and *L'Avant-scène opéra: Werther*, no. 61 (March 1984): 34–35.

### 6. POETIC EXPRESSION AND MUSICAL EXPRESSION

1. Act 4, sc. 2, no. 37, of the complete version of *Les Troyens*.

2. This version survives only in manuscript librettos in the Archives nationales. See Appendix 1.

3. See Hervé Lacombe, "Lakmé ou la fabrique de l'exotisme," *L'Avant-scène opéra: Lakmé*, no. 183 (March–April 1998): 68–73.

4. Castil-Blaze [F H. J. Blaze], *De l'opéra en France* (Paris: Janet & Cotelle, 1820), 1: 72.

5. Johannès Weber, "Critique musicale," *Le Temps*, October 6, 1863.

6. F.-J. Fétis, "Le Prophète," *Revue et Gazette musicale*, May 20, 1849, p. 154.

7. F. de L., "Revue musicale," *Revue des Deux Mondes*, March 15, 1875, p. 475.

8. Catherine Kintzler, *Poétique de l'opéra français de Corneille à Rousseau* (Paris: Minerve, 1991), p. 266.

9. Ibid., p. 267.

10. Charles Malherbe, "Auber, Meyerbeer," in *Encyclopédie de la musique et dictionnaire du Conservatoire...*, ed. Albert Lavignac and Lionel de La Laurencie, pt. 2, vol. 5 (Paris: Delagrave, 1930), p. 3235.

11. Ibid., p. 3236.

12. Ralph [Léon Escudier], "A propos de *La Muette de Portici*," *L'Art musical*, January 29, 1863, p. 67.

13. Paul Valéry, "Première leçon de cours de poétique," in *Variété* 5 (1944), reprinted in id., *Oeuvres*, ed. Jean Hytier, Bibliothèque de la Pléiade, 127 (Paris: Gallimard, 1957), 1: 1362. See also *Variety*, trans. Malcolm Cowley (New York: Harcourt, Brace, 1927).

14. Théophile Gautier quoted in *Grand Dictionnaire du XIX^e siècle*, ed. Pierre Larousse (15 vols., Paris: Administration du Grand Dictionnaire universel, 1866–76; vol. 16 [first supplement], 1877, vol. 17 [second supplement], [1879]), s.v. "Poésie."

15. Valéry, "Première leçon de cours de poétique."

16. Paul Valéry, "Poésie et pensée abstraite," *Variété* 5, reprinted in id., *Oeuvres*, ed. Jean Hytier, Bibliothèque de la Pléiade, 127 (Paris: Gallimard, 1957), 1: 1321.

17. Ibid., p. 1333.

18. Hector Berlioz, article in *Le Journal des Débats*, March 7, 1849, reprinted in id., *Cauchemars et passions*, ed. Gérard Condé (Paris: J. C. Lattès, 1981), p. 133.

19. Hector Berlioz, article in *La Revue et Gazette musicale*, January 1 and 8, 1837, reprinted in *Cauchemars et passions*, pp. 98–109.

20. Letter from Franz Liszt to Adolphe Pictet reprinted in *Pages romantiques*, ed. Jean Chantavoine (1912; reprint, Plan de La Tour: Editions d'aujourd'hui, 1985), p. 135.

21. Franz Liszt, article on *Tannhäuser*, *Journal des Débats*, May 18, 1849, reprinted in id., *Artiste et société*, edited from the French texts by R. Stricker (Paris: Flammarion, 1995), p. 333.

22. Ibid., p. 336.

23. F.-J. Fétis, "Le Pardon de Ploërmel," *Revue et Gazette musicale*, April 17, 1859, p. 126.

24. Franz Liszt, *F. Chopin* (Paris: M. Escudier, 1852), p. 2.

25. Charles Baudelaire, "Richard Wagner [et *Tannhäuser* à Paris]," *Revue européene*, April 1, 1861, reprinted in id., *Oeuvres complètes*, ed. Marcel A. Ruff (Paris: Seuil), p. 513.

26. All quotations from Berlioz on Beethoven's symphonies are from Hector Berlioz, "Etude critique des symphonies de Beethoven," in id., *A travers chants*, ed. Léon Guichard (Paris: Gründ, 1971), pp. 35–79.

27. Jean-Yves Tadié, *Introduction à la vie littéraire du XIX^e siècle* (Paris: Bordas, 1970), p. 111.

28. Hector Berlioz, article in *La Revue et Gazette musicale*, January 1 and 8, 1837, reprinted in *Cauchemars et passions*, pp. 98–109.

29. Ibid.

30. Massenet, *Esclarmonde*, stage direction from the libretto, reprinted in the orchestral score (Paris: G. Hartmann, n.d.), p. 13.

31. See Hector Berlioz, *Grand Traité d'instrumentation et d'orchestration moderne* (Paris: Schonenberger, 1843; expanded 1855); id., *Mémoires*, ed. Pierre Citron (Paris: Flammarion, 1991), p. 88. See also *The Memoirs of Hector Berlioz, Member of the French Institute: Including His Travels in Italy, Germany, Russia, and England, 1803–1865*, trans. and ed. David Cairns (rev. ed., New York: Norton, 1975), p. 73.

32. Georges Kastner, *Cours d'instrumentation considéré sous les rapports poétiques et philosophiques de l'art* (Textbook on orchestration viewed in the light of the poetic and philosophical relationships of that art) (Paris: Meissonier & Heugel, [1837]), pp. 10, 12, 13.

33. See Joël-Marie Fauquet, [Preface], in Hector Berlioz, *De l'instrumentation*, a series of articles from *La Revue et Gazette musicale*, November 21, 1841–July 17, 1842 (Paris: Le Castor Astral, 1994).

34. Letter from Bizet to Paul Lacombe (1867?), "Lettres inédites de Georges Bizet," in Hugues Imbert, *Portraits et études* (Paris: Fischbacher, 1894).

35. Camille Saint-Saëns, article in *Revue de Paris*, reprinted in id., *Portraits et souvenirs* (Paris: Société d'Edition artistique, 1900), and *Regards sur mes contemporains*, ed. Yves Gérard (Arles: Bernard Coutaz, 1990), pp. 111–52.

36. Hector Berlioz, "Feuilleton [*Sapho*]," *Journal des Débats*, April 21–22, 1851.

37. Ibid.

38. Hector Berlioz, "Feuilleton [Reprise de *Sapho*]," *Journal des Débats*, January 7, 1852.

39. Ibid.

40. Léon Durocher [Gustave Héquet], "Théâtre-Lyrique: Faust," *Revue et Gazette musicale*, March 27, 1859.

41. Unpublished letter from Gounod addressed to Jules Barbier. Bibliothèque nationale, Dép. de la musique, N.L.a. 24, II (109).

42. R. de Saint-Arroman, "Théâtre national de l'Opéra-Comique," *L'Art musical*, January 1884, p. 2.

43. Saint-Saëns, *Regards sur mes contemporains*, p. 120.

44. Ibid., p. 145.

45. The reference to a chalumeau is poetic; the theme is in fact played by an oboe. (Hervé Lacombe notes that the phrase "sighs of the chalumeau" [*les soupirs du chalumeau*] refers to "une évocation pastorale, que dans ce cas précis Gounod rend par un motif de hautbois." The term *chalumeau* "n'est pas à prendre comme terme musicologiquement exact."—Trans.)

46. Camille Bellaigue, *Gounod* (Paris: Félix Alcan, 1910), p. 48.

47. Reynaldo Hahn, "La Musique au théâtre sous le Second Empire," *Conférencia*, March 1, 1925, p. 287.

48. Léon Escudier, "Théâtre-Lyrique: Faust," *La France musicale*, March 27, 1859, p. 143.

49. J. d'Ortigue, "Théâtre-Lyrique: Faust," *Le Ménestrel*, p. 131.

50. Hahn, "La Musique au théâtre..." (cited n. 47 above), p. 288.

51. Saint-Saëns, *Regards sur mes contemporains*, p. 145.

52. R. de Saint-Arroman, "Théâtre national de l'Opéra-Comique," *L'Art musicale*, January 1884, p. 2.

53. Camille Bellaigue, article in *L'Année musicale* 1888–1889, quoted in P. Gillis, "Genèse d'*Esclarmonde*," *L'Avant-scène opéra: Esclarmonde, Grisélidis*, no. 148 (September–October 1992): 29–30.

54. A reference to the Grands Magasins Dufayel, a Paris department store associated with making a wide selection of goods available to people of all social classes.

55. Reynaldo Hahn, "La Musique au théâtre sous le Second Empire," *Conférencia*, February 15, 1925, p. 249.

56. Franz Liszt, "Revue musicale de l'année 1836," *Le Monde*, January 8, 1837, reprinted in *Artiste et société*, p. 222.

57. Gioaccchino Rossini, *Guillaume Tell*, ed. Elisabeth C. Bartlet (Pesaro: Fondazione Rossini, 1992). All the following citations are drawn from this critical edition.

58. Version, amended by Berlioz, of an article in *Revue et Gazette musicale*, nos. 41–44 (1834), edited by G. Condé, in *L'Avant-scène opéra: Guillaume Tell*, no. 118 (March 1989): 89.

59. Hector Berlioz, article in *Le Journal des Débats*, November 15, 1835, reprinted in *Cauchemars et passions*, p. 202.

60. Berlioz, *Mémoires*, ed. Citron, p. 103. See also *Memoirs of Hector Berlioz*, trans. and ed. Cairns.

61. Hector Berlioz, article in *Le Journal des Débats*, June 16, 1841, reprinted in id., *A travers chants*, pp. 247–48.

62. See Frank Heidlberger, *Carl Marie von Weber und Berlioz: Studien zur französichen Weber Rezeption* (Tutzing: H. Schneider, 1994).

63. This discussion uses Weber's score, not the revised version by Castil-Blaze. As noted, a more reliable edition had been published in 1824 (*Le Chasseur noir*). Moreover, despite the major changes, this scene retained its poetic significance, and the work was revived in various forms in 1824, 1835, 1841, and later.

64. The model of the infernal scene in Gluck's *Orphée*, which influenced E.-N. Méhul in his overture *La Chasse du Jeune Henri*, was no longer a valid example either for composers or for the Parisian public. Apart from Berlioz and a handful of others, they had forgotten the works of the composer of *Alceste*. For comments on the way Méhul constructed an "effects" scene, see P. Taïeb, "*La Chasse du Jeune Henri* (Méhul, 1797): Une Analyse historique," *Revue de Musicologie* 83, no. 2 (1997): 236.

65. P. D., [*Robert le Diable*], *Le Français*, December 19, 1831, quoted in Marie-Hélène Coudroy-Saghaï, *La Critique parisienne des "grands opéras" de Meyerbeer: Robert le Diable, Les Huguenots, Le Prophète, L'Africaine* (Saarbrücken: Musik-Edition Lucie Galland, 1988), p. 25.

66. Unsigned article in *Le Courrier de l'Europe*, November 23, 1831, quoted in Coudroy-Saghaï, *La Critique parisienne...*, p. 47.

67. Unsigned article in *Le Globe*, November 27, 1831, quoted in Coudroy-Saghaï, *La Critique parisienne...*, p. 48.

68. Castil-Blaze [F. H. J. Blaze], [*Robert le Diable*], *Journal des Débats*, December 16, 1831, quoted in Coudroy-Saghaï, *La Critique parisienne...*, p. 49. (Hervé Lacombe notes: "On peut ici traduire [chalumeau] par clarinette quoique ce ne soit pas exactement cela!"—Trans.)

69. Ernest Reyer, article in *Journal des Débats*, quoted in "*Hamlet* devant la critique," *Le Ménestrel*, March 22, 1868, p. 132.

70. P. Bernard, "Théâtre impérial de l'Opéra," *Revue et Gazette musicale*, March 15, 1868, p. 82.

71. Nestor Roqueplan, article in *Le Constitutionnel*, quoted in "*Hamlet* devant la critique," *Le Ménestrel*, March 22, 1868, p. 132.

72. F.-J. Fétis, "Le Prophète," *Revue et Gazette musicale*, May 20, 1849, p. 156.

73. F.-J. Fétis, [*Robert le Diable*], *La Revue musicale*, November 26, 1831, quoted in Coudroy-Saghaï, *La Critique parisienne...*, p. 61.

74. Hector Berlioz, "Feuilleton," *Journal des Débats*, March 26, 1859.

75. J.-M. Fauquet, "*Le Roi d'Ys*," in *Dictionnaire des oeuvres de l'art vocal*, ed. M. Honegger and P. Prévost, 3 vols. (Paris: Bordas, 1991–92).

76. The scene of Léïla's oath-taking, which had more than one commentator rigid with horror in 1863, was a crucial scene in terms of coordinating the interplay of tonalities and dissonant structures, marked by "figuralist" orchestration.

77. On this, with respect to Massenet, see Annegret Fauser, "L'Art de l'allusion musicale," *L'Avant-scène opéra: Manon*, no. 123 (September 1989): 126–29.

78. Interview with Jules Massenet, in "La Vie parisienne," *Le Figaro*, January 19, 1884.

79. See Léon Durocher, "Théâtre-Lyrique," *Revue et Gazette musicale*, January 17, 1858, p. 18.

80. "I thought the little pastorale sung by the same character disguised as a shepherd in the finale of the second act extremely pleasant; the rustic sound of

the oboe marries wonderfully well with the tenor's voice," Durocher wrote (ibid.).

81. See Jacques Joly, "Le XVIII<sup>e</sup> siècle dans l'oeuvre de Massenet," *L'Avant-scène opéra: Manon*, no. 123 (September 1989): 18–24. Even minor composers such as Clapisson used similar techniques. The composer of *La Fanchonnette* wrote variations on the "Folies d'Espagne" theme (also the basis of variations in the overture to Cherubini's *L'Hôtellerie portugaise*) at the beginning of act 3 of *La Figurante* (1838), which takes place in Spain. In *Le Code noir* (1842) he contrasts the rollicking music of the slaves with the urbane form of their masters' minuet (act 2, nos. 6 and 8).

82. See P. Gillis, "Manon: Le Rêve réalisé," *L'Avant-scène opéra: Manon*, no. 123 (September 1989): 36 and 38.

83. H. Moreno, "Semaine théâtrale," *Le Ménestrel*, January 27, 1884, p. 68. The architect Eugene-Emmanuel Viollet-le-Duc (1814–1879) restored Notre-Dame cathedral in Paris and the city of Carcassonne, among other monuments of the Middle Ages.

84. Gérard Condé, "Commentaire littéraire et musical," *L'Avant-scène opéra: Manon*, no. 123 (September 1989): 48.

85. Victor Wilder, "Semaine théâtrale," *Le Ménestrel*, January 28, 1877, p. 66.

86. Ibid.

87. Paul Scudo, *Revue des Deux Mondes*, May 15, 1863. F.-J. Fétis was less well informed and commented that "this effect, created in Germany in the singing clubs known as *Liedertafel*, was unknown in France when M. Limnander used it in his opera *Les Monténégrins* [in 1849]" ("*Le Pardon de Ploërmel*," *Revue et Gazette musicale*, April 17, 1859, p. 127). We find such use of a humming chorus in the dream scene of Auber's *L'Enfant prodigue* (1850); in the aria with chorus (no. 8) of Halévy's *Jaguarita* (1855); in the prayer (no. 8) of Fauconnier's *La Pagode* (1859); in act 2 (no. 9) of Meyerbeer's *Le Pardon de Ploërmel* (1859); in the chorus (no. 4) of Félicien David's *Lalla-Roukh* (1862); in act 4 (no. 20) of Ambroise Thomas's *Hamlet* (1868); and in other works.

88. See Hector Berlioz, "Théâtre de l'Opéra-Comique," *Journal des Débats*, April 10, 1859.

89. F.-J. Fétis, "*Le Pardon de Ploërmel*," *Revue et Gazette musicale*, April 17, 1859, p. 125.

90. Léon Escudier, "Théâtre impériale de l'Opéra-Comique," *La France musicale*, April 10, 1859, p. 163.

91. See G.R. Marschall, *Massenet et la fixation de la forme mélodique française* (Saarbrücken: Musik-Edition Lucie Galland, 1988), pp. 191, 274–76.

92. I follow the text of the autograph in the Bibliothèque-musée de l'Opéra de Paris, Rés. 542 (1–3), and of the piano-vocal score (Paris: Heugel, 1892).

93. Joël-Marie Fauquet, "Les Perles de la mémoire," *L'Avant-scène opéra: Les Pêcheurs de perles*, no. 124 (October 1989): 66.

94. See David Charlton, "The *Romance* and Its Cognates: Narrative, Irony and *Vraisemblance* in Early Opéra-Comique," in id., *Grétry and the Growth of Opéra-Comique* (Cambridge: Cambridge University Press, 1986); P. Taïeb, "Romance et mélomanie: Scènes d'opéra-comique sous la Révolution et l'Empire," in *Die Opéra Comique und ihr Einfluß auf das europäische Musiktheater im 19. Jahrhundert: Bericht über den internationalen Kongress Frankfurt 1994*, ed. Herbert Schneider and Nicole Wild (Hildesheim: Olms, 1997).

95. Letter from Bizet to Lacombe, 1866 or early 1867, in Hughes Imbert, *Portraits et études*, p. 167.

96. Berlioz, *Grand Traité d'instrumentation et d'orchestration moderne*, p. 122.

97. Ibid., p. 184.

98. Nestor Roqueplan, "Théâtres," *Le Constitutionnel*, October 5, 1863.

99. See Gabriel Fauré, account of the premiere of *Marouf*, in *Le Figaro*, May 15, 1914.

100. Lynne Thornton, *The Orientalists: Painter-Travellers, 1828–1908*, preface by William R. Johnston (Paris: ACR Editions, 1983), p. 13.

101. See Danièle Pistone, "Les Conditions historiques de l'exotisme musical français," *Revue internationale de la musique française* 2, no. 6 (November 1981): 11–12.

102. "Lettres sur l'Inde," *L'Illustration*, pt. 2, April 28, 1849, p. 135.

103. "Lettres sur l'Inde," *L'Illustration*, pt. 3, May 19, 1949, p. 183.

104. Denise Ledoux-Lebard, "L'Europe dans les meubles de Pharaon," in *Mémoires d'Egypte*, Bibliothèque nationale exhibition catalogue (Strasbourg: Editions La Nuée bleue, 1990), p. 62.

105. Jean Adhemar, foreword to *Les Joies de la nature au XVIIIᵉ siècle*, exhibition catalogue (Paris: Bibliothèque nationale, 1971), p. 19.

106. See the major anthology assembled and introduced by Jean-Claude Berchet, *Le Voyage en Orient: Anthologie des voyageurs français dans le Levant au XIXᵉ siècle* (Paris: Robert Laffont, 1985).

107. Thornton, *Orientalists*, p. 38.

108. Gérard de Nerval, *Le Voyage en Orient*, ed. Michel Jeanneret (Paris: Garnier-Flammarion, 1980), 1: 154.

109. Pierre Loti [Julien Viaud], *Le Roman d'un Spahi* [1881; 35th ed., Paris: Calmann-Lévy, 1893], pt. 2, ch. 4 ("Pedantic digression on music and on a class of people called griots").

110. Camille Saint-Saëns, *Harmonie et mélodie* (Paris: Calmann-Lévy, 1885), p. 13–14.

111. Camille Saint-Saëns, "Causeries sur le passé, le présent et l'avenir de la musique," paper read to the Académie française, October 25, 1884, reproduced in id., *Harmonie et mélodie*, p. 271.

112. Oscar Comettant, *Le Ménestrel* of December 1, 1867.

113. Gustave Bertrand, *Les Nationalités musicales étudiées dans le drame lyrique* (Paris: Didier, 1872), p. 289.

114. Thornton, *Orientalists*, pp. 14–15.

115. *Grand Dictionnaire universel*, ed. Larousse, s.v. "Méry." See also Pierre Jourda, *L'Exotisme dans la littérature depuis Chateaubriand*, vol. 2: *Du romantisme à 1939* (1956; reprint, Geneva: Slatkine, 1970), pp. 99–100, 137.

116. Henri Marchal, preface to the French-language edition of Lynne Thornton (cited n. 100 above): *Les Orientalistes: Peintres-voyageurs, 1828–1908*, trans. Jean de La Hogue (Paris: ACR Editions, 1983), pp. 10–11.

117. Paul Valéry, in preface to Roger Bezombes, *L'Exotisme dans l'art et la pensée* (Paris: Elsevier, 1953), p. vi. Méry wrote in connection with India, "I have a considerable advantage in painting this landscape. I have never seen it" (quoted in Jourda, *L'Exotisme dans la littérature française depuis Chateaubriand*, 2: 100).

118. Bertrand, *Nationalités musicales étudiées dans le drame lyrique*, p. 301.

119. Pierre Jourda, *L'Exotisme dans la littérature française*, vol. 1: *Le Romantisme* (1938; reprint, Geneva: Slatkine, 1970), p. 10. Félicien David explained to Sylvain de Saint-Etienne, "the Orient out there is so different from the one we construct here" (Bibliothèque nationale, Lettres autographes, no. 71 [undated]).

120. Berchet, *Voyage en Orient*, p. 15.

121. Jean-Marc Moura, *Lire l'exotisme* (Paris: Dunod, 1992), p. 3.

122. Ibid., p. 12.

123. See the works cited in ch. 2, nn. 60, 64, above. See also the exhibition catalogue *Voyage en musique: Cent ans d'exotisme: Décors et costumes dans le spectacle lyrique en France* (Boulogne-Billancourt: Centre culturel de Boulogne-Billancourt, 1990).

124. G. Bousquet, "Chronique musicale," *L'Illustration*, December 13, 1850, pp. 373–74.

125. D. A. D. Saint-Yves, "Théâtre impérial de l'Opéra-Comique," *Revue et Gazette musicale*, December 30, 1860, p. 447.

126. See Nicole Wild, "Eugène Lacoste et la première d'*Aida* au Palais Garnier, 22 mars 1880," in *L'Egyptomanie à l'épreuve de l'archéologie*, ed. Jean-Marcel Humbert, proceedings of conference held at the Louvre, April 8–9, 1994 (Paris: Musée du Louvre, Editions du Gram, 1996).

127. Johannès Weber, "Critique musicale," *Le Temps*, October 6, 1863.

128. F.-J. Fétis, "Théâtre de l'Opéra-Comique," *Revue musicale*, June 21, 1835, pp. 195, 197.

129. Jourda, *L'Exotisme dans la littérature française depuis Chateaubriand*, 2: 91.

130. Jean-Pierre Leduc-Adine, "Exotisme et discours d'art au XIX$^e$ siècle," in *L'Exotisme: Actes du colloque de Saint Denis de la Réunion* (Saint-Denis: Université de la Réunion, distr. Didier-Eruditin [Paris], 1988), p. 459.

131. In connection with Félicien David's piano fantasy *Le Harem*, which would be included in the collection *Mélodies orientales* (1836), Ralph P. Locke speaks of "a free alternation between barbaric and idyllic moods" (*Music, Mu-*

*sicians, and the Saint-Simonians* [Chicago: University of Chicago Press, 1985], p. 185).

132. G. Condé, "Lakmé de l'autre côté du mirroir," Opéra-Comique program, January–February 1995, p. 31.

133. Maurice Barrès, *Un Jardin sur l'Oronte* (1922; Paris: Gallimard, 1990).

134. Quoted in Jourda, *L'Exotisme dans la littérature française depuis Chateaubriand*, 2: 96.

135. "Chronique musicale," *Revue française*, November 1, 1863, p. 402. Subsequent quotations are from the same column.

136. L. Gatayes, [account of a January 18 concert at the Société nationale des Beaux-Arts], *L'Univers musical*, January 22, 1863, p. 26.

137. Victor Hugo, preface [January 1829] to id., *Les Orientales* (Paris: Seuil, 1972),p. 209.

138. Ralph [Léon Escudier], "A propos de *La Muette de Portici*" (cited n. 12 above), p. 66.

139. Joseph d'Ortigue, "Académie impériale de musique: Première représentation de la reprise de *La Muette de Portici*," *Le Ménestrel*, January 25, 1863, p. 60.

140. Ralph [Léon Escudier], "A propos de *La Muette de Portici*" (cited n. 12 above), p. 67.

141. Ibid.

142. Paul Scudo, *La Musique en l'année 1862* (Paris: J. Hetzel, [1863]), p. 36.

143. André Maurois, *René, ou la vie de Chateaubriand* (1938; reprint, Paris: Grasset, 1993), ch. 2, "Séjour en Amérique," pp. 44–46.

144. Bertrand, *Nationalités musicales étudiées dans le drame lyrique*, pp. 295–96.

145. Scudo, *Musique en l'année 1862*, p. 38.

146. Félicien David, letter dated May 11, 1835, to Sylvain de Saint-Etienne, written aboard a ship bound for Europe. Bibliothèque nationale, Dép. de la musique, Lettres autographes, no. 69.

147. Théophile Gautier, article dated December 16, 1844, reprinted in *Histoire de l'art dramatique en France depuis vingt-cinq ans*, vol. 3 (Paris: Hetzel, 1859), pp. 310, 315.

148. Saint-Saëns, *Harmonie et mélodie*, p. 131.

149. Leduc-Adine, "Exotisme et discours d'art" (cited n. 130 above), p. 461.

150. On exotic devices in music, see Peter Gradenwitz, "Félicien David (1810–1876) and French Romantic Orientalism," *Musical Quarterly* 62, no. 4 (October 1976): 503; Hellmuth Christian Wolff, "Der Orient in der französichen Oper des 19. Jahrhunderts," in *Die "couleur locale" in der Oper des 19. Jahrhunderts*, ed. H. Becher (Regensburg: Bosse, 1976); and Locke, *Music, Musicians, and the Saint-Simonians*.

151. A lowered leading tone adds a modal color to the orchestral introduction to the first chorus in act 1 of *Les Pêcheurs de perles*. In the contrasting orchestral dance, some measures also contain a tonal ambiguity owing to the

appearance of the lydian (F) mode with its raised fourth (here, E-flat major with an A-natural). Avoidance of the leading tone is also found in the chorus with dance, no. 13.

152. Paul Bernard, "Théâtre national de l'Opéra," *Revue et Gazette musicale*, May 6, 1877, p. 138.

153. Antoine Reicha, *Art du compositeur dramatique, ou Cours complet de composition vocale…accompagné d'un volume de planches*, 2 vols. (Paris: A. Farrenc, 1833), bk. 3,"Des airs de danse dans un opéra" ("Dance melodies in opera"), and bk. 4, "De la couleur locale" ("Local color").

154. Léon Escudier, "Théâtre de l'Opéra-Comique," *L'Art musical*, March 11, 1875, p. 73.

155. Unsigned column, "Semaine théâtrale," *Le Ménestrel*, April 29, 1877, p. 179.

156. J.-L.Heugel, "Opéra National," *Le Ménestrel*, November 30, 1851.

157. C. Koechlin, *Traité de l'orchestration*, vol. 1 (Paris: Max Eschig, 1954), p. 73.

158. Pierre Loti [Julien Viaud], *Le Mariage de Loti* (Paris: Jouve, 1880), ch. 24.

159. Moura, *Lire l'exotisme*, p. 78.

160. Ibid., p. 98.

## 7. THE PARISIAN OPERATIC WORLD

1. A. de Rovray [P. A. Fiorentino], "Revue musicale," *Le Moniteur universel*, October 7, 1863.

2. Wilhelm [Edouard Monnais], "Revue musicale," *Revue contemporaine*, September–October 1863.

3. A. de Rovray [P. A. Fiorentino], "Revue musicale," *Le Moniteur universel*, October 7, 1863.

4. Albert Wolff, "Chronique théâtrale," *Le Journal amusant*, October 10, 1863.

5. Adolfe Adam, *Souvenirs d'un musicien* (Paris: Lévy, 1857), p. 53

6. Steven Huebner, *The Operas of Charles Gounod* (New York: Oxford University Press, 1990), p. 26.

7. Ibid., p. 27.

8. See Albert Soubies, *Soixante-sept ans à l'Opéra en un page, 1826–1893* (Paris: Fischbacher, 1893).

9. See Stéphane Wolff, *L'Opéra au Palais Garnier (1875–1962): Les Oeuvres, les interprètes* (1962; Paris: Slatkine, 1983), p. 55.

10. G. Dumesnil, "Chronique musicale," *Le Courrier artistique*, October 11, 1863.

11. Camille Saint-Saëns, *Ecole buissonière: Notes et souvenirs* (Paris: Pierre Lafitte, [1913]), pp. 21–22.

12. P. Ferry, "Théâtres," *La Comédie*, October 4, 1863.

13. Nestor Roqueplan, "Théâtres," *Le Constitutionnel*, October 5, 1863.

14. Dr. Aldo [A. Azevedo], *Dictionnaire musico-humoristique* (Paris: Gérard, 1870), s.v. "Jeune compositeur."

15. A. de Rovray [P. A. Fiorentino], "Revue musicale," *Le Moniteur universel*, October 7, 1863.

16. Charles Gounod, *Autobiographie de Charles Gounod et articles sur la routine en matière d'art*, ed. Georgina Weldon (London: Mrs. Weldon [1875]), p. 73. The quotations in this book must be taken with a grain of salt.

17. Honoré de Balzac, *Le Cousin Pons*, vol. 7 of *La Comédie humaine* (1847; Paris: Gallimard, 1977), p. 487.

18. Ibid.

19. Ibid., p. 488. Still, the Prix de Rome competition had its earnest defenders, such as Edouard Monnais, writing under the pseudonym Paul Smith, who had only "one complaint about the Prix de Rome, ... the illusions it cannot fail to engender" ("De la liberté des théâtres...," *Revue et Gazette musicale*, February 7, 1864, p. 42).

20. Camille Saint-Saëns, *Harmonie et mélodie* (Paris: Calmann-Lévy, 1885), p. 199.

21. Ibid., p. 201.

22. A. de Lasalle, "Chronique musicale," *Le Monde illustré*, October 10, 1863.

23. Louis Martinet, *De la situation des compositeurs de musique et de l'avenir de l'art musical en France* (Paris: Imprimerie Claye, [1867]), pp. 24–25.

24. Johannès Weber, "Critique musicale," *Le Temps*, November 17, 1863.

25. Nestor Roqueplan, "Théâtres," *Le Constitutionnel*, November 9, 1863.

26. L. Augé de Lassus, *Saint-Saëns* (Paris: Delagrave, 1914), p. 132.

27. Charles Koechlin, "La Pédagogie musicale," in *Rapport sur la musique française contemporaine*, ed. P. M. Masson (Rome: Armani & Stein, 1913), p. 141.

28. Théodore Dubois, "L'Enseignement musical au cours des âges," in *Encyclopédie de la musique et Dictionnaire du Conservatoire...*, ed. Albert Lavignac and Lionel de La Laurencie, pt. 2, vol. 6 (Paris: Delagrave, 1931), p. 3449.

29. Adam, *Souvenirs d'un musicien*, p. 58.

30. Letter from Camille Saint-Saëns to an unknown correspondent, dated Saint-Germain-en-Laye, September 13, 1890, quoted in introduction to Saint-Saëns, *Regards sur mes contemporains*, ed. Yves Gérard (Arles: Bernard Coutaz, 1990), p. 24.

31. E. Desgranges, [Les Troyens], *L'Entracte*, November 5, 1863, p. 2.

32. Paul Smith [Edouard Monnais], *Revue et Gazette musicale*, June 28, 1863, p. 202.

33. Théophile Gautier, article dated October 9, 1843, reprinted in *Histoire de l'art dramatique en France depuis vingt-cinq ans*, vol. 3 (Paris: Hetzel, 1859), p. 108.

34. Paul Smith [Edouard Monnais], review of *La Musique au théâtre*, by A.-L. Mailliot (Paris: Amyot, 1863), *Revue et gazette musicale*, June 28, 1863, p. 202.

35. A. de Rovray [P. A. Fiorentino], "Revue musicale," *Le Moniteur universel*, October 7, 1863.

36. See Richard Wagner, "De la musique allemande," *Revue et Gazette musicale*, July 12, 1840, pp. 375–78; July 26, 1840, pp. 395–98. Published in German as "Über deutsche Musik." In English, see *Richard Wagner's Prose Works*, vol. 7, trans. William Ashton Ellis (1897; reprint, New York: Broude Brothers, 1966).

37. Ernest Reyer, "Souvenirs d'Allemagne," *Notes de musique*, 2d ed. (Paris: Charpentier, 1875), p. 158.

38. Paul Scudo, *Critique et littérature musicales: Deuxième série*, (Paris: Hachette, 1859), p. 270.

39. Honoré de Balzac, *Les Illusions perdues* (1837; Paris: Gallimard, 1976), 1: 63.

40. Mailliot, *Musique au théâtre*, p. 312.

41. Ibid., p. 346.

42. Ibid., p. 347.

43. Mary Jane Phillips-Matz, *Verdi: A Biography* (New York: Oxford University Press, 1993), p. 340.

44. Reyer, *Notes de musique*, p. 394.

45. Léon Escudier, *Mes souvenirs* (Paris: Dentu, 1863), p. 176.

46. Léon P., [*La Muette de Portici*], *La Vie parisienne*, February 14, 1863, p. 65.

47. Franck-Marie, "Revue musicale," *La Patrie*, October 5, 1863.

48. A. de Rovray [P. A. Fiorentino], "Revue musicale," *Le Moniteur universel*, October 7, 1863.

49. De Marcoux, "Causerie théâtrale," *Les Coulisses du monde*, October 15, 1863.

50. Franck-Marie, "Revue musicale," *La Patrie*, October 5, 1863.

51. A. de Rovray [P. A. Fiorentino], "Revue musicale," *Le Moniteur universel*, October 7, 1863.

52. Ibid.

53. G. Cesari and A. Luzio, *I copialettere di Giuseppe Verdi* (Milan, 1913; reprint, Bologna: Forni, 1968), p. 158

54. Hector Berlioz, *Le Rénovateur*, December 15, 1833.

55. Franck-Marie, "Revue musicale," *La Patrie*, October 5, 1863.

56. Franck-Marie, "Considérations sur la situation musicale des jeunes auteurs...," *La Patrie*, October 13, 1863.

57. Charles Desolmes, "Théâtre-Lyrique impérial," *L'Europe artiste* (weekly), October 4, 1863.

58. "Nouvelles," *L'Entr'acte*, November 14, 1863, p. 2.

59. Paul Smith [Edouard Monnais], "De la liberté des théâtres," *Revue et gazette musicale*, December 27, 1863, p. 409.

## 8. GENRE

1. Jean-Marie Schaeffer, *Qu'est-ce qu'un genre littéraire?* (Paris: Seuil, 1989), p. 65.

2. E. Desgranges, "Théâtre-Lyrique impérial," *L'Entr'acte,* October 1, 1863.

3. L. Lepaire, "Revue des théâtres," *Le Monde dramatique,* October 1, 1863.

4. Johannès Weber, "Critique musicale," *Le Temps,* October 6, 1863.

5. Castil-Blaze [F.H.J. Blaze], *Dictionnaire de musique moderne* (Paris: Egron, 1821), 2: 1825.

6. F.-J. Fétis in *La Musique mise à la portée de tout le monde,* éd. augmentée et suivie d'un dictionnaire de termes de musique (Paris: Duverger, 1834), s.v. "Opéra."

7. Arthur Pougin in id., *Dictionnaire historique et pittoresque du théâtre et des arts qui s'y rattachent* (Paris: Firmin-Didot, 1885), s.v. "Opéra."

8. Charles Simon Pascal Soullier in *Dictionnaire de musique complet* (Paris: Leduc, [1870]), s.v. "Opéra." The spoken portions of a few *opéras-comiques* were indeed in verse. Study of the sources reveals how the libretto of *Les Pêcheurs de perles* gradually came to be entirely in verse, i.e., matching the poetic form of *grand opéra.*

9. Castil-Blaze [F.H.J. Blaze] in *Dictionnaire de musique moderne,* s.v. "Opéra."

10. See Hervé Lacombe, "Définitions des genres lyriques dans les dictionnaires français du XIX^e siècle," in *Le Théâtre lyrique en France,* ed. P. Prévost, pp. 297–334.

11. H. Blaze du Bury, *Meyerbeer et son temps* (Paris: Lévy, 1865), p. 182.

12. Léon Escudier, "Théâtre impérial de l'Opéra-Comique," *La France musicale,* April 10, 1859, p. 162.

13. *Grand Dictionnaire universel du XIX^e siècle,* ed. Pierre Larousse (15 vols., Paris: Administration du Grand Dictionnaire universel, 1866–76; vol. 16 [1st suppl.], 1877, vol. 17 [2d suppl.], [1879]), s.v. "Opéra."

14. Ibid., s.v. "Opéra buffa ou Opéra-bouffe."

15. Albert de Lasalle, *Histoire des Bouffes-Parisiens* (Paris: Bourdilliat, 1860), p. 3.

16. R. Duhamel, "Deux maîtres de l'opéra-comique: Auber et Adam," *L'Opéra-Comique,* Revue trimestrielle de l'association des amis de l'Opera-Comique, 4, no. 1 (March 1932): 212.

17. Ibid. If we accept the validity of this definition, we can better understand the indignation of critics who expected an *opéra-comique* when they went to see *Les Pêcheurs de perles.*

18. See Richard Wagner, "Halévy et *la Reine de Chypre,*" pt. 1, *Revue et Gazette musicale,* February 27, 1842, p. 76.

19. "Théâtre de l'Opéra-Comique," *Le Ménestrel,* October 16, 1836.

20. R.O. Spazier, "Sur les récitatifs à ajouter à la partition du *Freischütz,*" *Revue et gazette musicale,* March 25, 1841, p. 186.

21. Albert Soubies and Charles Malherbe, *Histoire de l'Opéra-Comique: La Seconde Salle Favart, 1840–1887,* 2 vols. (Paris: Marpon & Flammarion, 1892–93), 2: 112–13.

22. Ibid., p. 192.

23. E. Viel, "Théâtre impérial de l'Opéra-Comique," *Le Ménestrel,* December 26, 1852.

24. Gottfried R. Marschall, "Manon," in *Dictionnaire des oeuvres de l'art vocal,* ed. M. Honegger and P. Prévost, 3 vols. (Paris: Bordas, 1991–92).

25. Soubies and Malherbe, *Histoire de l'Opéra-Comique...,* 2: 445–46.

26. In this connection see the ample bibliography drawn up by Anselm Gerhard in *Acta Musicologica* 59 (1987): 220–70. On romantic drama, see Anne Ubserfeld, *Le Drame romantique* (Paris: Belin, 1993).

27. See Richard Wagner, "Reminiscences of Auber" ("Erinnerungen an Auber"), in *Richard Wagner's Prose Works,* trans. William Ashton Ellis (1897; reprint, New York: Broude Brothers, 1966), 5: 35–55, and "Halévy et *la Reine de Chypre,*" four articles from the *Revue et Gazette musicale de Paris,* February 27, March 13, April 24, and May 1, 1842, reprinted in *Prose Works,* vol. 8.

28. Wagner, "Halévy...," pt. 1 (cited n. 18 above).

29. [Castil-Blaze], "Chronique musicale," *Journal des Débats,* March 2, 1828.

30. Ibid., March 3, 1828.

31. Claude Debussy, article in *Gil Blas,* May 19, 1903, in id., *Monsieur Croche, antidilettante,* reprinted in *Monsieur Croche et autres écrits,* ed. François Lesure (Paris: Gallimard, 1987), pp. 173–74.

32. See Albert Soubies, *Soixante-sept ans à l'Opéra en une page, 1826–1893* (Paris: Fischbacher, 1893), and Stéphane Wolff, *L'Opéra au Palais Garnier (1875–1962): Les Oeuvres, les interprètes* (1962; Paris: Slatkine, 1983).

33. See Dominique Patureau, *Le Palais Garnier dans la société parisienne, 1875–1914* (Liège: Mardaga, 1991), p. 152.

34. The 100th performance of *Hamlet* was given in 1874 and the 250th in 1889. But *Faust* was the most spectacular financial success, reaching its 500th performance in 1887, only eighteen years after its Opéra premiere, and its 1,000th in 1905.

35. Giacomo Meyerbeer, *Robert le Diable* [orchestral score] (Paris: Schlesinger, n.d.).

36. G. Bousquet, "Chronique musicale," *L'Illustration,* December 13, 1850, p. 373.

37. Letter from Scribe to Auber dated June 9, 1847, in *Correspondance d'Eugène Scribe et de Daniel-François-Esprit Auber,* ed. Herbert Schneider (Liège: Mardaga, 1998).

38. "Académie royale de musique," *Le Constitutionnel,* February 25, 1835.

39. Wagner, "Reminiscences of Auber," vol. 5.

40. Blaze de Bury, *Meyerbeer et son temps,* p. 130.

41. Gilles de Van, "Le Grand Opéra entre tragédie lyrique et drame romantique," *Il saggiatore musicale* 3, no. 2 (1996): 325–60.

42. Wagner, "Halévy…," pt. 1, pp. 76–77.

43. Wagner, "Reminiscences of Auber," vol. 5. The following quotations are from the same article.

44. These examples are given in de Van, "Grand Opéra," p. 340.

45. See Anselm Gerhard, *The Urbanization of Opera*, trans. Mary Whittall (Chicago: University of Chicago Press, 1998), pp. 162–77.

46. *Grand Dictionnaire universel*, ed. Larousse, s.v. "Opéra."

47. Ralph [Léon Escudier], "Les Trois Genres," *L'Art musical*, August 6, 1863, p. 281.

48. Louis Roger, "Les Compositeurs de musique devant le public, l'Etat et les privilèges de théâtre," *L'Univers musical*, October 22, 1863, p. 340.

49. Jane Fulcher, *The Nation's Image: French Grand Opera as Politics and Politicized Art* (New York: Cambridge University Press, 1987), pp. 2, 3.

50. Ministère de l'Instruction publique, *Cahier des charges du Théâtre national de l'Opéra*, March 30, 1893 (Paris: Paul Dupont, 1893), titre 1, article 1, p. 3.

51. See the *Cahier des charges de la direction de l'Opéra*, February 28, 1831, signed by Véron. Bibliothèque-Musée de l'Opéra, shelfmark P.A.

52. See Nicole Wild, *Dictionnaire des théâtres parisiens au XIX^e siècle* (Paris: Aux Amateurs de Livres [Klincksieck], 1989), p. 237.

53. Decree of June 8, 1806, supplemented by order of the Ministry of the Interior dated April 25, 1807, as ratified by the decree of July 29, 1807: "No theater may be established in the capital without our specific authorization, on the basis of a report that shall be prepared for us by our minister of the interior." See A.-F.-A. Vivien de Goubert and Edmond Blanc, *Traité de la législation des théâtres* (Paris: Brissot-Thivars, 1830), pp. 359–60.

54. Wild, *Dictionnaire des théâtres parisiens…*, p. 10.

55. Quotations in parentheses from decree of April 25, 1807, in Vivien and Blanc, *Traité de la léglislation des théâtres*, p. 363.

56. Wild, *Dictionnaire des théâtres parisiens…*, p. 239.

57. Ralph [Léon Escudier], "Les Trois Genres." *Les Pêcheurs de perles* must be seen as belonging to this third genre.

58. Jules Lovy, in *Le Ménestrel*, September 12, 1851.

59. Paul Scudo, *La Musique en l'année 1862* (Paris: Hetzel, [1863]), p. 2.

60. Léon Escudier, *Mes souvenirs* (Paris: Dentu, 1863), p. 318.

61. A. de Gasperini, [Chronique], *La Nation*, October 5, 1863.

62. Gaston de Saint-Valry, "Revue dramatique," *Le Pays*, October 5, 1863.

63. F. Baudillon, [*Les Troyens*], *Revue et Gazette des Théâtres*, November 8, 1863, p. 2.

64. Louis Roger, "Théâtre-lyrique impérial," *La Réforme musicale*, November 15, 1863.

65. Henri Lavoix *fils*, *La Musique française* (Paris: Librairies-Imprimeries réunies, [1891]), pp. 276–77.

66. Jean Mongrédien, *La Musique en France des Lumières au Romantisme, 1789–1830* (Paris: Flammarion, 1986), p. 88. In this connection, the chapter "Les Théâtres d'opéra-comique" is worth reading in its entirety. Translated by Sylvain Frémaux under the title *French Music from the Enlightenment to Romanticism, 1789–1830* (Portland, Oreg.: Amadeus Press, 1996).

67. Gustave Chouquet, *Histoire de la musique dramatique en France depuis ses origines jusqu'à nos jours* (Paris: Firmin-Didot, 1873), p. 306. According to Chouquet's definition, *Les Pêcheurs de perles* is a drama because of the raging passions that drive the characters, the "solemn and grandiose expression" of the oaths, and the "dark terror" of angry nature and of the final conflagration. Bizet's work was also related to genre opera because of its "poetic flights and inexpressible tenderness," which are among the score's most original elements. The work's ambivalent genre, which is exacerbated by its lack of spoken dialogue, was the cause of much negative criticism.

68. Lavoix *fils, La Musique française,* p. 278.

69. Morton Jay Achter, "Félicien David, Ambroise Thomas, and French 'Opéra Lyrique,' 1850–1870," diss., University of Michigan (University Microfilms International, 1972), analyzes three operas by David (*La Perle du Brésil,* 1851; *Lalla-Roukh,* 1862; and *Le Saphir,* 1865) and three by Thomas (*Le Songe d'une nuit d'été,* 1850; *Mignon,* 1866; and *Hamlet,* 1868); see esp. p. 4.

70. *Le Petit Robert* dictionary (Paris: Larousse, 1977).

71. Saint-Valry, "Revue dramatique," *Le Pays,* October 5, 1863.

72. Camille Bellaigue, *Gounod* (Paris: Félix Alcan, 1910), p. 207.

73. Paul Prévost, *"Faust,"* in *Dictionnaire des oeuvres de l'art vocal,* ed. Honegger and Prévost.

74. H. Moreno "Semaine théâtrale," *Le Ménestrel,* February 4, 1900, p. 35.

75. *Grand dictionnaire universel,* ed. Larousse, s.v. "Opéra."

76. *Dictionnaire historique et pittoresque du théâtre,* ed. Pougin, s.v. "Subvention."

77. A.-L. Mailliot, *La Musique au théâtre* (Paris: Amyot, 1863), p. 395.

9. THE AESTHETIC FOUNDATIONS OF NINETEENTH-CENTURY
FRENCH OPERA

1. Nestor Roqueplan, "Théâtres," *Le Constitutionnel,* November 9, 1863.

2. Théodore de Lajarte, "Courrier de la semaine," *La France musicale,* December 2, 1866, p. 374.

3. F. Baudillon, "Premières représentations," *Revue et Gazette des Théâtres,* October 4, 1863.

4. Gaston de Saint-Valry, "Revue dramatique," *Le Pays,* November 9, 1863.

5. *Les Huguenots,* for example, contains several scenes that evade the seriousness of the central drama: the banquet, "Bonheur de la table," act 1, no. 1 *d;* Marcel's Huguenot song "Piff, paff," act 1, no. 4; and Valentine's rejoinder in her duet with Raoul, "Ah! Si j'étais coquette," act 2, no. 10.

6. G. Chadeuil, "Revue musicale," *Le Siècle,* October 6, 1863.

7. Oscar Comettant, *Musique et musiciens* (Paris: Pagnerre: 1862), p. 367.

8. Emile Henriot, preface to Ernest Reyer, *Quarante ans de musique,* ed. Henriot (Paris: Calmann-Lévy, [1909]), p. vii.

9. A.-C. Bouyer, "Revue des théâtres," *Le Miroir parisien,* December 1863, pp. 88–89.

10. Stendhal, *Journal de Paris,* November 18, 1825.

11. Raoul de Saint-Arroman, "Théâtre national de l'Opéra-Comique," *L'Art musical,* January 1884, p. 2.

12. Ernest Reyer, *Notes de musique,* 2d ed. (Paris: Charpentier, 1875), pp. 93–94.

13. Louis de Romain, *Essais de critique musicale* (Paris: Alphonse Lemerre, 1890), p. 201.

14. Richard Wagner, "Reminiscences of Auber" ("Erinnerungen an Auber"), in *Richard Wagner's Prose Works,* trans. William Ashton Ellis (1897; reprint, New York: Broude Brothers, 1966), 5: 35–55.

15. *Mélodrame* (see chapter 2, n. 55, above) used contrasts and sharp juxtapositions to heighten emotions to their peak. Because he aimed for effect in every dimension of musical composition, Meyerbeer became complicated and overblown. For example, his melodic lines sometimes grew distorted and their complicated rhythms could destroy melodic momentum.

16. H. de Bonald, "Les Huguenots," *La France,* March 31, 1836.

17. *Grand dictionnaire universel du XIX^e siècle,* ed. Pierre Larousse (15 vols., Paris: Administration du Grand Dictionnaire universel, 1866–76; vol. 16 [1st suppl.], 1877, vol. 17 [2d suppl.], [1879]), s.v. "Opéra."

18. F.-J. Fétis, "Le Prophète," *Revue et Gazette musicale,* April 22, 1849, p. 124.

19. Théophile Gautier, article dated April 23, 1849, reprinted in *Histoire de l'art dramatique en France depuis vingt-cinq ans,* vol. 6 (Paris: Hetzel, 1859), p. 86.

20. See Anselm Gerhard, "Giacomo Meyerbeer et le *Thriller* avant la lettre," in *Le Théâtre lyrique en France au XIX^e siècle,* ed. Paul Prévost (Metz: Editions Serpenoise, 1995), pp. 107–18; Mattias Brzoska, "Historisches Bewußtsein und musikalische Zeitgestaltung," *Archiv für Musikwissenschaft* 45, no. 1 (1988).

21. Hector Berlioz, "Les Huguenots," *Journal des Débats,* December 10, 1836, quoted in Marie-Hélène Coudroy-Saghaï, *La Critique parisienne des "grands opéras" de Meyerbeer: Robert le Diable, Les Huguenots, Le Prophète, L'Africaine* (Saarbrücken: Musik-Edition Lucie Galland, 1988), p. 50.

22. See Max Milner and Claude Pichois, *De Chateaubriand à Baudelaire, 1820–1869* (Paris: Arthaud, 1985; rev. ed., Histoire de la littérature française, Garnier Flammarion [ser.], 963 (Paris: Flammarion, 1996), pp. 125–29.

23. Victor Hugo, Preface, *Cromwell* (Paris: Garnier-Flammarion, 1968), p. 69.

24. See Anselm Gerhard, *Die Verstädterung der Oper: Paris und das Musiktheater des 19. Jahrhunderts* (Stuttgart: J. B. Metzler, 1992), trans. Mary Whittall

as *The Urbanization of Opera: Music Theater in Paris in the Nineteenth Century* (Chicago: University of Chicago Press, 1998).

25. Giacomo Meyerbeer, *Robert le Diable* (Paris: Maurice Schlesigner, n.d.), p. 535.

26. Castil-Blaze [F H. J. Blaze], [*Robert le Diable*], *Journal des Débats,* December 16, 1831, quoted in Coudroy-Saghaï, *La Critique parisienne...,* p. 50.

27. Meyerbeer, *Robert le Diable* (cited n. 25 above), p. 543.

28. These descriptions are from L. Palianti, *Collection de mises en scènes* (Paris: E. Brière, n.d.). The list of instruments comes from the two-volume orchestral score (Paris: Brandus, n.d.).

29. See F.-J. Fétis, *Revue et Gazette musicale,* May 16, 1852, for this account of the original production of Halévy's *Le Juif errant* at the Opéra.

30. Fétis wrote that "this first, unparalleled, trial of ensemble music for the new instrument demonstrated that it could produce hitherto unknown effects in symphonic writing" (ibid.)

31. F.-J. Fétis, *Le Temps,* March 5, 1836.

32. F.-J. Fétis, "Du sort futur de la musique," *Revue musicale,* 2d ser., 3 (August–November 1830): 229.

33. L. D., *Le National,* March 15, 1836.

34. Heinrich Heine, *De la France* (Paris: Gallimard, 1994), pp. 309–10. Originally published as *Französische Zustände* (Hamburg: Hoffmann & Campe, 1833).

35. Claude Debussy, article in *Gil Blas,* May 19, 1903, in id., *Monsieur Croche, antidilettante,* reprinted in *Monsieur Croche et autres écrits,* ed. François Lesure (Paris: Gallimard, 1987), pp. 173–74.

36. See Gerhard, *Urbanization of Opera.*

37. See György Lukács, *The Historical Novel,* trans. Hannah Mitchell and Stanley Mitchell (1962; Lincoln: University of Nebraska Press, 1983).

38. The term *grandes journées* refers to the concept of decisive historical moments, such as occur during revolutions.

39. Raoul de Saint-Arroman, column in *L'Art musicale,* December 21, 1876.

40. See Jules Michelet, *Michelet par lui-même: Images et textes présentées par Roland Barthes* (Paris: Seuil, 1954; rev. ed., 1988), p. 67. And see also an English translation by Richard Howard (Berkeley and Los Angeles: University of California Press, 1992).

41. Jules Michelet, "Eclaircissements," in *Oeuvres complètes,* ed. Paul Villaneix, vol. 4: *Histoire de France. Livre IV* (Paris: Flammarion, 1974), pp. 613–14.

42. On Viollet-le-Duc, see chapter 6, n. 83, above.

43. Camille Saint-Saëns, *Ecole buissonière: Notes et souvenirs,* (Paris: Pierre Lafitte, [1913]), p. 13.

44. On this matter and its literary background, see Milner and Pichois, *De Chateaubriand à Baudelaire* (cited n. 22 above).

45. F.-J. Fétis, "Du sort futur de la musique," *Revue et Gazette musicale,* August 30, 1863.

46. Conversation between Debussy and Ernest Guiraud, reported by Maurice Emmanuel, quoted in Edward Lockspeiser, *Claude Debussy: Sa vie et sa pensée* (Paris: Fayard, 1980), p. 752. In English, see Edward Lockspeiser, *Debussy* (London: J. M. Dent & Sons, 1936), and id., *Debussy: His Life and Mind*, 2 vols. (New York: Cambridge University Press, 1978).

47. Louis Roger, "Théâtre-Lyrique impérial," *La Réforme musicale*, December 6, 1863.

48. See, e.g., Léon Durocher, "Théâtre-Lyrique impérial," *Revue et Gazette musicale*, October 4, 1863.

49. G. Schmitt, "Théâtre-Lyrique impérial," *L'Univers musical*, October 8, 1863.

50. Ibid. The trombone dissonances are heard in the scene of Léïla's investiture by Zurga, in act 1.

51. Broadly speaking, "aristocratic" reason may be contrasted with its diminished form, "middle-class" common sense, which is united with the concept of the happy medium that is hailed in politics.

52. Comettant, *Musique et musiciens*, pp. 361–62, 373.

53. E. Mathieu de Monter, "Eugène Scribe: Ses oeuvres complètes," pt. 2, *Revue et gazette musicale*, September 9, 1877, p. 284.

54. Camille Saint-Saëns, *Problèmes et mystères* (Paris: Flammarion, 1894), pp. 93–94.

55. H. Vignaud, "Revue musicale," *Le Mémorial diplomatique*, November 15, 1863.

56. Romain, *Essais de critique musicale*, p. 10.

57. T. Imbert, "Etude sur l'état actuel de l'art musical," pt. 6, *L'Univers musical*, May 28, 1863, p. 173.

58. Ralph [Léon Escudier], "A propos de *La Muette de Portici*," *L'Art musical*, January 29, 1863, p. 66.

59. Roqueplan, "Théâtres," *Le Constitutionnel*, November 9, 1863.

60. A. de Lasalle, "Chronique musicale," *Le Monde illustré*, October 10, 1863.

61. Xavier Aubryet, "Musique," *Le Nain jaune*, October 7, 1863.

62. See Albert Soubiès, *Le Théâtre-Italien de 1801 à 1913* (Paris: Librairie Fischbacher, 1913).

63. Hector Berlioz, *Le Corsaire*, January 11, 1824, reprinted in id., *La Critique musicale*, vol. 1: *1823–1834*, ed. H. Robert Cohen and Yves Gérard (Paris: Buchet/Chastel, 1996).

64. See Damien Colas, "Commentaire littéraire et musical," in *L'Avant-scène opéra: La Dame blanche*, no. 176 (March–April 1997).

65. Roqueplan, "Théâtres," *Le Constitutionnel*, November 9, 1863.

66. Paul Scudo, "Courier musical," *L'Art musical*, November 12, 1863, pp. 393–94.

67. A. de Lasalle, "Chronique musicale," *Le Monde illustré*, October 10, 1863.

68. Ibid.

69. Reynaldo Hahn, *Du Chant* (1920; reprint, Paris: Gallimard, 1957), pp. 151, 156. See also, in English, Reynaldo Hahn, *On Singers and Singing: Lectures and an Essay,* trans. Leopold Simoneau, ed. Reinhard G. Pauly (Portland, Oreg.: Amadeus Press, 1990).

70. Camille Saint-Saëns, *Harmonie et mélodie* (Paris: Calmann-Lévy, 1885), pp. 4–5, 46. Some of the articles in this collection bear dates. See also Stendhal, *Haydn, Mozart and Metastasio,* trans. and ed. Richard N. Coe (New York: Grossman, 1972).

71. Saint-Saëns, *Ecole buissonnière,* p. 133. Saint-Saëns had reread an article that criticized the lack of melody in Gounod's *Roméo et Juliette.*

72. Louis Roger, "Théâtre-Lyrique," *La Réforme musicale,* October 11, 1863.

73. Jean Mongrédien, *La Musique en France des Lumières au Romantisme, 1789–1830* (Paris: Flammarion, 1986), pp. 96–97. Translated by Sylvain Frémaux under the title *French Music from the Enlightenment to Romanticism, 1789–1830* (Portland, Oreg.: Amadeus Press, 1996).

74. Reyer, *Notes de musique,* p. 35.

75. E. Chapus, "La Vie à Paris," *Le Sport,* October 7, 1863.

76. Roger, "Théâtre-Lyrique" (cited n. 72 above). Emphasis added.

77. "Chronique musicale," *Revue française,* November 1, 1863.

78. Aubryet, "Musique," *Le Nain jaune,* October 7, 1863.

79. Gaston de Saint-Valry, "Revue dramatique," *Le Pays,* October 5, 1863.

80. J. Ruelle, "Théâtre national de l'Opéra," *L'Art musical,* May 3, 1877, p. 138.

81. P. Bernard, "Théâtre national de l'Opéra," *Revue et Gazette musicale,* May 6, 1877, p. 137.

82. L. Durocher, "Théâtre-Lyrique," *Revue et Gazette musicale,* January 17, 1858, p. 17.

83. Marie Escudier, "Mignon," *La France musicale,* November 25, 1866, p. 365.

84. J. Martin (d'Angers), "Revue des théâtres lyriques," *L'Univers musical,* April 1, 1859, p. 49.

85. The works of Shakespeare, which the Romantics claimed as their property, were often associated with those of German writers. Some critics wrote of an Anglo-German school. *Romeo and Juliet* and *Hamlet,* set to music respectively by Gounod and Thomas, were thus linked to *Faust, Mignon,* and, later, *Werther.*

86. This section draws on *"Faust* et *Mignon* face à la presse: Deux sujets allemands pour un nouveau genre lyrique français," in *Sillages musicologiques: Hommages à Yves Gérard* (Paris: CNSMP, 1997), pp. 101–9, an article I wrote in collaboration with Marie-Hélène Coudroy-Saghaï, whom I thank warmly.

87. G. Loiseau, "La Millième de *Mignon,*" *Le Figaro,* May 13, 1894.

88. G. Chadeuil, "Revue musicale," *Le Siècle,* November 27, 1866.

89. G. Chadeuil, "Revue musicale," *Le Siècle,* March 22, 1859.

90. One thinks of the apt title of Claude Digeon's book, *La Crise allemande de la pensée française,1870–1914* (Paris: Presses universitaires de France, 1959; 2d ed., 1992).

91. Albert Soubies and Charles Malherbe, *Histoire de L'Opéra-Comique: La Seconde Salle Favart, 1840–1887*, vol. 1 (Paris: Marpon & Flammarion, 1892–93), p. 88.

92. H. Moreno, "Semaine théâtrale," *Le Ménestrel,* December 2, 1866, p. 3.

93. Théophile Gautier, "Revue des théâtres," *Le Moniteur universel,* November 26, 1866.

94. Léon and Marie Escudier, "Ecole," in *Dictionnaire de musique complet* (Paris: Leduc, [1870]).

95. Roqueplan, "Théâtres," *Le Constitutionnel,* November 9, 1863.

96. Charles Poisot, *Histoire de la musique en France* (Paris: Dentu, 1860), pp. 308, 303.

97. Roqueplan, "Théâtres," *Le Constitutionnel,* November 9, 1863.

98. Raoul de Saint-Arroman, "Théâtre national de l'Opéra-Comique," *L'Art musical,* January 1884.

99. Marcel Rémy, "Chronique de la semaine," *Le Guide musical,* January 22, 1893, p. 42.

100. I. Philipp, "Théâtre," *Le Monde musical,* January 30, 1893, p. 305.

101. Interview with Jules Massenet in "La Vie parisienne," *Le Figaro,* January 19, 1884.

102. Honoré de Balzac, *Eugénie Grandet,* vol. 3 of *La Comédie humaine* (1833; Paris: Gallimard, 1976), p. 1125.

103. For an alternative translation, see *E. T. A. Hoffmann's Musical Writings: Kreisleriana, The Poet and the Composer, Music Criticism,* trans. Martyn Clarke, ed. David Charlton (Cambridge: New York: Cambridge University Press, 1989), p. 383.

104. Romain, *Essais de critique musicale,* p. 56.

105. Richard Wagner, "Halévy et *la Reine de Chypre,*" pt. 1, *Revue et Gazette musicale,* February 27, 1842, p. 76.

106. Ralph [Léon Escudier], "Théâtre-Lyrique," *L'Art musical,* November 12, 1863.

107. B. Jouvin, "Théâtres," *Le Figaro,* March 23, 1859.

108. Romain, *Essais de critique musicale,* p. 51.

109. Reyer, *Quarante ans de musique,* p. 48.

110. J. Pradella, article in *Le Sémaphore* (Marseilles), quoted by H. Moreno in "Semaine théâtrale: D.-F.-E. Auber," *Le Ménestrel,* January 29, 1862, pp. 67–68.

111. Hahn, *Du Chant,* p. 131.

112. Gabriel Fauré in *La Revue musicale,* February 1, 1922.

113. Henri Delaborde, *Eloge d'Auber* (Paris: Firmin-Didot, 1875), p. 3.

114. Saint-Saëns, *Harmonie et mélodie,* p. 292.

115. Victor Massé, *Notice sur la vie et les travaux de D.-F.-E. Auber* (Paris: Firmin-Didot, 1875), p. 21.

116. Romain, *Essais de critique musicale,* p. 59.

117. Claude Debussy, *Monsieur Croche, antidilettante,* reprinted in *Monsieur Croche et autres écrits,* ed. François Lesure (Paris: Gallimard, 1987), pp. 208–9.

118. Camille Saint-Saëns, article in *L'Echo de Paris* (October 12, 1912), reprinted in id., *Ecole buissonnière,* p. 270; id., *Regards sur mes contemporains,* ed. Yves Gérard (Arles: Bernard Coutaz, 1990), p. 172.

119. Victor Hugo, *Voyage aux Pyrénées,* in *Oeuvres complètes* (Paris: Robert Laffont, Collection Bouquins, 1987), pp. 820–21. Translated by John Manson under the title *The Alps and Pyrenees* (London: Bliss, Sands & Co., 1898), August 11, 1843.

120. Honoré de Balzac, *Autre étude de femme,* vol. 3 of *La Comédie humaine* (Paris: Gallimard, 1976), pp. 674–75.

121. Stendhal, *Journal de Paris,* February 26, 1826.

122. See Marc Fumaroli, *Trois institutions littéraires* (Paris: Gallimard, 1994). His three institutions are the Institut de France, known as La Coupole, which houses the Académie française in Paris; conversation; and the spirit of the French language.

123. Benoît Jouvin, *D.-F.-E. Auber: Sa vie et ses oeuvres* (Paris: Heugel, 1864), p. 74.

124. Gustave Chouquet, *Histoire de la musique dramatique en France depuis ses origines jusqu'à nos jours* (Paris: Firmin Didot, 1873), pp. 255–56.

125. Delaborde, *Eloge d'Auber,* p. 5.

126. A. Thurner, "L'Opéra-Comique...," *La France musicale,* 32d article, December 6, 1863, p. 382.

127. Hector Berlioz, "Théâtre de l'Opéra-Comique," *Revue et Gazette musicale,* December 10, 1837, p. 542.

128. Léon Escudier, *Mes Souvenirs* (Paris: Dentu, 1863), p. 182.

129. Gustave Bertrand, *Les Nationalités musicales étudiées dans le drame lyrique* (Paris: Didier, 1872), p. 250.

130. "Théâtre impérial de l'Opéra: *La Muette de Portici,"* *Revue et Gazette musicale,* January 25, 1863, p. 25.

131. Delaborde, *Eloge d'Auber,* p. 27. The parallel was taken up also by Lionel Dauriac in his operatic psychology course *La Psychologie dans l'opéra français (Auber, Rossini, Meyerbeer)* (Paris: F. Alcan, 1897), p. 20.

132. Saint-Saëns, *Ecole buissonière,* p. 236.

133. Heine, *De la France,* p. 340.

134. Bertrand, *Les Nationalités musicales...,* p. 250.

135. Massé, *Notice sur la vie et les travaux de D.-F.-E. Auber,* p. 23.

136. Reyer, *Notes de musique,* pp. 33–34.

137. "Opéra-Comique," *Le Ménestrel,* December 10, 1837.

138. Maurice Bourges, "Académie nationale de musique," *Revue et Gazette musicale,* December 8, 1850, p. 402.

139. Massé, *Notice sur la vie et les travaux de D.-F.-E. Auber,* pp. 19–20.

140. See Wagner, "Halévy...," pt. 1 (cited n. 105 above), and "Reminiscences of Auber" (cited n. 14 above).

141. *Grand Dictionnaire universel...*, ed. Larousse, s.v., "Motif."

142. Ibid.

143. Arthur Pougin writing on musical knowledge and on style in *Bellini: Sa vie, ses oeuvres* (Paris: Hachette, 1868), p. 197.

144. Letter dated Rome, March 19, 1859, from Bizet to his mother, in *Lettres de Georges Bizet: Impressions de Rome (1857–1860); La Commune (1871)*, 2d ed. (Paris: Calmann-Lévy, 1907).

145. Letter from Bizet to his mother, dated Rimini, August 17, 1860, in ibid.

146. Max d'Ollone, *Le Théâtre Lyrique et le public, avec des exemples musicaux* (Paris: La Palatine, 1955), p. 148.

147. Ibid., p. 182

148. Delaborde, *Eloge d'Auber*, p. 7.

149. Saint-Valry, "Revue dramatique."

150. Heine, *De la France*, p. 317.

151. Paul Bénichou, *L'Ecole du désenchantement: Sainte-Beuve, Nodier, Musset, Nerval, Gautier* (Paris: Gallimard, 1992), p. 500. Jeunes-France was the name adopted by a group of young Romantics after the July 1830 Revolution against Charles X. In 1833, Théophile Gautier published a set of "mocking romances" under that title; see id., *Les Jeunes France: Romans goguenards*, ed. Michel Crouzet (Paris: Séguier, 1995).

152. Louis Roger, "Les Compositeurs de musique devant le public, l'état et les privilèges de théâtre," *L'Univers musical*, October 8, 1863, p. 323. This long article was divided between two issues: October 8 and October 22.

153. Saint-Saëns, *Harmonie et mélodie*, p. 34.

154. Ibid., p. 49.

155. Ibid., p. 51. The last two quotations come from an article dated August 1876.

156. D'Ollone, *Le Théâtre Lyrique et le public*, p. 181.

157. Ibid.

158. Reynaldo Hahn, "Le Théâtre qu'aimaient nos pères...," *Conférencia*, February 15, 1925, p. 240. Paul le Kock (1793–1871) wrote popular, racy novels of Parisian life.

159. *La France musicale*, "L'Ecole parisienne," January 7, 1855.

160. Roger, "Les Compositeurs de musique devant le public," October 8, 1863 (cited n. 152 above), p. 323.

161. Letter from Jules Barbier addressed to Georges Loiseau in response to his query about the writing of *Mignon*, in "La Millième de *Mignon*," *Le Figaro*, May 13, 1894. Now very old and probably wishing to make the history of *Mignon* more interesting, Barbier undoubtedly simplified his testimony, which is nonetheless significant.

162. The contrast is more striking among composers than among writers. Clearly, Hugo's relationship to his audience was far less antagonistic than that of Berlioz; his plays owed a great deal to popular theater, including *mélodrame*. But, as Paul Bénichou reminds us, Hugo viewed the theater as a place for teaching, and his plays had a philosophical and symbolic dimension. Hugo "put into

play good, evil, human will and fate by using types that had a place in his value system. Hugo and what he was able to achieve must be judged in that light.... Hugo's drama, apart from the mixing of tones and milieus that is its most glaring aspect, is basically a Romantic and humanitarian realization of moral spiritualism, with a special character that is hostile to social convention" (Bénichou, *Les Mages romantiques* [Paris: Gallimard, 1988], pp. 300–301). The failure of *Les Burgraves* (1843) finally drove Hugo from the theater.

163. Hector Berlioz, "Feuilleton," *Journal des Débats*, April 21–22, 1851.

164. Jean-Claude Yon, "Eugène Scribe: La Fortune et la liberté" (thesis, Department of History, Université de Paris I, 1993), pp. 5, 7.

165. Paul Sc[udo], "M. Auber," *L'Art musical*, October 9, 1862, p. 355.

166. Reyer, *Notes de musique*, p. 135.

167. François Stroepel, "Essai pour servir à l'appréciation de la musique allemande," *Gazette musicale de Paris* 2, no. 42 (October 18, 1835): 337.

168. Reyer, *Notes de musique*, p. 204.

169. Honoré de Balzac, *Gambara*, vol. 10 of *La Comédie Humaine* (Paris: Gallimard, 1979), p. 510. Emphasis added.

170. *Mémoires, souvenirs et journaux de la comtesse d'Agoult*, ed. Charles F. Dupêchez (Paris: Mercure de France, 1990), 2: 127–28, journal entry for June 26, 1837.

171. See Marcel Brion, *Schumann et l'âme romantique* (Paris: Albin Michel, 1954), trans. Geoffrey Sainsbury as *Schumann and the Romantic Age* (New York: Macmillan, 1956).

172. Article by Robert Schumann quoted in André Boucourechliev, *Schumann* (Paris: Seuil, 1956), p. 52; trans. Arthur Boyars (New York: Grove Press, 1959).

173. Bénichou, *L'Ecole du désenchantement*, p. 67.

174. Baptiste-Augustin Hapdé, *Les Visions de Macbeth, ou les Sorcières d'Ecosse* (Paris: Delaunay, 1817). In his preface, the author asks forgiveness for the weaknesses of the play in its printed form: "A work that I read and one that I produce on stage are generally two different works; the critical thing is that they be successful. For my part, I would suggest that the theater is the best reading-room, once the outlines of the play have been sketched." The play includes a great serpent springing from a fire and a hideous bird. Music, which is used to underscore the high points, including the appearance of the three witches, who rise up from the half-open ground, and a terrifying landscape, with monsters and serpents, a chorus of sorcerers, a red moon, and shrill sounds, is featured in act 1, sc. 7.

175. Benjamin Antier and Théodore Nézel's *Le Chasseur noir: Mélodrame en 3 actes, à spectacle* (Paris: Bezon, 1828) had its first performance at the Théâtre de la Porte-Saint-Martin on January 30, 1828. Armand-Overnay and Frédérick Lemaître were involved in writing the play, which included music by Alexandre and a ballet by Coraly.

176. Antony Béraud and Jean-Toussaint Merle's *Faust* (Paris: J.-N. Barba, 1828) was performed at the Théâtre de la Porte-Saint-Martin on October 29, 1828, with music by A. Piccini, a ballet by Coraly, and scenery by Lefevre.

177. "Butin," *Le Corsaire,* December 30, 1825. *Robin des bois* (a French pastiche of Weber's *Der Freischütz*) was presented as a New Year's "spectacle" at the Odéon along with *Les Héritiers,* a comedy by Duval, and *Les Noces de Gamache,* an operatic farce—an *opéra bouffon*—by Savage and Dupin.

178. A. S., "Théâtre royal italien: Par la troupe allemande, *Fidelio," Revue musicale,* ed. F.-J. Fétis, 3 (1829): 441.

179. Stendhal, *Vie de Rossini* (Paris: A. Boulland, 1824); *Life of Rossini,* trans. and ed. Richard N. Coe (New York: Riverrun Press, 1985), ch. 40.

180. "Théâtre royal de l'Odéon," *Le Corsaire,* December 8, 1824.

181. Roqueplan, "Théâtres," *Le Constitutionnel,* November 9, 1863.

182. Alfred de Musset, in *Le Temps,* May 17, 1831.

183. Marcel Beaufils, *Comment l'Allemagne est devenue musicienne* (Paris: Robert Laffont, 1983).

184. Richard Wagner, "De la musique allemande," *Revue et Gazette musicale,* July 12, 1840, p. 376.

185. Richard Wagner, "Le Freischütz," pt. 1, *Revue et Gazette musicale,* May 23, 1841, p. 279.

186. Richard Wagner, "Le Freischütz," pt. 2, *Revue et Gazette musicale,* May 30, 1841, p. 287.

187. Ibid. Emphasis added.

188. See Jean Mongrédien, "La Pénétration de l'école allemande en France," in id. *La Musique en France des Lumières au Romantisme,* pp. 307–31.

189. Apart from his singspiels, Mozart wrote Italian operas and thus served as a kind of go-between.

190. The relationship between the libretto and the score in its way also reflects that between exteriority and interiority.

191. I borrow the phrase "s'évader d'Allemagne" from Jean Cocteau's *Le Coq et l'arlequin: Notes autour de la musique* (1918; reprint, Paris: Stock, 1979), p. 42.

192. Ibid., p. 79.

193. Conversation between Delibes and Lalo, transcribed by Pierre Lalo, quoted in Joël-Marie Fauquet, "Le Folklore breton dans *Le Roy d'Ys:* Un Antidote contre Wagner?" *L'Avant-scène opéra: Le Roi d'Ys,* no. 65 (July 1984): 20.

194. Letter from Lalo to Adolphe Jullien, dated Paris, May 19, 1888, in Edouard Lalo, *Correspondance,* ed. Joël-Marie Fauquet (Paris: Aux Amateurs de Livres, 1989), p. 289.

## CONCLUSION

1. Nineteenth-century French opera may thus be seen as a series of frames within frames. By "frame," I mean here a more or less well organized system that dictates structures or limits, such as the framework of genre, the framework of aesthetics, or the social framework.

2. This kind of thinking is reflected even in the programming of concerts. In the nineteenth century, a Parisian concert program combined diverse group-

ings of performers playing all kinds of works: Liszt broke away from that pattern by introducing the solo recital. At the turn of the twenty-first century, concerts need themes or guidelines; it seems that all we ever hear are the complete works of this or that composer.

3. To sum up these concepts, the first is marked by diversity (or, under the Second Empire, eclecticism) and mobility, and the second by stasis.

4. Claude Debussy, *Monsieur Croche, antidilettante*, reprinted in *Monsieur Croche et autres écrits*, ed. François Lesure (Paris: Gallimard, 1987), p. 63.

5. Sometimes as disillusionment. See Saint-Beuve as described by Paul Bénichou in *L'Ecole du désenchantement: Sainte-Beuve, Nodier, Musset, Nerval, Gautier* (Paris: Gallimard, 1992), pp. 14–15.

6. Camille Bellaigue, *Gounod* (Paris: Félix Alcan, 1910): "More poetic and more profound than the *opéra-comique* of the day, Gounod's opera was more intimate than *grand opéra*. The latter was no genre for an artist....Gounod was not a composer of bombastic spectacles, ceremonies, and processions. Marguerite's garden and Juliette's bedchamber were his favored refuges. He drove the crowds out of the cathedrals that composers such as Meyerbeer liked to fill. ...But what this music lacked in breadth, it made up in depth....Rich in its own resources, it abounded in, teemed with, inner life."

7. Philippe-Joseph Salazar, *Idéologie de l'opéra* (Paris: Presses universitaires de France, 1980), p. 129.

8. See Rodolfo Celletti, *Storia del belcanto* (Fiesole: Discanto, 1983), trans. Frederick Fuller as *A History of Bel Canto* (New York: Oxford University Press, 1991).

9. See C.-L. de Montesquieu, *De l'Esprit des lois*, bks. 14 and 18. Montesquieu sets out the idea that climate affects the temperament, feelings, and character of the individual, and thus defines peoples. See the quotation from Pradella's article on Auber in chapter 9 above (pp. 283–84).

10. Victor Hugo, excerpt from *Tas de pierres*, quoted in Pierre Larthomas, "Hugo et le langage," *Romantisme* 24, no. 86 (1994): 70.

11. See Marc Fumaroli, *Trois institutions littéraires* (Paris: Gallimard, 1994), esp. pp. 45, 213–15, 283, 297–98, 304, and 308.

12. Germaine de Staël, *De l'Allemagne* (1810; Paris: Garnier-Flammarion, 1968), p. 202. "The French are depriving themselves of an endless source of impressions and emotions by reducing tragic characteristics, as though they were musical notes or colors of the spectrum, to a few salient features—and always the same ones" (ibid., p. 282).

13. Stendhal, *Vie de Rossini* (Paris: A. Boulland, 1824); *Life of Rossini*, trans. and ed. Richard N. Coe (New York: Riverrun Press, 1985), ch. 46.

14. Mme de Staël, *De l'Allemagne*, p. 247. Hence, "those who consider themselves to be persons of taste are more arrogant than those who think themselves geniuses."

15. Ibid., p. 248.

16. Ibid., p. 249.

17. See F. Lesure, *Claude Debussy avant Pelléas* (Paris: Klincksieck, 1992), pp. 94–96.

18. Arthur Pougin, [on *Carmen*], *La Chronique musicale,* March 15, 1875.

19. Paul Landormy, *La Musique française de Franck à Debussy,* 4th ed. (Paris: Gallimard, 1943), pp. 147–48.

20. Letter from Bizet to Mme Halévy dated [June?] 1871, in *Lettres de Georges Bizet: Impressions de Rome (1857–1860); La Commune (1871),* 2d ed. (Paris: Calmann-Lévy, 1907).

APPENDIX 1. THE SOURCES OF BIZET'S *LES PÊCHEURS DE PERLES*

1. See L. A. Wright, *"Les Pêcheurs de perles:* Before the Première," *Studies in Music* 20 (1986): 27–45.

2. This was used for performances at the Opéra-Comique on January 29, 30, and 31 and February 2, 3, 8, 10, 12, 16, and 20, 1991, thanks to the goodwill of Thierry Fouquet and Editions Choudens.

3. See Winton Dean, "Bizet's Self-Borrowings," *Music and Letters,* 1960, pp. 238–44.

APPENDIX 2. THE VERSIONS OF *LES PÊCHEURS DE PERLES*

1. V. Joncières, "Revue musicale," *La Liberté,* April 22, 1889, p. 1.

APPENDIX 4. PASSAGES CUT IN THE COURSE OF PERFORMANCE

1. J. Ruelle, "Chronique musicale," *Le Messager des Théâtres et des Arts,* October 8, 1863.

APPENDIX 6. THE STAGING OF *LES PÊCHEURS DE PERLES*

1. L. Durocher, "Théâtre-Lyrique impérial," *Revue et Gazette musicale,* October 4, 1863.

2. P. Mahalin, "Semaine théâtrale," *La Presse théâtrale et musicale,* October 15, 1863.

3. G. du Taillys, "Revue musicale," *Revue de l'Empire,* October 10, 1863.

4. Johannès Weber, "Critique musicale," *Le Temps,* October 6, 1863.

5. Ibid.

6. Three sketches for the final scene, probably dating from one of the first Paris revivals of *Les Pêcheurs de perles,* are in the Bibliothèque de l'Arsenal, Paris; they may be used to fill out this brief description.

7. A. de Rovray [P. A. Fiorentino], "Revue musicale," *Le Moniteur universel,* October 7, 1863.

8. Weber, "Critique musicale" (cited n. 4 above).

9. H. L. d'Aubel, "Théâtre Lyrique impérial," *L'Europe artiste* (weekly), October 11, 1863.

10. Hector Berlioz, "Feuilleton," *Journal des Débats*, October 8, 1863.

11. For information on the performers at the premiere, see the introduction to *Dossier de presse des Pêcheurs de perles de Bizet*, ed. Hervé Lacombe (Heilbronn: Musik-Edition Lucie Galland, 1996).

# Index

| | |
|---:|:---|
| Text: | 10/13 Aldus |
| Display: | Aldus |
| Composition: | Impressions Book and Journal Services, Inc. |
| Printing and binding: | Edwards Brothers, Inc. |
| Index: | Jean Mann |